D0085498

The Restoration Mode
from
Milton to Dryden

Written or Edited by the Same Author

(In This Series)
The Metaphysical Mode from Donne to Cowley
The Cavalier Mode from Jonson to Cotton

(Other Books)
The Japanese Tradition in British and American Literature
Nihon o Utsusu Chiisana Kagami
Dryden's Poetry
The Fables of Aesop Paraphras'd in Verse by John Ogilby
Restoration Dramatists
An Introduction to Japanese Court Poetry
Japanese Poetic Diaries
Selected Poetry and Prose of John Dryden
Seventeenth-Century Imagery
English Criticism in Japan
Stuart and Georgian Moments
John Dryden
The Works of John Dryden (Editor, Associate General Editor)

Written with Robert H. Brower

Japanese Court Poetry
Fujiwara Teika's Superior Poems of Our Time

The Restoration Mode from Milton to Dryden

BY EARL MINER

PRINCETON UNIVERSITY PRESS
PRINCETON, NEW JERSEY
1974

Library of Congress Catalog card number: 73-14865

ISBN 0-691-10019-5

Library of Congress Cataloging in Publication data
will be found on the last printed page
of this book.

Printed in the United States of America

For

ERIK AND LISA

PREFACE

In the middle of the seventeenth century the poetic genres were reordered as a major shift occurred in views of human experience. Narrative and other larger forms displaced the lyric as the chief means of expression of what was thought to be most important in life. Although older styles continued to show vitality after 1640, they are themselves affected by the change in view, and hence the "Restoration Mode" may be said to cover a period from about 1640 to 1700, overlapping as it does considerable achievements by Metaphysical and Cavalier poets.

As I have said in the two books preceding this one (*The Metaphysical Mode from Donne to Cowley* and *The Cavalier Mode from Jonson to Cotton*), my aim can be defined in one sense as an effort to steer between such larger abstractions as the "Renaissance" or "Seventeenth Century" and such smaller ones as single author canons or single poems. From reviews of the second of these three volumes, it appears that the brief remarks on my theory and method in its "Postscript" have helped clarify what was not so clear in the first volume. I had not given any sustained explanation of my modal conception of literature, trusting to example and to inference by readers. In these prefatory remarks to the last of the three volumes, I shall seek to remedy the omission.

I assume as axiomatic that any literary discussion, whether of history, biography, canon, or single work, constitutes an abstraction; or, if "abstraction" be too formidable, it is certainly evident that to talk about literature or a given work we must stop reading and rely on our memories. When we start a discussion, we set our level according to the purpose in mind. We do not need at all to have a conscious notion that we will now talk about such a "structure" as that large generalization, "The Seventeenth Century," or that much smaller one, *Hudibras*. On the other hand, explicit aims may not assist us. For some years past it has been clear that much as we might wish to write literary histories of an earlier kind or practical criticism of the kind known by such labels as "New Criticism," it has become increasingly difficult to do so with very much faith shared by the historian or critic and readers. Recently literary theory thrives as it has not for a very long time. One hypothesis for such criticism is that in a single poem or canon a full structure or system can be ascertained and discussed. In his *Literature as System* (Princeton, 1971), for example, Claudio Guillén so discusses a poem by Machado in an essay called "The Poetics of Silence," taking into account elements seemingly not present "in the text" (that old abstraction) but present in the "system" that the critic can describe for us.

In the prefaces to the two preceding studies I sought to emphasize my respect for discussions more minute than mine in the sense of focusing on single poems or poets, and discussions grander than mine by virtue of their undertaking to deal at once with the whole "Seventeenth Century." All three of these studies do give attention to poems as well as to interests common to the century, and to that extent I have trespassed on the grounds of others. It very much seems to me that literary study of seventeenth-century poetry has been more distinguished in the last few decades for the minute than for the grand. That seems a tribute to the poems and poets, as if people writing have wanted to recapture by mental effort the valuable nature of the experience of reading. All of us appreciate that. It also seems very likely that it is much easier to talk about single examples than to distinguish larger "structures" or "systems," to use the jargon of today. The difficulty does not imply any lack of importance. None of us is likely to stop talking about such entities as "seventeenth-century poetry," "Renaissance literature," "English literature," "European literature," or "literature." Why should we? And yet all these abstractions get larger and larger, farther and farther from the remembered experience of reading. Curiously, when we reach the largest abstraction, "literature," we discover again that our contemporaries find their subject as congenial as the discussion of individual poems or canons. In many respects, the spectrum of literary study today is bright at the extremes and dim in the great middle range of hues.

I take it as a singular kindness that reviewers should have been generous to the two earlier studies in spite of their evident sense that my literary discussion did not wholly honor contemporary conventions as to analytical discussion. I felt certain that my main purpose would be achieved and, like any writer, had to take my chances otherwise. In fact, I think that the modal approach I am about to describe has to recommend it the virtue of being simple and accordant with experience. The simplicity also was caught by some reviewers, and I shall explain one aspect of it by saying again that I do not assume a conflict between "critical" and "historical" approaches to literature—one plaintiff, the other defendant, and only one of them logically right. To me they represent different kinds of abstraction from our memory of reading, for reading (or hearing, seeing a play) is the only fully literary experience we can have. Moreover, our minds are not *tabulae rasae*, and each of us inevitably brings to bear in literary experience all that we find evoked by the act of reading from our total experience or culture. In that sense reading a poem involves "historical" or autobiographical considerations far more than allowed by the explicit critical shibboleths of not such bygone times. But are there not some dangers in "criticism" and "history"? Surely divorcing them from the complex act of creation and the complex act of reading takes us to a purer criticism or history but away from reading and our memory of what we have read. Running such dangers myself, I criticize no one else. But I have tried to account for the (modal) terms of creation and therefore of our reading in a fashion hospitable to criticism and history but centrally involving *my* experience of reading, and in a fashion applicable to literature of other periods and cultures.

My aim is, then, to provide a literary discussion developing a middle ground between the "critical" (remembered single work or canon) and the "historical" (seventeenth-century poetry, etc.). My modal approach involves certain easily explained ideas, as I believe the first chapters of each of these studies show. I had thought at first of writing on "the Metaphysical race," a phrase used by Dr. Johnson, but was deterred by editors who understandably thought the phrase ambiguous. On reflection, I decided that since each study would be defined by its first chapter, I would take the idea of mode to characterize the whole as well, recognizing some awkwardness in using a crucial word both in the title and the first chapter. It seemed to me likely that a reader's first response on encountering "The Metaphysical Mode" would be to conceive the crucial word to mean "style" or "the way of doing something"; that would not mislead him. But I also had in mind something much more philosophical, adapting to my own ends a dictionary definition of "mode" as "a thing considered as possessing certain attributes that do not belong to its essence, and may be changed without destroying its identity" (*Oxford English Dictionary*). My "thing" was obviously seventeenth-century poetry, a mode differing from Romantic poetry or the Chinese novel. That mode itself possesses attributive submodes that I was setting about to distinguish in a few studies, just as each submode varies from poet to poet.

Plainly, the attributive modes required something more substantive than names alone, and from previous study or intuition or hypothesis I had derived a third concept of mode: the definition of the self in relation to other people and the "world." Human perception refers one's self-consciousness to the other two terms, just as those two outside terms are taken to refer to oneself and to assist in defining the self. It follows that there must be as many such perceptions as there are perceivers. That total perception of innumerable individual examples may or may not be desirable to know, but we cannot know it any more than we can find access to all the individual perceptions. Both philosophically and congenially I sought a middle set of generalizations referring on the one hand to major writers who seemed to perceive in similar ways and on the other hand to a modal conception of the interrelations in those perceptions between the self, others, and the world. I did this the more readily because I had found in the study of Japanese poetry that the modal hypothesis had been corroborated by its utility in explaining important matters in a quite different poetic tradition from that for which the hypothesis had been formed.

My hypothesis about the submodes of the seventeenth-century mode means then, that the forms of perception demonstrably involved in the poetry of Donne and Herbert, of Jonson and Herrick, and of Milton and Dryden constitute three distinctive ways of regarding the self, others, and the world. As I have said in *The Cavalier Mode*, the social submode practiced by the Cavalier poets seems to me the direct inheritance from the Elizabethans, whereas the private mode is a direct reaction to the one side and the public to the other. Such major shifts imply, I believe, profound disquiet about the self in the seventeenth century, and in that I think we discover something about the larger "seventeenth-century mode." Most of the important poets considered in these three studies altered their religion at least once, and so also their politics and their direction in life. In other words, the modal explanation turns not just on perception and knowledge but also on values, on assessment of what the world is all about, and on feelings of hope or despair. In Donne's attempt at public poetry in a few of his occasional pieces, in Vaughan's inward voyage from a Cavalier style to lonely Metaphysical meditation, and in the tendency of poets like Cowley and Marvell to write in all three poetic submodes I find something greatly moving about the century's search for itself, for others, and the world. The causes for such uncertainty, or, to use more modest words, the symptoms of such uneasiness, can be found in religion, politics, and economics, as I suggested a moment ago. Avoiding for the most part the "historical" effort to relate these things to "The Indifferent" or *Corinna's Going a Maying* or *Hudibras*, and avoiding also the "critical" effort to posit a "structure" of meaning from the images (for example) of those poems, we can discover, I believe, in the modal approach something of that "thing" or "structure" we call seventeenth-century poetry. By attention to its three attributes or variables on a middle level of abstraction, we are able to postulate features of the "essential" mode.

The kinds of matters that prove especially important to such an approach also relate to the higher or lower levels of abstraction. One must read critically, as it were, in order to observe that after Donne lyrics tend more and more to lose the dominant sub-characteristic of his poems, a dramatic quality, and to take on a narrative sub-characteristic. And yet the observation moves along a historical scale: Donne and after. Or again, in *The Cavalier Mode* I remarked on a shift in attitude from suspicion of the court to idealizing of it when the Cavalier cause went down in defeat. Unlike the other observation, this one requires no poems to substantiate it and so can be called "historical" in some sense. And yet it provides a basis for distinguishing between the kinds of experiences offered in a number of Herrick's poems. How was one to fit such observations as this into any coherent "structure" or "thing"? I presumed that by examining and characterizing the definition of self against others and the world, and vice versa, it would be possible to account for both the perspective of an individual poet in an individual poem and "structures" of such perspectives in seventeenth-century poetry.

In practice, one must define certain larger limits and then choose what seems the most useful number of sub-units in the larger. My modal hypothesis about the larger unit should explain diachronic matters as well. Something new comes into poetry with Donne, and something new happens in an accelerating way after 1688. Before Donne, lyricism was so concerned with form and social convention that it could not express that private sensibility which is certain that it is right and real, that the world is wrong and perhaps unreal. After 1688 the heroic ideal we see so clearly yet once more in Dryden's *Fables* wanes increasingly and the novel with its socially lower, non-heroic individuals comes about. The "Seventeenth Century" makes sense as a poetic "thing" or "structure."

Given "seventeenth-century English poetry" as a meaningful historical entity, we have the various poems and poets that provide that entity with its existence: one cannot speak of the seventeenth-century English novel, because there are no novels or novelists to refer to. A modal approach requires either that we address ourselves to the whole or to modes within the whole, and it will be evident that for the most part I have chosen the latter approach. I have done so in order at once to discriminate elements within the whole and to discuss the whole in terms other than a ticking-off of poems and poets. Of course it makes good sense to talk about poems by Donne, Milton, or Dryden, and many of us have done so before, just as it makes sense to talk about seventeenth-century poetry. But if we assume that some poets regarded that perceptual triad of the self, other people, and the world differently within the whole, then it also makes sense to identify different modes. One's choice is perforce governed by what one understands to be the modes actually embodied in poetic practice, and it can be said that my choices largely but not entirely reflect usual conceptions. One possible exception is a major one, Milton, who usually finds himself dubbed some sort of lingerer into an alien age or else a writer who fits with no one else. It will be plain that I think it futile to argue with history and that I believe that his narrative achievement distinguishes him from private and social modes that are not conducive to narrative. Or positively, that his narrative gifts fit with the public mode of numerous other writers from Henry More to Dryden.

I have returned to my earlier observation that about 1640 narrative conceptions of experience begin to replace lyric conceptions, or to my point that after Donne and Jonson, lyricism begins to take on a narrative sub-characteristic. Such reordering of the genres modally presumes a profound shift in human attitudes toward experience. Milton and Dryden are part of the larger entity of seventeenth-century English poetry in that they wrote distinguished lyric poems, even if that lyricism required for them the public mode of Milton's mature sonnets and Dryden's odes. The eighteenth century has given us the highly distinguished public poetry by Pope and the lesser but valuable poetry by Dr. Johnson, Gray, Goldsmith, and others. But the fact that lyric poetry of whatever kind proved impossible (by normative standards) whereas, on the other hand, the novel suddenly emerged as a reality practiced with distinction tells us that "eighteenth-century English literature" also comprises a meaningful entity, even if we must define it in such historically overlapping terms as roughly 1690 to 1790.

If we relate the public mode to the historical emergence of narrative poetry, we must also acknowledge that the modal conception is not something restricted to literature. If it were, we would have cause to doubt the validity of the conception itself. Just as the concept of the public mode as a determinant of the "Restoration" must be validated by the numerous "critical" and "historical" details that this volume dwells upon, so we require validation in other kinds of writing to show how far public and narrative emphases predominated. The proof comes in works such as Clarendon's *History*, ecclesiastical histories by Stillingfleet and others, Pepys's *Diary*, the *Pilgrim's Progress*, and Burnet's *Theory of the Earth*. Although there may be nothing new under the sun, these works are highly novel in many respects, and all of us must agree on their individual importance and on the considerable significance of their being narratives written at about the same time.

By definition, then, "mode" is not a merely literary term. In fact, if its claim for use in poetry is to be substantiated, it is necessary to assume the existence of other forms of writing that exhibit the common properties. Metaphysical private religious poetry and the religious meditation show such a relation, as do the relations between Cavalier poetry and the more or less "familiar" letter. For this study, it seems significant to me that one can find in the modal impulse to narrative something uniting an Anglican like Clarendon, an Anglican Latitudinarian like Stillingfleet, and a Dissenter like Bunyan. Or that *Paradise Lost* and *Mac Flecknoe* share essential things with Pepys and Burnet. The modal hypothesis does become literary when it is directed to literature, but like any other hypothesis about the nature of human experience it should retain validity when directed to other matters. For such reasons, I prefer "mode" to "aesthetic distance," although that concept certainly has utility.

Any form of literary discussion in which we engage ought to honor claims for numerous kinds of literary discussion, whether "critical," "modal," "historical," or some other. And quite apart from the requisites for success in any of these, one owes it to oneself and one's readers to develop some degree of competence in the three I have named. More than that, I think that outside theoretical disquisition some impurity in any discussion helps us to gain in terms of a fuller sense of literature what may be lost in terms of philosophical rigor. Since I find myself well embarked on a set of criteria that may be used to judge my performance, I shall add that simplicity or clarity of style seems preferable to more "ambitious" kinds of writing, even if clarity more readily reveals one's faults. Another aim I have set in these studies is mutual trust with my readers. For example, in *The Metaphysical Mode* I mentioned, among other debts that I owe, one to the three-volume study by Robert Ellrodt. The reader deserves to know these things, and I underlined that debt by some references in the text. One reviewer remarked that I should also have said in specific detail what I owed to Ellrodt's study, which she oddly described as being "in progress." That immense "thèse principale" has sections headed by such phrases as "Le temps et l'espace," "Les modes de l'attention à soi," etc. I am inclined to think that anybody who has even glanced at Ellrodt's work and mine would think it impertinent of me to dwell on connections. Or again, the rich use of classical authors by the Cavalier poets, and of both classical and biblical writings by Restoration authors, poses a problem of tact. In my view, representative examples illustrating important matters are much to be preferred to saying all that one knows on each topic.

Therefore, in *The Cavalier Mode* I was fairly liberal in providing classical detail on matters concerned with the good life and friendship but, as I said (disappointing one able reviewer), I could not see any point in giving my pages of notes on the lore of roses from antiquity to the Cavaliers. Similarly, in this present study much might be said about the relation between *Paradise Lost* and other epics or between Dryden's poems and the Bible. But I have thought it more to the purpose to deal only with the relation between *Paradise Lost* and the *Aeneid* and with Dryden's use of religious typology, because these matters are central.

My first chapter, then, deals with that modal characteristic of poetry that defines the "historical" mode: what I have termed the public mode. Instead of defining oneself in opposition to the world by finding just one Other, as in the private mode, and instead of defining oneself in terms of a social group of a few choice spirits, as in the social mode, the public mode tends to suspect what is valuable only apart from all others and to prize what men and women share. One defines oneself optimistically or necessarily against other people and the world. Of course a private lyric may speak of grief, and a public poem may be a satire of public nuisances and menaces. But they arrive at their unhappiness from quite different directions. It will be evident that the public mode differs from the private more radically than does the social mode from either of the others. But it will also be clear that the three modes I have distinguished merely generalize on three areas of a finely graded spectrum.

In each of these studies, the chapters following the first have explored what I think are the so-to-speak special descriptive consequences of choice of mode and the kinds of values actually achieved in the poems. Certain variables require manipulation: the state of the art in respect to Jonson *vs.* Donne, our customary wisdom about literary history, our current prejudices as to what purposes the poets had, their relative merits, and so on. I delayed until *The Cavalier Mode* the hint that this was to be a three-part study, partly because the announcement would not have got by a publisher, but also because it was necessary for me to feel my way in *The Metaphysical Mode*, in which I was attempting something for the first time.

In this last volume, "The Public Mode" constitutes the sole chapter of the first part. There follow two far longer parts. The middle deals with narrative and its variants, with experiments from about 1640 onwards, and with the rich harvest beginning some twenty years later. The third part concerns values, with a chapter on libertine poetry followed by one on satire. The last chapter concerns positive values dealing, as do the longest individual chapters in the second part, with Butler, Milton, and Dryden.

This study much exceeds the length of its predecessors, in spite of my reducing the scale and omitting whatever I felt I dared to do. I have only touched, for example, on Milton's *Poems* of 1645 and on Dryden's *Virgil*. On the other hand, the lack of fresh discussion of the narratives by Davenant and Cowley required lengthier treatment, and as usual I have said what I think. In each volume it has been my good fortune to propound a neglected poet. After Cowley and Charles Cotton I now bring, with a few other not very familiar fruits, *Pharonnida* (1659). This lengthy heroic narrative by William Chamberlayne is a bizarre triumph if there ever was one, but it is also in my opinion (following George Saintsbury) the finest narrative poem between Spenser at the one end, and Butler, Milton, and Dryden at the other. In some other respects the common wisdom and current prejudice remain intact by the end of this study: Milton is the greatest poet considered in this volume, in all three for that matter. I have tried to make clear why and how that is so, as I also have my views on the other poets.

It is clearly impossible to treat so large a body of often very long poems in the same detail that was possible for the shorter poems and smaller canons of poets in the two preceding volumes. As a kind of compensation, I have amplified the annotation somewhat. Whatever such decisions, they will now be evident enough to all, and my task is done. One is sustained in an enterprise such as this not merely by the desire to put into practice a modal study of poetry. One is sustained by the quality of the poems themselves, by one's students close to hand, and by one's colleagues in various countries. Of the poems I shall confess to a prejudice. They seem to me to represent a variety and scale for which we can find no English parallel for a period like that from Donne to Dryden. Of my students I shall say that they have had to bear with my ideas for some time, whether in undergraduate courses or graduate seminars, and that they have participated in the development of those ideas in ways I have tried to acknowledge. As for my colleagues in this country and abroad, the more they know about my subjects, the more they will be able to distinguish what I owe them and what I offer them that is fresh. On reflection, I recall that my immediate debts are owed not only to colleagues in this country and Canada, but also to others in England, Australia, and New Zealand, and beyond those countries to colleagues in Norway, Germany, France, and Japan. I could not possibly have set down all my immediate obligations. Those to whom I am in debt will recognize as much, and take it as a species of admiration and thanks, with their being welcome to what they find here. My ultimate debts are wholly incapable of describing, but in lieu of thanking a person who qualifies better for that than anyone else, I am dedicating this book to our son and daughter. Some acknowledgements of particular assistance on this book follow. I shall only add that I have simply ignored those with whom I disagree, unless I especially respect them or find the nature of our disagreement itself illuminating. I look upon literary study more as a cooperative voyage than a combat and, having felt at times on this voyage like Odysseus, I am happy to have arrived at my destination.

The Clark Library E.M.
Summer, 1972

ACKNOWLEDGMENTS

THE PREFACE touches on my indebtedness to numerous scholars and critics, and signs of such debt will be found in the footnotes. The Bibliography includes the editions on which I have relied, and once more I thank my friend Philip R. Wikelund for giving me the text for a poem by Waller in advance of the publication of his edition. It gives me pleasure to acknowledge other forms of assistance. This book was completed during my tenure as Clark Library Professor at UCLA. I wish to express my gratitude to the Clark Library Committee for the honor and the opportunity given me by the appointment, and once again to the staff of the Clark Library for its invariable kindness and assistance. Miss Ellen Cole, head of the Central Stenographic Bureau at UCLA, oversaw the typing of this manuscript, as she did that of my first book over fifteen years ago. I thank her and her staff for long-continued assistance. Work on the book was also aided by funds from the Committee on Research at UCLA.

I wish to thank the Clarendon Press and the editors of the *Modern Language Review* for their permission to reprint in the Appendix to this book two summaries of the plot of Chamberlayne's *Pharonnida:* George Saintsbury's from his *Minor Poets of the Caroline Period* (Oxford, repr. 1968); and A. E. Parson's from his article, "A Forgotten Poet: William Chamberlayne and 'Pharonnida' " printed in *MLR* (1950).

To Michael Wilding and Michael Seidel I am indebted for advice, general and particular, concerning Samuel Butler and *Hudibras,* and to Maurice Kelley for advice on a theological issue in *Paradise Lost.* William S. Conway has troubled himself to check my citation of a passage in a book at the Clark Library.

I am grateful to Susan McCloskey and Frederick Gray

for checking some of the quotations, titles, and references in this book, and to Pamela White for her devoted help.

I wish to thank Princeton University Press for sustaining its interest in this three-volume series of studies of seventeenth-century poetry. Such thanks go particularly to Herbert S. Bailey, Jr., and R. Miriam Brokaw. The Press has also been good enough to allow me a colophon at the end of each volume. This device provides a last attraction to the customary standards of the Press's book design and it also provides recognition to the editor as well as designer of this book. This is a good time to thank Jan Lilly for the design of all three volumes. At the climax of these expressions of gratitude, I thank George Robinson, the copy editor. I appreciate the opportunity to work with him, and he will know what I mean in saying that his help has been essential rather than substantial.

In all these matters, I cannot imagine an author being better served.

TABLE OF CONTENTS

CONTENTS

PART THREE: COLORS OF GOOD AND EVIL

PART ONE
THE PUBLIC MODE

THE PUBLIC MODE

it appeares that Poesy hath for its naturall prevailings over the Understandings of Men . . . been very successful in the most grave, and important occasions that the necessities of States or Mankinde have produc'd.

—Davenant, Preface to *Gondibert*

as the epic poet, if he is scrupulous and disinclined to break the rules, undertakes to extol, not the whole life of the hero whom he proposes to celebrate in his verse, but usually one event of his life (the exploits of Achilles at Troy, let us say, or the return of Ulysses, or the arrival of Aeneas in Italy) and passes over the rest, so let it suffice me too, as my duty or my excuse, to have celebrated at least one heroic achievement of my countrymen.

—Milton, *Second Defence of the English People*

At the end of his *Second Defence of the English People* (1654) Milton compared his prose defenses of the Commonwealth and Protectorate to the literary epic. Public events are treated as if they were literary, just as literature to Milton deals with those exploits that men may share in groups of "countrymen." Seventeenth-century writers never wearied of connecting "art" and "nature," and with Milton's remark we see that he has considered nature in a specific way: the life and times of John Milton, Englishman. So far do his literary emphases differ from those of Donne and Jonson, that we discover not so much a new literary subject (although we do discover that) as a new language, a new sense of man's relation to other men and the world, new forms for recreating experience, and a large reordering of literary priorities. All these subjects are the concern of this study as a whole, but two of them are treated in this chapter under the heads of "Life as Art, Art as Nature" and "The Reordering of the Genres." Since all such concerns involve a prior relation between poet and reader, and of the poet and reader with that experience which makes up their world, some decision must be made about the kind of address to be made. My first concern, therefore, will be with the relations of men and women to the world in the poems of men like Davenant, Milton, and Dryden speaking to their "countrymen," and through them to readers in other places and other times.

i. Public Voices

Just as Donne's poetry seems to inhabit various private rooms, and as Jonson's speaks in many social tones of approbation or censure to his closely knit group of friends, so does public poetry have many voices. A fourth of the way through *Paradise Lost*, we suddenly hear a new accent:

> O for that warning voice, which he who saw
> Th' *Apocalyps*, heard cry in heaven aloud,
> Then when the Dragon, put to second rout,
> Came furious down to be reveng'd on men,
> *Wo to the inhabitants on earth!* (IV, 1–5)

Milton looks ahead from the scene of Satan arriving in Eden to what will prove the successful attempt to seduce Eve and

Adam. He looks also to the other limit of history, the Apocalypse, when the fruit of that forbidden tree will at last be fully gathered by man. As he stands between creation and Apocalypse in seventeenth-century England, he wishes without hope to warn Adam and Eve, knowing full well that his "warning voice" can speak only to that far larger audience he writes to, all of us readers who share in the fall that Milton's voice could not prevent. The audience that might attend is perhaps few though fit, but the warning of which Milton is capable involves all who will read.

About a decade and a half after *Paradise Lost* came into the world, Dryden sought to warn his "countrymen." Before proceeding to set forth his own principles of government in *Absalom and Achitophel*, he pauses for reflection:

> Thus, in a Pageant Show, a Plot is made;
> And Peace it self is War in Masquerade.
> Oh foolish *Israel*! never warn'd by ill,
> Still the same baite, and circumvented still!
> Did ever men forsake their present ease,
> In midst of health Imagine a desease;
> Take pains Contingent mischiefs to foresee,
> Make Heirs for Monarks, and for God decree?
> What shall we think! (751–59)

Dryden does not here envision all of human history but rather that of two kingdoms, Israel and that other elect nation (as Milton had also believed), God's Englishmen. What shall we think indeed of foolish Israel, of ourselves, and the constant human falling-away from a divinely appointed moral order? So foolish is man that peace itself is war—in the masquerade of man's desire to deceive others and his willingness to deceive himself.

Every reader recognizes that in many respects the voices we hear in Milton and in Dryden's poems differ considerably.

But they differ among voices of the same kind. Another difference, one of kind, can be found by contrast with Donne and Jonson. Donne sometimes addresses real or fictional women in his secular verse:

> And now good-morrow to our waking soules,
> Which watch not one another out of feare;
> For love, all love of other sights controles,
> And makes one little roome an every where.[1]

On other occasions Donne addresses himself or God in divine poetry:

> What if this present were the worlds last night?
> Marke in my heart, O Soule, where thou dost dwell,
> The picture of Christ crucified, and tell
> Whether that countenance can thee affright . . . ?[2]

More of the present world exists in Jonson's poetry, more of society. On a minutely graded scale of aesthetic distance, on which the radically private of Donne's poetry and the radically public of Dryden's are extremes, Jonson's occupies a middle, or social relation of people to each other. Here, then, is Jonson in a very characteristic vein, addressing a good woman:

> Beautie, I know, is good, and bloud is more;
> Riches thought most: But, *Madame*, thinke what store
> The world hath seen, which all these had in trust,
> And now lye lost in their forgotten dust.
> It is the *Muse*, alone, can raise to heaven.[3]

Donne and Jonson shine in such passages, and in them are also at their most universal, most comprehensive. Yet to

[1] "The good-morrow," 8–11.
[2] Holy Sonnet 9 (1633), 1–4.
[3] *To Elizabeth Countesse of Rutland*, 37–41.

Donne the reality of consciousness and private psychological need is so great that the universe contracts itself to his chamber and the world's last night to a picture in his heart. Jonson works with other, equally pressing concerns. He contrasts the world's customs with inner truth, the misdirections of the times with what endures. Above all he addresses a woman known to be real in a world felt to be real as to time and place. The woman and the world, for both Jonson and Donne, assist in defining the personality as well as the experience of the poet, just as the reverse is also true. For Jonson, a "real" world emerges, and so does a poet defined by time and place and a historically real person addressed. Beyond that situation, we sense an implied group of friends, a small group of good people among a far larger group of foolish or vicious ones. Both have defined themselves in relation to the world by means that poets must always use, but the definitions and workings of the relations are very different.

Milton and Dryden also must define themselves in relation to their worlds. Milton, wishing for a warning voice to admonish that man and that woman in whose behavior the destiny of all mankind is bound, or Dryden, wondering what we should think when men prove so tragically wayward, clearly looked upon themselves as poets dealing with versions of historical truth. Neither shrank from consideration of himself, but those selves are premised on the historical existence and public validity of the world outside their own consciousness. It turns out that everything else is, and that the Muse-assisted poet can range over all time as one to whom the truth is so far known that he assumes he shares it with his readers. Today we might debate the historicity of the Book of Revelation or of Second Samuel, and certainly we find it difficult to prove philosophically the objective existence of that which lies in the so-called external world outside our own consciousness. But to these public poets, the

Bible was a kind of proof of man's existence in an objectively knowable world. The Creator of man and that world had, after all, revealed much of His truth in the Book of His Word and something, too, in the Book of His Works, the creation. For Milton and Dryden in the public mode, or for poets using other means of defining themselves in terms of their worlds, there are necessarily kinds of reality and kinds of convention. Public poetry is distinguished by its assumptions that the world is as real as the poet and that understanding of the world and oneself is shared with other men. Public poetry concerns itself with personalities as much as does Cicero in excoriating Cataline, but it avoids the idiosyncrasies of the little room and, rather than address solely a single woman, "Madame," or a group of friends, it addresses all.

It was with some irritation that T. S. Eliot termed Milton and Dryden "the two most powerful poets of the century." [4] Such power comes not from the public mode in itself but from what they made of it. In its making we discover a far larger number of named individual characters than we do in private or social poetry, and in such characters as Satan and Adam, Achitophel and Palamon and Arcite the sense of personality swells. It must also be said that by their diminishing of the importance of the private and intimate, Milton and Dryden lost no little of that delicacy and fineness of perception that marks, however differently, Donne and Herbert, Jonson and (much of) Marvell. Only in the drama, and then with effort, can both the private and the public worlds mingle. Milton seems sometimes to speak to the Greek Areopagus, or its Christian equivalent, and Dryden to the Roman Senate, or its English counterpart. Milton and Dryden could not, or in any event did not, write the songs that individuals were to sing thereafter: "Goe and catch a falling star,"

[4] "The Metaphysical Poets," in *Selected Prose*, ed. John Hayward (Harmondsworth, Mddx., 1963), p. 111.

"Drink to me only with thine eyes," or unset poems that seem to provide their own music for the chamber. Nor could they celebrate the soul's voyage into itself, where its meditations become "A green thought in a green shade."

By the same token, Milton and Dryden, along with less gifted poets of the public mode, could discover things that their great predecessors could not. They could write for the music of public performance. By the loss of delicacy and fineness they could gain in strength and scope in the treatment of powerful passions of fear and trust, anger and triumph, despair and hope. I cannot believe that my students and I are unusual in finding ourselves near tears, or in tears, on reading the ending of *Paradise Lost.* Nor can it be strange in us to feel profound disquiet over the words of Jesus in rejecting Athens in *Paradise Regained* or over Dryden's white-lipped anger in *The Medall.* If we possess sufficient faith in our responses and in our poets, we shall think that Milton and Dryden expected us to feel such great sadness or disquiet when we attend to what they wrote.

Public poetry like Milton's and Dryden's also gains in that higher mimesis that Erich Auerbach sought.[5] In that larger realism, art testifies to a shared world in which words and action, the *lexis* and *praxis* of the Greeks, are harmonious in a real world validated by the experience of many minds. Donne earlier and Bishop Berkeley later gave strong reasons for considering the importance of the human subjectivity and reasons as well for doubting the value or the reality of "the world." The assurance for the higher "realism" of the public poets presents one of the strongest fulfillments we can find of the profound human need to believe that the world is real and that we are real in it along with other real persons. Those who look in public poetry for valued intimate details or for the number of the streaks of the tulip will be able

[5] *Mimesis: The Representation of Reality in Western Literature* (Princeton, 1953).

with effort to find them, just as private poetry will also sometimes gaze on public vistas. But what is characteristic is what is convincing, and the rich details of the private and social modes seem more convincing, indeed more necessary to them, because of their lesser security in the belief that the whole exists as a valued norm. The world certainly exists to Davenant and Butler, Milton and Dryden. That existence is more than descriptive, because the things that fill such worlds are not merely mechanical. The reality is primarily one of people and of other creatures given meaning by a transcendent order and an intelligible scheme of value. Again and again in Milton, Butler, and Dryden we find ourselves faced with a powerful challenge: we can deny if we choose the reality presented but, if we do, we discover that the order they celebrate is so encompassing and so filled with values that denial entails sacrifice of major elements in our lives. Such are the problems encountered, because self-created, by Hudibras, Satan, and Achitophel. In a sense not wholly alien to that of the Neoplatonists of the century, each of these great public poets created "intelligible worlds," worlds governed by great ideas and therefore assured as to their existence, understandable in their inner relationships, and clarified by their moral orders.

Something in us all leads us to wish to ask why such poetic changes take place in a century of great poetry, why the public mode should so decisively replace the private and social. (Some of these issues are also touched on in the Preface.) It does not avail logically to say merely that political and other changes of importance occurred, since that just removes the question by one step. But analogy between the arts, or between literature and what else was done, emphasizes that literature did not exist in a vacuum. The closer we look, even at literature alone, the more we are apt to see survival and change together, compromise and many-facetedness. In the period from 1640 to 1660, perhaps the least studied for its literature of all periods of the century, many wonderful and many distinctly odd things were going on. It is difficult to discover in those two decades that steady direction of change, almost year by year, that we can discover in the prose and verse of a Milton. Henry Vaughan begins very much as a royalist and Cavalier poet, but ends as a practitioner of that private mode first explored by Donne and Herbert. Marvell said in 1674 of his reaction to *Paradise Lost* that he was "Held . . . a while misdoubting" of Milton's aims. And yet in *The Character of Holland* (ca. 1653) he had seemed to have resolved all doubts in malice, as he did otherwise in his panegyric on Cromwell and his Restoration satires. Dryden's career begins, as far as we know, with a schoolboy poem, "Upon the death of the Lord Hastings" (1649). We do not know what else he may have been writing in those years, except that Dr. Busby set him to translate Persius at Westminster. The tortured conceits of the Hastings poem and its heavy pumping of feeling mark that late Metaphysical style which Dryden transcends, without wholly forgetting, in his mature work.

One of the few explanations we possess for such different changes can be understood by simply attending to what *Hudibras* represents: the Civil Wars and the experience of the Interregnum. Nothing could ever be the same in England after that upheaval. Yet, as the careers of Vaughan, Waller, and Marvell show, different poets responded variously. The vicissitudes in the kingdom of letters do not exactly parallel those in the political realm. The next sections of this chapter will seek to define the bases of changes and their results leading to public poetry, but we may linger a moment to consider those ways in which events in the two kingdoms of letters and politics resembled each other.

One great energy of the Renaissance was spent on unifying the state. In some European principalities the process was completed relatively quickly; in others the centralizing process awaited the Romantic or later periods for achievement. For better and for worse, English rule between Henry VII and Charles I was highly personal in symbol and in fact. With the Civil Wars we find strong personalities to be sure, but we also discover enterprises on a hitherto unrealized scale. One such was the execution of a king by his own subjects, an event (as Milton might have said) "Of which all Europe talks from side to side." The execution of Charles I necessitated other grand conceptions: the New Model Army, Blake's navy, the Commonwealth, and the Protectorate. Not since the Reformation in England had the grand conceptions of man seemed so evident a capacity, and to some of them we can give names: Hobbes' *Leviathan*, Harrington's *Oceana*, *Hudibras*, *Paradise Lost*, *Absalom and Achitophel*.[6] Similarly, a Royal Society is chartered, Wren remodels London, Purcell creates *Dido and Aeneas*, Burnet designs a *Theory of the Earth*. The emergence of political parties organizes men's ideas about politics, and Newton's *Principia* organizes scientific thought. The English epic is at last fully realized, drama takes such grandiose forms as the heroic play, Petty writes about political arithmetic, and Locke about human understanding. The Columbia edition of Milton's works runs to twenty-one volumes without annotation or index; the California edition of Dryden's works will require twenty volumes. Even the lesser writers were often surprisingly prolific: Davenant at one end, and Bishop Ken or Blackmore at the other. The Civil Wars fostered a prodigious bursting forth of cultural achievement in a late phase of the English Renaissance.

Public poetry did not die with Milton and Dryden, nor

[6] On Hobbes see Sheldon S. Wolin's excellent Clark Library Seminar Paper, "Hobbes and the Epic Tradition of Political Theory" (Los Angeles, 1970). My point complements Wolin's: poems like *Paradise Lost* or *Absalom and Achitophel* create like Hobbes a polity, a part of what I shall subsequently call the great idea.

even with Pope. Dr. Johnson, like Arnold later, may fairly be claimed a humanist, although neither belongs to the world of Butler, Milton, and Dryden. Many of us are coming to believe that the shift of energy and taste for which the crudest of labels is "the Civil Wars" has another crude label for its ending, "the Glorious Revolution." Dryden clearly felt as much in his late years (and in later chapters we shall see how much that he represents finds its ending with him). Of course Dryden's sense of change from what he knew and hoped for differed in many respects from Milton's. After 1688, however, Elizabeth I, once an ikon of the Whigs, begins to serve a similar purpose for the Tories under Bolingbroke, and the ideal of the Augustan empire is displaced by another of the Roman republic.[7] In three nations of Europe in the seventeenth century, dreams of empire filled minds, as they had earlier those of the Portuguese and the Spaniards. But even as England was beginning to push out France and Holland from the imperial stage, the conceptions required seemed to overshadow man. Sometime around the turn of the century the most creative literary talents seemed to turn away from the grand conceptions of imperial enterprise: the Bank of England, National Debt, heavy systematic taxation, the armies of William III and Marlborough, the growth of London as a commercial emporium. The political arithmetic that Petty had argued for, and the empire of trade that Dryden like others had envisioned, really came into being. The argument was won and the vision was realized, but at a considerable cost to the creative imagination as it had been taught to express itself.

The novel turned attention from the heroic to the diurnal, so opening a whole new literary world to men and women. *The Dunciad* judges the new world by values of the old, so

[7] See Isaac Kramnick, *Bolingbroke and His Circle* (Cambridge, Mass., 1968), and Zera Silver Fink, *The Classical Republicans* (Evanston, Ill., 1945).

telling us more about the details of the modern world we know than had *Hudibras, Paradise Lost,* or *Absalom and Achitophel.* The feeling grew stronger that man was becoming smaller, that old values were being lost. "The gloom of the Tory satirists" no doubt responded to the loss more than to the gain, which was reaped by families wealthy on a new scale, families able to create their own little, far more manageable worlds on hedged estates with elegant houses and beautiful gardens. Before that day, that is, between 1640 and 1690 or 1700, it had been the special achievement of poetry to attain a variety and scale of large works such as only the bustling Victorian novelists would exceed. The Restoration poets had achieved a scale that measured man's reality as well as the world's in ways compatible with each other. It is significant that most of the works attempted were actually brought off, and the achievement of the central figures was sufficiently real to contain the countercharge of those Sons of Belial who have occupied the society pages of literary histories in their scandals. Of course the achievement was a struggle, and much of what was hoped for was frustrated. More than that, in pursuing things yet unattempted in prose and rhyme, poets nonetheless adhered to ancient models in the Renaissance way. They also found not seldom what they had not expected, and most found it impossible to keep consistently on the wing. But they did speak with full certainty in one conviction that poets seldom enjoy: they knew that men and women were listening, that others would seek to rival and excel them, or that shortly they would endure the tributes of parody in verse or in "transprosing."

Men had been taught to listen to other men out of a conviction that what was said mattered. To the Puritans England owed the lively sense that human acts and speech, contemporary events, were as much a part of history under God's eye as the famous acts of haughty Rome or chosen

Israel. With such assurance in themselves and their world, and with no little nervousness over what would come next, they could achieve a great deal by way of creation and disagreement. Above all, knowing that they would be attended to, poets could assert *themselves* before others, could speak in a public voice. As Milton presents it, it was not so terribly difficult to be a poet. One invoked the true Muse:

> What in me is dark
> Illumin, what is low raise and support;
> That to the highth of this great Argument
> I may assert eternal Providence,
> And justifie the wayes of God to men.
> (*Paradise Lost*, I, 22–26)

Poets so inspired held special status among men, at least when the trumpet would sound and the dead would be raised.

> The sacred Poets first shall hear the Sound,
> And formost from the Tomb shall bound:
> For they are cover'd with the lightest Ground
> And streight, with in-born Vigour, on the Wing,
> Like mounting Larkes, to the New Morning sing.

So Dryden, predicting as he loved to do, on the slender evidence of Anne Killigrew (188-92) and the stronger evidence of faith. To Milton, concluding his second defense of the English people during a particularly unruly and disputatious time, their high endeavors became a real epic in his celebration of them. As he embarks on *Paradise Lost* he assumes that he can and must accommodate the human epic to the unsearchable disposition of divine providence. To Dryden, writing of a woman who was a small poet and a not much larger painter, it is clear that his own function as a poet is sufficiently high to merit the term "sacred," and to believe that the species of the poet was enough to enable him to include even Anne Killigrew among the human representatives of a supernal order. The connections between art and life are always complex beyond total unraveling. But each generation requires some kind of concept of that relation, and public poetry no less. What made the public mode the radical of a new poetry was its faith in the relation between men and their world. That faith involved as one tenet the definition of art by life, and life by art. As another tenet, it involved belief that the divine and human creators possessed comparable functions, just as the divine and human creations were believed to resemble each other.

ii. Life as Art, Art as Nature

Those accumulating energies in poetry and other spheres of life which strengthen and take on new forms after 1640 required certain leading motives if anything new and enduring was to come of them. Like all generations, the two between 1640 and 1700 discovered that the sharing of grand conceptions did not prevent rivalry among them. In the political forum, words often portended bloodshed, and although it seems to be part of the English genius to expend in words energies that might otherwise tear the state apart, real and incipient revolutions in the state gave a continuing sense of crisis and upheaval. In prose, such great achievements as Milton's total defense of the Puritan Revolution, Hobbes' *Leviathan*, Clarendon's *History of the Grand Rebellion*, and Locke's treatises on government are compatible only as great if alternative visions of the state. The royalist nostalgia kept alive that very English sense of a constitution unwritten but endlessly to be written about. Both the royalists and the Puritans included people who supported the Royal Society. The Puritans themselves were empirical, dedicated to work in this world, and impatient with schemes that promised no fruit. At the same time, they were also millenarian in the 1640's, and their sense of hope at hand affected not only preachers and politicians, soldiers and astrologers, but also the optimists of the Royal Society and those poets like Milton, Marvell, and Dryden who held to an eschatological belief and hopes of either reform or human progress.

Numerous other motives might be mentioned, but the most important to define rightly or for the age to grasp was the search for dynamic order. At the end of the period Newton of course provided the world as well as England with a conception of an abstract or "geometric" space in which the void made attraction possible, in which order made motion possible, and in which God made all possible by previous creation and constant repair of what He had created.[8] It has grown fashionable among literary students to dismiss the concept of dynamic order as a soul-less "mechanics." But for two generations at least the music of the spheres yielded to another image, to what Dryden in a "Copernican" mood called "The dance of Planets round the radiant Sun." [9] Similarly, in a series of astronomical passages somewhat ambiguous as a group, Milton comes at last to Raphael's well-known question:

> What if the Sun
> Be Center to the World, and other Starrs
> By his attractive vertue and thir own
> Incited, dance about him various rounds? [10]

[8] See Alexander Koyré, *Newtonian Studies* (Cambridge, Mass., 1965), chs. I, III, and Appendix L.

[9] In *Of the Pythagorean Philosophy* (in *Fables*), 94.

[10] *Paradise Lost*, VIII, 122–25. Cf. III, 571–87 and V, 171–79, 618–27. Milton never quite commits himself to any cosmogony. Dryden uses whichever makes his poetic point, tending to more "Copernican" references later in life. Davenant is the only poet of importance in the century who seems to have made up his mind that the universe is heliocentric: see *Gondibert*, II, v, sts. 18–20, a fine passage.

As the song image for world harmony was leaving men's minds along with the "Ptolemaic," earth-centered universe, the dance image became more prominent. This idea, too, was an old one. For Plato and others, the stars moved in "choric dance," χορεία,[11] and the concept was common in illustrations of Job 38:7, "When the morning stars sang together, and all the sons of God shouted for joy."[12] From ancient ideas and symbols of *harmonia mundi,* a new age was taking means for expressing a fresh conviction in the existence and importance of a dynamic world order. That order was thought to obtain both in the world and in man, and music with its temporal rhythms supplied the symbols for the *musica mundana* and *musica humana* as accompaniment of the stellar dance.[13]

The motions of the heavenly bodies and the elements of matter are described in terms of three human arts: dance, music, and song. Their creation must, therefore, be from a musical source, the *musica divina,* the divine voice bespeaking harmony. And the harmonious act of creation culminates in the most harmonious of the creatures, man, on a diapason or full concord, as Dryden shows in *A Song for St. Cecilia's Day.*

> From Harmony, from heav'nly Harmony
> This universal Frame began.
> When Nature underneath a heap

[11] *Timaeus,* 40C; see also *Ion,* 1080; *Laws,* 942D.

[12] See Plate VI in my *Dryden's Poetry* (Bloomington and London, 1967), opposite p. 273, illustrating music, dance, and song in various orders of angels and stars.

[13] An excellent account is given by Leo Spitzer, "Classical and Christian Ideas of World Harmony," *Traditio,* II (1944), 409–64; III (1945), 307–64. For further studies touching on seventeenth-century literature, see Earl R. Wasserman, "Denham: *Cooper's Hill,*" reprinted in *The Subtler Language* (Baltimore, 1959), ch. III; John Hollander, *The Untuning of the Sky* (Princeton, 1961); and H. T. Swedenberg, Jr., *et al.,* eds., *The Works of John Dryden,* III (Berkeley and Los Angeles, 1969), 459–67.

Of jarring Atomes lay,
And cou'd not heave her Head,
The tuneful Voice was heard from high,
Arise ye more than dead.
Then cold, and hot, and moist, and dry,
In order to their stations leap,
And MUSICK's pow'r obey.
From Harmony, from heav'nly Harmony
This universal Frame began:
From Harmony to Harmony
Through all the compass of the Notes it ran
The Diapason closing full in Man. (1–15)

The tendency to use images of the arts for the creation, divine and human, must be counted one of the central and fertile motives of our larger Restoration from 1640 to 1700. We have seen, and we shall have occasion to see again, that the novelty of the images lies not in themselves but in what they function for. By believing that the creatures of God, or more generally the total creation, were analogous to human creation, writers like Dryden revived the idea of God as poet,[14] and of His creation as poem, song, dance, or picture. The St. Cecilia Day festivities after the Restoration of 1660 came to feature poems and sermons in which these and related topics were often treated. And we must not consider that the ideas were the property only of a few lingering Hermeticists, Neoplatonists, and others who perceived things invisible to sight. Here is a fair example:

'Twas thus th'Almighty Poet (if we dare
Our weak, and meaner Acts with his compare)
When he the Worlds fair Poem did of old design,
That work which now must boast no longer date
than thine . . . .

[14] See God's "tuneful Voice" in the passage just quoted.

I rather doubt that most people, who tend to look upon the Restoration with the inheritance of customary wisdom, would identify the poet as John Oldham, or the topic, *Upon the Works of Ben Johnson* (st. xii). Similarly, when describing Jonson's work (st. xiii), Oldham naturally compares it to the Creator's poem, the creation in old images of perfection and royalty.

. . . 'twas a solid, whole, and perfect Globe of light,
  That shone all over, was all one bright,
And dar'd all sullying Clouds, and fear'd no darkning night;
  Like the gay Monarch of the Stars and Sky,
    Who whereso'er he does display
  His soveregn Luster, and majestick Ray,
  Strait all the less, and petty Glories nigh
    Vanish, and shrink away. . . .

"Art" was used by these writers more widely and more richly than by later poets. One must be alert for uses in areas as seemingly remote as the *ars rhetoricae* or *ars memoriae* or, even to the point of parody, *The Art of Cooking* modeled on Horace's *Ars Poetica.* Rhetoric was commonly defined as the art of speaking persuasively or the art of speaking well. That is, like every art, it was thought of not merely in terms of its means, but also in terms of its end or effect. In this sense of poet-Creator (along with some other senses), Dryden depicts James II as the orator-divinity who creates the state, as God's "tuneful voice" had created the world. (James had a reputation for keeping his word, which is also involved.)

Thus *Britain's* Basis on a Word is laid,
As by a Word the World it self was made.[15]

In effect, James says, "I will be true" (giving his "Word") and the integrity, or "privity" as it was described, of the

[15] Epilogue to *Albion and Albanius,* 33–34.

king's body natural with his body politic (his subjects) was ensured. By such a rhetoric, we are also reminded, by such a *logos*, the world was created. And as that "Word was made flesh" in Jesus the Christ after having been with God "in the beginning" (John 1), so kings are God's vicegerents on earth, and so the Son of God is, in Milton's term, "*Israel's* true king."[16]

Such examples show how associations, analogous relations, reciprocations, and substitutions work among a few fertile concepts. By "Word" Dryden signifies a meaningful uttered sound, fidelity to one's promises, the divine *logos*, and the human analogue, the king, as the animating, soul-giving principle. No doubt in such an art of poetry there was more of the art of rhetoric than of the art of logic. But these images of art for life, for creation, and for the divine and human creations served to integrate diverse experience into those grand conceptions that the age spent its energies upon and made real. Even the dyspeptic Butler was highly learned and used the concepts in deliberately debased forms in his fury with man and the world. Neither *Hudibras* nor the *Leviathan*, neither *Paradise Lost* nor Dryden's *Fables*, would have been possible without the means of integrating the grand conception. How often do we recall that the progress of the *Leviathan* is from man and his faculties to "The Kingdom of Darkness"? Or that Hobbes follows his description "Of Commonwealth" with one "Of a Christian Commonwealth," ending with "what is necessary for a Man's Reception into the Kingdom of Heaven"? There are those who consider Hobbes the worst enemy of poets since Plato, and there are those who think with Dryden that Hobbes took up the study of poetry (to translate Homer) as he did geometry, too late. But if imaginative integration of large tracts of experience and a vision of the world in central images has

[16] For much of the lore behind kingship, see the excellent study by Ernst H. Kantorowicz, *The King's Two Bodies* (Princeton, 1957).

something to do with poetry, then if Hobbes, like Plato, be not a poet, where is poetry to be found?

A problem often encountered by poets of the general Renaissance persuasion is that the art of rhetoric was dependent upon the art of memory. Although most of us would recall at once that Memory was mother of the Muses, it has been shown how closely the *ars memoriae* is related to the theatre, and how meaningfully the theatre could be taken to image the world.[17] The world's great theatre was variously regarded for many generations as *theatrum mundi, theatrum orbis,* and *theatrum vitae humanae.*[18] Milton uses the actual word, "theatre," only two or three times in his poetry. But the usages, and related words, are of great importance. For instance, in *Paradise Lost,* there is Eden:

> A Silvan Scene, and as the ranks ascend
> Shade above shade, a woodie Theatre
> Of stateliest view.[19]

At that theatre there was played the drama of all mankind. Similarly, the "theatre" is everything to the place where Samson *acts* (1605). In Milton's mind, *theatre, scene,* and *temple* merge or diverge as he finds reason for them to do. Marvell's poem most in the Restoration mode is his *Horatian Ode upon Cromwel's Return from Ireland,* and in it we have two *actors.* Foremost of course there is Cromwell who gave up "the inglorious Arts of Peace" (10), who perhaps would "ruine the great Work of Time" (34), but who "had

[17] See Frances Yates, *The Art of Memory* (London, 1966) and *Theatre of the World* (London, 1969), to whom students of Milton and Dryden must be indebted although she says nothing much about the later seventeenth century.

[18] The standard study of the world-as-stage topos is that by E. R. Curtius, *European Literature in the Latin Middle Ages* (London, 1953), pp. 138 ff. See also Yates, *Theatre of the World,* ch. IX, for further elaboration and citation.

[19] IV, 140–42.

[a] wiser Art" (48). Charles I is the other, the "*Royal Actor*" who plays his last role on the "*Tragic Scaffold*" (53–54). As Marvell says with a play on the noun and a remarkable meiosis, it was a "memorable Scene" (58). That creature of the wars and fortune (113), Cromwell, must "March indefatigably on," for

> The same *Arts* that did *gain*
> A *Pow'r* must it *maintain.*
>
> (114, 119–20)

Such art for war's sake, or power's sake, no doubt expresses the trope with some obliqueness or at least freshness. But it must also be said that the sense of public reality is also very explicit. Unlike Shakespeare writing about Richard II and Bolingbroke back in the age of Chaucer, however, Marvell is writing about the momentous events of his own today, about the arts of reality. His art tells us that the world exists, and that men exist in it.

The art of memory functioned by giving topics a kind of associative reality. By associating a topic with a physical place such as a part of a theatre or other building, one could remember the parts of one's subject without difficulty and spend one's immediate energies on speaking most effectively. The physical associations of topics was natural enough, given that Greek *topos* and Latin *locus* meant "place" before they meant "commonplace." To most seventeenth-century poets, however, the "commonplaces," *loci communes,* were usually well-tried metaphors carrying a range of possible signification. So the theatre was not so much an aid to memory as the commonplace of the theatre was an emblem of life. To return to Dryden's "Song for St. Cecilia's Day," after the opening stanza depicts creation in terms of divine "tuneful" fiat and the achievement of world harmony, the middle stanzas depict the history of man in terms of progress pieces and ages of man represented by musical instruments.[20] And so to the third such set of long-tried poetic figures in the Grand Chorus:

As from the pow'r of sacred Lays
The Spheres began to move,
And sung the great Creator's praise
To all the bless'd above;
So when the last and dreadful hour
This crumbling Pageant shall devour,
The TRUMPET *shall be heard on high,*
The Dead shall live, the Living die,
And MUSICK *shall untune the Sky.*

Dryden uses the trumpet of doom as variously referred to in the Bible (e.g., Isaiah 27:13; Joel 2:1; 2 Corinthians 15:52; Revelation 8–9) as a climax to the progress piece of instruments and to usher in eternity again. But he does not stop with that. The trumpet must sound from somewhere, and as he says it "*shall be heard on high.*" That must mean from the heavens. Dryden does not say so, and the "heavens" of the Elizabethan theatre had yielded to a new architecture. But the musicians of the Restoration theatre occupied a similar place above the stage. Hence, the earth is the stage below, the *theatrum mundi: "This crumbling pageant."*

To give an example of one public voice in the preceding section of this chapter, I quoted a passage from *Absalom and Achitophel,* beginning with these lines:

Thus, in a Pageant Show, a Plot is made;
And Peace it self is War in Masquerade.

We can now observe the kinds of ideas Dryden develops. On the stage of the world, a false plot is played and, in the special terms of artful disguise, what is presented as peace is

[20] See *The Works of John Dryden,* as cited in n. 13 above.

war with a vizard-mask. As the seventeenth century never tired of doing, Dryden develops here some of the complex relations between art and what was then termed nature, or reality. Sometimes they were at one, sometimes in strife, and usually complementary in some fashion. The best art, according to the widely accepted proverb, was that which concealed itself. But such concealment also could suggest corruption, deceit, falseness. Achitophel comes to use "studied Arts" on Absalom, but only after he has been introduced with this line at the head of what is said of him: "Of these the false *Achitophel* was first" (150). That magnificent, almost Satanic falseness cannot be claimed by the giddy Zimri, who

> in the course of one revolving Moon,
> Was Chymist, Fidler, States-Man, and Buffoon:
> Then all for Women, Painting, Rhiming, Drinking;
> Besides ten thousand freaks that dy'd in thinking. . . .
> In squandring Wealth was his peculiar Art:
> Nothing went unrewarded, but Desert
>
> (549–52; 559–60)

An inimical art that equates science with fiddling and womanizing with painting—the whole giddy round consists of "freaks," aberrations from nature as much as meaningless art. On the other hand, a good character has "heavenly eloquence":

> The Prophets Sons by such example led,
> To Learning and to Loyalty were bred:
> For *Colleges* on bounteous Kings depend,
> And never Rebell was to Arts a friend.
>
> (869–73)

The Church, the many arts taught in the universities, and loyalty: heaven, art, and political life. No one need think that

Dryden's stand on these matters can go unquestioned, but no one should doubt that they derive from and strengthen a whole scheme of thought. Coming after an age when royalists had been ejected from colleges and pulpits, when the stained glass of most churches had been smashed, organs had been removed, and even much of St. Paul's had been let out for shops, Dryden's conservative assessment of the relation between various kinds of art and various aspects of life possesses a felt meaning.

Other people had equal passions for other meanings, and although there was no Dryden among them, there was an even greater poet who found his meaningful versions of the art-and-nature trope. As an epigraph for this chapter reveals, at the end of his *Second Defence,* Milton represents himself as an epic poet for having defended the English Puritan cause. As we assented with reservations to Dryden's world, so can we to Milton's, observing that his analogy also works in more than one way: not only has Milton written a prose epic, but the events themselves were of epic character, making their historical embodiment heroic. Milton had in a sense anticipated that observation as early as 1642 in his *Apology for . . . Smectymnuus:*

> And long it was not after, when I was confirm'd in this opinion, that he who would not be frustrate of his hope to write well hereafter in laudable things, ought him selfe to bee a true Poem, that is, a composition, and patterne of the best and honourablest things; not presuming to sing high praises of heroick men, or famous Cities, unlesse he have in himselfe the experience and the practice of all that which is praise-worthy.[21]

Ideally, life becomes art, the poet himself the fair poem. As Milton first fashioned himself into a composition and pat-

[21] *An Apology . . . ,* in *The Complete Prose Works of John Milton,* vol. I, ed. Don M. Wolfe (New Haven and London, 1953), p. 890.

tern, so from 1642 to 1660 he sought in prose to find a composition and pattern designed by God and executed by an elect nation. We shall see that Milton's hopes were repeatedly falsified by the national execution of that grand design and that, with perfect justice, he at last required the art of *Paradise Lost* to give a meaningful order to life.

So closely were art and nature related in the seventeenth century and so encompassing were they that, in Donne's phrase, "Nothing else is." A dialectician might distinguish between natural reasons and artificial reasons (devised by human art); and critics arguing for unity of time in plays could distinguish between a natural or an artificial day. No other kinds existed. As a result, when the proud emperor of dulness, Flecknoe, asks, "What share have we in Nature or in Art?" (176), the inference clearly is that they have no share in anything. The poets could relate divine and human creation in the dual sense of the act of creation and the creation resulting from the act. As Dryden and Milton have already suggested, art itself was nothing (in certain formulations) but another nature. As late as Goethe it could be said: "Kunst: eine andere Natur." [22] Sidney's account of the poet in his *Defence of Poetry* could only have been known to Milton and Dryden as a familiar truth very well stated:

> There is no Arte delivered to mankinde that hath not the workes of Nature for his principall object . . . [and Sidney goes on to mention how the astronomer, the mathematician, musician, philosopher, and others draw upon nature]. Onely the Poet, disdayning to be tied to any such subjection, lifted up with the vigor of his owne invention, dooth growe in effect another nature, in making things either better then Nature bringeth forth, or, quite a new, formes such as never were in Nature . . . so as hee goeth

[22] See the discussion of Goethe's phrase by Hermann Meyer, "Zum Problem der epischen Integration," *Trivium*, VIII (1950), 299–318.

hand in hand with Nature, not inclosed within the narrow warrant of her guifts, but freely ranging onely within the Zodiack of his owne wit.[23]

In that great march of ideas in what Alfred North Whitehead called the century of genius, there were many captains who carried such slogans, and who proclaimed their slogans to many ends. Here is Hobbes in the opening of his Introduction to *Leviathan:*

> Nature, the art whereby God hath made and governs the world, is by the *art* of man, as in many other things, so in this also imitated, that it can make an artificial animal. For seeing life is but a motion of limbs, the beginning whereof is in some principal part within; why may we not say, that all *automata* (engines that move themselves by springs and wheels as doth a watch) have an artificial life? For what is the *heart*, but a *spring;* and the *nerves*, but so many *strings;* and the *joints*, but so many *wheels*, giving motion to the whole body, such as was intended by the artificer? *Art* goes yet further, imitating that rational and most excellent work of nature, *man.* For by art is created that great LEVIATHAN called a COMMONWEALTH, or STATE, in Latin CIVITAS, which is but an artificial man; though of greater stature and strength than the natural, for whose protection and defence it was intended; and in which the *sovereignty* is an artificial *soul*, as giving life and motion to the whole body; the *magistrates*, and other *officers* of judicature and execution, artificial *joints; reward* and *punishment*, by which fastened to the seat of the sovereignty every joint and member is moved to perform his duty, are the *nerves*, that do the same in the body natural; the *wealth* and *riches* of all the

[23] In *Elizabethan Critical Essays*, ed. G. Gregory Smith, 2 vols. (Oxford, 1904), I, 155–56.

> particular members, are the *strength; salus populi,* the *people's safety,* its *business; counsellors,* by whom all things needful for it to know are suggested unto it, are the *memory; equity,* and *laws,* an artificial *reason* and *will; concord, health; sedition, sickness;* and *civil war, death.* Lastly, the *pacts* and *covenants,* by which the parts of his body politic were at first made, set together, and united, resemble that *fiat,* or the *let us make man,* pronounced by God in the creation.[24]

And here is Dryden's Crites in *Of Dramatick Poesie an Essay,* asking a momentous question.

> Is it not evident, in these last hundred years (when the Study of Philosophy [i.e., science in particular] has been the business of all the *Virtuosi* in *Christendome)* that almost a new Nature has been reveal'd to us? [25]

Hobbes, like Sidney, conceives of a single, seemingly timeless creation. Dryden, surely echoing Sidney, adds a historical dimension. For if art can reveal a *new* nature, then nature itself exists in history. With Dryden the idea of art another nature has for the first time, at least in English criticism, become part of that public possession in time for which history is the only simple name.

In his poetry, Dryden frequently embodies history and nature in progress pieces, accounts of the growth of an art. In his most general progress piece, that at the beginning of "To the Earl of Roscomon," he wonders about the doubtful beginnings of the "Arts."

> Whether the fruitful *Nile,* or *Tyrian* Shore,
> The seeds of Arts and Infant Science [knowledge] bore,

[24] *Leviathan,* ed. Michael Oakeshott (Oxford, 1960), p. 5.
[25] *Works,* ed. Swedenberg, *et al.,* XVII, 15.

'Tis sure the noble Plant, translated first,
Advanc'd its head in *Grecian* Gardens nurst.

Images of nature convey the growth of the arts, and hardly any concept here lacks a second meaning. Dryden plays, for example, on various English and Latinate meanings of "translation" in the poem, because it is dedicated to his noble friend "on his Excellent Essay on Translated Verse." The translation of the arts in history implies changes in the arts and a hope that the change is for the better. Dryden always treats such hope as possible or real, and in *To My Dear Friend Mr. Congreve,* he makes clear that a new age requires the effort to make "a new Nature." What had gone before in what Dryden usually terms "the former age," is now past. He has discovered that if there is to be something new, then the pastness of the past must be equally a reality:

Theirs was the Gyant Race, before the Flood;
And thus, when *Charles* Return'd, our Empire stood.
Like *Janus* he the stubborn Soil manur'd,
With Rules of Husbandry the rankness cur'd:
Tam'd us to manners, when the Stage was rude;
And boistrous *English* Wit, with Art indu'd.
Our Age was cultivated thus at length.[26]

The "Empire" spoken of is that of the kingdom of letters. The meagre soil required the working of hands ("manur'd") in order that the art of civilized cultivation could be realized. In the poems to Roscommon and Congreve, art and nature exist historically in progress pieces involving a cultivation that includes both terms.

The cultivation metaphor includes art and nature while relating both to a historical scheme in mini-narratives of

[26] *To . . . Congreve,* 5–11. According to Virgil, *Aeneid,* VIII, 306–56, Saturn took cultivation to Italy. Since Janus welcomed Saturn, Dryden depicts the Latin god doing what Saturn had taught.

the course of civilization. Beyond such matters, Dryden is creating the myth of the Restoration. Again and again, he relates that myth of revival as well as return. As return, Dryden emphasizes what is most conservative in him, his belief in the necessary reconstitution of the forms and institutions of civilizations. As revival, Dryden emphasizes as had no major poet before him the hope for progress and the faith in man's capacity to improve on his inheritance. Both Dryden's conservative and radical sides find numerous other versions between the middle and the end of the century, because other poets might place their radical hopes in new institutions or might hold to a conservative view of man's capacities. Whatever the variation, however, the world's stage is now that of the public theatre, the forum, and the state. Such formulations of the public version of the various tropes of art and nature obviously enabled poets to integrate individual passages or to play on certain well-tried commonplaces. But as Dryden shows, the public versions of art and nature also tended to give the poet a narrative emphasis and to give a historical coherence far larger than any incidental or even striking effect. Enrichment of style at its best suggests heightened experience, just as integration of whole works implies a clearer view of a larger world.

In the whole of that larger Renaissance in England that runs from the twelfth century to Dr. Johnson, nature and art have yet another set of relationships. It is a set explored with the rigor and the detail of modern science or linguistics, and it involves theology and natural philosophy as well as the operations of the mind, rhetoric, and what we today refer to as the arts. My aim does not require a discussion of that great whole, but is rather to emphasize the importance of the art of rhetoric in dealing with nature. Because nature, or reality, was itself not a neutral, cold, and factual thing but a divine creation, it was thought to entail values, hierarchies, and inner correspondences between steps in the hierarchy. In a somewhat similar way, rhetoric was thought to enable men to discuss what was real in ways that would move men's minds and arts in the presentation. Setting aside the ancient quarrel between philosophy and rhetoric, men like Milton, Dryden, and Butler believed that in dealing with what was common to men, what was public, reality could be manipulated without falsifying it. In simple terms, the rhetorical procedure most taken advantage of was amplification. *Amplificatio* presumes a norm of truth, nature. It also presumes that within limits the poet could raise or lower without transgressing the bounds of truth. Milton of course shows us better than anyone else how amplification to the greater could serve poetic truth. Before "Longinus" became known in England, Milton's *Paradise Lost* had become a demonstration of the treatise *On the Sublime*. Satan's career in *Paradise Lost* has no equal for gradations of amplification, but most of Dryden's career was spent in enlarging or belittling amplifications within a general presumption of epic. The great master of belittling amplification, the man whose genius was predicated on diminution, was Samuel Butler.

Hudibras provides few moments when the art of falling is intermitted. Butler's plain conviction is that nature—reality and human nature—is squalid, and his art is dedicated to sinking the low yet farther. Three of the most memorable episodes of *Hudibras* include that of the bear-baiting (I, ii and iii), the Skimmington procession (II, ii), and the visit to the astrologer, Sidrophel (II, iii). I shall consider the poem at greater length subsequently, but the point worth making here is that all three episodes deal with art forms illustrative of life as understood so infuriatingly by Butler. Bear-baiting represents one of the crudest forms of English art and pastime, which is enough to explain Butler's choice of it for the first major episode in the poem. Hudibras and Ralph are shocked by what Puritans called the carnal nature of the sport. They included maypoles and observance of Christmas among carnal practices deserving parliamentary ban. Butler simply chooses as debased a form as possible in order to reveal the yet more debased responses of his two anti-heroes. A Skimmington procession mocked a couple in which the henpecked husband was ridiculed on horseback along with his shrewish wife. For a wife to rule the husband was so preposterous (in theory) to the century as to constitute a major symbol of disorder. The disorderly, ridiculous spectacle revealed a disorder in nature. Similarly, Butler's astrologer practices one of the arts that burgeoned during the Interregnum (and which was practiced with a supposedly greater rigor by those enlightened souls, Dryden and Sir Isaac Newton). Butler takes pain that we understand that Sidrophel is a charlatan. Although, like Milton's Galileo in *Paradise Lost*, he possesses a telescope, his tawdry art is far removed from Milton's conception of study of

> the Moon, whose Orb
> Through Optic Glass the *Tuscan* Artist views
> At Ev'ning from the top of *Fesole*,
> Or in *Valdarno*, to descry new Lands,
> Rivers or Mountains in her spotty Globe.
>
> (I, 287–91)

To Butler astronomy and astrology (which were hopelessly entangled for most minds during the century) are an equal hoax. Sidrophel offends yet more by pretending to predict the future, because his "art" pretends to an impossible command over "nature." Even the stupid and superstitious Hudibras is not taken in and, in his one unquestionable victory in the poem, he beats up the dingy astrologer. Man must not, as Butler said, "strive nature to suborn" with such false art. And yet Butler is sufficiently a man of his time to have the Widow, or Lady, tell her malformed, greedy wooer at the end of the poem:

> The whole World without *Art*, and *Dress*,
> Would be but one great *Wilderness*.
> And Mankind but a Savage Heard,
> For all that Nature has Conferd.
>
> (*The Ladies Answer*, 233–36)

Butler's terms of reference are not strange, but his satire leaves man only a tragically marginal existence in the only world that we know.

With Milton and Dryden the amplifying spiral usually takes us up to increasing heights. But with *Hudibras*, and with nearly all else by its author, the relations between art and nature are such that the human creature deludes himself over the realm of art and yet falls into something like savagery without it. The motif we have been following in this section, and its uses, remains the same for Butler as for Milton and Dryden: art and nature invest public poetry with significance and provide a degree of integration. The difference with Butler turns out to be qualitative, a negative rather than a positive amplification.

We may take as a final example of the exchange of roles between art and life (or nature) one that illuminates the kind of thinking behind various seventeenth-century usages, and especially the public. When Davenant inscribed the Preface to *Gondibert* to the man Dryden rather disparagingly termed the Sage of Malmesbury, both that very Thomas Hobbes and he were in Parisian exile. The second and third paragraphs of Hobbes's "Answer" must be given in their entirety.

> As Philosophers have divided the Universe (their subject) into three Regions, *Caelestiall*, *Aeriall*, and *Terrestriall*; so the Poets, (whose worke it is by imitating humane life, in delightfull and measur'd lines, to avert men from

vice, and encline them to vertuous and honorable actions) have lodg'd themselves in the three Regions of mankind, *Court, Citty,* and *Country,* correspondent in some proportion, to those three Regions of the World. For there is in Princes, and men of conspicuous power (anciently called *Heroes*) a lustre and influence upon the rest of men, resembling that of the Heavens; and an insincerenesse, inconstancy, and troublesome humor of those that dwell in populous Citties, like the mobility, blustring, and impurity of the Aire; and a plainesse, and (though dull) yet a nutritive faculty in rurall people, that endures a comparison with the Earth they labour.

From hence have proceeded three sorts of Poesy: *Heroique, Scommatique,* and *Pastorall.* Every one of these is distinguished againe in the manner of *Representation,* which sometimes is *Narrative,* wherein the Poet himselfe relateth, and sometimes *Dramatique,* as when the persons are every one adorned and brought upon the Theater, to speake and act their owne parts. There is therefore neither more nor lesse then six sorts of Poesy. For the Heroique Poeme narrative (such as is yours) is called an *Epique Poeme;* The Heroique Poeme Dramatique, is *Tragedy.* The Scommatique Narrative, is *Satyre,* Dramatique is *Comedy.* The Pastorall narrative, is called simply *Pastorall* (anciently *Bucolique*) the same Dramatique, *Pastorall comedy.* The Figure therefore of an Epique Poeme, and of a Tragedy, ought to be the same, for they differ no more but in that they are pronounced by one, or many persons. Which I insert to justify the figure of yours, consisting of five bookes divided into Songs, or Cantoes, as five Acts divided into Scenes has ever bene the approved figure of a Tragedy.

Not many readers will think literary study in need of such geometry (the only science, Hobbes said, that God has yet seen fit to bestow on man). But for all the excessive rigor ("neither more nor lesse then six sorts of Poesy") Hobbes has got at something profound in seventeenth-century thinking and feeling. He has imaged all public life by the court, the city, and the country, and Davenant's epic makes use of all three. To our way of thinking, the country hardly represents public endeavor, and its poetic expression seems to require a Romantic celebration of a wholly different "nature." Poets like Vaughan and Marvell sometimes satisfy such expectations. But we should recall that Donne's private world normally assumes the anonymity of the city. More than that, philosophical and scientific speculation for human good involved, as Bacon said, retirement, not so much a pastoralism as a "georgics of the mind," to use his phrase. In addition, the experience of royalists during those years was making the wintering of the cold season on private country estates into a political act.[27] If any of Hobbes's terms is surprising, given usual attitudes in the century, it is the city. Even moderate royalists like Denham and Davenant were apt to regard the city as something of a threat to court and country. It remains a fact, however, that they included it rather than the court alone in what they termed "heroic song." The city really had to be included, partly because of the example of the ancients and the Church fathers, and partly because it was a real force in men's lives since the early stages of the Reformation. Especially on the Continent, but in London as well, the city was the center of an evolutionary, sometimes revolutionary, religious, political, and economic activity.[28] The court and its military avatar, the camp, were of course normal in epic poetry for centuries.

[27] See *The Cavalier Mode* (Princeton, 1971), ch. IV.

[28] The complex and central role of the city in these matters has been well discussed by Basil Hall, "The Reformation City," *Bulletin of the John Rylands Library*, LIV (1971), 103–48.

The notoriety earned by Hobbes in his day has continued to ours, but even his modern enemies must concede that he certainly found a way to make art and nature unite in a single view. That he was not eccentric can be understood by recalling the expulsion scene of *Paradise Lost* in the plate designed by Medina for the first illustrated edition of the poem (1688). Adam and Eve have come down a few steps from a gate in a wall on their way "To the subjected Plaine" of postlapsarian life. It is of course the plain into whose midst Bunyan's pilgrim runs, his fingers stopping his ears from his family's entreaty, while he cries for "Life! Life! Eternal Life!" But what is it that Adam and Eve depart from in descending those few steps? Does the wall represent a court? The evidence suggests that it does. Milton treats Adam's naming of the animals in the traditional Judaeo-Christian way as indicating his lordship over them. When they parade by him in *Paradise Lost,* it is to pay him "fealtie" (VIII, 344; see Genesis 1:26). His sin has lost him his full dominion over God's other creatures, and Milton's words near the end convey something of a lost castle divided from Adam and Eve by the celestial guard.

> They looking back, all th' Eastern side beheld
> Of Paradise, so late thir happie seat,
> Wav'd over by that flaming Brand, the Gate
> With dreadful Faces throng'd and fierie Armes.
>
> (XII, 641–44)

The portcullis, as it were, will not be raised by human hand.

At the same time, the wall is that of a city, the great subject of many an epic from the *Iliad* onward. Looking at Carthage, Aeneas can exclaim, "O fortunate they whose walls already rise" ("O fortunati quorum iam moenia surgunt"). But from Jewish experience, Jerusalem was also God's chosen city, and Christians merely adapted it typologically to the

New Jerusalem, the second paradise. Significantly, in *Paradise Regain'd* Jesus wins man the chance to regain the *civitas dei* by rejecting Satan's last temptation on a pinnacle in Jerusalem. A few biblical passages will clarify what Milton had in mind.

> But now they desire a better country, that is, an heavenly: wherefore God is not ashamed to be called their God: for he hath prepared for them a city.
>
> But ye are come . . . unto the city of the living God, the heavenly Jerusalem.
>
> . . . the name of the city of my God, which is new Jerusalem.[29]

In this sense, by recapitulation, paradise was a city, and there would be Sodom and Gomorrah or the evil cities of the plain, and finally the city of God, the new Jerusalem. Paradise provides a type of the heavenly city, just as St. Augustine's earthly city, Rome, is a corrupt version of the *civitas dei.* Medina well interpreted Milton to mean that Adam and Eve left a city as well as a court.

It will be obvious that they also leave a garden, the Garden of Eden, an inner portion of that larger Eden from whose east side they depart. Eden is walled and enclosed because of European habits of walling certain gardens, and because the walled or enclosed garden *(hortus conclusus)* was an emblem of the contemplative life and the meditating soul, just as many allegorically minded exegetes of the Eden story treated the garden as the soul of man.[30] Moreover, given the allegoriz-

[29] Hebrews 11:16; 12:22; Revelation 3:12. The concept of Jerusalem as God's chosen city of course emerges in the Psalms: e.g., 46:4, 48:1, 87:3.

[30] See Stanley Stewart, *The Enclosed Garden* (Madison, Milwaukee, and London, 1966); and J. M. Evans, *Paradise Lost and the Genesis Tradition* (Oxford, 1968), especially pp. 74–77.

ing of the principal other garden in the Old Testament, that of the Canticles, and given the treatment of Christ as the second Adam in the Gospels, a single verse from Solomon's song exerted enormous effect on the European imagination:

> A garden enclosed is my sister my spouse; a spring shut up, a fountain sealed. (Canticles 4:12)

In the first enclosed garden, Adam and Eve lived as one until they sinned. In the heavenly garden (but also city and court), Christ will live as one with His Church. Medina's illustration provides a brilliant exposition of the significance of the Expulsion in *Paradise Lost.* It is perhaps significant of the passing of a kind of thought shared by Milton and Hobbes that the wall and steps in illustrations of the Expulsion gradually fade away during the eighteenth century.

Hobbes and Milton share major images with each other and with their contemporaries. Such commonplaces represent but a few of the great stock related to art and nature; and to an age that esteemed commonplaces as part of perennial wisdom, the task was to render new. Milton proceeds to use all three emblems of court, city, and country (and temple, omitted by Hobbes but not Davenant) to invest his Eden with symbols of value that comprised all of civilized life. Hobbes in his philosophical way chose rather to divide them into three and to multiply by the two of narrative and dramatic genres.[31] To many of us, he is too imperious in dividing all his subject, as Caesar did Gaul, into three parts. But we should attend to what he and his contemporaries were doing, however foreign it may seem. Looking about at nature, that is, at human life, he found it possible to draw three distinctions of locale that answered to radical forms of experience. What was true of such a nature must be also

[31] The pastoral had of course always been associated with the country. It is also true that *rex* in Latin has associations with the epic. But it took Hobbes to categorize everything of importance to him.

true of art if it is to represent nature faithfully. Hobbes concluded—with a logic impeccable on his own presumptions—that therefore the court, city, and country of life must represent divisions of art, specific genres. I believe that we can find some sense in this mimetic logic and madness. Certainly one of the major implications of what Milton as well as Hobbes are about is a fundamental reordering of the genres.

iii. The Reordering of the Genres

A chief aim of literary history is to relate the development of a genre such as epic or lyric, to investigate some subspecies, or to discuss relations between genres in a given age. And literary theory has long been occupied with genres, their characteristics, their requirements, and their implications. In either enterprise, explicit or hidden assumptions from the other are necessarily entailed. In the first section of this chapter, certain more theoretical presumptions of literature between 1640 and 1700 were considered, those presumptions about the relation of man to other men and the world which make for a literary mode distinct from others being practiced at the same time or in different times. And in the second section, a representative and major feature of the relation between the literary mode and reality was discussed in terms of concerns that can be seen to have received major attention from poets of the seventeenth century. If it has not been evident, I must say now that the polarity of art and nature is not a concern confined to the public poets of the seventeenth century, any more than are such other polarities as nature and grace, the one and the many, or that commonplace unifying polarity, *discordia concors*. What distinguishes the poets considered in this volume is that such widely held concerns of the century found expression in public poetry rather than in poetry private or social. Once so radical a change had taken place (with of course many poets still faithful to private or social modes), the relations among the traditional genres could only be seen in different terms. The actual development of literature in time entails a conscious or unconscious, a slow or rapid reordering of the genres.

What can be seen among the genres can also often be seen in individual genres. Lyric poetry, for example, the great prize of earlier seventeenth-century styles, does not die in 1640 or even in 1700. But it does become relatively less important in the total relationship, which is to say that as a genre in itself it wanes in the old terms, both in terms of relative quantity and quality, and its best examples acquire characteristics from the dominant literary mode. To put it very curtly for the moment, Milton's sonnets become progressively more public, and those of Dryden's lyrics that live in the canon of English poetry are public, for the most part odes and elegies on historical individuals.

In part of the sentence following the two rather lengthy paragraphs quoted from Hobbes a few pages ago, we find lyricism dismissed:

> They that take for Poesy whatsoever is Writ in Verse, will thinke this division imperfect, and call in Sonnets, Epigrammes, Eclogues, and the like peeces (which are but Essayes, and parts of an entire Poeme) . . .[32]

None among us would dismiss the Metaphysical and Cavalier —or the Elizabethan and Romantic—achievements so airily. It may be true that the Donnes and Jonsons were unable to sustain long poems without the "stanzaic" repetition of the *Anniversaries*, for example.[33] But because post-Romantic critics have tended to cut up long poems on the shorter

[32] Hobbes, "Answer," in *Gondibert*, ed. David F. Gladish (Oxford, 1971), p. 46.

[33] See *The Metaphysical Mode* (Princeton, 1969), pp. 185–86. Similarly, Jonson's *Celebration of Charis* appears to seek to make a whole of individual lyrics written at different times.

procrustean bed of lyrics does not mean that we should fall into the opposite error and abuse lyric poetry for inability to go the whole distance. To apply more widely Jonson's criticism of Donne, any poet, any genre, any age can only aspire to be first in the world for some things. Contra Hobbes, lyric poems are no more fragments of larger poems than are larger poems simply amalgamations of smaller. We must consider differences in kind.

In depreciating lyricism, Hobbes has an importance as a sign of a change in which not only theory but actual practice demonstrate that poets are beginning to think differently in some major respects. To return for the moment to lyric poetry, it is significant in the gross that Milton and Dryden, or Rochester and Sedley, continue to find need of lyric poems. In that respect, they differ from their greatest eighteenth-century successors. But the change in the kind, quantity, and quality (alternatively in the descriptive and the evaluative senses) implies that lyric poetry has been reordered and that other genres have been placed above it. From about 1640 a new energy is moving in literature, not at first dominant nor ever exclusive of lyricism. But as Hobbes shows in one way, and Davenant's *Gondibert* and plays in another, the genres are being reordered so that varieties of narrative and drama claim the respect not only of theory but also of practice. Sir Philip Sidney had, in theory and in practice, far more sympathy than did Hobbes for "that Lyricall kind of Songs and Sonnets," and he placed that kind independently among the other genres.[34] In theory, however, Sidney shares with Hobbes and other critics of the larger Renaissance the view that the more extensive genres surpass the lyric. Like Hobbes, Milton, Butler, and Dryden, he believes the "Heroicall" to be the greatest. It is only fair to recognize that Sidney wrote in a historical context, as we all must.

[34] Sidney, in Smith, I, 201, 159.

England was still "so hard a step-mother to Poets" (I, 193), although before long *The Faerie Queene* and a drama magnificently varied in achievement would erase Sidney's doubts over *The Shepheardes Calendar* and assign his much admired *Gorbuduc* to the cabinet of historical curiosities.

An even profounder change occurred in attitudes toward the worth of poetry. The inheritance from the Elizabethans and the first half of the seventeenth century was a rich one. Critical theory had moved ahead, thanks to growing English awareness, to the rise of biblical and classical scholarship in England, and to their assistance to understanding of vernacular literature. And public poetry tended to short-circuit the arguments that poetry was frivolous or deceitful. One of the profoundest changes that had occurred by the second half of the seventeenth century will be found in the fact that unlike their Elizabethan predecessors, critics and poets no longer felt themselves in a vulnerable position, at least not until the end of the century when the drama fell into the censorious hands of the Colliers. Butler, Milton, and Dryden were sure of their art. It was no longer a "whining poesy" and it was no longer necessary to devote the chief critical effort to defense.[35]

They had only to write it. Of course many an aspirant found that the art of poetry was by no means less difficult than the art of defending poetry had been. In writing his "Answer" to Davenant, Hobbes was in the happy position of the critic. He could give voice to an emerging sense of that reordering which once again placed the epic as the highest and the normative genre. But he tried to do more. He tried to legislate the forms, the subjects, and the parts of life that each genre would treat. As his own poetic efforts show all too well, his attempt, remote from that of the practicing

[35] On the difficultics of the Elizabethan critics in defending poetry, see Smith, Introduction, III, "The Defence," pp. xxi–xxxi.

poet, resembled nothing so much as identifying six poetic vessels to be filled, three with red wine and three with white, before he had grown his literary grapes. In spite of his translations of Homer and his *De Mirabilibus Pecci,* his scheme resembled many philosophical schemes in being something perfectly amenable to logic but belied by practice. The only work in which he deserves to be thought a true poet is *Leviathan.*

If we choose to discount Hobbes's less tolerable fiats in mid-century, we still discover that he was well aware of a change of direction in the poetic winds. His description in Paris of the relative merits of poetic genres shortly became widely accepted doctrine in England, before long became the prescription of rules in France, and yet later caused reaction in England. The process is one common to all critical orthodoxies. What cannot be disputed in this great movement of sensibility is the displacement of lyricism from the pinnacle in favor of versions of narrative and drama. And as a part of this process we recognize that the Metaphysical poets wrote no plays, although their somewhat junior Calavier contemporaries did—without succeeding, however, in narrative.

In 1674, more than twenty years after *Gondibert,* René Rapin wrote and Thomas Rymer translated the *Reflections on Aristotle's Book of Poesie.* The opening paragraphs testify to that enduring French belief that practical concerns are so important that the critic owes it to the practitioners to tell them the rules of art. The sense does not vary that much from Hobbes, although the tone and style of Rapin-Rymer is a species of praise of Hobbes:

I.

ARISTOTLE distinguishes POESIE into Three divers kinds of perfect POEMS, the *Epick,* the *Tragick,* and the *Comick. Horace* reduces these Three into Two only, One

> whereof consists in *Action*, the Other in *Narration;* all the other Kinds whereof *Aristotle* makes mention, may be brought to these Two, the *Comedy* to the *Dramatick*, the *Satyr* to the *Comedy*, the *Ode* and *Eclogue* to the *Heroick* Poem; for the *Sonnet*, *Madrigal*, *Epigram*, &c. are only a sort of *imperfect* Poems; it is the Poets part to consult his Strength in the different ways he must hold in the different *Characters* of *Verse*, that he may not do violence to his *Genius*.
>
> II.
>
> The *Epick* Poem is that which is the *Greatest* and most *Noble* in *Poesie;* it is the *greatest Work* that Humane Wit is capable of. . . .[36]

Reading this, we wish to return to Hobbes as a liberating spirit. What it shows above all else is that a profound change of view has taken place, a radical reordering of the genres. If Donne had written literary criticism, he would no doubt have expressed views consonant with that general neoclassicism that runs in English from Chaucer to Dr. Johnson, although one would expect certain witty and neo-Platonic divagations.

Be the consensus what it may, however, the most profound critical assertion is found in the practice of the best poets, and it will be clear that lyric poetry (and dramatic) carried the prizes before there appeared the major works of the three principal poets considered in this volume, Butler, Milton, and Dryden. Donne could write of the world and Dryden could write lyrics. But Donne wrote of the world to reject it, and Dryden's finest lyrics are public in conception, often in the literal sense of being cantatas for public performance. The reordering of the genres, then, is not simply

[36] Rymer, trans., *Monsieur Rapin's Reflections on Aristotle's Treatise of Poesie*, 2nd ed. (London, 1694), pp. 76–77.

a matter of downgrading lyric forms and placing the heroic poem at the summit once more. The reordering offers a symptom that poets and readers were looking in new ways at themselves, their world, their fellow men, and religion, and also that out of such new approaches were being created new ideas and new values.

The higher regard for the heroic ideal and for a number of forms related to narrative suggest certain important preferences. Action now replaces vision as a prime ideal. Along with that, personality matters more than intimacy. Rather than seeking intense moments at which time seems to vanish, or than lamenting the evanescence of things, poets and readers have come to concern themselves with a historical scale, the sense of a *now* clearly related to a past and a future. All these relate to the fundamental assumption of the public mode, that what men share is what is most important, their likenesses, their civilized and other human inheritances. Without such an assumption, poets could believe in the Fall of Man and in all men's sharing in Adam and Eve's sin. And they could refer to the truth in their poems, developing a sense of sinfulness, perhaps, or writing in the *de contemptu mundi* vein. But without the public mode, *Paradise Lost*, a long narrative, an epic treating of our "general" parents, would have been impossible. Whatever grand vistas and ethical power we may discover in Donne and Jonson, the private or social lyric simply does not lend itself to Milton's "great Argument."

Hobbes and Rapin-Rymer represent the new temper in its more regulatory versions. A respect for the rules, or principles for writing literature, will be found to be sure in Sidney, Milton (see the epigraph to this chapter), and Dryden. Milton's little prefaces to *Paradise Lost* and *Samson Agonistes* resemble Protestant doctrine both by being doctrinaire and by insisting on our getting back to the pristine purity of the ancients. But Milton gives us a great paradox. He is the best classical scholar of all our great poets and a neoclassicist in critical utterance as well as choice of literary kinds in his mature work. At the same time, however, he alters the classical epic and the classical tragedy so far by giving them a Christian soul that their temper and meanings have been entirely altered. Other critics, like Dryden, were simply less rigid to begin with. For example, in 1682 the Earl of Mulgrave (John Sheffield, later Duke of Buckingham) not surprisingly prefers epic above other genres. But his *Essay on Poetry* shows no fuss or animus in ordering the genres. His series runs: songs, elegies, pindaric odes, satire (which is followed by an excursion into the drama that does not concern us here), and lastly epic. Three of the five non-dramatic categories are lyrical. That the highest of these is the pindaric ode tells us something of the shift to public poetry even in lyricism, but the balance in Mulgrave's series pretty well reflects the quantitative practice of the Restoration canon.

By the last decade of the century, we can observe an important shift in taste. The taste for regulation in formal matters that had originated in France is shown (as Dryden had said earlier) to be a product of its country of origin, not so much wrong as superfluous and self-regarding. Writing *On Poetry* in 1690, Sir William Temple comments:

> The modern French Wits (or pretenders) have been very severe in their censures, and exact in their rules, I think to very little purpose; for I know not, why they might not have contented themselves with those given by Aristotle and Horace, and have translated them rather than commented upon them . . . so as they seem, by their writings of this kind, rather to have valued themselves, than improved any body else.[37]

[37] *The Works*, 3 vols. (London, 1814), III, 417.

Here we encounter the urbane amateur of the next century, an empiricist who lowers the temperature of literary discussion. The gain is very great, but so is the loss. In fact Aristotle and Horace had been translated, Horace frequently. But if they were really to matter, their importance to a new age, other languages, and historically new forms would have to be shown, and that is what the best commentary and criticism on both sides of the Channel had been about.

Temple's preferences resemble those of his predecessors in that the epic is of course the acme of poetic achievement. Like all changes in taste, his involves tolerance in areas that had been previously thought to need close control and control in other areas that had been thought to require freedom. Here is his tolerance and his rigidity:

> When I speak of poetry, I mean not an ode or an elegy, a song or a satire, nor by a poet, the composer of any of these, but of a just poem; and after all I have said [concerning what is required of "just" poetry], it is no wonder there should be so few that appeared in any parts or any ages of the world, or that such as have should be so much admired, and have almost divinity ascribed to them, and to their works. (III, 415).

Such a high value on poetry seems to bring all ages and all persuasions together without fret over local rules or this or that little prejudice and insistence. Such tolerance differs greatly from the English patriotism, or chauvinism, that runs so strongly from Sidney to Dryden. But rigidity of a new kind is also here. It turns out that there are probably no more than two just poets, Homer and Virgil. Calliope, the Muse of the epic, does not have much to look after, and Erato and her lyric poets seem not to exist. In his *Preface* to Rapin, Thomas Rymer had shown no such urbanity, but a very large number of poets ancient and modern, French as well as English, had seemed to matter. Hobbes, Rapin, and Rymer (also Milton and Dryden) would not have bothered over the rules and principles of poetry if they thought that poetry was no longer possible. Temple represents, then, yet a further reordering of genres, or rather the first stage of development of a new taste.

The reordering of the genres begins with some now little read poets in the 1640's and 1650's, even while the great lyric energy was still spending itself and finding private or social presumptions about man the most satisfying. Gradually the new understanding becomes more widely available, turning in the pre-Romantic way for justification to a different set of classical writers from those drawn on most directly by earlier English poets. By the first and second decades of the Restoration, the public mode is in unquestioned triumph. So simple an account is true enough, but we must also acknowledge that no higher degree of tidiness prevailed then than ever exists. Vaughan and Cotton are late flowers of earlier kinds; Donne and Jonson still enjoy high reputation. Milton, the greatest classicist among our poets, refuses in his epics to invoke Calliope, calling instead upon Urania, the Muse of astronomy, by whom Milton of course means one of "Voice divine" (VII, 1–2), the Muse of Christian poetry. In fact his mentioning of the Muses proves very rare: four times in his longest poem and not at all in *Paradise Regain'd*. Dryden, another enthusiast for the ancients as well as the moderns, invokes the Muse only once, using the term frequently enough, but almost always to mean rather the poet's mind, character, genius—the poet himself. On that sole occasion that he invokes one of the Nine, it is in a pindaric ode rather than an epic, but the Muse is not therefore Erato but Clio, who presides over history. Being sufficiently at ease with the classical tradition, Butler, Milton, and Dryden feel free to treat it liberally. Of all the breathtaking freedoms taken, none rivals that of the first line of *Paradise Regained*: "I who e're while the happy Garden sung." We have seen what a resonance a word like "garden" or "court" could have, but to speak of that grand epic, *Paradise Lost*, covering eternity and all time, as a pastoral ditty focuses our minds just as Milton wishes us to with the startling statement: from garden to wilderness to the heavenly garden. Plainly the creation of a public poetry and the reordering of the genres did not render all one. Poetic individuality remained as much a determinant as ever. But a major change had certainly occurred.

PART TWO

THE TRIUMPH OF NARRATIVE

THE SEARCH FOR NEW LANGUAGE AND FORM: NARRATIVE POETRY FROM MORE TO CHAMBERLAYNE

And his Attendants, such blest Poets are,
As make unblemish'd Love, Courts best delight;
And sing the prosp'rous Batails of just warre;
By these the loving, Love, and valiant, fight.

O hyreless Science! and of all alone
The Liberal! Meanly the rest each State
In pension treats, but this depends on none;
Whose worth they rev'rendly forbear to rate.
— Davenant, *Gondibert*

The story of Loves civil Wars.
. . . no place for words,
The various business of the World, to see
What wondrous Change dwells in Eternitie.
— Chamberlayne, *Pharonnida*

The gradual definition of the public mode, the discovery of new means of using old commonplaces relating art to life, and the reordering of the genres constitute changes of such importance that numerous writers and readers were required to assist in the enterprise. Inevitably, much proceeded by fits and starts, and lesser works in the new vein were required before the greatest works began to appear. By the criteria of quality, the great works appear to stand by themselves, self-sufficient achievements. But the great works in the new mode are not short. Very many are narrative or quasi-narrative in nature, involving an unusual command over considerable bodies of experience. It does not surprise us, then, that Milton and Dryden are poets unusually mature in age when they write the works by which they are remembered. Even the precocious Cowley began with lyrics, essaying his finest public poetry only relatively late in life. No doubt narrative poets like others are born rather than made, but they also require time for maturing sufficiently to give their "art" command over the vast tracts of "nature."

Milton's admiration for Cowley tells us that any consideration of Milton, or of Butler and Dryden, requires attention to a number of poets whose efforts to create a new poetry came before the triumph of the 1660's and later. Such poets are the concern of this chapter. Their names will not be those often spoken of, and their works are even less often read. But some of them do exercise serious claim to attention, and their fall from currency owes as much to the post-Romantic predilection for lyric poetry as to their own limitations. The limitations are often considerable, and two or three of them must be confessed not a little odd. The oddness does not insure a claim on attention, but neither does it warrant unconsidered dismissal. If this were an account of seventeenth-century criticism, the explicit and implicit presumptions of narrative poets in the seventeenth century would require examination. Such consideration is out of place here, but it is hardly possible to consider the problems of narrative in the seventeenth century without some attention to language. By "language" is meant not just the kind or level of diction but also, and more than that, linguistic sets or strategies, prosody as a symptom of a larger poetic, and assumptions about how one speaks to others and organizes in words large forms of story. The search for narrative possibilities required the discovery of a new language of poetry.

Most critics agreed with Aristotle that the language of literature was among the last things to be considered.[1] Sidney termed diction to be merely the "out-side" of poetry, and Dryden had some words on Hobbes' translation and praise of Homer:

> Mr. *Hobbs,* in the Preface to his own bald Translation of the Ilias, (studying Poetry as he did Mathematicks, when it was too late) Mr. *Hobbs,* I say, begins the Praise of *Homer* where he should have ended it. He tells us, that the first Beauty of an Epick Poem consists in Diction, that is, in the Choice of Words, and Harmony of Numbers: Now, the Words are the Colouring of the Work, which in the Order of Nature is last to be consider'd. The Design, the Disposition, the Manners, and the Thoughts, are all before it: where any of those wanting or imperfect, so much wants or is imperfect in the Imitation of Humane Life; which is in the very Definition of a Poem.[2]

Dryden here follows Aristotle with some fidelity. The terms "design" and "disposition" of course correspond to Aristotle's central concern with plot, as does "manners" (i.e., moral conduct) to Aristotle's second concern, character portrayal. Dryden's "thoughts" translates Aristotle's third term. Aristotle placed language fourth and all but ignored the last two elements he distinguished in tragedy, song and spectacle. Since the last two were irrelevant to narrative poetry, Dryden does not bother to consider them.

Because literature of all kinds is a creation in language, we

[1] Aristotle, *Poetics,* VI. See Gerald F. Else, *Aristotle's Poetics: The Argument* (Cambridge, Mass., 1967), pp. 232–80.

[2] Sidney, *Apology,* ed. G. Gregory Smith, *Elizabethan Critical Essays,* 2 vols (Oxford, 1904), I, 201; Dryden, "Preface" to *Fables, The Poems of John Dryden,* ed. James Kinsley, 4 vols. (Oxford, 1958), IV, 1448–49.

may well wonder at the relatively low status given "words" by Aristotle and Dryden. And equally we may be baffled that Milton, that great master of a language totally his own, should not bother to comment on it in his prefaces. Such depreciations or omissions can only be explained by the principle of prior assumption. Aristotle, Milton, and Dryden simply assumed that a poet had command of his whole linguistic world. That was an unspoken premise from which all else began. For the same reason Dickens, master performer that he was on the page as well as in the theatre, does not trouble himself over language. It is a happy assumption to be able to make. We shall also see that to poets entertaining large works, Aristotle's priorities might seem right. All the same, many of the predecessors of Butler, Milton, and Dryden spoke their own tongues and yet found great difficulty in managing what Dryden terms "design," "disposition," and "thoughts."

The assumption that the poet, by definition, commands language conceals a very considerable seventeenth-century uneasiness over language. No one put the matter more succinctly than Edmund Waller in the fourth and fifth stanzas of his poem, "Of English Verse":

> Poets that lasting Marble seek
> Must carve in *Latine,* or in *Greek;*
> We write in Sand, our Language grows,
> And like the Tide our work o're flows.
>
> *Chaucer* his Sense can only boast,
> The glory of his numbers lost,
> Years have defac'd his matchless strain,
> And yet he did not sing in vain.[3]

[3] 13–20. Once again I acknowledge with gratitude the kindness of Philip R. Wikelund in furnishing me the text of these lines by Waller from his forthcoming edition.

Something of Chaucer was left, but English poets looked with envy at the reforms in French spelling and usage. Poets sighed for the seeming perfection of Latin and Greek. But they were after all English and so wrote in English, and since they were poets they invented as it were new languages (a term, as Dryden shows, including prosody). Butler's Hudibrastics, Milton's blank verse paragraphs, and Dryden's couplet or stanza paragraphs represent the three most distinguished languages in non-dramatic poetry of the time. But we shall see that other languages were being written if not spoken. And in our assessment we shall also see the importance of action, character, and thoughts.

i. Beginnings in More and Kynaston

The revival of narrative poetry coincided with deep political strains and the outbreak of civil war. Such coincidence was not necessary, but it was a factor that affected poets differently, making some concerned with glancing at the troubles of the day and others looking inward to the consolations of philosophy. Above all, however, there was a struggle to achieve something great, something commensurate with the scale of contemporary events. The most useful of predecessors at first were Spenser and the Fletchers, who soon yielded to a tradition of romance going back as far as Chaucer but more and more wrought with aspirations for the heroic. A constant problem facing these narrative poets was that facing all writers of narrative: creation of a story that seemed at once interesting and important. From our beginnings in Henry More and Sir Francis Kynaston we can see this problem. At one extreme, a writer may invest his narrative with all the philosophical or other significance in his mind, and so lose hold of simple plot. Or at the other extreme, he may write a plot that moves so jauntily and quickly that when it is over one doubts that it has meant a blessed thing. It is astonishing that in the two decades preceding the appearance of *Hudibras* (Part One, 1662) a whole art of narrative had been devised.

The Christian, or Cambridge, Neoplatonist Henry More first produced a narrative entitled ΨΥΧΩΔΙΑ *Platonica: or A Platonicall Song of the Soul* at Cambridge in 1642. More's scientific interests emerge more clearly in a collection supplementary to the former poem in 1646: *Democritus Platonissans, or an Essay upon the Infinity of Worlds out of Platonic Principles.* Epicurus, Ficino, Descartes, and Christianity mingle in an allegory. In 1647 *Democritus Platonissans* was printed with Psyche's *Song* under the general title of *Philosophical Poems.* By now, however, More had woven the two together in a way requiring, for full explanation, the reader to have a copy in his hand. Suffice it to say that the working title of the whole is *A Platonick Song of the Soul* and that More himself usually refers to his work as the *Song of the Soul.* The 1647 *Philosophical Poems* is of capital importance to understanding More, because he added to it an index of characters and ideas, "The Interpretation Generall."

Among most students of Renaissance literature, the possibility of Neoplatonism increases at once the value of a literary work. If ever there was a Neoplatonic English poet, Henry More was the one. Of course his Neoplatonism has very little connection with Plato, who was not fully extracted from Ficino and other interpreters until the last century. But Psyche's *Song* is unquestionably "platonick." In "To the Reader," More sets out an analogy between Neoplatonism and Christianity.

> *Ahad, Aeon,* and *Psyche* [his heroes and heroine] are all omnipresent in the World, after the most perfect way that humane reason can conceive of. For they are in the world all totally and at once every where.
>
> This is the the famous Platonicall Triad: which though

> they that slight the Christian Trinity do take for a figment; yet I think it is no contemptible argument, that the Platonists, the best and divinest of Philosophers, and the Christians, the best of all that do professe religion, do both concur that there is a Trinity. In what they differ, I leave to be found out according to the safe direction of that infallible Rule of Faith, the holy Word.[4]

The first part of the poem has the separate title, *Psychozoia, or The Life of the Soul;* and this part "has," we are told, "the first spontaneous glow of the satisfying revelation the author's passionately hungry soul had sought and found"; it is further reassuring that "The most Spenserian and most attractive of these poems" is *Psychozoia,* because I confess it difficult to get much beyond it.[5] Since the poem is not widely read, I shall undertake a brief characterization. Ahad is the Neoplatonic One, from which the multiplicity of creation derives, and is analagous to God the Father in the Christian Trinity. Aeon is eternity, but since he is described as "My first born Sonne" (I, 34), we have no difficulty in recognizing the analogy with God the Son. Psyche is "Soul, or spirit," in More's Neoplatonic sense not of an individual but of the whole universe. Since Ahad calls her "my Daughter dear" (I, 34), she is less perfectly analagous to God the Holy Spirit. The poem begins with the argument: "No Ladies loves, nor Knights brave martiall deeds . . . [but] *Psyche,* I'll sing" and something of an invocation. The first real action occurs when Ahad marries his son Aeon to his daughter Psyche (I, 33). The remainder of Canto I (which is made up of sixty-one Spenserian stanzas) is given over to description of the ceremony and of Psyche's garments—the material world—one of the commonest of Neoplatonic ideas at the time.

[4] *Philosophical Poems* (Cambridge, 1647; Scolar Press facsimile), sig. B 7^r.

[5] Douglas Bush, *English Literature in the Earlier Seventeenth-Century,* 2nd ed. (Oxford, 1962), pp. 92, 91.

At the beginning of Canto II our poet takes us rather at surprise by changing some of the names, as for example Aeon to Autocalon, and then by revealing to us:

> When *Psyche* wedded to *Autocalon*,
> They both to *Ahad* forthwith straight were wed:
> For as you heard, all these became but one,
> And so conjoyn'd they lie all in one bed,
> And with that four-fold vest they be all overspred. (II, i)

The unity of the Neoplatonic trinity emerges from this, and of course the "four-fold vest" represents Psyche's garments described at length in the preceding canto. To the liveliness of brother-sister incest in the first canto, More has added in the second father-daughter incest, not to mention father-son incest in what proves to be a plot developing suddenly after scarcely moving through the first canto. The pace is sustained after a fashion, because by the sixth stanza the poet begins to tell us of Psyche's progeny. It must be understood that More is talking about the visible world, or at the least lower orders of creation, because otherwise the reader might be surprised that such unexceptionable parentage brings forth, among others, that evil pair, Daemon and Duessa, along with their sons Autophilus (self-love) and Philosomatus (love of the body).

At this point More introduces Mnemon, and memory, it turns out, is one thousand years old; whether at birth or in a sudden temporal leap of the plot is not really clear. Mnemon gets the mundane plot under way by relating the first of his travels, in Psittacusa (the land of parrots) and his conversation there with Don Psittaco. Don Psittaco subsequently introduces Mnemon to Corvino (Roman Catholicism) and Graeculo (extreme Protestantism). Traveling on, Mnemon encounters cities representing various political schemes. Then Simon, the hero of what follows in *Psychozoia*, is suddenly introduced to us. He travels with Mnemon and others on a journey representing the progress of the good individual soul, Simon, to perfection. So *The Life of the Soul* comes to its close with its third canto.

It seems improbable to me that any reader of *The Life of the Soul* will single out its plot for praise. But that the poem has had readers can be demonstrated by the echoes of More's Hyle in Milton's chaos, and of More's Pandaemoniothen in Milton's Pandemonium. The difference between the two poems is more radical than these connections. If proof of that be necessary, we need only compare More's evil characters with Milton's fallen angels in the first two books of *Paradise Lost*.

> That rabble rout that in this Castle won [dwells],
> Is irefull-ignorance, Unseemly-zeal,
> Strong-self-conceit, Rotten-religion,
> Contentious-reproch-'gainst-Michael-
> If-he-of-*Moses*-body-ought-reveal-
> Which-their-dull-skonses[-]cannot-eas'ly-reach,
> Love-of-the-carkas, An[-]Inept-appeal-
> T'uncertain[-]papyrs, a-False-formall-fetch-
> Of[-]feigned-sighs, Contempt-of-poore-and-sinfull-
> wretch. (III, 13)

The charms of Neoplatonism hardly extend to a character named Contentious-reproch-'gainst-Michael-If-he-of-*Moses*-body-ought-reveal-Which-their-dull-skonses[-]cannot-eas'ly-reach. (How much finer are Bunyan's conjugate names.) More is not done, for he has more—two stanzas of this nonsense in which I find it particularly difficult to detect "the first spontaneous glow of the satisfying revelation" of anything poetic. These evil ones are later defeated by "the mighty warlick Michaels host," and in one stanza (except for its bathetic last line) we hear true poetry.

In perfect silver glistring panoply
They ride, the army of the highest God.
Ten thousands of his Saints approachen nie,
To judge the world, and rule it with his rod.
They leave all plain whereever they have trod.
Each Rider on his shield doth bear the Sun
With golden shining beams dispread abroad,
The Sun of righteousness at high day noon,
By this same strength, I ween, this Fort is easily wonne.

(III, 27)

All Henry More need do is turn from religious action (the Angels Militant under Michael) to platonick allegory and the art of sinking is mastered. In spite of Aristotle, Sidney, and Dryden, we believe that when the "language" of the poem is so palpably incompetent, any discussion of further issues seems superfluous. Anyone who can marry brother to sister and both to father, bedding them at once under the world (Psyche's robe), leads us to ask why he wrote a poem when he might have written a prose treatise. I fear that the answer is that writers of the Neoplatonic persuasion fancy themselves poetic *ipso facto,* as do many of their admirers, but that the kind of poet wholly attracted to such beliefs usually lacks the requisite talents. More's poem (of which we have considered the first, best part) shows the extraordinary difficulties that lie in the way of anyone seeking to be a narrative poet, even if he knows full well what he designs his poem to mean. There is something, in the end, altogether pathetic about More's attempt to write a fully philosophical poem.

Sir Francis Kynaston's *Leoline and Sydanis* also appeared in 1642, also in stanzas (rhyme royal). The poem is a delight. It deals with matters often naughty or incredible with such aplomb and zest that I have found myself rereading the whole thing again when I looked at its beginning. It begins, like

More, where many poems end. Within twenty stanzas Leoline and Sydanis (accent on the first syllable) are married. Then a vile Frenchman rejected by Sydanis casts a spell on Leoline.

> For by it was he maleficiated
> And quite depriv'd of all ability
> To use a woman, as shall be related,
> For Nature felt an imbecility,
> Extinguishing in him virility:
> The sad events where of to set before ye
> Is as the dire Praeludium to our story.
>
> (I, xxix)

What follows is comic in one of Chaucer's veins, and the reader will have recognized in Kynaston's last two lines quoted an echo of the first stanza of *Troilus and Criseyde*, some parts of which Kynaston succeeded in putting into Latin rhyme royal. Everything amuses or interests the reader of Kynaston's story, and we must accord high marks to the vital presence it exerts. I am unaware, however, of any significance it may possess.

Still, Leoline's excuses on his wedding night are very funny. After that night, Sydanis' Nurse posts to a Druid's cave for a potion to help Leoline to raise "Venus's standard." Alas, the potion puts him into a deathlike sleep, much like Juliet's. So Sydanis, thinking Leoline dead, is persuaded to flee suspicion in disguise as a man. She does so and, assisted by a druidic spell, is conveyed to Ireland. There she (still in disguise) serves the princess as a favored courtier until, of all people, Leoline shows up. Possessing more virility than he does virtue for women other than Sydanis, he seeks out the princess. Sydanis thwarts him by bedding herself rather than her rival with Leoline. This time all works according to nature and before long the whole plot—which is sustained to the end by larks and hijinks of many kinds—closes. In the last stanza but two, Kynaston with feigned surprise recalls that he had left the Nurse, Merioneth, in dungeon.

cdlxxxii

Who albeit that she long dead was thought,
And in the dungeon starv'd for want of food,
Yet to Duke Leon [Sydanis' father] she again was brought,
From whom he divers stories understood,
And now in fine all sorted unto good:
Whose wonderful relations serve in Wales
To pass away long nights in winter's tales.

cdlxxxiii

And lastly for to consummate all joy,
Ere Phoebe nine times had renew'd her light,
Fair Sydanis brought forth a Prince, a boy,
Heaven's choicest darling, and mankind's delight:
Of whose exploits some happier pen may write,
And may relate strange things to be admir'd:
For here my fainting pen is well near tir'd.

It is difficult to imagine a poem on which glosses would seem more pedantic. It would be superfluous to gloss the fourth line from the last stanza quoted with Suetonius on the emperor Titus, "amor ac deliciae generis humani," or with the description of the king in *Absalom and Achitophel*, "Mankinds delight" (318). Yet it is worthy of notice that Kynaston's style has something of the rapid energy of Dryden's, no doubt moving the faster for not being burdened with ideas. *Leoline and Sydanis* is one of those works that means very well by the reader without meaning much of anything in itself. In a sense, Kynaston is as bankrupt of narrative as More, since his failing on the other side is equally radical. But he is incomparably more readable. He ticks off a night-piece here, an inexpressibility-topos there, inventing fern-seed elsewhere, and in general writes a poem that adds a spark of divine fire to the unstrained intelligence of a sophomore. One can do far worse than read *Leoline and Sydanis*, which is probably the best of the "good reads" provided by the seventeenth century.

ii. Narrative Experiment: Quarles, Davenant, and Cowley

We must linger a moment with Francis Quarles before considering Sir William Davenant and Abraham Cowley. The most popular poet of the century, Quarles belongs to a rather earlier time. His *Divine Poems* first appeared in 1633, and its "Fifth Edition" in 1643, about the same time that More and Kynaston appeared as poets. Quarles' collection includes paraphrases of certain biblical stories: Esther, Job, and Samson. They are not devoid of interest. The combination of occasional experiments in versification, of royalism, emblems, and sententiae makes it a revealing product of its time. But Quarles' means of achieving significant movement prove better worth contrasting with the gains sought and the losses accepted by More and Kynaston. *The Historie of Ester* begins with a prayer, "To the Highest," in six-line stanzas. There follow twenty parts, each of which possesses three constituents: an "Argument" made up of two tetrameter couplets, a "Section" retelling the biblical story in pentameter couplets, and a "Meditation" on the biblical story, also in pentameter couplets. In religious terms, Quarles adapts the major tradition of English Protestant meditation: on a biblical text. In narrative terms, he neatly separates the story from the significance he derives from it. Or, more charitably, he juxtaposes the two. There is much in Quarles' methods worth comparing with Donne's meditative verse, although the quality of mind functioning differs considerably. By devising a workable method and by writing with some art on religion,

Quarles assured himself of popularity. Meditations continue to be written into the eighteenth century, but the new outward looking sensibility emergent in More and Kynaston gropes toward worlds that Quarles did not very much concern himself with in his biblical narratives.

Davenant and Cowley, writing a decade or so after More and Kynaston, advanced much farther toward the creation of a meaningful world of heroic romance. Neither finished his principal English poem, but both made considerable progress in narrative language and conception. More and Kynaston betrayed a tie with the Spenserian and romance past by their use of complex stanza forms. Davenant took a step forward by using a simpler stanza, the heroic quatrain, and Cowley moved yet farther by choosing the heroic couplet; both, but especially Cowley, achieve a degree of stylistic clarity that seems to have been prerequisite to any higher developments. Dryden was to acknowledge that Davenant's quatrains were his model in *Annus Mirabilis,* and Cowley holds an important place in the slow redevelopment of ordonnance in the heroic couplet. I believe it true to say that all readers feel that Milton's blank verse implies a different view of the world through poetry than does rhymed verse, and that is the kind of thing I mean when I speak of "languages" of narrative, of organizing the expressive systems of major poems. No doubt there is something demotic about the languages being considered thus far, but the shift from More's Spenserian stanzas to Cowley's couplets represents among other things an urge to leave celebration and to cultivate action and description. Once English poets had convinced themselves that the "heroic poem" told them most about themselves, and once they believed that such poetry was possible, they had of necessity to turn to such fundamental questions as prosody.

Davenant possessed the advantages and the disadvantages

of having been a practicing dramatist before 1642, when the theatres were closed. Dramatic plots resemble those of narrative in certain ways while yet differing in others (to stage Books III, V-VI, or other parts of *Paradise Lost*, would be an absurdity). It seems clear to me that Davenant took up *Gondibert* when he was denied the opportunity to do what he liked best, work in the theatre. After all, he had ample opportunity to complete *Gondibert* when he got out of prison. Instead, he was at work on dramatic productions, even before the Restoration. Of all the men who wrote narratives in verse or prose supposedly modeled on the five-act structure of drama, Davenant most convinces me that he knew best what the five-act structure was. He has sometimes been criticized for his design of one genre in the terms of another, and in some ways the criticism may be deserved. But it will not be amiss to hear him out:

> I have drawn the body of an Heroick Poem: In which I did . . . observe the Symmetry, proportioning five bookes to five *Acts*, and *Canto's* to *Scenes* (the Scenes, having their number ever govern'd by occasion).

Davenant goes on to describe the five-act development of English plays:

> The first *Act* is the generall preparative, by rendring the cheefest characters of persons, and ending with something that lookes like an obscure promise of designe. The second begins with an introducement of new persons, so finishes all the characters, and ends with some little performance of that designe which was promis'd at the parting of the first *Act*. The Third makes a visible correspondence in the Underwalks (or lesser intrigues) of persons; and ends with an ample turne of the maine designe, and expectation of a new. The fourth (ever having occasion to

> be the longest) gives a notorious turne to all the Underwalks, and a conterturne to that maine designe which chang'd in the Third. The Fifth begins with an intire diversion of the mayne, and dependant Plotts; then makes the generall correspondence of the persons more discernable, and ends with an easy untying of those particular knots, which made a contexture of the whole; leaving such satisfaction of probabilities with the Spectator, as may persuade him that neither Fortune in the fate of the Persons, nor the Writer in the Representment, have been unnaturall or exorbitant.[6]

Davenant gives us real insight into the craft of playwriting in the century, and it seems possible that a narrative could be fashioned along such lines. To those two observations must be added a third, however, and that is that *Gondibert* does not conform to the pattern. The second book/act does not begin "with an introducement of new persons," and the third does not end "with an ample turne of the maine designe, and expectation of a new." No one could say absolutely how well the fourth and fifth parts would have conformed to the supposed pattern, but this much is clear: one of the most experienced dramatists of the time essayed narrative modeled on the five-act structure and failed both to complete his narrative and to follow the proposed model. If Davenant had not told us of his model, we should not have supposed it. It may be that the poet required the supposition of such a form in order to write non-dramatic poetry of such length. But I suspect that what was in Davenant's mind, and those of others, was

[6] *Sir William Davenant's Gondibert*, ed. David F. Gladish (Oxford, 1971), p. 16, with change by me in confusing punctuation. For other studies of the "five-act structure" of narratives, see p. xx. Book I of *Gondibert* has six cantos, II eight, and III six—or seven, including the so-called "lost canto" printed later and surviving in but two known copies.

a theoretical desire to combine the two noblest genres, narrative and drama.

Looking at *Gondibert* without dramatic presumptions, one readily sees a characteristic Renaissance attempt to make an epic of the verse romance. The romance usually has a title that sets before the reader the names of the hero and heroine. The readers of Saintsbury's *Minor Caroline Poets* will recall John Chalkhill's *Thealma and Clearchus* (1683, but written much earlier), Patrick Hannay's *Sheretine and Mariana* (1622, merely two cantos), and Nathaniel Whiting's *Albino and Bellama* (1638, a naughty poem for a man who was to become a rabid Puritan). In the same year that *Gondibert* appeared, 1651, there also appeared William Bosworth's *Arcadus and Sepha*. We might also recall Kynaston's *Leoline and Sydanis*. Chamberlayne's *Pharonnida* (the subject of the next section of this chapter) might well have had "and Argalia" added to its title. Davenant appropriately does not add the heroine's name to his poem, because the poem as we have it leaves off with Gondibert committed to two women. His contemporaries presumed that Gondibert would marry the sweet Birtha of the country, and perhaps her name could be added to his in the usual style.

The point of the usual practice is that it helps distinguish between the romance and the epic elements in verse narrative. Sometimes the distinction is difficult, and at other times it is unnecessary. But as the titles show, the romance can be distinguished from the classical epic by the centrality of love as a subject. Conversely, the classical epic is distinguished from the romance by the centrality of valor and strenuous high purpose to an important end. Tasso's *Jerusalem Delivered* enjoyed great popularity in England, in considerable measure for his very successful fusion of love and valor. As we are told early in *Gondibert*, "Beauty and Valor native Jewels are, / And as each others only price agree" (I, i, 69).

Davenant's situating of his poem in "Gothic" Lombardy accords well enough with both subjects, but his "Preface" makes clear that revival of the heroic subject was prominent in his mind. He writes that "the most effectuall Schooles of Morality, are Courts and Camps." And again, "I may now beleeve I have usefully taken from Courts and Camps, the patterns of such as will be fit to be imitated by the most necessary Men." [7] As a single concept, "Courts and Camps" implies rule and intrigue as well as valor, so that Davenant's "patterns" argues for a courtesy-book intent. In none of this does he have Tasso's clarity of mind and integrative powers. We need only remind ourselves of the valor of Tasso's *women* and the relation between love and war in *Gerusalemme Liberata* to understand Davenant's relative failure to bring off *Gondibert*. The poem as we have it divides markedly into a portion concerned with valor and a portion with love. Prior to the fifth canto of the second book, valor is the concern. There follow the two fascinating Astragon cantos (II, v and vi), and after them the poem as we have it turns on love. Dividing the poem in this fashion, we discover many versions of honorable or crafty warriors and courtiers in the first part and numerous versions of lovers in the second. Davenant has made very considerable advances upon More and Kynaston in terms of making significant movement out of movement and significance, but he could not bring the whole together consistently or even finish it.

A précis of the poem will not be amiss. Aribert, a Lombard king ruling ca. A. D. 750, has a daughter, Rhodalind. Prince Oswald, the heroic villain of the former part of the poem, and Duke Gondibert are thought to be rivals for the princess. While Gondibert and his men are engaged in a hunt, Oswald appears in great strength to catch his rival by surprise and defeat him. Being discovered, Oswald parleys, and single

[7] In Gladish, pp. 12, 13.

combat is agreed upon. The duel between Gondibert and Oswald shortly becomes a battle. Although he slays Oswald, Gondibert is himself severely wounded and is borne to the palace of "sage *Astragon*" for treatment. The first book ends there.

The second book begins with a description of Verona and its noble inhabitants, who react strongly but diversely to news of what has happened. Princess Rhodalind and the other ladies of the court do not rival in interest the passionately angry Gartha, sister of the dead Oswald and no less ambitious than he. She storms off to Oswald's camp and is about to fire his men into attack on Verona when old Hermegild visits the camp and counsels guile. Hermegild is motivated both by ambition and by his passion for Gartha. She is wise enough to accept his counsel without committing herself to him. We are now come to the Astragon cantos, the poem's third major shift in scene. Davenant first describes the house of Astragon as a scientific establishment (II, v) and then as a religious temple (II, vi). The former recalls Bacon's Solomon's House and presents the first clear English poetic advocacy of the "Copernican" heliocentric universe. The religion seems to be a Socinian version of Anglicanism, in that it does not mention the second or third persons of the Trinity, and yet very much unlike the Puritans it emphasizes "*Pray'r, and Penitence, but most . . . Praise.*" [8]

An important shift in the plot occurs in the next canto (II, vii). Gondibert and Birtha, Astragon's sweet and innocent daughter, fall in love. They subsequently inform her father, and so the second book ends. The third book, written by Davenant while imprisoned by Commonwealth authorities and under sentence of execution, returns to Verona and the

[8] "Argument," II, vi. The Puritans were criticized for being "petitionary," for always asking God for favors. See *The Cavalier Mode from Jonson to Cotton* (Princeton, 1971), pp. 194–95.

cast of minor characters as well as a few major ones. The climax of the love plot as we have it occurs when Aribert, accompanied by Rhodalind and his train, makes a royal progress to Gondibert, offering his daughter and inheritance of the throne. Gondibert equivocates with the King and thereafter seals his vows to Birtha with a miraculous emerald whose color will change if he changes in faith to her. After this inconclusive episode, there follow two or three cantos situated in Verona, again featuring minor characters.

We read the poem, then, finding epic assumptions better satisfied by the first portion of the poem, and romance expectations better fulfilled in the second. And we find a philosophical interlude between. It seems most likely that if Davenant had continued, romance would have continued to dominate. It really is quite remarkable how agreed Davenant's contemporaries were in considering the romance element the important thing in the poem. Henry Vaughan wrote "To Sir William Davenant on his *Gondibert*" almost immediately on reading the poem (Vaughan's verses appeared in *Olor Iscanus* in 1651, the year *Gondibert* was published). He emphasized Davenant's success in obtaining verisimilitude in his "wonders" and especially love as the poem's topic. Vaughan devoted a whole passage (35-48) to Birtha, assuming that she will marry the hero. Such assumptions were made by the wits in attacking Davenant. One laughed at him for preferring "this simpling Girle" to a princess.[9] For all such agreement, it is not clear that Davenant could have gone any farther with the romance plot than he had with his heroic plot or his philosophical digression.

The poem invites other approaches than those of plot, how-

[9] See, for example, Davenant in Gladish, p. 274. Gladish very well says that "Perhaps Gondibert will turn out to be a long-lost son of Aribert or Astragon and will be able to love both women, one as a sister" (p. xxii).

ever. Many a reader has suspected that the poem shadows in some fashion contemporary English events. The first person to hint of such matters was the poet himself. In his "Postscript," for example, he returns to his favorite image for the poem, a building: "I was now by degrees to present you (as I promis'd in the *Preface*) the severall Keys of the main Building; which should convey you through such short Walks as give an easie view of the whole Frame. But 'tis high time to strike Sail. . . ." [10] Readers of mid-century narratives as well as of poems in other genres must be prepared for such hints, for allusion to, or comment on, contemporary events. But it is also necessary to recognize the denials, evasions, and sudden shifts of what the writers seem at pains to establish. Davenant does not entirely suggest what he means by "Keys," and in any event he shifts direction as easily as metaphor. The so-called "lost" canto was dedicated to Charles Cotton the Younger, and Cotton responded with a poem in which he remarks, "Blest be my Father, who has found his Name / Among the Heroes, by your Pen reviv'd." It has been suggested that Cotton's words imply that the characters of the poem stand for Davenant's contemporaries, but Cotton may have meant no more than that Davenant had included his father's name in the dedication.[11]

The issue involved is very important, because it determines our sense of the significance of *Gondibert* and, beyond that, how we are to read much of the poetry written between 1640 and 1660. In *Gondibert*, as in numerous other poems, we do sense intermittent political or historical pressures. Davenant is much given to applying a maxim on public behavior to an event just completed in his story. He seems to wish to place

[10] In Gladish, p. 250.

[11] "To Sir William Davenant," 17–18, in Gladish, p. 287. Gladish draws attention to these lines in arguing for a historical allegory he is unable to outline clearly.

both the time of happening in *Gondibert* and the time of his age into clear relationship. He uses praise or satire of individuals and groups, and many of his pithy observations suggest that they stem from what he has seen himself. A fair sample of what is involved comes at the end of the very first canto:

> Ah how perverse and froward is Mankinde!
>   Faction in Courts does us to rage excite;
> The rich in Cities we litigious finde,
>   And in the Field th'Ambitious make us fight:
>
> And fatally (as if even soules were made
>   Of warring Elements as Bodies are)
> Our Reason our Religion does invade,
>   Till from the Schools to Camps it carry Warre.[12]

It seems to me incontestable that those lines are inspired by the events of the reign of Charles I and the Interregnum. Any dispute must consider how much farther topical interpretation can validly go. Davenant's temper in the two stanzas does remind us of Denham's in *Cooper's Hill*. Like that poem near its end, *Gondibert* includes a stag hunt in its second canto. The usual modern reading of the slaying of the stag in Denham's poem identifies the animal with Strafford, and the slaying hand with Charles I.[13] Here is Davenant's version of the climax of the hunt:

> But now the Monarch Murderer comes in,
>   Destructive Man! whom Nature would not arme,

[12] I, i, 79–80. Although I follow Gladish's very accurate text verbally, I indent the second and fourth lines of a stanza as in the original.

[13] See the interpretations by Earl R. Wasserman, *The Subtler Language* (Baltimore, 1959), pp. 35–88; and by Brendan O Hehir, *Expans'd Hieroglyphicks* (Berkeley and Los Angeles, 1969). But unpublished work by John Wallace, dating the poem very carefully, puts such an allegorical interpretation in doubt.

As when in madness mischief is foreseen
  We leave it weaponless for fear of harme.

For she [Nature] defencelesse made him that he might
  Less readily offend; but Art armes all,
From single strife makes us in Numbers fight;
  And by such art this Royall Stagg did fall.
(I, ii, 52–53)

The epithet for the stag in the last line quoted perhaps is best glossed by an earlier description: "A Stagg made long since Royall in the Chace, / If Kings can honor give by giving wounds" (I, ii, 32). The simple fact that Gondibert slays the stag and that he is not royal must defeat any attempt at consistent allegory. Davenant is using the emblems and commonplaces of his age to comment partly on the experience of his age. But that experience is not to be taken as the history of the time so much as the nature of human life, its failings and its hopes, in an age of trial. *Topical events illuminate the narrative, not the reverse.*

Until we know much more than we do about the years before Charles II returned and about specific connections between poetic details and specific events, we shall lack the keys to parts of the buildings of many poets. I am far from certain that *Gondibert* would turn out to be a *roman à clef* in any event. Our tendency to read mid-century poems in such fashion is really a tribute to what Dryden made of poetry responding to contemporary experience. That we should see through his vision provides a better testimony to his achievement than it does an explanation of earlier poets.

At the other extreme from allegory, there is a danger that a Davenant will be thought merely inconsistent or of no fixed purpose. As I have said, I think that too true in the large. But in another respect, of attitude toward what is described, Davenant is consistent. He directs praise and satire (or criticism, if satire is too strong a word) at almost everything he treats: princes and courts, cities, warriors, and man himself. With one or two exceptions, Davenant raises a number of symbols of value, or celebrates the values themselves, in such ways that their limits become as clear as their scope. He practices an art of intellectual and moral discrimination. Distrusting the primacy, or exclusiveness, of any of the world's rival schemes, he exhibits that desire for moderation that the best mid-century poets showed. In other words, Davenant and, I believe, most of his contemporaries responded in poetically general ways to specific experiences. He excuses himself from writing a lengthy postscript "when I am interrupted by so great an experiment [experience] as Dying." As Dr. Johnson observed, such a prospect wonderfully concentrates the mind, and Davenant was much more succinct than he had been in the "Preface," now telling his readers that what he has been up to should be obvious enough:

> I shall not think I instruct Military Men, by saying, That with *Poesie*, in *Heroick Songs*, the Wiser Ancients prepar'd their Batails; nor would I offend the austerity of such, as vex themselves with the mannage of Civill Affairs, by putting them in minde, that whilst the Plays of Children are punish'd, the plays of Men, are but excus'd under the title of business.[14]

Even here there is sententious observation and the recommendation to hold moderate views of oneself and the world.

Davenant must be credited with writing from genuine "experiment" and with seeking to find meaning in such experience. I cannot pretend that in themselves distrust of extremes and advocacy of moderation are especially profound, but everyone knows that the widespread failure to understand such things repeatedly convulsed England during the

[14] In Gladish, pp. 250–51.

seventeenth century. In such, his most general ideas, Davenant proves very sound. His problems arise in features of the immediate and the intermediate. A major immediate problem involves style in the sense of a sustaining, expressive conception. There are seldom very many stanzas together that do not suffer either from sudden deflation or from obscurity. In both respects of narrative movement and significance, Davenant is attempting something larger than More or Kynaston, and he deserves credit for the clarity he achieves within larger purposes and for a reasonably successful style. Praise cannot be greater in this realm, however, because the reader does miss that continuous force and presence that narrative requires, both because Davenant allows himself to be distracted and because his style is too uniform. What is deficient in the immediate experience of the poem is also deficient in the intermediate or somewhat deeper experience. Davenant fails to carry things through. Valor, philosophy, and love might have made an impressive whole, as *The Faerie Queene* is a whole by virtue of the integrity of what has been conveyed.

Gondibert involves us, then, in some hesitation as to what is being done in the poem and to mixed evaluation of its achievement. Because so little exists in the way of suggestion about contexts for the poem, I feel obliged to make some effort to provide a thematic context. If we can give up Hobbes' compulsion to approach literature as if it were geometry, I think that we can find in his three "Regions" the proper contexts for understanding *Gondibert*, and I suspect that there in Paris Hobbes and Davenant had been talking about heroic poetry before they set their pens to paper. In other words, I attribute in principle some of Hobbes' ideas to Davenant's "Preface" and some of Davenant's to Hobbes' "Answer."

Gondibert amalgamates three regions: court-and-camp, city, and country. And as we saw in the previous chapter, such distinctions were common ones. Davenant varies somewhat from other writers in distinguishing warriors (the camp) rather more than usual from the court, but in that he better reflects the experience of the Civil Wars, when not all soldiers could be seen in terms of the court. The distinction also allows him to distinguish more clearly faults in the heroic region. The court may prove impotent with its warriors removed from it, as Aribert explicitly is and as Charles had proved to be. And the camps may prove excessively active and threatening, as is the case with Oswald and, perhaps Davenant thought, the armies opposed to Charles the Martyr. At the court of Aribert we see indecision, intrigue, and general weakness. In the camps, including Gondibert's, we see too great violence and, in Oswald's case, treachery and civil war. No closer agreement between Davenant and Hobbes can be imagined than in their seeing how much is shared by the heroic world with what for Hobbes was its narrative counterpart, tragedy.

The city—Verona, but also London and Paris—claims even less respect. It is regarded by Davenant as by Denham as an economic center and moral sink. Denham had used the device of a satiric prospect:

> I see the City in a thicker cloud
> Of business, then of smoake; where men like Ants
> Toyle to prevent imaginarie wants;
> Yet all in vaine, increasing with their store,
> Their vast desires, but make their wants the more.
> As food to unsound bodies, though it please
> The Appetite, feeds onely the disease;
> Where with like haste, though severall waies they runne:
> Some to undoe, and some to be undone:
> While Luxurie, and wealth, like Warre and Peace,

Are each the others ruine, and increase,
As Rivers lost in Seas some secret veine
Thence reconveies, there to be lost againe.
Some study plots, and some those plots t'undoe,
Others to make'em, and undoe'em too,
False to their hopes, affraid to be secure,
Those mischiefes onely which they make, endure,
Blinded with light, and sicke of being well,
In tumults seeke their peace, their heaven in hell.
(1642 "A" text, 28–46)

For his part, Davenant seeks to create a series of narrative scenes, and as befits the greater length of his poem has a great deal to say about his city. Dawn is just breaking:

From wider Gates Oppressors sally there;
Here creeps th'afflicted through a narrow Dore;
Groans under wrongs he has not strength to bear,
Yet seeks for wealth to injure others more. . . .

Here through a secret Posterne issues out
The skar'd Adult'rer, who out-slept his time;
Day, and the Husbands Spie alike does doubt [suspect],
And with a half hid face would hide his crime. . . .

Here stooping Lab'rers slowly moving are;
Beasts to the Rich, whose strength grows rude with ease;
And would usurp, did not their Rulers care,
With toile and tax their furious strength appease.
(II, i, 15, 18, 20)

Davenant pulls aside the curtain of time and lets us see more of what happened on that great stage of the seventeenth century than does almost any other poet. And as we can see from that rare glimpse of "Lab'rers," he is far from reposing any more trust in them than in the oppressive rich. But for Davenant the mass of men in groups is the traditional "Monster, the Multitude," whom he compares to wolves.[15]

At one point Davenant refers "To Streets (the People's Region)" (II, ii, 1), using Hobbes' very word.[16] Moreover, most of what Davenant depicts of the city employs the narrative genre that Hobbes had distinguished, satire. Yet Hobbes had merely voiced the century's usual view of urban life. Jonson's comedies illustrate the idea perfectly, as do Dryden's London comedies or his contempt for the urban and "suburbian" Muse in *Mac Flecknoe*. Davenant's best comic scene (comedy being that other literary avatar of the city) comes when young Goltho is taken in by the experienced courtesan, "Black Dalga" (III, vi). The long English connection of aristocracy and gentry to landed estates developed a hostile impulse to London, where a man would have to go to raise a mortgage or engage a lawyer to settle disputes over property. Of course London continued to act as an irresistible lodestone on the very men who decried the city, but its filth, its underworld, and its spawning of capital and new ideas filled many people with grave misgiving.

Davenant's point proves to be less simple than Hobbes' scheme or even than Denham's brief dismissal of the city. To Hobbes, the three regions are distinct, and to Denham the city contrasts with Windsor Palace. Just as the division of courts and camps had made it possible for us to understand the limits Davenant set for heroic values, so in fact does his city, Verona, play a dual role as urban center and

[15] "Preface," ibid., pp. 12–13.

[16] See Hobbes, "Answer," ibid., p. 45: "the three Regions of mankind, *Court, Citty*, and *Country*." But the coincidence in language provides a symptom of prior discussion between Davenant and Hobbes.

as site of Aribert's court. City and court merge here, as country and court merge in *Cooper's Hill*, and all three in *Paradise Lost*. A scene very characteristic of Davenant occurs when a priest refuses to allow burial for Oswald in consecrated ground. As the priest argues:

Here the neglected Lord of peace does live;
Who taught the wrangling world the rules of love;
Should we his dwelling to the wrathful give,
Our Sainted Dead would rise, and he remove.
(II, i, 45)

The all but unparalleled introduction of Jesus Christ into the poem (see II, vi, 72 for the other instance) exerts a powerful challenge to the heroic ideal Oswald represents, and one feels that something of Davenant's urge to moderation also is given voice. But he refuses to leave things at that, and with another half turn what had seemed so brightly lit moves into ironic shadows. The priest gets a reply from an "Orator," or demagogue, who starts up. "We know," he says,

We know, though Priests are Pensioners of Heav'n,
Your Flock which yeilds best rent, is this dull Crowd.
(II, i, 50)

First shorn by the rich, the poor are shortly fleeced by the Church. The allegation carries conviction. The leader Tybalt then speaks with feeling and eloquence about man as a religious creature, arguing also, as had Davenant himself in the Preface, that the role of arms is that of the court: to make human justice effective.[17] And so, in the city, the limits of

[17] II, i, 67–73; the whole speech is excellent. Cf. Davenant, "Preface," in Gladish, pp. 12–13.

city-dwellers and the troubles of the court have added to them the defects of institutions like the Church. Tybalt has finished his address.

> This said, Warrs cause these Priests no more debate;
> They knew, Warr's Justice none could ere decide;
> At that more specious name [Justice] they open strait,
> And sacred Rites of fun'ral they provide.
>
> How vain is Custom, and how guilty Pow'r?
> Slaughter is lawful made by the excess;
> Earth's partial Laws, just Heav'n must need abhor,
> Which greater crimes allow, and damn the less.
>
> (II, i, 74–75)

Once again Davenant bears upon us his conviction of man's tragic limitations. We may take nothing too far on trust. Our knowledge, our society, our Church, our passions—all—require distrust at the least sign of excess. He tells us as much in an important section of his "Preface."

> Therefore wee may conclude, that Nature, for the safety of mankinde, hath as well . . . given limits to courage and to learning, to wickednes and to error, as it hath ordain'd the [underwater] shelves before the shore, to restraine the rage and excesses of the Sea.[18]

The image of the sea for destructive anarchy reminds us of the image of the Thames in flood at the end of *Cooper's Hill.* Both because it is a narrative and because it is better known, I have tried to use it to clarify aspects of *Gondibert.*

Denham also provides us with our next topic for Davenant in the lines following those Denham had written on the city:

[18] In Gladish, p. 9, with a spelling correction from the quarto. Davenant's remark on human limits—for good or evil—follows his criticism of earlier heroic poets and is of first importance for understanding his intellectual temper.

Oh happinesse of sweete retir'd content!
To be at once secure, and innocent.[19]

The country, the third region distinguished by Hobbes, provides Davenant as it had other writers with his most secure values. Gondibert is borne to Astragon for care and enlightenment, much like a Spenserian knight toward the end of his story. The concern with knowledge and science in the first of the Astragon cantos (II, v) once again associates retirement with philosophical study, and we feel that an unprecedented degree of excitement has come into the poem:

And wisely *Astragon*, thus busy grew,
  To seek the Stars remote societies;
And judge the walks of th' old by finding new;
  For Nature's law, in correspondence lies.

Man's pride (grown to Religion) he abates,
  By moving our lov'd Earth; which we think fix'd;
Think all to it, and it to none relates;
  With others motion scorn to have it mix'd:

As if 'twere great and stately to stand still
  Whilst other Orbes dance on; or else think all
Those vaste bright Globes (to shew God's needless skill)
  Were made but to attend our little Ball.

(II, v, 18–20)

Although Davenant seems to derive his sage's name from *astra-gone* or *ἀστέρ-γονή*, the man of the starry race, or family of the stars, Astragon's branches of learning include all that Davenant wishes to include, especially poetry. Poetry leads

[19] 1642 "A" text, 47–48, as in O Hehir's ed., n. 13 above (substantially the same in later versions). Denham uses the country at this juncture to effect a shift to the court at Windsor.

him, as so often, to David and so to a conception of the poet as a kingly figure of divine function:

O hyreless Science! and of all alone
  The Liberal! Meanly the rest each State
In pension treats, but this depends on none;
  Whose worth they rev'rendly forbear to rate.

The praise of science in Astragon's house ends with this stanza (68), with poetry.

Today poetry is not considered a science (although of course Davenant has in mind the seventeenth-century sense of a species of knowledge), and today both are not associated with the country. Davenant associates poetry at this juncture, and natural science completely, with the country, because it involves the scene of the retired or contemplative life as opposed to the active life of the court, camp, and city. The best introduction to such assumptions will be found in Cowley's delightful essays. In the country, as Cowley argues, virtue is achieved more easily, and the honest man is not subject to shows of greatness or to temptations of great things. In retirement, a man may be himself, and he may ponder such knowledge as is either poetic or scientific. Only by understanding such things can we make sense of the fact that the "Attendants" of the Psalmist do not write bucolic poetry.

And his Attendants, such blest Poets are,
  As make unblemish'd Love, Courts best delight;
And sing the prosp'rous Batails of just warre;
  By these the loving, Love, and valiant fight.

(II, v, 67)

So *Gondibert* arrives at a moment when it mirrors its own ideal, and the public world of love and valor is attendant upon David.

The next canto (II, vi) describes Astragon's temple. As

early as the "Preface" Davenant had made clear the tripartite motif of this section of *Gondibert:* praise, penitence, and prayer. There is more than that, and very much in the seventeenth-century vein. Among the old motifs we discover a hexaemeron (sts. 53–61), a creation piece especially interesting, as all such commonplace topics are, for an idiosyncratic touch. Two lines could have been written in no other century: "Then Motion, Nature's great Preservative, / Tun'd order in this World, Life's restless Inn" (II, vi, 55). The combination of the new dynamics with the *harmonia mundi* and the Stoic image of the world as "Inn" microcosmically sets forth Davenant's eclecticism.

And what of credibility? Birtha's role develops fully only after these cantos. There is nothing at all wrong with a character of importance entering an epic or romance at an advanced stage. But her entry brings a change in the hero from Gondibert Furioso to Gondibert Innamorato. That change, like the division of what we have of the poem into sections on valor, Astragon, and love, is not complete. More positively, as I have tried to suggest, Davenant has a consistent attitude favoring moderation, distrusting the ultimate truth of anything human; and he organizes experience according to the three "Regions" of mankind. In all this he advanced the art of narrative considerably, but he did not succeed in the large. We discover his limitations both in the poem and in the fact that he could not, or would not, complete his "heroic song."

Five years after *Gondibert* had appeared, Cowley wrote in the Preface to his *Poems* that "a warlike, various, and a tragical age is best to *write of*, but worst to *write in*." [20] Cowley is no doubt right as far as certain kinds of poetry are concerned, and his *Davideis* was perhaps written between

[20] Cowley, in J. E. Spingarn, ed., *Critical Essays of the Seventeenth Century*, 3 vols. (Bloomington, 1963), II, 80.

1650 and 1654. If so it is contemporary with *Gondibert*. I think myself that of the two poems, *Gondibert* better deserves title to being the "heroic song" of mid-century. For one thing, it is the better poem. Beyond that crucial fact, however, Davenant was far better able to give a sense of that "Warlike, various, and tragical age," England in the Puritan Revolution.

In Cowley's great breadth of interest, in his learning, in his capacity for innovation, in his ease in handling various literary kinds, and in his excellence in prose as well as verse, he very much reminds one of Dryden. Unlike Dryden, however, he showed his abilities at a very early age, and either he or his readers thereafter have lacked staying power. It always seems difficult to form a just estimation of writers like Davenant and Cowley, but I have made my own preference clear as far as narrative poetry is concerned. I shall say with the same candor that I think Cowley a finer poet than Traherne and that the revival of his reputation awaits little more than a proper edition of his poems. He has been called the Muses' Hannibal, and no doubt he sometimes labors poetic elephants over difficult Alps. At present, those of his victories which we can celebrate seem minor skirmishes, and if I cannot promise a Roman triumph for his *Davideis*, that is not to say that he is negligible.

Cowley's best modern critic has well said that the poet's ideal sought an "intersection of the truly august and the truly humble" in a style of the "conversational baroque." [21] Such aspiration and such modesty have an appeal otherwise difficult to describe. The qualities manifest themselves not only in his epic on "The Troubles of David" but also in his generosity to other writers. Cowley's poem "To Sir William Davenant" appears to have been written after he had seen

[21] Robert B. Hinman, "The Apotheosis of Faust: Poetry and the New Philosophy in the Seventeenth Century," in *Metaphysical Poetry*, ed. Malcolm Bradbury and David Palmer (London, 1970), p. 170.

only the first two books of *Gondibert* in manuscript, and on that basis he had every right to expect a major narrative of a specific kind.

> Methinks *Heroick Poesie* till now
> Like some fantastick *Fairy Land* did show,
> *Gods, Devils, Nymphs, Witches* and *Gyants race,*
> And all but *Man* in *Mans chief Work* had place.[22]

Whatever else narrative may aspire to, it requires some form of normality to insure credibility, as Vaughan had also recognized. It is such praise that Cowley generously bestows on Davenant. We recall that the magic emerald inherited by Gondibert appears in the third book that Cowley apparently had not yet seen. Typically, he never wrote in dispraise of the remainder of Davenant's epic.

In 1679 someone, probably Cowley's friend Thomas Sprat, published Cowley's *Poem on the Late Civil War*. This narrative reviews English history, selecting for chief attention those kings who had been great abroad, leading Cowley to ask, "What Rage does *England* from it self divide, / More than the Seas from all the World beside?" [23] Domestic peace and foreign triumphs are shattered by the Grand Rebellion, whose progress Cowley then proceeds to follow through most of the poem, emphasizing battles for the most part. A very royalist tone informs the poem. Like the *Davideis* it is incomplete, in this instance probably because after the royalists were so obviously losing the war Cowley lost heart in his

[22] *Poems*, ed. A. R. Waller (Cambridge, 1905), p. 42. My earlier point about the shift in emphasis in *Gondibert* after the Astragon cantos is borne out by Cowley's downplaying of love and his failure to mention Birtha.

[23] Cowley, *Essays and Plays*, ed. A. R. Waller (Cambridge, 1906), p. 467, the opening lines. The second line echoes Virgil, *Eclogues*, I, 66 ("penitus toto divisos orbe Britannos"), as Dryden's second line does in *Astraea Redux*—part of the classical lore once so widely shared by poets.

narrative. The closing moments of the poem begin with a question addressed to the rebels.

> Why will you die fond Men, why will you buy,
> At this fond rate, your Countreys slavery? [24]

He rejects the Puritan claims that they fought for liberty, property, and religion. For, if the last were true,

> Why are all *Sect's* let loose, that ere had Birth
> Since *Luther's noise* wak'd the *Lethargick Earth,*
> *The Author went no further.*

Cowley's point here provides a version of the lasting concern of his work, the need for a harmonious, creative order.[25] As with the *Davideis,* however, here also the desire for creative order fails to produce a whole poem.

Cowley's ideal led directly to Dryden's great idea animating his work, but both men discovered with their contemporaries of many persuasions that what an individual may regard as creative order other individuals may regard as tyranny or anarchy. So it ever is, although the ideal is well worth the effort to strive for convincing statement. We can see from Cowley's writings that one of the reasons for the appeal of science in the seventeenth century and later was the conviction that God in His works had given man an opportunity for discovery of what was truly creative and harmonious, far better opportunity than in the tumultuous affairs of men in the century. Cowley's interest in science is known to most people by virtue of his ode published in Sprat's *History of the Royal Society* in 1667, that *annus mirabilis* which also brought, in addition to Dryden's poem of that title, *Paradise Lost.* In the next year Cowley's *Poemata Latina* was pub-

[24] Ibid., p. 480.

[25] This point is well established in Robert B. Hinman, *Abraham Cowley's World of Order* (Cambridge, Mass., 1960).

lished and in it his *Sex Libri Plantarum,* or *Book of Plants,* as Nahum Tate and his colleagues subsequently put it for their translation. Cowley's real distinction as a neo-Latin poet is unlikely to bring discovery by most of us today. Few of us are capable of proving or disproving, or even discussing intelligently, Dr. Johnson's preference for Cowley over Milton as a Latin poet.[26] But classicists agree that the distinguishing feature of his Latin poems is his anglicizing of Latin to the point, say his critics, of its being no longer classical or, said Johnson, of its being no longer dead. The point is made in the very title of his volume: *Abrahami Couleii Angli, Poemata Latina.*

One need not be a classicist to find some charm in the opening of Cowley's modified georgic, "Infima regna cano, sed longè maxima *Vitae.*"[27] Cowley's versification also has charm. For the first two books, he uses the elegiac distich. That seems a strange choice until one encounters the loving attention to herbs mostly of feminine gender in their names. Salvia, Melissa, Cochelaria, Cassytha, and so on do seem to fit in with Corinna, Celia, and Amanda. The third and fourth books, devoted to flowers, contain poems in various measures, elegiac and lyric measures predominating, as again is appropriate for the feminine gender of most names for flowers.

The fifth and sixth books constitute Cowley's finest epic, which is concerned with the political plant, the tree.[28] Cowley begins with a description of the Fortunate Isles, that earthly paradise or *locus amoenus* celebrated by many writers

[26] For comment on Johnson and other verdicts, see G. B. Hill, ed., *The Lives of the English Poets,* 3 vols. (Oxford, 1905), I, 12, 66.

[27] "J. O.'s" is loose: "Lifes lowest, but far greatest Sphere, I sing" (Cowley, *The Works,* Third Part [London, 1700], p. 1). The key concept, *regna,* has been lost: nature offers man the image of a perfect kingdom.

[28] On Waller's and James Howell's use of tree lore to such ends, see *The Cavalier Mode,* pp. 24–37.

but probably best known in England from Tasso's *Jerusalem Delivered,* whose translation by Fairfax had such renown. Cowley's version unequivocally renders new by making the earthly paradise a realm ruled by Pomona:

> Hanc sapiens mundi mediam veterísque novíque
> Pomiferis statuens umbrosam gentibus urbem,
> (Arborei caput imperii sedémque verendam)
> Conscriptis ab utroque replevit civibus orbe.
>
> (V, 34-37)

> Betwixt th' old World and new makes this retreat
> Of her Green Empire the Imperial Seat:
> And wisely too, that Plants of ev'ry sort
> May from both Worlds repair to fill her Court.[29]

The monarch tree and forest kingdom are lively topoi in the seventeenth century. The first notable expression of it in terms like Cowley's is James Howell's two-part allegory, ΔΕΝΔΡΟΛΟΓΙΑ. *Dodona's Grove, or The Vocall Forest* (1640, 1650), which is evidently Cowley's source. In mid-century such lore was heightened further by Charles II's hiding in an oak at Boscobel after royalist defeat at the Battle of Worcester. There are political implications to the trees in Milton's paradise and hell; and Dryden sums up much of the lore in the "Monarch Oakes" of *Mac Flecknoe.* Howell's frontispiece is emblematic, and his afterpiece showing himself leaning on a tree labels it *Robur Britannicum,* the British oak. Such sources and the history of the Interregnum combine in Cowley's poem. In the words by Sprat, quoted by Nahum Tate,

> the sixth Book is wholly dedicated to the Honour of his Country. For making the *British* Oak to preside in the Assembly of the Forest Trees, upon the occasion he en-

[29] Cowley, *Poemata,* p. 204; *Works* (1700), Third Part, p. 106.

> larges on the History of our late Troubles, the King's Affliction and Return, and the beginning of the *Dutch* Wars; and manages all in a Style, that (to say all in a Word) is equal to the Valour and Greatness of the *English* Nation.[30]

A considerable portion of the sixth book rehearses the events treated in *A Poem on the Late Civil War*, but much more interestingly and successfully. In terms of emphasis, the fifth book may be said to take the kingdom as an excuse to write about trees and the sixth to take trees to write about the kingdom. The two books are at least as complementary as *L'Allegro* and *Il Penseroso* and give us Cowley's finest narrative writing. Even in the translation of one book by Tate and the other by Aphra Behn, we understand the conception they share. For the first time in this survey of English narrative poetry after 1640 I can say that the narrative is whole, that significance and movement have become significant movement.

The *Book of Plants* was said by Sprat to have been begun when Cowley returned to England in the Interregnum. Apparently Cowley had taken up medicine (of which herbalism was a part) to put Parliamentary watchdogs off the scent. But it could not have been completed until the Second Dutch War had at least begun (1665). The *Davideis* was begun earlier, while Cowley was up at Cambridge, according to Sprat. Whatever the exact dates, the poem has been thought Cowley's chief claim to be more than a lyric poet, and it certainly provides a less exotic narrative than that concluding the *Sex Libri Plantarum*. In addition to passages of interest and a characteristic theme, the poem has undeniable historical importance. But so uneven is it, at times so flat, at

[30] *Works* (1700), Third Part, sig. a 2ᵛ. On the British oak or *Robur Britannicum*, see *The Cavalier Mode*, p. 31, text and n. 16.

times so inflated, and above all so lacking in intelligible movement, that it fails to exercise any lasting claim as a narrative. As we shall see, the poem does, however, possess a clarity that is not epidemic in mid-century narrative. The clarity extends from the style to the episodes.

Because the action is not widely familiar, and because Cowley's handling of a biblical subject sets off Milton's and Dryden's, a précis may be useful. The poem begins with the epic proposition and invocation. The action begins with an account of a temporary patching-up of the strained relations between Saul and David. The brief account is interrupted for a description of Hell and the devil (the visit-to-the-underworld motif). The Father of Lies has been upset by David's thwarting of his plans to subvert Israel. Envy interrupts his raging to suggest a plan. She rekindles Saul's jealousy in the next short episode, which is followed by another brief scene in Heaven in which God speaks. God sends an angel to tell David to play before Saul. This leads to a brief digression on music and to a fine versification of Psalm 114 as David's song. Saul, however, attempts to kill David. Flying the court, David goes home and shortly, with help from his wife Michal, escapes to the prophets' "College" at Ramah. The scene then changes back to Saul in rage, and then back again to the college and a digression on its activities. Saul sends officers to capture David at the college, but they are so taken by life there that they remain. Finally Saul appears himself, and he too lives for a time among the prophets, being compared to Balaam, a song by whom ends the book. The summary makes clear how fragmentary Book I is. Put another way, Cowley has not imagined an epic conception that will make his action one.

Book II has a far better narrative execution. True, there are digressions, two labeled as such, a third describing Fancy, and a fourth tracing in a vision the descent from David to Christ. But these are far better carried by the basic narrative, which moves naturally from an account of the love between David and Jonathan, conversation between them, and Jonathan's return to court in David's interest at the time of the "Feast of the New Moon."

Books III and IV are set among the Moabites, to whom David has had to flee for safety. Book three gets moving slowly, although the digression on Lot and more especially Melchor's song are in themselves well worth the delay. Book III is mostly taken up, however, by Joab's relation of David's life to Moab. In this relation the poem achieves its best conceived and executed narrative. The perennial interest of the duel with Goliath is sustained, and my favorite passage in the whole poem is the wonderfully amusing one on David confronting the giant:

> Now in the Valley'he stands; through's youthful face
> Wrath checks the Beauty, and sheds manly grace.
> Both in his looks so joyn'd, that they might move
> Fear ev'n in Friends, and from an En'emy Love.
> Hot as ripe Noon, sweet as the blooming Day,
> Like July furious, but more fair than May.
> Th'accurst Philistian stands on th'other side,
> Grumbling aloud, and smiles 'twixt rage and pride.
> "The Plagues of Dagon! a smooth Boy," said he,
> "A cursed beardless foe oppos'd to *Me!*
> Hell! with what arms (hence thou fond Child) he's come!
> Some friend his Mother call to drive him home.
> Not gone yet? if one minute more thou stay,
> The birds of heav'en shall bear thee dead away.
> Gods! a curst *Boy!*" the rest then murmuring out,
> He walks, and casts a deadly grin about.[31]

[31] In *Poems*, Waller, p. 338. Many of the other outstanding passages are quoted by Hinman (see n. 25, above). Cowley's text is much disfigured by italics, and in this instance I have removed such stress for all but two words and have added quotation marks.

If only Cowley always wrote like this! In lapsing into humor, he also falls into real poetry. Perhaps we should infer that the rest of his poem might better have shunned its sobriety. But the admission of humor into the epic, without toppling the statues, requires an uncommonly soft footfall of a poet.

Book IV involves a long and not very credible tale of Jewish history told by David to Moab as they rumble across the country in the royal chariot. The book ends with an account of Jonathan's heroism in battle and with David's saving of his friend from a rash curse by Saul. So the *Davideis* ends inconclusively. Clearly, it is a failure as an epic or a narrative, although it does have attractive features.

Cowley's ideal of creative order provides the major thematic focus of the poem in both negative and positive versions. Saul's unstable personality, like the intervention by the Devil and Envy, creates disorder where it should not exist: between father and son, king and subject. David's attempts to heal Saul's instability with music clearly represent one version of harmony, just as the friendship between David and Jonathan has philosophical and political implications of harmony.[32] Reflecting as it does major interests of the century, the poem might have given the age what it sought for had Cowley been able to find narrative expression for his themes.

Cowley's most important achievement in the poem, at least as we follow the history of narrative poetry in the century, is clarity. At long last, language seems to be under control. Cowley is sure and we are sure at every moment about what is being said and done. Because we shall be considering shortly a poem that kicks clarity in the shins, and because the three stylistic revolutions of Butler, Milton, and Dryden depend on clarity to make complexity allowable, for such

[32] See *The Cavalier Mode*, ch. VI.

reasons Cowley has an honorable historical place. The example of the biblical epic in English also has importance, because Quarles's paraphrases do not have epic pretensions. As biblical narrative, however, the *Davideis* does not match his pindaric ode, *The Plagues of Egypt*. The use of narrative in that lyric fulfills a shift begun earlier from a "dramatic" emphasis in the lyric to a "narrative." [33]

We shall have occasion to see later how Dryden took advantage of such a procedure in his lyrics, but perhaps the most extreme example of mingled genres is also worth mentioning. Three years after the Glorious Revolution, "Tho. Heyrick, M. A. *Formerly of* Peter-*House* in Cambridge," brought out *The Submarine Voyage. A Pindarick Poem in Four Parts*. Some sixty-seven quarto pages long, this narrative in the Cowleyan pindarics tells how the narrator was changed in form, swam all about the world and into it to see its wonders, returned to England, and resumed his original shape. One of the imaginary voyages of the century, this bizarre poem excited enough interest for the author's friends to write some commendatory poems. The inheritance of Cowley's loose pindaric form from Dryden to Wordsworth certainly includes some very exotic flowers.

Two marked characteristics of the *Davideis* are its frequent digressions and its frequent epic similes. The digressions prove difficult to assess, because although they impede the action and often seem to have no reason for being, they still contain much of the best writing of the poem. Perhaps they illustrate the poem into which they intervene in being symptomatic of a failure of the whole but of an interest in many parts. Cowley's similes usually prove more interesting than the narrative they illustrate, but only on a few occasions do they suggest that Milton was taking note and seeing how

[33] See *The Metaphysical Mode from Donne to Cowley* (Princeton, 1969), pp. 93-99.

such comparisons could function proleptically or forecastingly of ensuing events.

> As midst the Main a low small Island lies,
> Assaulted round by stormy Seas and skies.
> Whilst the poor heartless Natives every hour
> Darkness and Noise seems ready to devour:
> Such Israels state appeared, whilst ore the West
> Philistian clouds hung threatning . . .[34]

Echoes of lines or techniques also show that Milton and Dryden had read attentively. Only Cowley before Milton gets to the underworld so quickly, and with the example of a Christian conception of Hell. Dryden's echoes of the *Davideis* in *Mac Flecknoe* have long been recognized, and Dryden must have assumed that some readers at least would have recognized them. Certainly the idea of a biblical epic must have interested Milton, and the idea of a poem on "The Troubles of David" equally certainly interested Dryden. But for successful narrative, we must go to the last two books of Cowley's *Book of Plants*. The fanciful appears to have found greater coherence and significance in his imagination than did more usual conceptions of the heroic.

iii. Love in Fantastic Triumph: *Pharonnida*

Between Cowley's *Davideis* and Butler's *Hudibras* there appeared a very remarkable narrative poem little known to most readers. In 1659 William Chamberlayne brought out *Pharonnida* with the further title, A *Heroick Poem.* In his "Epistle to the Reader," the author explains: "I have made bold with the *Title* of *Heroick*, but have a late example that deters me from disputing upon what grounds I assumed

[34] In *Poems*, Waller, pp. 375–76. Cowley's note shows that he was echoing Seneca, *Thyestes.* I have again removed italics.

it." [35] Such cryptic assertions accompanied by an indifference as to explanation do not violate the spirit of the poem itself. But presumably Chamberlayne refers to *Gondibert* with its "Preface" and "Answer," as also to the brief flurry of ridicule Davenant received from self-styled friends. Those wags could not contain themselves over such humor as calling the poet Daphne or gloating over his use of such hard words as "abstersive." If any of these humorists saw *Pharonnida* he must have died of instant apoplexy.

It is unknown exactly when Chamberlayne began or completed his poem. The conclusion of the second book (II, 513–36; p. 172) speaks of "*Britains* blushing Chronicle," which is marginally glossed "*Newberries* Second Fight." With true Cavalier aplomb Chamberlayne wrote, "I leave the Muses to converse with men" at that second Battle of Newbury (October, 1644). When he returned to medical practice in Dorset is uncertain but he appears to have been wounded during the war.[36] His royalism continued unabated. He was perhaps involved in the 1655 Rising, although that is conjectural. He certainly was deep in the plot to raise an army for Charles II, who was to land and reign in 1659 if all went according to plan, which it did not.[37] After the Restoration Chamberlayne was thrice mayor of Shaftesbury, circumstances suggesting that he was not as poor as is suggested

[35] *Pharonnida* (London, 1659), sig. A 2ʳ. Chamberlayne's royalism and Anglicanism emerge very forcibly in this grumpy introduction. The "Epistle Dedicatory" (running head) is more equable, and since it is dated "*May* 12. 1659," it offers a *terminus ad quem*.

[36] See A. E. Parsons, "A Forgotten Poet: William Chamberlayne and 'Pharonnida,'" *Modern Language Review*, XLV (1950), 296–311: 301–302. Saintsbury's introduction and Parsons' essay constitute nearly the entire body of criticism on *Pharonnida*. The rest is mostly recounted or included in Ernst Kilian, *William Chamberlaynes "Pharonnida"* (Königsberg, 1913). I shall be returning to Parsons' essay frequently, with indebtedness and with doubt on various points.

[37] Parsons, pp. 301–303.

by his being taxed on but two chimneys and having left no hitherto discovered will.[38] Whenever it was that he returned to his poem, he effectively changed the subtitle at the head of the *third* book from that of a "Heroick Poem" to "A *Tragi-comical POEM.*" To confuse things further, the 1659 edition changes typography, arrangement, and pagination at the beginning of the *fourth* book. All in all, it seems most likely that by 1646, when Dorset was under the control of Parliament, he returned to his poem (finishing it sometime before 1659). In the prefatory matter to the book, Chamberlayne wishes rather perversely that any strictures on his poem would have come to him "whilst these *Papers* were private" rather than "now they are publisht" (sig. A 5^{v}). He does not explain how readers might have had access to private papers. Whether heroic or tragi-comical, *Pharonnida* is then a poem modeled on the five-act structure of plays (to no discernible effect), with each book again divided into five parts on the analogy of scenes (again without effect). Written about 1640 to 1659, the poem deserves recognition for being *complete* in the nearly five hundred (misnumbered) octavo pages of the first edition or the almost 280 pages of Saintsbury's text. It is a full, long poem whose extraordinary conception and yet more extraordinary style found a large arena for play.

Such details about the author of a bizarre but in many ways great poem may seem frustratingly meager. Such paucity of genuine information, and confusion over what little exists, conform to the spirit of the poem. Chamberlayne closes his "Epistle to the Reader" with a line from Pindar's eighth Olympian ode: "But nothing shall be equally pleasant among all men." [39] If not "all men," then at least those who read

[38] Ibid., pp. 303–304.

[39] *Olympic Odes*, viii, 70, with alteration, translation from the Loeb ed. Chamberlayne's title-page motto (*Odyssey*, XIX, 203, also askew in his Greek), runs as follows in the Loeb translation: "He spoke and made the many falsehoods of his tale seem like the truth." There are times when the reverse seems true of Chamberlayne.

his poem would be pleased to have a great deal more information than we possess. As an example of his prose, and as an example of saying a great deal without saying what we wish to know, here is Chamberlayne's sentence in the "Epistle Dedicatory" on that very important matter, the subject of *Pharonnida:*

> For my *Subject* (it being *Heroick Poesie*) it is such as the wiser part of the World hath alwaies held in a Venerable Esteem, the *Extracts* of *Fancy* being that noble *Elixer,* which Heaven ordain'd to Immortalize their *Memories,* whose worthy *Actions* being the *Products* of that nobler part of *Man,* the *Soul,* is by this made, almost Commensurate with Her [the soul's] *Eternity;* which otherwise (to the sorrow of succeeding *Ages*) who are in debt for much of their *Vertue* to a noble Emulation of their glorious *Ancestors,* had either terminated in a Circle of no larger a *Diameter* then Life; or like short breath'd *Ephemera's,* only surviv'd a while in the Aiery Region of *Discourse.*[40]

We learn that the subject is heroic, and that the heroic poem immortalizes its subject. But we do not learn what Chamberlayne's subject aspires to treat. Apart from the unusual generality of language, however, the spirit—and heaven knows the syntax—answers to his poetic style. Every major and even minor poet deserves to be called special. As far as style is concerned, Chamberlayne deserves something more, to be thought *sui generis* like the phoenix. Every reader will have to cast very far to recall anything comparable, and I confess that the only style I know which resembles Chamberlayne's in complexity is that of the Japanese prose syntax of *The Tale of Genji.* If some difference exists between the two, I suspect that it comes down to my belief that the

[40] "Epistle Dedicatory" (1659), sigs. A 2^v–A 3^r.

Japanese is closer to normality and that Chamberlayne simply could not be translated.

I have been going on at some length about matters that may seem extrinsic to the poem, however, and the season has come to quote Chamberlayne and let the reader decide for himself. The following period opens *Pharonnida,* III, ii. (Saintsbury broke up the sentence for reasons that will not seem wholly willful.)

> If angry [age], the Enemy to Love,
> Tels thy grave pride—thy Judgment is above,
> What with contempt (although it injure truth)
> Thy spleen miscals the vanity of youth,
> If harsh imployment; gross society,
> That feast of Brutes, make thee an Enemy
> To love, the Souls Commercive Language, then
> Remove thy Eye, whilst my unenvied Pen,
> That long to Passion hath a Servant been,
> Confines the fair *Pharonnida's* within,
> These paper limits; frozen still she lies
> Beneath opposing Passions, her bright Eyes;
> Those Stars whose best of influence scarce had power
> To thaw what grief congeald into a shower
> Of heart dis-burthening tears, their influence spend
> In sorrow's polar Circles, and could lend
> No light to beauties World; ith' vigorous reign
> Of this pale Tyrant, whilst she did remain
> Unlighten'd with a beam of comfort, in
> A Bower being sate, that formerly had been
> Her seat, when she heard the unhappy news
> Of parting with *Argalia;* whilst she views
> She blames the guiltless shadows, who to ask
> Pardon in trembling murmures did unmask
> Their naked Limbs, and scatterd at her Feet

The fragrant Vail, in's death-bed sate the sweet
But pining Rose, each Grass its heavy head,
Laden with tears did hang, whilst her Eyes shead
A pattern to instruct them: hence, whilst she
Looks thorough on a way conceiv'd to be
The same her Lord marcht with his Army, when
He left *Girenza*, with a hast more then
A common Traveler, she sees one post
Towards her Court, whose Visage had not lost
Its room within her Memory, he's known
Argalia's Page, and now each minute grown,
A burthen to her thoughts, that did defer
A neerer interview, the Messenger
Arrives, and to her eager view presents
His Masters Letters, whose inclos'd Contents,
Are now the Object, her expecting Soul
Courts with desire, nor doth she long controle
Their forward hast; A diamond being by
The Messenger returnd, whose worth might vie
Price with an *Indian* Fleet, when it sails slow
With's glittering burthen; though each word ore-flow
With joy, whilst her inquisitive discourse,
Was on this pleasing theam, time did enforce
The Pages swift departure, who with all
Affected Epithetes, that Love can call
To gild Invention when it would expresse,
Things more sublime than mortal happinesse,
Is gone to carry his expecting Lord,
What pleasure could, when rarified afford. (1–54) [41]

[41] Pages 190–92. For reasons shortly to be given, and turning on Chamberlayne's normal practice of indenting both lines of a couplet for each sentence-period-paragraph, it is quite possible that this 54-line flight should be thought to continue through the 122nd line, something that even a printer of 1659 would have found unusual. All 122 lines make a splendid passage. Saintsbury's valiant efforts to modernize the text

Anyone who admires Chamberlayne as much as I do must confess that his style represents an advanced form of excess and often grows rather obscure as to grammar, syntax, and sometimes (though rarely) of general meaning. Yet in the best narrated episode of the poem, Chamberlayne tells how the hero, Pharonnida's lover Argalia, falls into the hands of the Turks. In a retelling of the story of Joseph and Potiphar's wife, Chamberlayne plays on English imaginings about the sexual attractions that European men were supposed to have for Turkish women. So the concubine, Janusa, of the Turkish sultan Ammurat, attempts to seduce Argalia, but in vain, he proving another Joseph. The following passage relates the reactions of Argalia and Janusa when the determinations of both have come to stalemate, and as her departure is followed by the entry of her servant and bawd.

  To have the spring-tyde of her pleasures, sweld
  By Lusts salt-waters, thus by force expeld
Back to Confusions troubl'd Sea, had made
Such troops of Passion ready to invade,
An ill defended Conscience, that her look
Like a cast Felons, out of hopes of th' book,
Was sad with silent guilt; the Room she leaves
To her Contemner, who not long receives
The benefit of rest, she that had been
The Prologue unto this obstructed sin,
With six arm'd Slaves was enterd, thence to force
Him to his dismal Jayl, but the Divorce

---

have not wholly succeeded. Because of that and because of Chamberlayne's being such a strange one, I have kept to the 1659 text (with some bracketed changes); but in view of the confusing pagination of the original edition, my citations of book, canto, and line will identify a passage in George Saintsbury, ed., *Minor Poets of the Caroline Period*, 3 vols. (Oxford, 1968), I, 17–303, to which I have added page numbers from the 1659 edition, in which pagination begins afresh with Book IV.

Of life, from those which first approacht, joynd to
The others flight had put her to renew
That scatterd strength, had not that sacred tye
(His solemn Oath) from Laureld Victory,
Snatcht the fair wreath, and though brave Valour strives
To reach at Freedome through a thousand Lives:
At her Command more tamely made him yield,
Then conquerd Virgins in the Bridal Field.

(III, iii, 504–524; pp. 226–27)

This somewhat extreme example shows that sometimes we must read a passage more than once to get such things as pronouns and their references straight. But in some fashion, which one hopes will never be imitated, the complexity of the style answers to the complex situation of the narrative.

Chamberlayne has unusual powers for unusual description. He not only describes often, something that itself distinguishes him from most seventeenth-century poets, and not only at length, which is yet rarer. He also describes with his heart in it.

The Stars cloath'd in the pride of light, had sent
Their sharp beams from the spangled firmament,
To silver ore the Earth, which being embost
With hills, seem'd now enamel'd ore with frost,
The keen winds whistle in the justling trees,
And cloath'd their naked limbs in hoary frees.
When having pac'd some miles of crusted earth,
Whose labor warm'd our blood, before the birth
O' th' sluggish morning from his bed had drawn
The early Villager, the sober dawn
Lending our eyes the slow salutes of light,
We are encountred with the welcom sight
Of some poor scatter'd Cottages that stood
In the dark shadow of a spacious wood

That fring'd an humble valley, towards those,
Whilst the still morn knew nought to discompose
Her sleepy infancy, we went, and now
Being come so near we might discover how
The unstir'd smoke stream'd from the Cottage tops,
A glim'ring light from a low window stops
Our further course . . .

(IV, iv, 270–90; pp. 78–79)

His night pieces and dawn pieces rival those by Virgil, and they come more frequently. Sometimes, admittedly, they are overdone.

Now from Nights swarthy Region rose that day,
'Gainst which Invention taught her Babes the way
To level at delight, though she flew high
As Monarchs breasts . . .

(III, v, 353–56; p. 250)

But usually they prove beyond cavil, at least the cavil of any enthusiast of seventeenth-century poetry.

'Twas the short journey 'twixt the Day and Night,
The calm fresh Evening, Times Hermaphrodite.
The sun on Lights dilated Wings being fled,
To call the Western Villagers from Bed:
Ere at his Castle they arrive, which stood
Upon a Hill, whose Basis freng'd with wood,
Shadowed the fragrant Meadows, thorough which
A spatious River, striving to enrich
The flow'ry Valleys, with what ever might
At home be profit, or abroad delight,
With parted streams that pleasant Islands made,
Its gentle Current to the Sea conveyd.

(I, i, 139–50; p. 6)

I would accept the criticism that such a style can hardly be termed narrative in any ordinary sense. But if Chamberlayne does not deserve the title of narrative poet, he certainly should be thought an outstanding describer of narrative. His plot derives from episodes and, more important, from the model of the romance from Heliodorus to Barclay's *Argenis* and Sir Philip Sidney's *Arcadia.* So also does much of his manner of relating it. Sudden shifts, coincidences, prophecies, repetitions of motifs, and disguises abound—surely these and similar things must and can be accepted. What Chamberlayne adds proves far more difficult to define. Pharonnida's father is sometimes styled a prince and sometimes a king. Because the two were synonymous in the Renaissance that is no great problem. Yet no discernible obligation kept Chamberlayne from naming the man before his third book, and no necessity entailed his reintroducing a character who had earlier seemed to have been slain. Saintsbury was forcibly struck by Chamberlayne's alternately referring to the kingdom ruled by Pharonnida's father (who turns out to be named Cleander) as Morea and Sicily, and he wrote that he read the poem three times in order to be able to provide his précis. In the Appendix to this book are both Saintsbury's account of what happens in the poem and that of Chamberlayne's most studious critic, A. E. Parsons. In all this, we cannot deny a wholeness to *Pharonnida,* and while conceding that Chamberlayne perhaps describes a narrative, he describes silences as well as actions. Here, for example, we discover Pharonnida and Argalia at one of their rare moments of quiet and happiness.

> Here whilst their sweet imployment was discourse
> Taught in the School of Vertue, to divorce
> Those maiden brides, their twisted eye-beams, sleep
> Which flies the open gates of care, did creep

In at their cristal windows to remove
The lamp of joy, fill'd with the oil of love.
The Princess spirits fled from the distress
Of action into calm forgetfulness
Having the Curtains drawn, *Argalia's* head
Softly reposing on her lap (that bed)
Of precious odours, there receives a while
A rest, for sweetness such as Saints beguile
Time [with], in their still dormitories till
Heavens summons shall their hopes on earth fulfil.

(IV, i, 309–22; pp. 13–14)

That precious moment seems no less lovely for a latinism like "dormitories." Other fine passages develop the traditional topoi of Renaissance poetry. In one fine dawn piece, for example, the princess' eyes properly outshine the stars.

Whilst here the learnd Astronomers of Love,
Observ'd how Eyes (those wandring Stars) did move,
And thence with heedful Art did calculate
Approaching changes in that doubtful state;
The Princess (like the Planet of the day)
Comes with a luster forth that did betray
The others beams into contempt, and made
The Morning Stars of meaner beauties fade,
Sadly confessing by their Languisht light,
They shone but when her absence made it Night:
Stately her look, yet not too high to be
Seen in the Valleys of Humility;
Clear as Heavens Brow was hers, her smiles to all,
Like the Suns comforts, Epidemical.
Yet by the boldest Gazer, with no lesse
Reverence ador'd, then *Persians* in distresse;
Do that bright power, who though familiar by,
An airy *Medium*, still is thron'd on high.

(III, v, 393–410; p. 251)

Such lengthy quotations seem to me the only way to convey the extraordinary character of Chamberlayne's style, and those effects which such a style works in us. Quite apart from what has been said, certain things distinguish him from the other narrative poets discussed in this chapter. For one thing his very elongated syntax testifies to a capacity for sustained thought like nothing before in the seventeenth century and like nothing after, except for Milton. Also, the intelligence directing such a style, perverse though it is, cannot be denied. In addition, it will have been recognized that the continuous syntax accommodates imagery often so conceited that we are torn between the forward pressures of the period and the arresting image or phrase. Here from a few pages (231–33) are examples of his phrases.

> that ball of earth, the hart
>
> vertue (the Souls motion)
>
> Great Loves mysterious Riddles
>
> Despair (Loves Tyrant)
>
> he stood red with flaming anger
>
> his wild eyes stood
> Like Comets
>
> think not to out-live
> This hour, this fatal hour, ordain'd to see,
> More then an Age before of Tragedy
>
> Sins that, till fear their guilt did aggravate,
> Bore Vertues Frontispiece.[42]

[42] In his note on one passage, III, iv, 207–70, which includes the last two selections, Saintsbury comments (p. 162) that it provides "A remarkable and almost unique example of a passage where poetry is absolutely 'above grammar.' "

Conceited imagery and witty phrasing formerly led critics to associate Davenant with the Metaphysical poets. If such be the criteria, Chamberlayne's title to that association is better. Or again, if the use of definition and dialectic be taken as central features of Metaphysical wit,[43] Chamberlayne qualifies by virtue of his constantly defining by apposition or juxtaposition: "that ball of earth, the hart." He diverges from earlier lyric poets, however, in employing a "dialectic" of narrative and description that moves a story ahead and that moves characters out of their private worlds onto the great stage of the public scene. The conceits, bizarre though they often are, and the other resemblances to Metaphysical techniques effectively slow the narrative and give the poet some remove. This was implied earlier by the remark that Chamberlayne does not so much narrate as describe a narrative. And if we look yet further into his poem, we shall see that after all if any age belongs to him, it is the future when there will be other poets like him able to complete full narrative enterprises. What is true of the larger capacity is also true of the smaller: more even than Davenant, more still than Cowley, Chamberlayne elaborately proclaims his mastery of extended poetic narrative style. Like Lyly in the prose of *Euphues*, Chamberlayne demonstrates that he can make poetry do just about anything he wishes it to.

A poet reading *Pharonnida* in 1659 could have inferred from it three partial but by no means necessarily compatible "rules." Chamberlayne's first principle involves a very strong tendency to a coincidence between the sentence, the rhetorical period and, for want of a better word, the stanza. Such units begin (in the 1659 edition) with the indentation of the first *couplet*. The next such indentation comes at no stipulated number of lines later (hence the inadequacy of "stanza") and begins a new syntactic, periodic, stanzaic unit. Sometimes within a unit there will be more than one sentence, whether

[43] As they are in *The Metaphysical Mode*, ch. III.

because Chamberlayne wanted it that way, or because the printer so understandably felt intervention necessary from time to time. The feature of coincidence between sentence, period, and "stanza" suggests that Chamberlayne had learned something from Spenser without choosing to go the whole distance.

The second principle of Chamberlayne's prosodic style is the iambic pentameter couplet. The indentation of a whole couplet at the head of a sentence-period-stanza quite markedly advertises the couplet. In *Pharonnida*, however, what is most obvious is not necessarily most important, as this altogether common example shows:

> When in their stretch Extentions reaching to
> Justice, which can through reverst Opticks view
> Giants . . . (III, iv, 211–13; p. 233)

Even more than Donne, Chamberlayne seems to call for "versifying" before the couplet could pass muster with a Pope. Yet Chamberlayne seems to find the presence of rhyme necessary to assure himself and us that those long periods are under control.

The third principle of his style, the verse paragraph, claims greatest attention, since it organizes his poetry and prophesies Butler, Milton, and Dryden. The depreciation of the couplet, like the coincidence of sentence, period, and "stanza," shows that Chamberlayne wished to subordinate all to the third principle; but he also needed the resources of the other principles to help hold together a verse unit at once so lengthy and so loaded with poetic freight. His empery over these narrative sub-units earns him high marks. But his sway is hardly absolute: the paragraph requires the unending sentence, and the sentence or period a rhyming couplet intermittently honored for its existence. Three separate principles function, none with any dominant claim, except perhaps the paragraph of verse. Although adventurous, his flight above the Aonian mount requires desperate flapping of wing in pursuing things unattempted yet in prose or rhyme.

And what does all that nervous agitation of plot, imagery, and style signify? Chamberlayne himself and we readers owe to Saintsbury's sure insight the availability of *Pharonnida* today. But Saintsbury would not or could not say what world of meaning Chamberlayne created, although the "poetic moment" mentioned by Saintsbury certainly has power. In the light of the failed epic ambitions of a Davenant or a Cowley, we can only assume that some guiding conception must have led the poet of *Pharonnida* to bring off his long poem. In the most complete discussion we have of the poem, A. E. Parsons argued for two guiding purposes. One was the "Heroic code" as developed by Heliodorus (Chamberlayne's first scene appears to derive from the *Aethiopica*), or in other words from the Greek romance and its numerous imitations and adaptations.[44] Although that apparently, and convincingly, is the "main theme," it is argued that upon it are embroidered "unmistakably topical passages." [45] From such acceptable terms Parsons' interpretation rises higher to include a "historical allegory," which is supposed to have been included in the poem in terms of an original conception and a subsequent revision or revisions. In the earlier stage,

> Pharonnida represents the English Succession as well as typifying the rights and liberties of the English Constitution. She was courted by an Epirot Prince, Zoranza, as well as by Argalia, a hero of royal bearing but unknown birth. Zoranza, who represents the Welsh line, is ultimately killed, and after a formidable series of adventures and achievements Argalia, who represents the Scottish line, is found to be of royal birth, inheriting in his own person the rights

[44] Parsons, p. 304; see also Kilian, as in n. 36.

[45] Parsons, p. 298. He instances such passages as II, i., 204–23 (p. 97) as pictures of the countryside in wartime disorder.

> of the Epirot prince (the direct male line being extinguished) just as the hereditary right to the Welsh line was vested in the Stuarts by virtue of their descent through Banquo. By his marriage with Pharonnida the three crowns were united.[46]

Such, it is argued, was Chamberlayne's original conception.

> This theme was subsequently enlarged and modified. . . . Pharonnida still represents the English succession whose marriage with Argalia will unite three kingdoms, but she comes increasingly to symbolize the constitutional rights of the country, threatened first by her royal father (Chamberlayne treads delicately here) and secondly by Parliamentary power, represented by [the archvillain] Almanzor, who has tried all along to possess herself of her person. The two themes are, perforce, intermingled and Argalia's adventures at times reflect the misfortunes of the Stuart line down to and including the execution of Mary Queen of Scots.[47]

Almanzor represents Cromwell, then (but "down to . . . Mary Queen of Scots"?) and *Pharonnida* in its final form is modeled on the political allegory of Barclay's pastoral—and influential—romance, *Argenis.*

Such in outline runs this interpretation, although the argument supporting it adduces evidence of parallels of certain

[46] Ibid., p. 308. See also the quotation following next in the text. The uniting of three kingdoms is a detail in the poem's two prophecies (I, v, 153–382, pp. 75–82; and II, iii, 548–59, p. 136), but is clear only in the second. Parsons assumes that the latter was written first and the former later inserted: one would have thought that the inserted passage would then be the clearer as to any political implication. I accept his argument in terms of historical touches but not for an allegory. His argument rests on his interpretation of stages of composition in the poem as we have it.

[47] Ibid., pp. 308–309.

kinds that cannot be entered into here. Topical interpretations of mid-century poems do meet general resistance today. When the literature written between 1640 and 1660 is better understood, we shall not find ourselves wandering among confusions and disagreements such as trouble discussion now. At present, we must be grateful to careful readers who are willing to take risks, and we must not think that in a generation that could read about Astragon or about Dryden's version of the troubles of David, such a political allegory was an impossible thing. That said, however, one must take his own stand. Anyone with a knowledge of seventeenth-century history, with *Pharonnida* before him, and with a pencil in his hand will, I feel, follow Parsons and myself in making notes or marginalia about possible topical allusions. In the vein of Lovelace, Denham, and Davenant, Chamberlayne does (I believe) write "topical passages." But I cannot accept the allegory offered. If Pharonnida represents the English succession or, later, also the rights and liberties of the English constitution, and if Argalia represents the Stuarts, then it seems very strange that Pharonnida's father, very much the prince of Morea (or of Sicily)—and of the English constitution, etc.—should be presented as trying to have the Stuart line murdered. Nor can I find it in my heart to believe that the Turkish would-be seductress Janusa, or Jhanusa, will have the Stuart line slain if it does not go to bed with her. With so many characters and so full, so episodic a plot, a Dante would have been required to sustain an allegory. In short, I think that the topical allusions function with the many episodes, descriptions, and images as part of a more general theme of human and personal government; and that historical details are natural concomitants of narrative and the public mode.

By giving an example or two of the ways in which topical glances seem to be invited and limited, it should be possible to move to the larger theme. Pharonnida responds to the false news of the "losse" of Argalia with

> Such formes of Griefe, as Princes that have been
> Hurl'd from the splendent Glories of a Throne
> Into a Dungeon . . .
>
> (III, ii, 450–53; pp. 204–205)

For a work published in 1659 by an ardent royalist, it is impossible not to think of the fate of Charles I, even if his fate seems to have been mingled with the dungeon death of Marlowe's Edward II. In the same canto the place of Argalia's confinement is described as

> The Princes tower, a place whose strength had stood
> Unshook with danger, when that violent flood
> Of warre rag'd in the land.
>
> (499–501; p. 206)

One's mind not unnaturally turns to the Tower of London, especially on reading further that there is "at its depth a Lake / Supply'd by'th neighbouring sea" (511–12; p. 206), not unlike the Tower at Thames-side. Again, however, Chamberlayne generalizes (as was perhaps only prudent for a poem completed during the Interregnum), and such other details as location on an isthmus, high cliffs, etc., do not allow for any simple identification. In other words, the sufferings of Argalia can be given meaning by a glance at those of Charles I, Strafford, and Laud without Argalia's standing for any of them. After all, he loves Pharonnida, the daughter of Cleander, who has imprisoned our hero. If we are meant to recall Charles I in the previously quoted passage, we do so only in a description of the reaction of Pharonnida.

The poem presents us with a much fuller plot of episodes including kingdoms, rebellions, intrigue, heirs, thrones, and instances of good as well as bad government. In so various a story Chamberlayne sometimes has occasion to write against the court. As Jonson and others show, there need be nothing inconsistent with royalism in that. Chamberlayne has an epic simile of sad truth on "becoming gratitude":

> as in
> Relation to servility, a sinne
> In the great souls of Princes, who can be
> If they remain in debt for curtesie
> But Captives in the throne, too oft the cause
> Why meritorious Subjects meet the Lawes
> Harsh Rigour for Reward, when their Deserts
> Many and great, o're fill their Princes hearts.
> (III, v, 141–48; pp. 243–44)

In this simile kings are impotent, and in the poem as a whole Cleander is so readily deceived by Almanzor that the two of them combine to obstruct the fulfillment of the love shared by Pharonnida and Argalia.

Like many a poem written between 1640 and 1660, *Pharonnida* possesses political elements at once suggestive and cryptic. *Gondibert* and two or three poems by Marvell share the possession of what may be termed political concern without political allegory.[48] Let it be said again that we should not allow the method and success of *Absalom and Achitophel* to convince us that Dryden's is the only way for a poet to respond to events of his own time in terms of the events of a poem. Like other poets in mid-century, Chamberlayne enjoys establishing a connection between contemporary experience and the very different world of his poem. One world of nature or life and another of art existed, but no law decreed

[48] My discussion of Marvell's *Nymph complaining for the Death of her Faun* in *The Metaphysical Mode* (v, iii) misled some reviewers into thinking I argued for a historical allegory. As n. 28 in that chapter and the argument as a whole was intended to show, the historical allusions only contribute to the treatment of innocence.

that the imitation of one by the other should involve constant equivalence.

In other words, Chamberlayne does not weave an artistic tissue into an allegorical veil. His episodes do not figure forth his times. As with Davenant and others, it is the reverse: the times are drawn upon to heighten and illuminate the meaning of his episodes. For example, at one point (IV, ii; p. 42) Pharonnida is rescued from the captivity of Almanzor by Ismander and is taken to

> his Palace that of late
> With's absence dimm'd in her most beauteous age
> Stood more neglected then a Hermitage
> Or sacred buildings, when the sinful times
> To persecution aggravate their crimes.
>
> (471–75)

Again we observe that Chamberlayne draws on the troubled experience of his time to present, in a simile, sufferings in a world of Heliodorian romance.[49] In other words, nature, actual seventeenth-century experience, is made to correspond to the golden world of romance, rather than romance to reality. What is presented by simile helps explain the real-seeming character of Chamberlayne's "Heroick" world. This process of elucidating the heroic by the real seems to me one particularly important mid-century procedure. The technique was used earlier and later, but seldom in ways that employed topicality in the simile. Of course we must take a further step to the realization that the intellectual force generated by the simile tends to work backwards as well: we are conscious of two terms in the comparison. In other words, if Ismander's palace is compared in its neglect to churches abandoned or

[49] Another such simile among many applied from contemporary experience to the romance world concludes the passage: see 487–95, pp. 42–43.

desecrated during the Interregnum (when much of St. Paul's was let out to shops), then Ismander's palace suggests as well to some extent the neglected churches of England, and in her rescue Pharonnida is being taken not merely to a refuge in a heroic world, but to a refuge in a heroic world with English overtones.

To argue for more than this seems to me to strain too far the over-colored tapestry of the poem. I must confess that my marginalia and notes support Parsons' point about "unmistakably topical passages." Within 250 lines, for example, I have queried whether a reference to a Syracusan army often victorious in the cause of rebels might not refer to the Scots; I have underscored *Rebellion* in a passage telling how Fate has overthrown a righteous cause; and when I read of Argalia's princely father having had to take on plebeian disguise, I have noted a connection with the King's-disguise poems by Cleveland, Vaughan, and others. But glancing allusions, or connections in simile, do not create a systematic allegory. On the other hand, if we reject the interpretation that Pharonnida represents the English Constitution, or English rights and liberties, and so on, we reject as well the one coherent theme ever attributed to the poem. Either we must return to Hobbes' three areas of court, city, and country or search farther still for the poem's intellectual significance.

The interpretation I shall advance includes both the Hobbesian areas as foci of value and contemporary references as part of a more pervasive, larger theme. Chamberlayne certainly gives us many court scenes. These provide us with a world at once glorious and given over to giddy intrigue, rebellion and war, not to speak of some ridiculous "Platonick" lovers (II, v). As is usual at this point in the century, we do not see too much of the city, but what we do usually merely extends the worse sides of the court. And of course we have the much loved countryside discovered for England by the defeated royalists. The triple polity (again a fourth, that of the temple, is not absent) is revealed to us when Ismander takes Pharonnida to his palace, giving her—which is to say the poet and us—an opportunity to see the countryside less in terms of a physical presence than in terms of a set of values. Chamberlayne introduces the country-piece with care, first with one of his dawn pieces (IV, ii, 408–19; pp. 39–40), then with a river piece (420–31). And so the country (pp. 40–41):

> Rounded with spacious meads, here scatter'd stood
> Fair Country-farms, whose happy neighborhood,
> Though not so near as justling Palaces
> Which trouble Cities, yet had more to please
> By a community of goodness in
> That separation. Natures hand had been
> To all too liberal, to let any want
> The treasures of a free inhabitant,
> Each in his own unrack'd inheritance
> Where born expir'd, not striving to advance
> Their levell'd fortunes to a loftier pitch
> Then what first stil'd them honest, after rich.
>
> (IV, ii, 432–43)

Here is the "mean" estate, here "rural happiness." And here are the commonplaces of retirement, the "Agriculturae Beatitudo" motif associated with Horace's second epode.[50] In other words, long tradition and an idealized version of the English countryside, with its gentry and yeomanry, have been made to yield a vision of how things might be. The rural ideal contrasts with "justling Palaces" and cities troubled by them. We must not think from this, however, that the theme

[50] See Maren-Sofie Røstvig, *The Happy Man*, I, rev. ed. (Oslo, 1962), p. 28. For citations on the *Rustica vita optima* commonplace, see *The Cavalier Mode*, p. 151 (n. 35). For discussion, see pp. 150–52, 179–89; and Røstvig *passim*.

of *Pharonnida* concerns simply the country and what it may stand for. That offers but part of a larger theme. The lovely and ideal rural setting provides Pharonnida not a place to stay but a topography over which she passes with Ismander on the way to his non-urban palace. She does not settle in the palace until there have been two similes from the times suggestive of the overthrow of monarchs (473–75, 488–95; pp. 42–43). The country represents a partial polity, a partial alternative of values for a way of life. Pharonnida is a princess rather than a farmer; she requires a courtly equivalent of the peace and fullness of life enjoyed by those farmers, just as much as the farmers require something of the strength of the court. The latter point emerges forcefully in the next canto (IV, iii). There another countryside is described. Its farmers do not have the wise protection of the good Ismander and so suffe: miserably under the grinding of usury and other oppression. It seems clear that Chamberlayne uses the Hobbesian regions, as he uses topical allusions, to illuminate parts of a larger whole.

The topical references and use of the regions distinguished by Hobbes testify that Chamberlayne aims to treat government, in the widest sense of human control of life. The romance movement of the poem—with abductions, sieges, blessed hours, and all—images the vicissitudes of life, for all of which Chamberlayne's recurrent word is "fate." Chamberlayne's views prove to be less radical than his style, but the agitation in the latter answers to a profound mid-century sense of the agitation of life.

We may continue with Book IV as a representative choice within the poem, and also as a part written fairly late and so expressive of the poet's mature views. The first canto of this book opens with a scene of rebellion by a stirred-up multitude. Pharonnida is led by Argalia toward escape, but at a critical moment his sword breaks, he falls wounded, and she is abducted by Almanzor. Although not Chamberlayne's most lucid paragraph, the last in the canto has clear import.

> To this sad separation leaving them
> Whom innocence had licenc'd to condemn
> Fortunes harsh discipline, *Almanzor* goes
> Fates dark enigma's, by the help of those
> That took her to unvail, but 'twas a work
> Too full of subtil mysterie . . .
>
> (IV, i, 553–58; p. 22)

Chamberlayne no more than we ourselves always attaches the same meanings to words, but here clearly fortune accounts for the sudden, especially unhappy, turns in our lives, whereas fate represents the obscurer long-term ends toward which our lives move. The important thing not to miss is the moral control seen but dimly here in "innocence." That virtue in Pharonnida and Argalia presently yields them to fortune but in the end will also allow them control of fate.

In canto iv, the hermit who reveals to Argalia the secret of his royal birth speaks of the disasters of war that had overwhelmed his father's kingdom. The hermit concludes that the kingdom had so far decayed morally as to make it prey to outside forces, subjecting it, in other words, to fortune and fate. Chamberlayne is especially good in showing that even the virtue of a few good men will not necessarily save them from the general tragedy. They will necessarily die for the right,

> when their righteous cause
> Condemn'd by fates inevitable laws,
> Lets its religion, vertue, valor, all
> That heaven calls just, beneath rebellion fall.
>
> (IV, iv, 172–75; pp. 74–75)

As the hermit observes subsequently, "our fears / Became our fate" (IV, v, 96–97; p. 88), once virtue had left the body politic.

What holds for the body politic holds true also of the human creature. Both are considered realms requiring government, and consequently the social, moral, and psychological government required in one is also required in the other. In Book IV, Canto ii, 129–47, the confined Pharonnida wonders whether perhaps Argalia's love has carried his fear for her to "An unknown world of passions," scorning to return "to its Center, Reason" (p. 29). Happily, she errs in her speculation, for Argalia remains rational throughout the work. If one required an allegory in the work, the old psychomachia would surely be the best model. On such a reading, Pharonnida and Argalia would represent reason, her father Cleander will, Almanzor the passions, Florenza affections, the hermit memory, and so on. There is much to validate the interpretation, especially as regards the two lovers representing reason, but Chamberlayne's aim to create characters as credible as possible in the "heroick" terms of romance entailed using such faculty psychology for its reiterated suggestiveness rather than as an all-explaining allegory. A further passage will demonstrate how the theme of reason and virtue integrates with that of fate. As day comes to Pharonnida in Almanzor's captivity, "Groans . . .

> Fly toward the throne of Reason, to inform
> The pensive Princess, that the last great storm
> Of fate was now descending.
>
> (IV, ii, 193–96; p. 32)

As in many illustrations of the faculties of the mind, Reason (feminine *ratio*) is an enthroned queen. Our "pensive Princess" is also royal, rational on reason's throne, deliberating how rightly to withstand the adversities bearing upon her in that storm of fate. The passionate Almanzor responds very differently when Pharonnida rejects him in order to confirm her love of Argalia:

> This, with a heat that spoil'd digestion, by
> The angry Tyrant heard, rage did unty
> The curles of passion, whose soft trammels had
> Crisp'd smooth hypocrisie [to that point].
> (IV, ii, 174–77; p. 31)

The political associations remain: an evil man, his will corrupted by passion, must be termed a "Tyrant" in the way he seeks to govern others without having governed himself. The effects are physiological in spoiling his "digestion" and balance of humors.[51] The effects work outward as well, leading the access of passion to betray openly what he had hitherto disguised (by the art of curling the naturally straight hair of hypocrisy!).

Chamberlayne's narrative conveys—by its movements, its characters, its descriptions, its imagery, and its generalizations—a concept of life found in much of Renaissance and seventeenth-century literature. An ancient idea, it had been put succinctly by Heraclitus: "A man's character is his fate."[52] The idea works in contrary ways, allowing both for determinism (what one is one inescapably becomes) and for freedom (one's character rather than outside forces has power over one's ends). Chamberlayne's version follows a common Renaissance adaptation: the good and reasonable are free, the evil subject to fate. In Book IV such ideas are represented best by Pharonnida herself. Here she asserts herself against Almanzor's advances, so leading to his response as described a moment ago. She declares:

[51] Chamberlayne was a physician, a fact that may have led him to this psychosomatic depiction.

[52] *On the Universe*, CXXI.

I live but to die his, and will attend
Him with my pray'rs (those verbal angels) till
His soul's on th' wing, then follow him, and fill
Those blanks our Fate left in the lines of life
Up with eternal bliss. (IV, ii, 151–55; p. 30)

In addition to such "blanks" left to man, the rational, virtuous soul may control fate. When Euriolus rescues his "royal Mistress" from her dark confinement, her

free soul exprest
As much of joy as in her clouded fate
With reason at the helm of action sate.
(IV, ii, 375–77; p. 38)

A lengthy passage toward the end of Book IV (v, 271–360) brings much of this together by relating the stars, fate, and fortune; faith and reason; as well as politics, mercy, and action.[53] Such are the staples of Chamberlaynes' intricate romance plot, unfolded to create a design of life marked by sudden and extreme changes, suffering and joy, trial and final reward.

Such significance must be counted original in the sense that it derives from a particular version of common thought a fully realized narrative poem, one that differs moreover from some of the same concerns in tragedies by Chapman and Dryden. In the 1640's and 1650's, Chamberlayne had reason to feel that the kingdom of England, and the realm of that royal creature, man, had been seized by disturbances well represented by his complex adventures and madcap style. Yet through all the variety, or even excess, the themes of government find repeated development in their emphasis

[53] Pages 94–97. See also IV, v, 181–82: "Those that know how to rate / Their worth, prize it by vertue, not by fate" (p. 91).

on reason, endurance, fortitude, prudence, and love. In the end they triumph who endure, right reason is queen, and love conquers all: "Vincit qui patitur"; "Recta ratio regina"; "Amor vincit omnia"—the old tags are given renewed life. Chamberlayne brought to life the world as it was regarded by most educated people in the middle of the seventeenth century, with whatever royalist prejudices of his own. He also made that new life whole by completing a long narrative poem. No one in England had done so on his scale since the Middle Ages. Pharonnida and Argalia have, then, many generations before them, as well as collateral lines in the major western European countries. For his part Chamberlayne created his world of heroic romance by shaping tradition with his extraordinarily nervous style, by response to events in his own day, and by using features of the intellectual system and historical experience of his time.

Such features can be illustrated most readily by the poem's two prophecies. The second is discovered by Argalia, when, leading his troops after rebels, he comes upon a cave whose horridness has previously kept men out, but in whose fastnesses Argalia discovers a glorious room, an image of a wealthy monarch of a size beyond that of most men today, and a prophecy written in antic rhyme. The prophecy declares that the triple crown of old Morea will be pulled down; that it will be placed subsequently on one head; but that further suffering will be necessary before all will come right (II, iii, 417–617; pp. 131–38). And shortly the grand image crumbles into dust. As Parsons argued, it is difficult not to think of the three kingdoms of England, Wales, and Scotland. To my view, this allusion to the British kingdom (for it does seem to me to be such an allusion) functions as a prediction of that state of unity and completeness which will result, not merely on a national or historical scale, but more fundamentally on all scales of values, at the end of the poem. Morea (alternatively Sicily in the poem) represents the total state of human endeavor and being, not just Britain; it represents to my view the human estate as well, for which the British allusion represents one symbolic exemplar.

Pharonnida's earlier dream (I, v, 153–382; pp. 75–82) follows the same outline of prophesied hope with additional warning of sufferings to come. But the symbolism of prophecy takes a different form. The most memorable symbol in the long passage comes about halfway through. The first section of the dream (153–67) promises a revelation to faith transcendent of, but compatible with, reason. In the next section (168–74) the sacred truth is presented in astronomical or astrological imagery suggestive of time and eternity as well as space. What follows next (175–90) deals with the Neoplatonic world of spirits intermediary between the angelic and the mortal, with Nature working through love as the formative principle. A longer passage (191–237) deals with two brothers, one the favorite of this world, the other escorting souls to death and the underworld. After the crucial section comes a long passage (279–382) comparable to the second dream, although less clearly allusive to the three kingdoms of Britain. In any event the final unity and wholeness predicted next includes a vision of Argalia severely wounded, and lastly a vision of the hero and heroine united on a throne. With that Pharonnida wakes.

The passage I have termed crucial (237–78) includes as its central symbol a triangle surrounding a square, and a perfect circle surrounding and including those forms. Such a symbol can only be deliberate and be derived from some tradition of a kind broadly spiritual or mystic. The three figures enter repeatedly into representations of alchemical process, with the circle sometimes being found within the square (and the triangle the outside figure), or sometimes the circle outside and the square within. At yet other times we find both a circle within and a larger circle without.[54] The inner circle (when present) designates the "chaos" or *prima materia* with which the alchemist must begin. The square, triangle, and outer circle are the three ensuing stages leading to perfection, which is spoken of as the philosopher's stone and other designations. Crucial to the entire process is the marriage of the king and queen (sometimes Mercury as Hermaphrodite), without which conjunction (unity, wholeness, joining of complements) the process will fail. Various other details in the process might be mentioned as seemingly entailed by Chamberlayne's story: the death of the prince (real in Cleander's case, seeming in Argalia's) and the devouring of one's child (metaphorical in the case of Cleander's mistreatment of Pharonnida). But the main importance of the symbolism is that it represents a process leading to perfection and entailing the union of Argalia and Pharonnida as the necessary condition. That union does not come till the very end, providing as it were the last circle drawn about the whole story.

Danger lies pretty equally in dismissing such lore with impatience or in dwelling on it as the single explanatory factor. To avoid the former error, we may recall earlier and later uses of alchemical lore. Donne obviously uses it in "Loves Alchymie," "Twicknam Garden," and "A Nocturnal upon S. Lucies Day," as any modern edition and much commentary will show. Dryden uses alchemy pervasively in *Annus Mirabilis*, most obviously at the end with London rising from "this

[54] For illustrations, see C. G. Jung, *Psychology and Alchemy, Collected Works*, XII, 2nd ed. (Princeton, 1968). The illustrations on pp. 125 and 126 show the circle enclosed successively by a square, triangle, and larger circle. That on p. 393 gives a representation of a Hermetic transformation, presenting the symbol described by Chamberlayne, a square enclosed successively by a triangle and a circle.

Chymick flame," "from her fires" into a new existence like the Phoenix.[55] The full flower of such lore bloomed most lavishly, however, in mid-century, as two notable examples show: John Everard's translation of *The Divine Pymander of Hermes Mercurius Trismegistus* (1650) and the various alchemical and mystical writings of Thomas Vaughan (1650–55). Any impatience we feel with such cloudy speculations must not prevent our realizing that during the Interregnum many men voyaged inward in ways traditional, however misty. On the other hand, we err if we think that alchemy was the central concern of Donne in love poems, of Dryden in *Annus Mirabilis,* or of Chamberlayne in *Pharonnida.* For Chamberlayne, a passage of prophecy in a dream happened to be a moment when symbols were useful, and those we have been considering were brought to him on the currents of seventeenth-century thought, especially in the flood of such writings during the middle decades of the century.

Pharonnida sees the symbols as but one of her visions in the Mansion House of Fate. After the brief but striking depiction of the square triangulated and encircled, she next has a vision of the three Fates, or Parcae, and subsequently of poets and historians ensuring immortality. We return to the point made more than once about topical allusions. Like them the alchemical or mystic symbols function to elucidate Chamberlayne's larger themes of government, virtue, love, and fate. So long a heroic, or tragi-comical, poem requires a great deal of illustrative, intellectual, and affective lore if its action is to rise above the well-told but insufficiently meaningful tale Kynaston relates in *Leoline and Sydanis.* Conversely, lore of alchemy or topical allusion must be fully subordinated to the movement of the poem if we are to get

[55] 1169, 1178. See Bruce A. Rosenberg, "*Annus Mirabilis* Distilled," *Publications of the Modern Language Association of America,* LXXIX (June, 1964), 254–58, for a useful discussion.

something more truly poetic than More's fairly ridiculous and cumbersome allegory.

Chamberlayne's conception and talents also proved sufficiently effective for him to be able, amid adversity, to complete his long poem, as Davenant and Cowley were not able to do. I am haunted, I confess, by two doubts. Surely the neglect of this splendid madcap implies an unspoken sober judgment by the sober world. I must remember that unknown masterpieces are not strewn here and there for discovery by literary students, although unrecognized by generations of knowing readers. Such a doubt strongly implies that something is missing or that something is not wholly sound in *Pharonnida.* As Chamberlayne himself would have put it, fate's stenography is not thoroughly written in the poem. As I have put it, the poem seems to me untranslatable. And yet a second doubt troubles me, especially as I read the praise of those two modern manipulators of language, James Joyce and Vladimir Nabokov, not to mention lesser writers. If I could see as well into the scheme of things as dreaming Pharonnida, I would be more certain. Since I cannot, I shall hazard the guess that *Pharonnida* occupies a sphere between Joyce and Nabokov. To put it another way, I feel some uneasiness in having discussed Chamberlayne along with More and Kynaston, Davenant and Cowley. Thinking of them, I can only conclude that he very much excels. Thinking ahead, however, of the writers we shall now consider, I must with reluctance conclude that, sadly and after all, he also does not belong with Butler, Milton, and Dryden. *Pharonnida* has gone with me to England, to France, and around this country. A strange and compelling poem, it shares with the Wife of Bath the status of something other than a golden vessel. The poem's first words are "The Earth," and its last words come after talk of "joy's exalted harmonie," the uniting of hearts and crowns, and of the marriage of the hero and heroine. At last the themes we have been following come to transcendent resolution:

> Thus after all the wild varietie
> Through Fates dark labyrinths, now arriv'd to be
> Crown'd with as much content as ere was known
> By any that death did enforce to own
> The frailties of mortality, we leave
> Our celebrated Lovers to receive
> Those blessings which heaven on such Kings showers down,
> Whose vertues add a lustre to the Crown.
>
> (V, v, 801–808; p. 113)

So, too, does Chamberlayne's poem on the Restoration the following year end with thoughts about the King's marrying, about peace, strength, and resolution in "the triumphs of Eternity!" [56] "Earth" and "Eternity" are very much first and last words. I should be delighted to be taught that this strange poet is as great as I hope he is.

[56] In Saintsbury, I, 303.

THREE LANGUAGES

Wov'n close, both matter, form and stile.
— Milton, Sonnet XI

[*I wish the government to*] *consider me as a Man, who have done my best to improve the Language, & especially the Poetry* [*of England*].
— Dryden, in a letter, 1699

With the publication of *Pharonnida* in 1659, English narrative poetry might have headed in various directions, not excluding triumph or disaster. Chamberlayne's language—that is his expressive resources of words, syntax, metaphor, and prosody—startles those readers he still finds. Even at the end of nearly five hundred pages we find ourselves astonished at Chamberlayne's unflagging ability to hustle high-astounding terms and to stretch English syntax into unwonted and thitherto unnecessary shapes. Untranslatable his language may be, but we understand it, and something in us receives an equally strenuous workout. To be interested in literature is to be interested in language, especially in the languages possessed by different poets, or the several possessed by the same poet. Donne conveys two wholly different meanings by the distinct languages of "Sweetest love, I do not goe" and "For Godsake hold your tongue, and let me love." Milton does the same in the shift of language between *Paradise Lost* and *Paradise Regained.* Dryden's shift in serious drama from the heroic couplet to the strict but lyric blank verse in *All for Love*, and thereafter to a much rougher medium, provides symptoms of three very different kinds of experience.

Critics whose chief interests lie with earlier literature tend to make unwarranted assumptions that major literary achievement is not possible after such-and-such a date. Critics most concerned with the modern or contemporary make a comparable mistake in assuming that there can be found nothing experimental or radical in older literature. Like Spenser before him, Donne radically altered poetic language, although their alterations were very different. Like Jonson and Dryden after him, Donne bent the language of poetry more closely to the natural rhythms of speech. Chamberlayne shares Donne's sudden shifts, conceits, and juggling of logic. But what works so well for Donne in his brief "dialogue of one" appears startling in the public and narrative modes of *Pharonnida.* Chamberlayne's talent, like his language, includes a pervasive eccentricity, an intellectual tic providing our sense at once of his appeal and his limits. After a number of poets had sought unsuccessfully to bring off a whole narrative by means of lesser measures, Chamberlayne succeeded with extreme measures. Some such thoroughgoing reordering as his was probably necessary if narrative was ever again to achieve greatness. But some kind of naturalness, a normative humanity and language, would also be required. And, the seventeenth century being what it was, the requirements would also include learning.

Although the learning of Butler, Milton, and Dryden has sometimes been exaggerated by critics, and sometimes underestimated, it has not so far been equaled by any other three poetic contemporaries. The knowledge they possessed was often untrue or confused in detail, but it had the great advantage for the knower of holding together as a multifarious but inner-related whole. Numerous national languages, the arts (including logic and rhetoric), history, philosophy, science, and religion provide the main components outside literature. The translation of such knowledge into poetry, and poetry often recalling in some fashion the Latin and Greek poets, leads many readers to think that a Milton is a classic. At the same time, anyone studying his expressive resources can only acknowledge that the classic is profoundly radical. No other English poet except Chamberlayne ever used a poetic language of such extended syntax, and it is a tribute to Milton that Chamberlayne seems affected by comparison. Any really great work, old or new, can only be profoundly timeless or normative and profoundly radical in its transforming art. The innovations in language made by the three greatest poets of the latter half of the seventeenth century should tell us something about what is central to their understanding of our world.

Samuel Butler made "Hudibrastics" into a new language of poetry quickly imitated by other writers of his time for burlesque and by Henry Higden even for translating Juvenal's thirteenth satire. No one ever wrote the Hudibrastic tongue better than its inventor, however, and his combination of prosody, diction, drive of thought, and tone was essential to the success of *Hudibras*. Butler wrote enough in other forms for us to see that Hudibrastics provided him with his finest language. Yet he is a man of his time in writing the heroic couplet, the loose pindaric ode, and various ballad measures. We may consider the two versions of *The Elephant in the Moon* (in which a Royal Society virtuoso thinks he discovers that great beast through his telescope only to have it prove a mouse that had crept in). The version in "short verse" runs to 520 lines, whereas that in "long verse" extends to 538 lines. Since each of the long lines is some twenty percent longer to begin with, we can readily see how much more pointed and efficient was Butler's "short verse."

A comparison of two passages will not only demonstrate

the relative merits of the two verses or languages but will also show something of the purpose for which Butler devised his languages. First, a passage in long verse:

> And what has *Mankind* ever gain'd by knowing
> His little Truths, unless his own Undoing,
> That prudently by *Nature* had been hidden,
> And, only for his greater Good, forbidden?
> And therefore with as great Discretion does
> The *World* endeavour still to keep it close:
> For if the Secrets of all Truths were known,
> Who would not, once more, be as much undone?
> For *Truth* is never without Danger in't. . . .
>
> (431–39)

Something of the accent of Butler's country of the mind can be heard there, but little of the province of *Hudibras.* Significantly, we hear the language of Butler's masterpiece much more clearly in the "short lines." The most cursory inspection will show how superior this "short" version of *The Elephant in the Moon* is to what we have just seen.

> For, what has Mankind gain'd by knowing
> His little Truth, but his Undoing,
> Which wisely was by Nature hidden,
> And only for his Good forbidden?
> And, therefore, with great Prudence does,
> The World still strive to keep it close;
> For if all secret Truths were known,
> Who would not be once more undone?
> For Truth has always Danger in't. . . .
>
> (419–27)

More minute inspection of both versions would show that this passage sounds more like *Hudibras* than does any other section of the poem. The significant thing proves to be this:

that Butler's work sounds most like *Hudibras* when the language is telling the same story about man. For the most part *The Elephant in the Moon* satirizes Butler's much-detested scientists for their ability to deceive themselves over a matter that a boy could understand. In terms of human response, the poem generally sounds with derisive laughter. But in the passage chosen, laughter is absent, as it is absent from *Hudibras*. Folly, knavery, and delusion are only nominally held under the rule of that poor shriveled thing, reason, who seldom dares to look into her own mirror. Most of mankind are fools, but Butler does not, like Swift, define happiness as the state of being a fool among knaves. He does not, because he does not believe that happiness exists. The fools delude themselves and suffer. The knaves delude and exploit the fools, but they also delude themselves and conduct themselves into suffering. Even more than Chamberlayne, Butler is obsessed by the need for a rational understanding of man, and his reason perpetually shows him and us how hideously irrational all is. Butler strips away the tawdry dress from imagination, pretense from tenderness, self-interest from fellow feeling, and delusion from hope, revealing each to be, like Duessa, all filthy, foul, and full of vile disdain. All this will be familiar to readers of *Hudibras,* by which I mean of the whole poem rather than a bit from the first part. Readers acquainted with the whole will know what I mean in saying that it is a truly terrible great poem. The one standard, reason, proves in the end to be hideously paltry and tragically insufficient. In the end, after we have known our "little Truth," all we have gained is our "Undoing." Not to know or to reason is to run directly afoul of life. To know is to be disappointed endlessly at the paltriness of what can be known. More than that, to know is to court the full tragedy of reason, insanity: "For Truth has always Danger in't."

In a work as pervasively debasing as *Hudibras,* we look

for various ways of saving our self-regard or of escaping unnoticed. One of the ways is to enter into collusion with an author, agreeing that he and we are exceptions. Another way would posit that Butler's scepticism was but a first stage to his fideism, so that optimism might prevail after all. Or it might be said that the consciousness displayed by Hudibrastics entails a view of human sinfulness and limitation, the better to reveal our need of divine grace. The possibility of exception will be considered in the next chapter, but for the moment this much will suffice: for all the religious harangue of *Hudibras,* God is not mentioned. No character in the poem sets foot in church or prays. The language Butler devised tells us of a world in which there is no hope. He does have a little poem entitled "Hope," to be sure. It begins with an image of death and ends with an image of the gallows.

Butler's language presses devaluation on us. He takes from life any pretense to meaningfulness, decency, or beauty. To talk about such a world, Butler devalued language. His humor and learning often won him praise in the eighteenth century, but laughter is gone from the one and relevance from the other.

> From that blest Bed the *Heroe* came,
> Whom *France* and *Poland* yet does fame:
> Who, when retired here to Peace,
> His warlike Studies could not cease.

On the occasions when Marvell grows flatulent (here *Upon Appleton House,* 281–84) his tetrameter lines begin to sound like *Hudibras.* But Marvell does not have Butler's language nor does he use his own tetrameter accent to Butler's ends. Whether successful or not, these four lines are meant as praise of Fairfax. If we found them in *Hudibras,* they would be utterly sarcastic. And lest we take refuge in the language itself, Butler will have been sure to jumble it up with odd rhymes and throw-away feminine rhyme syllables. Nor is that enough. He likes to lay hands on something generally considered to be of price, or some bit of erudite lore that must be explained in a footnote. Then he brings it in at the least propitious moment, rhymes it with something suitably deflating, and shows his indifference to language treated otherwise.

When *civil* Fury first grew high,
And men fell out they knew not why;
When hard words, *Jealousies* and *Fears*,
Set Folks together by the ears,
And made them fight, like mad or drunk,
For Dame *Religion* as for Punk,
Whose honesty they all durst swear for,
Though not a man of them knew wherefore:
When *Gospel-trumpeter*, surrounded
With long-ear'd rout, to battel sounded;
And Pulpit, Drum Ecclesiastick,
Was beat with fist, instead of a stick:
Then did Sir *Knight* abandon dwelling,
And out he rode a Colonelling.

So the familiar beginning of *Hudibras*. The language steadily deteriorates in the passage describing the Good Old Cause that Marvell later said was too good to have been fought for. Men should have trusted God and the King. God and the King are not mentioned here at all. Precisely. There was no more reason ("they knew not why") for the Civil Wars than there ever is for men to do something. Religion, Punk; "ecclesiastic" rhymes with "a stick." Nothing whatsoever except the redundant and sarcastic "Sir *Knight*" exists in the passage to hold any pretense of goodness or attraction. None of Butler's imitators had so rich a fund of learning and thoughts as he. Consequently, none had so much to devalue as he. Nor were their hearts in it the way that Butler's was. He really believed anything good said about man is untrue. To reveal its untruth, he debased *Don Quixote* and the tradition of romance. To debase them, he debased his own mother tongue. The only difference between universal human debasement and that of Butler's language and his poem is this: his was controlled, deliberate.

Saintsbury well said that "The verse of Butler is scorn made metrical" [1] and he might have added metrics debased. Looking back beyond Butler to Chamberlayne and Davenant, we sense something of the mastery of Butler in gaining control and exercising it. All that power and more, but with enlargement of language, would be required in any attempt to create a serious epic world. Again to recall Saintsbury, whose ear was so well tuned, Milton brought off two achievements: "He tightened up the metre without unduly constricting it; he refined the expression without making it jejune." And Milton's verse paragraph "was to be perhaps his greatest contribution to the English *Ars Poetica*." [2] In another passage, looking back on the prosodic deterioration of Caroline drama and on Chamberlayne's brave but frantic gestures, Saintsbury credits Milton with making something positive of the decline in verse.

> Milton, especially devoting himself to the good sides of these various [earlier] lawlessnesses, created, to an extent not surpassed or sensibly enlarged to the present day, a form of blank verse at once infinitely various and extremely precise, capable, by the further elaboration of the verse-

[1] George Saintsbury, *A Short History of English Literature* (London and New York, [1898] 1966), p. 479.

[2] Ibid., pp. 401, 395.

> paragraph, of being made to subserve almost every purpose of poetry except the lyrical.[3]

Whereas Butler's language was devised to remove by debasement, Milton's was created to include by magnificence.

Saintsbury recognized, as others have since, how much Milton owed to Italian critics and poets.[4] Anyone familiar with Virgil will know that Milton took English syntax as far toward the Virgilian as possible. He may have taken it too far, but he certainly took it farther than anyone would have thought possible. He works in great movements, as we all recall from the familiar period-paragraph that opens *Paradise Lost*. Such period-paragraphs involve unusually constant enjambement, unusually heavy and radical use of subordinate syntax, frequent suspensions of predicates and other key elements, rearrangement of basic English syntax so that the object of a sentence comes first, and displacement of such elements as adjectives. This set of principles, which anyone will have no difficulty whatsoever in recognizing, enabled Milton to achieve not only Virgilian splendor but also extraordinary capaciousness. It is also true, however, that they constitute a recipe for disaster, and proved as much to more than a few enthusiasts of the blind bard in the following two centuries.

Milton in heroic couplets is unthinkable. *Paradise Lost* in prose is impossible. His prosodic language counts, and its version of English differs markedly from Latin and Italian. Virgilian quantitative prosody and the trochaic cadence of Italian could not provide Milton with the language he sought, although lessons of other kinds might be learned.

[3] Ibid., p. 476. Saintsbury would have allowed for lyric elements in *Paradise Lost*, but his point is clear.

[4] After Saintsbury, there are two fine studies: F. T. Prince, *The Italian Element in Milton's Verse* (Oxford, 1954); and Irene Samuel, *Dante and Milton* (Ithaca, New York, 1966).

Contrary to recent criticism, discussion of Milton's language must return to what our predecessors knew: the prosodies of *Paradise Lost* and *Paradise Regained* use iambic pentameter. We have been told that Milton's prosody has but two "laws":

I. The line has a theoretic ten syllables (not eleven, as in Italian).

II. The tenth syllable must always have, or be capable of being given, a stress; one other stress must fall, in any one line, on either the fourth or the sixth syllable.[5]

That is, Milton's verse has no meter, is purely syllabic, with two exceptions of stress. Those stresses fall, however, just where iambic stress may be expected. Now it is noteworthy that a *truly* syllabic prosody like Japanese has *no* such stresses anywhere. A conception of English prosody based on so simple a conception of stress as that held by the critic quoted could not possibly describe any English verse, except perhaps that in *Gorbudoc*. Phonologists distinguish degrees of stress somewhat arbitrarily in terms of three or four degrees. In other words, if four is highest, we could have two successive iambs 1–2, 3–4. In the second iamb, the "weak" syllable would be stronger than the "strong" syllable in the first. Once so simple a principle is grasped, along with the possibility of variation from the norm, English iambic prosody need excite no fears.

Since my return to the wisdom of our fathers counters a great deal said about Milton's language of poetry today, I feel it incumbent on me to follow the matter of prosody a bit farther. The Elizabethans, who were obsessed with prosody for good reason, used various terms to describe what they believed to be the bases of English verse. They agreed that it required a set number of syllables, that it must be harmonious, and that it was metrical. Except for some

[5] Prince, *The Italian Element*, p. 143.

dranting attempts to refine a fools' gold of quantitative meter, they were agreed fully that accent determined meter in English. The evidence is consistent and constant: from Sidney, Spenser (letter to Harvey), Puttenham, Gascoigne, Stanyhurst, Webbe, and Daniel.[6] When Jonson declared to Drummond that Donne was the first poet in the world for some things, but that for not keeping of accent he deserved hanging, the point is clear. Contrary to all that, we *may* presume, of course, that the nature of English prosody is something different from what the Elizabethans thought, and we *may* still wish to argue whether Milton believed English prosody was metrical and accentual, or syllabic. Moreover, apart from what he thought, it *is* possible to argue over his practice.

We have two pieces of evidence about Milton's thought, one direct and the other secondhand. Clearly, in the seventeenth century the publication of a nondramatic poem without rhyme was a radical thing, as it would have been any time since Chaucer. There should be no cause for surprise that Milton's printer, Simmons, asked Milton for some comment on his reasons for departing from almost universal practice. The request elicited from Milton a somewhat peremptory paragraph, "The Verse," defending his use of blank verse in an English narrative poem: [7]

[6] See those critics as printed by G. Gregory Smith, ed., *Elizabethan Critical Essays*, 2 vols. (Oxford, 1904). If this book did not have so much else to consider, the central point about English prosody could be developed at Saintsburyian length.

[7] The *Oxford English Dictionary* gives no examples of the phrase "blank verse" from the seventeenth century, which is no more reason to think that Milton failed to write it than that because Elizabethan and Stuart critics fail to mention the word "accent" very often, and instead use "number" and "measure," they knew nothing about accent in English prosody. John Aubrey mentions "blank verse" more than once: see J. E. Stephens, ed., *Aubrey on Education* (London and Boston, 1972), pp. 57, 68, and 92.

> Rime [is] . . . a thing of itself, to all judicious ears, triveal and of no true musical delight; which consists onely in apt Numbers, fit quantity of Syllables, and the sense variously drawn out from one Verse into another, not in the jingling sound of like endings. . . .

Milton's business lies in defining "musical delight," not prosody, and obviously he does not accord any delight to rhyme. In passing, however, he does give three characteristics of delightful verse (like his own), and he seems to suggest that the features he mentions are the sole requirements for prosody in an English epic. His third attribute, enjambement, gives merely the accent of his own verse language and does not now concern us. The second, "fit quantity of Syllables," could mean one or both of two things: either the proper number of syllables (ten, with supernumerary syllables when "fit") or, possibly, effects akin to Greek and Latin prosody (enriching of English sound effects with something like the longer and shorter syllables of classical prosody). It seems clear enough to me that although Milton may have meant a classical quantity additionally, he certainly meant number of syllables. English poetry has, then, in Milton's narrative practice, lines of ten syllables. It also has what he first mentions, "apt Numbers." Like the other phrases, this entails evaluation ("apt" numerosity), but it also works descriptively to emphasize "Numbers." From the Elizabethans on, that word and "measure" are the two commonest terms for designating accentual metrics and their units. Certainly Milton does not mean number of syllables by his phrase, since he immediately proceeds to enter that as a second requirement. The simplest explanation should be preferred: like others before him, Milton believed in accentual metrics as the basis of "Numbers," along with a requisite skill to vary and make "apt."

The indirect evidence comes from Milton's closest poetic

and personal friend during the Restoration, Andrew Marvell. Marvell's commendatory verses prefixed to *Paradise Lost* (in 1674) conclude:

> Thy Verse created like thy Theme sublime,
> In Number, Weight, and Measure, needs not Rhime.

In rhyming himself, Marvell uses not only "Weight" (which does not enter here) but both "Number" and "Measure." Whether he means by both terms an accentual prosody well deployed, or whether he means accent by one and line-length by the other, it is clear that he means iambic pentameter. We need only attend to Marvell's own music:

> In Number, Weight, and Measure, needs not Rhime.

It is iambic pentameter all right, closing for climax with syllables relatively high in stress even in the ill-named "unstressed" positions. Here is another strain.

> Of that Forbidden Tree, whose mortal tast . . .

Here the tension comes, as it so often does in Milton's blank verse, not at Marvell's end of the line but in the middle, at the caesura. Surely anyone can scan the line as iambic pentameter?

My question has brought me to the most important consideration of all, the prosody Milton actually used, whatever he may have thought he was doing. (I am embarassed to proceed as if a Sidney or a Milton did not know well enough what they were about, but I seek to beg no questions.) One of the best kinds of evidence will be found in the evident accenting of polysyllabic words. We are aided in the effort by the fact that in the seventeenth century some of these words were pronounced consistently but differently from modern versions, and yet more because some polysyllabic accenting was variable. Here are two instances of Milton's use of the noun "contest" in *Paradise Lost:*

Not likely to part hence without contest (IV, 872)

In sharp contest of Battel found no aid (XI, 800).

Any reasonably attentive reader would pronounce both usages *contést.* He will do so for the simple reason that both lines are very regular: meter requires it.[8]

Sometimes we may wonder whether the modern pronunciation should be used or not, as with the first word in the following line from *Paradise Lost:*

Concours in Arms, fierce Faces threatning War (XI, 641)

The imputed iambic norm calls for an unmodern *concóurs.* (The common initial trochaic substitution might be thought to give modern *cóncours* some likelihood.) The matter seems settled by a line in *Paradise Regained* (IV, 404), which makes Milton's iambic stress amply clear:

Wherever, under some *concoúrse* of shades.[9]

We find ourselves in uncertainty over the line from *Paradise Lost* only where a trochaic variant from the iambic norm is traditionally acceptable. We find clarity where it is not.

The best evidence, which is irrefutable, will be found in Milton's usage of those polysyllabic words whose pronunciation varied in the seventeenth century, for example, "triumph" and "commune." [10] All that should be necessary is to set forth examples:

[8] See also *Paradise Lost,* VI, 124: "Victor; though brutish that contest and foule," where a traditional initial trochaic version is followed by four iambs, including that of *contést,* with its strong stress in the eighth syllable, *not* in Prince's fourth or sixth.

[9] See the *Oxford English Dictionary, s. v. Concourse* on Milton's use of this older accenting.

[10] The accenting, *triúmph* as opposed to *tríumph,* is sometimes used by Shakespeare (e.g., 1 *Henry IV,* V, iv, 14) and sometimes by Dryden (e.g., *The Hind and the Panther,* III, 566). Both also use the modern accenting. As for Milton's accenting of *commune,* see the *Oxford English Dictionary.*

I through the ample Air in Triumph high
(*PL* III, 254)

In Triumph and luxurious wealth, are they
(*PL* XI, 788)

least the Adversary
Triumph and say; Fickle their State whom God
(*PL* IX, 948)

Turnd to exploding hiss, triumph to shame
(*PL* X, 546)

The *Pontic* King and in triumph had rode
(*PR* III, 36)

The third example poses a real problem, because once again a trochaic inversion would be possible at the beginning of a line. The position after the caesura in the fourth line may also create doubt. Otherwise, the first two obviously call for *tríumph*, the last two for *triúmph*. Anything else would make a hash of the last example given. Milton uses the verb "commune" but twice in his verse:

Then commune how that day they best may ply
(*PL* IX, 201)

Commun'd in silent walk, then laid him down
(*PR* II, 261)

The evidence requires no analysis. It should be clear that Milton's paragraph on "The Verse" and his own evident practice show that in his epics he used, and knew he used, an iambic pentameter that would have been clear to Chaucer and Spenser, Pope and Wordsworth. Certain things are possible, and others impossible, unaesthetic, in given national languages. In prosody as in so much else to do with his narrative language and his total practice, Milton begins with the traditional and standard so that he may radically alter for our experience what we had thought to be confirmed as orthodox and fixed.

Everyone knows how Milton admits many Latinisms as well as occasional Grecisms and Hebraisms into his style. But in forging his language of epic he does much more than that. His essentially Virgilian form is baptized into Christian meaning and so celebrates the Augustinian city of God rather than Rome. Having made such an alteration in epic he then turns back to the pagans for means. Milton's language is, then, one of constant admission and revision; his syntax is indeed transformational. As with Chamberlayne, the point of such extended periods turns on their being able to admit the maximum amount of words, of phrases, and of clauses, which is to say ideas and subjects and predications. In theory, at least, narrative syntax moves in basically conjunctive and continuously coordinating fashion: and, and, because, for, but, since, and. . . . If we consider such to be the natural language of narrative, then we must admit that Butler follows it much better than Milton, driving us nearly mad with inconsequence after inconsequence.

In Milton's narrative syntax we discover so much juxtaposition, so much that is subordinated and gerundive, that a counter-narrative force is powerfully at work. And in this simple fact, observable in the largest as well as the smallest aspects of his narrative linguistic structures, we discover the genius of his language. For one thing, the counter-narrative does function as usual in the best narratives to give significance. Milton's large syntax admits so much from his great range of knowledge that the subordinating counter-narrative is essential to discriminate and revise what has been admitted. A Miltonic sentence (whether we consider it in a literal or adapted sense) admits almost anything, but only on its own terms. The most familiar examples of such functioning no doubt are the epic similes in which classical lore is invited to contribute all that it can to the heightening of experience, only for us to discover after all that "thus they relate, erring," and that having had the semblance we must now learn the reality of truth, or that having learned what was fabled we can now understand what will happen in the poem. But as we shall have occasion to consider at greater length, the large syntax, if so it may be termed, of *Paradise Lost* and *Paradise Regained* also combines narrative and counter-narrative elements. More than that, the syntaxes of the two poems differ. In *Paradise Lost* Milton presents us with what may be termed a gigantic initial subordinate clause lasting through Book VIII; a principle clause in Books IX and X; and a descending last clause in Books XI and XII. In the subordinate first clause we discover no small amount of inner conjunction or parataxis, with two series of introductions of the fallen angels (repeating $a + b + c \ldots n$) involving repetition and accretion in Books I and II. But whether we consider such matters syntactically or in terms of a start *in medias res* that requires retrospection for eight books, either way Milton provides us with a form perfectly mirroring the lesser syntax of his periods in the manner by which it admits so much in order to discriminate and revise what is admitted.

Paradise Regained has a very different larger syntax, one basically simpler as befits the length of the poem and the predication intended. Again at the beginning we discover complications or lesser movements with a complementary effect. Where in the earlier poem those involved conjunction or parataxis in an essentially subordinate construction, in *Paradise Regained* the complements are subordinate (the hopeful around John the Baptist, Mary mother of Jesus, Satan's consult in the air, etc.) in a very strongly conjunctive or paratactic main structure. That main structure, with numerous complexities in its early stage, bears down on repetition to an extraordinary degree in what may be termed a series of parallel subject clauses. Each involves one of Satan's temptations. So that the syntax runs something like: Jesus resisting *a*, Jesus resisting *b*, . . . resisting *n* up to what is very nearly the last moment of the poem. At almost the last words of the "sentence" we find it completed logically, grammatically, and as narrative: Jesus said and stood, but Satan with amazement fell.

I do not present such discussion of the language of Milton's epics with any pretense to "deep structures" or of "homology" between sentences and total work, but as a convenience for our appreciation of Milton's poetic art. It would be very nearly impossible to describe the larger syntax of *Pharonnida*. Yet Milton's two great syntactic achievements are wonderfully clear. That to my view represents an aspect of his greatness. Not only does he admit so much more than other poets, and not only does he admit what he welcomes into structures of unusual range and complexity, but most of all he does these things in ways that prove wholly understandable. Much of modern criticism has devoted itself to study of what may be called in my terms Milton's intermediate process of discrimination and revision, the stage between admission and that luminous clarity of the whole. The processes involved have been scrutinized and debated. It is to my present purpose only to agree that this process is important, because much of its operation in so long a poem cannot be readily dealt with under the head of language. But a further observation must be made: the process of admission and discrimination is one in which the reader as well as the poet engages. As we read the first eight books of *Paradise Lost*, or as we follow the successive temptations of Jesus in *Paradise Regained*, we find an enormous amount of *discriminated* experience (feeling, idea, concern, hope, fear) readied to be brought down upon the essential predication of the poem. That is not all. In the process of discrimination and refinement Milton gradually leads us to relegate the less important to its due status. And he assists us in identifying those things that are far the most important, although in any other context they might be of baffling, if not banal, simplicity: "She took and eat." "Hand in hand." "He said and stood." We can agree with those critics who have spoken of Milton's affirmation of a few central things like love.[11] Students are always surprised on finishing *Paradise Lost* how fully they understand that imposingly complex poem. That is the point. Milton devised a language of enormous complexity in order that we might understand essential things clearly. No wonder Raphael (who resembles Milton in this) appeals so much to Adam, to Milton, and to us.

Dryden's narrative language differs from Butler's in being but one of several distinguished languages created by a single poet. Like Milton, Dryden had also a lyric language for odes. He had also three or four dramatic languages for the heroic play, tragedy, and comedy. The dramatic languages are completely distinguishable, being founded respectively on couplets, blank verse, and prose (with some interchanges). Dryden's narrative language differs from Milton's chiefly in that its operations differ in themselves and in the ends to which they drive. But Saintsbury was not far wrong in terming one of Dryden's languages "a splendid *carroccio* for invective, for argument, and for narrative." [12] That combination well suits some of the poems of the 1680's (*MacFlecknoe*, *Absalom and Achitophel*, and *The Medall*, but not

[11] See C. S. Lewis, *A Preface to Paradise Lost* (Oxford, 1952); and Joseph H. Summers, *The Muse's Method* (London, 1962). Among the few central subjects for which we owe emphasis, however adverse, to Milton's critics in this century is obedience, and that important matter will concern me later.

[12] Saintsbury, *A Short History*, p. 476.

Religio Laici and *The Hind and the Panther*). Other combinations would need to be made for earlier and later poems, however, and it must be confessed that with Dryden so many poems call for attention when we seek to frame any generalization that we must resign ourselves to distinctions and to development.

If any one thing distinguishes the development of Dryden's language, both as a principle from which he began and as the end toward which he worked, that was his desire to make his poetic language English. This aim distinguishes him from both Butler and Milton. Like Donne and Jonson, Dryden created a great natural language for poetry. In art even the natural is a creation, of course, but like his predecessors Dryden was interested in founding his poetry on deeds and language such as men do use, or as he said in reference to Oldham, in creating the numbers of his native tongue. Most poetic revolutions turn either toward the more natural or the more artistic ("artificial" is the right Renaissance word), so that Dryden was merely siding (as it were) with Donne and Jonson rather than with Spenser and Milton. As we have seen with Milton, the choice of where one begins is not necessarily the place where one ends. So that Dryden was simply making a choice basic to his attitude toward language. Most of his career was spent in the effort to make numbers and his native tongue one single thing, and it is really the last decade and a half of his life in which the mastery is complete.

Well then; the promis'd hour is come at last;
The present Age of Wit obscures the past.

To Threats, the stubborn Sinner oft is hard:
Wrap'd in his Crimes, against the Storm prepar'd;
But, when the milder Beams of Mercy play,
He melts, and throws his cumb'rous Cloak away.

Lightnings and Thunder (Heav'ns Artillery)
As Harbingers before th' Almighty fly:
Those, but proclaim his Stile, and disappear;
The stiller Sound succeeds; and God is there.

A Patriot, both the King and Country serves;
Prerogative, and Privilege preserves:
Of Each, our Laws the certain Limit show;
One must not ebb, nor t'other overflow:
Betwixt the Prince and Parliament we stand;
The Barriers of the State on either Hand:
May neither overflow, for then they drown the Land.
When both are full, they feed our bless'd Abode;
Like those, that water'd once, the Paradise of God.[13]

The first example shows how closely Dryden's poetic language has come to resemble our shared English language in its basic form. The second and third examples show how that basic syntax is developed beyond the line, the couplet, and the simple declarative sentence to a more complex syntax that nonetheless moves with complete ease through the motions of English. To speak one's native tongue so fluently is no easy thing in prose. To do so in poetry that yet sounds like, and is, poetry is to do, as Donne said, one greater thing.

Dryden's effort to purify the well of English accords with that very strong conservative instinct in him. Obviously no one can read Dryden without responding to that sense of keeping pure and preserving what is one's own special possession as a nation and a culture. In this respect, his attitude toward language differs almost diametrically from Milton's, and so also does what is made with the principle. Starting with his conservative impulse to preserve and keep pure,

[13] Dryden, *To . . . Congreve*, 1–2; *The Character of a Good Parson* (in *Fables*), 34–41; *To My Honour'd Kinsman, John Driden* (ibid.), 171–79.

Dryden then moves out upon large tracts claiming them in the name of the laws of nature and of England. For example, although no one need be surprised that Dryden, like Donne and Jonson, should create a natural language, what is revolutionary is that such a natural language should seize public poetry. Public poetry had long been the possession of ritual, wonder, and the hieratic. To take away public poetry from all that incense and ecclesiastical Latin, to bring it into the sunshine and make it speak natural English—that was Dryden's revolution. Donne used natural language precisely to cut his lovers off from the ceremonies of the world. Jonson used his to distinguish the few good from the many evil. Both were altogether successful. But public poetry concerns itself with what is shared, and Dryden's decision to make sharing possible in natural English made it possible for public poetry to become the general property of all those who shared the language. Beginning with exclusions of what is not natural, Dryden moves toward inclusion in his intermediate processes, and his "world" comes to seem historically real. Again, we see in his language a counterpart of Milton's.

We may therefore return to our starting point with Milton, prosody. If we follow the history of the English iambic pentameter couplet from Chaucer to Chamberlayne and from Dryden to Robert Lowell, it becomes perfectly clear that, contrary to received opinion, couplet prosody has proved a more varied thing than blank verse. Where there are more phenomena, they may occur in more numerous ways. The first and in some ways the most striking effect of Dryden's language (whether in its naturalness or its prosody) is its unusual rapidity, its "energy divine." Few poets *think* more quickly in poetry than does Dryden, so natural is his language. Milton is one of not very many English poets more intelligent than Dryden, but Milton's concern is with magnificence, in the proper Latin sense, and that is a slow process. Dryden's poetic language is above all a thinking language, one which possesses more than any other in English what Jane Austen called the wonderful velocity of thought. That this is so can be confirmed by our strong impression that his lines are somehow shorter than they are, or than Chamberlayne's or Pope's seem. Partly that is due to the reflection of rapid thought in language, but it is also due to his reliance on active verbs in stressed, often rhyming, positions, so impelling the verse yet faster. In this rapid movement, the resources of the couplet as such are not fully exploited. If he had completely developed that interior music, he would have been Pope. But he was not, and he sped on. He seems to have been wholly conscious of his rapidity, since he frequently slows things down with a triplet or an alexandrine, or both together, or even heptameters. If the image may be used, Dryden's is not the music of the fountain but rather of the varied plash of a rapid current streaming through its banks of rhyme in large, undulating verse paragraphs.

Mean time, when thoughts of death disturb thy head;
Consider, *Ancus* great and good is dead;
Ancus thy better far, was born to die,
And thou, dost thou bewail mortality?
So many Monarchs with their mighty State,
Who rul'd the World, were overrul'd by fate.
That haughty King, who Lorded o're the Main,
And whose stupendous Bridge did the wild Waves restrain,
(In vain they foam'd, in vain they threatned wreck,
While his proud Legions march'd upon their back:)
Him death, a greater Monarch, overcame;
Nor spared his guards the more, for their immortal name.
The *Roman* chief, the *Carthaginian* dread, }
Scipio the Thunder Bolt of War is dead, }
And like a common Slave, by fate in triumph led. }
The Founders of invented Arts are lost;
And Wits who made Eternity their boast;

> Where now is *Homer* who possest the Throne?
> Th' immortal Work remains, the mortal Author's gone.[14]

The difference between Dryden's rapid current of thought and the additive accumulations of grandeur by Lucretius (III, 1024–38) can scarcely be believed.

Dryden's prosody contributes to his narrative language in yet another way. The basic natural language we have been considering is essentially a language of narrative in contexts other than the lyric and the drama. That is, it suits narrative by definition better than does Milton's very complex and wholly adjusted language. And yet, paradoxically, in most instances Dryden proves to be less the narrative poet than does Milton. The element of significance-bestowing counter-narrative is yet more powerful in his work than in Milton's, precisely because it counters a style of such rapidity. (That is not to say that Dryden's best known poems are ultimately more significant than Milton's, but that they are more pre-occupied with signifying.) To bring this consideration to smaller details, in Dryden's couplets we of course discover rhyme. His do not chime, however, as do Pope's in constant and essential juxtaposition, balance, antithesis. As we well know from reading Dryden's couplets, they do not use rhyme to identify or to define but to proclaim *with-ness* and *like-ness*. Here is how he addresses his *Honour'd Kinsman, John Driden, of Chesterton*, on hunting, and in particular on the coursing of hares:

> The Hare, in Pastures or in Plains is found,
> Emblem of Humane Life, who runs the Round;
> And, after all his wand'ring Ways are done,
> His Circle fills, and ends where he begun,
> Just as the Setting meets the Rising Sun.

[14] Dryden, tr. Lucretius, ". . . Against the Fear of Death" (in *Sylvae*), III, 236–54.

Thus Princes ease their Cares: But happier he
Who seeks not Pleasure thro' Necessity,
Than such as once on slipp'ry Thrones were plac'd,
And chasing, sigh to think themselves are chas'd.
So liv'd our Sires.... (62–71)

To ears trained by Pope's fine music, the first couplet surely sounds harsh. The syntax should be:

The Hare
—who runs the Round
—in Pastures or in Plains is found
Emblem of Humane Life.

But Dryden pursues an ending where we begin, slipping from what is high, turning the chaser to the chased. It is important that the found/Round rhyme be heard but also that it should have to compete with three other alliterative rhymes that cut straight through the narrative progress of the couplet to give significance:

Pastures / Plains = Hare
runs / Round = Humane.

And of course this inner coupleting has its own rhyme of ideas and parts of speech in the basic thought: Hare / Humane.

Following the passage, we observe that "Round" metamorphoses into "Sphere," both terms being emblematic of perfection. The perfection here proves imperfect, because instead of giving us fullest realization or utter completion, it takes us back to where we began. Before long we lose track of what is being compared to what. The Hare, we remember, is "Emblem of Humane Life, who runs the Round." What is the antecedent of "who" if not "man" somehow extracted from "Humane"? But perhaps it is the Hare as emblem of the human? Then, somehow, we find ourselves worked into the temporality of setting and rising suns. If the sun sets and rises, it circles the earth: "his Circle fills," as we recall. Since the sun is also an emblem of royalty—"Thus Princes . . ."—happier he who is not constrained to be happy. Constraint transforms into slipperiness ("on slipp'ry Thrones were plac'd") in a swish of sibilants, "And chasing, sigh to think themselves are chas'd." We must, it seems, think of princes and suns, hares and men—but we are not given a moment's rest by Dryden to consider any longer what is being compared to what, because the point is that whatever is compared to what, the experience (being circular) is the same. Once the hunter can become the hunted and dawn dusk we have even more than circularity: the metamorphosis of one thing into its complement, an emblem.

After such complicatedly inter-likened comparisons, Dryden nearly sends us giddy with "So liv'd our Sires. . . ." We are jolted into recalling that the poem *has* been developing all along a larger context or mini-narrative that we are moving through. We are considering in the larger passage the good life, how it may be maintained by exercise and devotion to one's estate. We are shortly hurtled on to modern doctors (by contrast with "our Sires") who kill even Homer's Muse. Eighteen lines after "our Sires" we are back with "our long-liv'd Fathers" maintaining health by means of the chase and what is natural: "God never made his Work, for Man to mend" (95). Which by association leads to the "The Tree of Knowledge," reminding Dryden in turn how man fell because of woman and how ever since men have continued to search out knowledge for which they are not fit, how,

> yet wandring in the dark,
> Physicians for the Tree, have found the Bark. (100–101)

That is, irreligious physicians miss "the better Plant of Life" and find "The Tree of Knowledge," or rather its mere surface, what was called "the Jesuits' bark," quinine.

To My Honour'd Kinsman includes a number of semi-narratives and two larger procedures. The one we have just been considering functions in a counter-narrative fashion by endlessly likening elements that come in sequence but whose relations cut across sequence. The combination of unusually rapid movement and of constant likening creates a language Dryden's own. The celerity of thought and syntax operates in an immediate way contrary to Milton's large and carefully inclusive periods. Although Milton's intermediate procedure involves discrimination and ordering, Dryden's intermediate procedure runs counter to Milton's intermediate discrimination and ordering. Dryden constantly likens what the speed of his verse-thought separates or disperses, so insisting on the inclusion and sharing of what otherwise might have been excluded and have seemed alien. Dryden's immediate effect in his language seems conjunctive: this and this and this. The intermediate operation does not subordinate but draws together, relates, connects, likens. As a result a narrative of events turns out to be a sequence of interconnected ideas; ideas require a semi-narrative of events; and both are further connected by transformations into emblems, metaphors, images, comparisons, and analogies.

The other larger procedure is the largest of all. The rapidity of thought covers much quickly. The process of likening relates what is covered. And the end of it all is a sense of *reality* and *totality*. The "Hare" is real as an animal hunted at Chesterton. "Humane Life" has the same claim, and so also has the sun. "Princes" exist, and to Dryden's regret one of them had recently found himself placed on a particularly slippery throne. Bad doctors exist; in fact Dryden names more than one. We assent also to God, man, Eden, quinine, and apothecaries. Dryden hurries us in consent as we encounter one "reality" after another. Observing each, we see that it is likened and related to the others. And the assurance of the language leads us to assent that a total reality is there. We recognize something essentially Donnean in "My five gray haires, or ruin'd fortune flout." And something essentially Jonsonian in "For he that once is good, is ever great." But one cannot distill the essence of Dryden into a line. His essence does not exist in the line or couplet. A poet who drives so forcefully leaves us little time to tick off characteristic elements, and when we think we have them they turn out to be real in themselves but fundamentally, because meaningfully, most real in relation to other elements. We recognize Dryden as we do Mozart, by the style, the rhythms, and the characteristic sounds. But we understand Dryden only so far as we comprehend an articulated and inner-related whole. It is just such considerations that make Dryden's a narrative language in spite of the frequent absence of a "story" in any usual sense. *Absalom and Achitophel* obviously entails a plot, but it is not so much a narrative as a subject, not so much a story as a Popish Plot, one that Dryden is so far from narrating that he begins "In pious times." And yet the whole amalgamates, likens, and relates biblical and Restoration history. Both claim full reality, but instead of addressing himself principally to relating either, Dryden situates his narrative in the likening of the two. The important thing for the languages of Butler and Milton is that comparison implies *difference*. The point of almost every predication in *Hudibras* seems to be that anything other than the naked and filthy truth about man, which we so constantly pretend to be clean or to dress up in the trappings of knight-errantry or astrology, simply is not what we pretend. Milton is much given to connecting by denial, to comparing great things to small. Thus they relate, erring. But wide remote from this Assyrian garden. Dryden's comparisons *relate* realities. He may require us to distinguish between MacFlecknoe and Ben Jonson, but both are dramatists, and we apply both names to historically real playwrights who differ essentially from Hudibras or Eve.

Butler was often imitated. Milton found many would-be imitators, and he has found parodists. Outside his early plays, Dryden can neither be parodied or imitated. Pope, who almost seems to have all Dryden by heart, does echo Dryden with some constancy. But like Keats later, he paid the highest tribute, which is not imitation but learning what could be learned from a master and going one's own distinct way. Natural languages like those fashioned by Donne and Dryden are particularly difficult to ape. Of course the experience in ideas and feelings can never be seized by one poet from another, but in prose and verse Dryden's language is so near the naked thew and sinew of English, as Hopkins said, that all a poet seeking lessons can do is look into his own thew and sinew and write. We readers are another matter. Seeking to retransform in our own lives what the poets have transformed from theirs, we hazard something important in ourselves. Milton rewards us with simple magnificence, Dryden with vital reality, or, to use one of his favorite words, harmony. With Butler our risk in hazarding anything proves to be fundamental. What we hazard we are sure to lose. The worst poet in the world for too many things, Samuel Butler produced one masterpiece. That great beast, *Hudibras*, does not slouch toward Bethlehem to be born but induces in us a lasting fear that at the center of our hopes we shall discover degradation. The discovery is not quite all, because the one assurance Butler gives us is that we do exist. Degradation of his radical kind is a degree above nothing.

IV

BUTLER: HATING OUR PHYSICIAN

They that endeavor to redeeme the world from Error and Imposture, have a very ungrateful Imployment, for if they do any man good it is against his will, and therefore they must not only reward but thanke themselves: For as Mad men always hate their Physitians, the People can never endure those, that seeke to recover them from their deare Dotage.

— Butler, *Characters & Notebooks*

THE COMPOSITION of *Pharonnida* coincided with the Civil Wars and the Interregnum, and poetic evidence of those events testifies to the positive theme of government developed by Chamberlayne. *Hudibras* also connects with events of significance to it and its poet: the "Puritan Revolution" from 1642 to 1660, the Restoration in 1660, the reestablishment of the Anglican Church in 1661, the chartering of the Royal Society in 1662—and the appearance of *Hudibras. The First Part* in 1663.[1] It is essential to our understanding of *Hudibras* that we know the kinds of connection to make between it and Butler's experience. The poem does *not* celebrate Charles II's return. It does not extol the Anglican

[1] "The First Part" of course suggests that Butler had more on hand or in his mind. The former is the more likely, since the second part was published the next year. In 1674 the first two parts were issued together. "The Third and Last Part" was published in 1678, and the three parts were not published together before Butler's death in 1680.

Church. And, consistent with Butler's other works, it attacks the Royal Society. That is, we must understand that the poem gives allegiance to little except itself, and it often betrays itself. On the other hand, Charles II and the Anglican Church claimed Butler as their poet. With evident delight, Charles would recite portions of *Hudibras* from memory, and the Anglican divines busy persecuting Dissenters relished Butler's portraiture of their recent oppressors. Yet in keeping with the negative air attendant on Butler, his contemporaries believed that the King and the Church had mistreated a loyal poet. Dryden's Catholic Hind rebukes the Anglican Panther on just this score.

> Unpitty'd *Hudibrass*, your Champion friend,
> Has shown how far your charities extend.
> This lasting verse shall on his tomb be read,
> *He sham'd you living, and upbraids you dead.*[2]

That curious epitaph, that twisted praise, cannot be bettered for the personality of the author of the worst great poem in the language. It certainly describes exactly what happens to the reader: shame and upbraiding of our very humanity.

Most readers of *Hudibras* look on it in terms of its opening cantos, regarding it as a rather long-winded but still funny attack on those two religious hypocrites and political fanatics, the Presbyterian knight Hudibras and his Independent squire Ralpho. The reader familiar with the whole poem will accept only some of this. He will think the poem not so much long-winded as harangue unremitting. He will believe that it does indeed attack hypocrisy, but he will not think that the truth it reveals has much more to recommend itself than that it is the "truth." The question of politics proves to be one of the most difficult of all in interpreting the poem. And as for humor and mirth, the poem constitutes one chief and many

[2] *The Hind and the Panther*, III, 247–50.

subordinate jokes told at very unfunny length and to the end of our wishing the poet would be either more or less serious. Something of the distance between the seventeenth-century sensibility and our own can be measured by the fact that *Hudibras* was thought a joke of scorn upon the enemies of crown and mitre. It was read as a poem of revenge, much like that Tory collection, *Ratts Rim'd to Death.* Although such an interpretation narrows too far the application of the poem's negativism, it has validity in reminding us that *Hudibras* forces on us not a theatre of the absurd but an arena of the grotesque and the cruel.

Another version of the seventeenth-century view of the poem emerged very forcibly in Zachary Grey's excellent 1744 edition. With his mostly "religious" friends—that is, Anglican divines—Grey made a Toriad of the poem so successfully that his view has been held by almost all subsequent critics. Truth resides in that view, and we owe to Grey and his friends the resuscitation of names and events to which Butler alludes, often most obliquely. The importance of Grey's Tory view resides chiefly, however, in the fact that it was essential to the minds of the eighteenth-century "country" and religious establishment. How important Butler was to legitimizing Anglican Toryism can be judged by the fact that Grey's distinguished edition in 1744 precedes Thomas Newton's of *Paradise Lost* by five years and Samuel Derrick's edition of Dryden by sixteen.[3] Subsequent scholars and critics accept Grey's interpretation, which is expressed in his address "To the Reader," in his "Preface," and above all in his notes. Butler was rich in "Wit and Learning" (p. ii). The poem presents "a SERIES of Adventures that did really happen" (p. ii). And the character of Hudibras

[3] I bypass as unworthy of comparison with Grey's edition the 1695 *Paradise Lost* annotated by Patrick Hume, and the 1732 edition edited by Richard Bentley; and for the same reason I pass over the 1742 or 1743 edition of Dryden's *Original Poems*, edited by Thomas Broughton.

> might suit many of those busy, meddling, pragmatical Fellows who were put into COMMITTEES then [during the Interregnum] set up in every county, and the COMMISSIONS of the PEACE, that they might oppress all such as were believed to be Friends to the King, and the Ancient Government in Church and State. (p. iii)

Dr. Johnson spent effort writing Grey large and also seeking to gain a literary perspective on *Hudibras*. He implies that Butler's knowledge equals that of Rabelais.[4] And he follows Grey in giving a character of the hero. Hudibras

> is a Presbyterian Justice who, in the confidence of legal authority and the rage of zealous ignorance, ranges the country to repress superstitution and correct abuses, accompanied by an Independent Clerk, disputatious and obstinate, with whom he often debates, but never conquers him. (I, 210)

And of course Dr. Johnson subscribes to the Tory view of what had happened in the middle of the preceding century.

> It is scarcely possible, in the regularity and composure of the present time, to image the tumult of absurdity and clamour of contradiction which perplexed doctrine, disordered practice, and disturbed the publick and private quiet in that age, when subordination was broken and awe was hissed away; when any unsettled innovator who could hatch a half-formed notion produced it to the publick; when every man might become a preacher, and almost every preacher could collect a congregation.
>
> The wisdom of the nation is very reasonably supposed to reside in the parliament. What can be concluded of the

[4] *The Lives of the English Poets*, ed. G. B. Hill, 3 vols. (Oxford, 1905), I, 212. Hill cites Hume's *History of England*, where it is said that the poem is perhaps one of the most learned in any language.

> lower classes of the people when in one of the parliaments summoned by Cromwell it was seriously proposed that all the records in the Tower should be burnt, that all memory of things past should be effaced, and that the whole system of life should commence anew? (I, 214–15)

In those three sentences, Johnson's passion takes on eloquence. He is talking about two matters central to his view of life: social subordination or class structure, and the preservation of the civilized past. Butler must be a great poet to be able to stir Johnson to such depths.

The traditional view of *Hudibras* as a revenge on the enemies of those possessed of civilization, reason, and the right to rule cannot be ignored. The interpretation has been held since 1662, and therefore has been worth setting forth in such detail. To a point, we who live at some remove in time from Toryism can regard *Hudibras* in such light. But the poem is far greater than the Tory view holds it to be, and primarily because it and the kind of Tory view it expresses are far worse than has been admitted. Most poems and novels exploring the darker sides of human life offer brighter alternatives or refuse to go the whole distance. Not *Hudibras*. We must say to its credit that it exploits to the full certain neglected passions that daily animate mankind: fear, anger, envy, gluttony, self-regard, deceit and, above all, hatred. Grey and Dr. Johnson were no doubt right in that the actual Restoration of Charles II was less important to the milieu of *Hudibras* than events occurring just as he was readying his poem for publication.

Early in 1661, before the reestablishment of the Anglican Church, there was a revolt by the miserable and deranged Fifth Monarchy men. They and the Quakers were at once visited by persecution. John Bunyan had been arrested within six months of the King's return, was convicted illegally (without witnesses) in 1661, and spent the next eleven years in prison, enjoying considerable freedom or suffering great rigor, according to the times and the jailers. In the early years of the Restoration, those prelates against whom Milton had campaigned so bitterly were back in power, determined to extirpate dissent by destroying, or at least imprisoning, Dissenters. That Anglican reaction must be regarded to a considerable extent as a human one to what had been endured. That is, fear and hatred are powerful passions, all too natural to us, and no one has embodied them quite so powerfully in a poem of political and religious association as has Butler. His hatred of Dissent is unrelieved. Worse still, almost nothing can be found in the poem to suggest that the world contains any hope of man's rising above such detestable states to any dignity or lasting self-esteem.

Hudibras is not so well known that readers may be counted on to remember the events in their order. Because of that, and because study of the connection between the poem and its author's times requires great care, it will not be impertinent to offer a summary of the poem. From summary we can move to larger considerations.

The First Day

Part I

Canto i: The introduction of Hudibras and Ralpho (*alias*, Ralph, Rafe) with "characters" of their appearance and dispositions. The two of them fall into their first debate. They set out.

Canto ii: Hudibras and Ralpho encounter a bearbaiting. After speeches on that carnal activity, they attack the bearbaiters, accidentally overcome them, and put the peg-legged fiddler Crowdero into the stocks.

Canto iii: The other bearbaiters return in force. Trulla and Cerdon rescue the bear. In a duel Trulla conquers Hudibras fairly. She has him and Ralpho put into the stocks, and there the two of them again fall into disputation.

Part II

Canto i: The Lady, whose property Hudibras seeks, is greatly amused by Hudibras's discomfiture, and she goes at once to taunt him. After various arguments between them and considerable logic-chopping by him, she agrees to have him released on condition that he will whip himself.

The Second Day (see II, ii, 29–32)

Canto ii: Once released, Hudibras and Ralpho find reasons in various religious and logical evasions why he need not keep his word to whip himself. So satisfied, they set out once more. Encountering a rabble in a Skimmington procession, they harangue against it but wisely flee the mob.

Canto iii: The knight and squire go to visit the astrologer Sidrophel to learn the future, and in particular the future of Hudibras's suit with the Lady. After first being unreasonably impressed by the astrologer, Hudibras falls into an argument with Sidrophel. As violence threatens, Ralpho flees. Hudibras beats up the astrologer and leaves him on the floor as dead.

Digression

An Heroical Epistle of Hudibras to Sidrophel: In this taunting and insulting letter, Sidrophel effectively changes from an Interregnum astrologer into a virtuoso of the Royal Society.

Part III

Canto i: Informed by Ralpho of Hudibras's deceit over the whipping, the Lady quizzes the hero and then has him tormented in a dark room by "devils," who make him confess his many duplicities.

Digression

Canto ii: This canto offers a digression from the main action and a transition from the rule of the Saints (with focus on the role of Shaftesbury in the Protectorate) to the Restoration.

The Third Day (III, iii, 43–74)

Canto iii: Hudibras and Ralpho are reunited. They decide that Hudibras should win the Lady by going to law. They consult a lawyer who agrees to take the case.

An Heroical Epistle of Hudibras to his Lady: Abusing logic as usual, Hudibras seeks to evade guilt for his lies. Rising in his false eloquence to the Lady, he proclaims on the subject of love and, in the climax, tells her in almost so many words that she *must* love him.

The Ladies Answer to the Knight: She rejects his logic, and his person, telling him that he is a fraud. Moreover, she says at length and with eloquence, women should rightly rule men and the state, and in fact they do. So the poem ends.

Boswell reports Dr. Johnson's saying that a man who read Richardson for the story would hang himself. We must read him, Johnson said, for his sentiments. As for *Hudibras,* its plot also entitles the author to such a dry death, although we readers are far more likely to take our lives over the sentiments. The debasement of plot expresses Butler's general sentiment about everything. A fine example of debasement, and one that tells us something about Butler's relation to his age, comes in the "Heroical Epistle of Hudibras to Sidrophel," concluding Part II. A heroic epistle is of course a love epistle following the model of Ovid's *Heroides,* in which great women write to their lovers with high passion, as for example Dido to her faithless Aeneas. No precedent existed in the genre for a man to write a man, or to change the atmosphere from love to hatred. So much for the form of greeting. In that verse letter, the ragtail cheat, the astrologer Sidrophel, is transformed into a Royal Society virtuoso. To Butler as to Swift, modern notions of the Royal Society would have been incomprehensible. The virtuoso did not herald an age of rationalism, empiricism, and mechanistic clarity, but rather mad notions, superstitions, belief in magic and chimerical projects, and an avoidance of what common sense knew to be the real nature, the needs of man.

Many views existed in the Restoration, as they do in all periods of which we know, and by no means all men thought as Butler did. But that Sidrophel should be thought to degenerate in the change from Interregnum astrologer to Royal Society virtuoso tells us a great deal about the Restoration that modern critics, tiresomely repeating Thomas Sprat and each other, have failed to comprehend. We now understand that scientific creativity resembles literary or any other kind in its proceeding by fits and falls, by intuitions and odd courses. Butler knew in his bones what we have only lately understood, and he hated it. Butler accounted for that line of scientific spiritualism that can be drawn from Robert Fludd's Rosicrucian (and much otherwise) *Utriusque Cosmi . . . Historia* (1617) to William Lilly's *Christian Astrologer* (1647), still the best book on the subject in our language; from such to the Hon. Robert Boyle experimenting with gases and "spirits," conceiving *The Christian Virtuoso*, and writing on the style of Holy Scriptures; from him to Sir Isaac Newton, casting nativities, practicing alchemy, and interpreting Ezekiel as well as mathematical principles. Butler hated all such.

And he would have hated even the sober and seemingly inoffensive John Evelyn, if he had had access to things that Evelyn reveals in his diary. Perhaps the most moving part of the diary is its account of the death of that angelic prodigy, Evelyn's son Richard.[5] The boy could pronounce four languages by the age of two and a half years, had "a strange

[5] *The Diary*, ed. E. S. de Beer, 6 vols. (Oxford, 1955), III, 206 ff.

passion for *Greeke*" by five, along with "a wonderfull disposition to *Mathematics*, having by heart, divers propositions of *Euclid*." Among "these and the like illuminations" were the boy's extraordinary sweetness, kindness, and saintliness. Here we have Evelyn's religious rhapsody on his loss:

> Such a Child I never saw; for such a child I blesse God, in whose boosome he is: May I & mine become as this little child, which now follows the Child Jesus, that Lamb of God, in a white robe whithersoever he gos. Even so, Lord *Jesus, fiat Voluntas tua,* Thou gavest him to us, thou hast taken him from us, blessed be the name of the Lord, That I had any thing acceptable to thee, was from thy Grace alone, since from me he had nothing but sinn; But that thou hast pardon'd, blessed be my God for ever Amen.

Butler would never have believed that such a child existed. But he would have believed that a person who believed as much could add in the next entry, "On the *Saturday* following, I sufferd the Physitians to have him opened. . . ." Only by understanding an age inclusive of Butler and Evelyn and Bunyan, as well as of Milton, Dryden, and Rochester, shall we be able to make sense of the literary works of any of them or of the ways in which those works may become part of our lives.

The degeneration of Sidrophel into a Royal Society virtuoso tells us something as well of the chronology of *Hudibras*. A double time-scheme operates in parallel if somewhat dim fashion. The action of the poem, such as it is, covers three days. The first day's events are related from Part I, Canto i through Part II, Canto i. The second day runs from Part II, Canto ii through Part III, Canto i. Part III, Canto ii constitutes a digression. The third day receives only Part III, Canto iii and, apparently, "The Heroical Epistle of Hudibras to his Lady" and "The Ladies Answer." With characteristic indifference to design, Butler manages to make the three days fail to coincide with his three parts, and of course fills the parts with various odd lumber.

And what of a political chronology? From Zachary Grey the view has persisted that the adventures in the poem "did really happen," and that therefore the characters must represent real people. Once again it is necessary to remind ourselves that Butler writes before Dryden's *Absalom and Achitophel.* We ought also to consider whether the gross misshapenness of the poem implies a careful, clear design *à clef.* I just cannot think that anyone like Butler, so contemptuous even of art itself, would strain himself to such ends. Modern scholars have come up with very little new information about Butler, but both what has been discovered to be true and what has been discovered to be false has inspired increasing uncertainty in Butler's editors about a historical or political allegory. In my opinion it is vain to argue that in Hudibras Butler shadowed one single person, although it seems quite likely that his two principals began with historical models and departed from them the more artistic life was given them.[6] I see no value at all in trying to find a political allegory in the bearbaiting or Skimmington episodes. None of this denies that Butler was responding to experience in his time, between about 1641 and 1642 on to almost the time of writing. But our necessity must be to discover how he sets forth the times and what interests him in them.

Butler makes many allusions to events and to individuals, usually by mentioning something particularly absurd that was said or done, and which the diligent efforts of Grey and others have been able to date. By following such allusions, we can discover a pattern or sequence of time that has a pretty firm consistency, although exceptions do exist in every part. The

[6] See *Hudibras,* ed. John Wilders (Oxford, 1967), p. xxxviii. Butler admitted to being inspired by real people only for the characters of Hudibras and Ralpho, and he admitted nothing of the kind for the other characters.

pattern involves three decades, which divide up, surprisingly, just as the three days do:

I, i–II, i	1640's
II, ii–III,i	1650's
III, ii	Transition
III, iii	1660's

Butler's manner of conveying the sequence can best be set forth in terms of examples that prove that he does use the sequence.

1640's (I, i–II,i)

"When *civil* Fury first [*sic*] grew high" (I, i, 1).
The Western setting, where Charles I held out longest.
Challenge to bearbaiting: reference to the attacks on sports and amusements culminating in the Parliamentary ordinance of 3 June 1647 banning such pastimes.
See allusions in I, i, 721 ff.
I, iii: Hudibras and Ralpho fall out: Presbyterians and Independents fell out 1647–49 on what to do with Charles I and other issues.
See II, i, 885 ff. and notes in Grey or Wilders, the issue being whether or not try Charles I (1649).

1650's (II, ii–III, i)

II, ii, 129 ff: Ralpho now expounder. The Independents have taken over after the execution of Charles.
769 Operatic detail suggests Davenant's efforts in the 1650's (e.g., *Siege of Rhodes*), before which there was no opera in England.
II, iii: Allusions in this canto range from 1646 to 1659, with emphasis on the Long Parliament (1647–1653): see iii, 139 ff. and Butler's note on 165–66.
Hudibras to Sidrophel: This is a digression, but it moves from astrologers and other devotees of the occult during

the Commonwealth and Protectorate to virtuosi of the Royal Society (from 1662). Since the historical time scheme has not developed so far in the main action, this digression gives a kind of double vision. Butler may have felt this section offered a prediction appropriate for abusing an astrologer. But I suspect he just did not care.

Transition (III, ii)

Really a digression like the preceding, it covers the same time, but in ways clearer than anywhere else in the poem. Lines 1557–1630 describe the Rump Parliament and 1665–66 allude to the Restoration, with the Parliamentary cause put to "the Rout."

1660's (III, iii and the exchange of verse letters)

This section glances as far ahead as 1675 (see the allusion in 145–46).

But Butler's main purpose appears to be showing that after the Restoration Presbyterianism (Hudibras) is once again a stronger force than Independency (Ralpho).

Although foiled as always, Hudibras finds himself in a new world where he must go to law or appeal directly in hopes to gain the lady. He fails.

Even from this brief summary it will be plain that Butler's sequence entails prevailing terms of reference rather than a matching of one historical fable to another as in *Absalom and Achitophel.* In fact we must really ask whether any importance at all attaches to the sequence of three days and three decades. The three-day pattern seems to me of minimal significance. It testifies, I suppose, to some degree of order in the poem, but the fact that nobody seems ever to have asked how much time the action covers seems to me to show rather pointedly that the chronology of plot has not been very keenly felt by readers of *Hudibras*. Or, to take the matter from Butler's point of view, it might have been awkward to squeeze the events into two days. In any case, what difference would four days have made, or even a week? The variance in sequence between the days and the Book-Canto pattern (also three each) suggests that the three-day pattern was a kind of scaffolding for Butler's building of the poem, that he has left it there to hold up an unusually shaky pile, and that the reader is advised less to rely on that old timber than to beware the fall of mortar and mossy stone.

The three-decade pattern has rather more importance, although it also is far from crucial. Again, no one before seems to have troubled himself to look into the pattern of chronological allusions, and one can only assume people have not done so because they did not *feel* that pressure in the poem. The single important thing implied by the three-decade sequence is that the world of *Hudibras* includes the Restoration. The extraordinary metamorphosis of Sidrophel from Interregnum astrologer to Royal Society virtuoso, however, has striking poetic and historical significance and therefore requires further consideration. To take the historical first, anyone trying to assess the intellectual history of the middle and later part of the seventeenth century must come to terms with Butler's sense of what had happened. Butler may not be right in thinking the Royal Society descended from astrologers. But that he thought so, believing enough others also did for him to write of that metamorphosis, seems to me a fact that no one writing about the Interregnum and Restoration has grasped. Milton and Dryden were far more positive about science than was Butler, but perhaps Raphael's clear advice about limiting human inquiry and Dryden's accusation that the irreligious physicians have missed the Tree of Life and got instead the bark of the Tree of Knowledge testify to a nervousness over the limits of knowledge that Butler makes much more plain.

The poetic importance has connection of course with the historical. The metamorphosis of Sidrophel testifies to Butler's poem's having a far wider than anti-Puritan outlook. Hudibras himself may have been transformed out of Sir Samuel Luke, as the earlier editors securely thought. Sidrophel may have been modeled on William Lilly or some other of the plethora of astrologers and spiritualists who kept the occult pot boiling during the Interregnum. All this and more may be so, but poetically and humanly Butler lays before us in Sidrophel transformed the central truth of his poem: that he is concerned with man, not a man, with the Restoration as well as the rebellion, with humanity itself rather than the purely seventeenth-century *homo infelix*. The transformation of Sidrophel is one of the important moments in seventeenth-century poetry and thought, a passage every way worthy of the attention of an Erich Auerbach.

In this instance, the absence of comment from others seems to me to testify to the tyranny of conventional opinion. Our commonplace presumptions have barred us from the obvious. Moreover, if we set aside for a moment Butler's hatred for astrology-science, we must grant the truth of what he says. Perhaps, given old views, it is not so strange that Milton speculates on the diet and sex life of angels (who can assume either sex), and is quite sure that both give them pleasure. But the fact that neither Milton nor Dryden could wholly make up his mind whether the earth went around the sun, the sun around the earth, or whether appearances should be saved by juggling the two systems—that surely gets us nearer Sidrophel. And when we think of Dryden casting nativities, and the unscientific and even mystic activities of Boyle and Newton, then surely we must admit that Butler has found out something that we have ignored too long.

Science in the Restoration was very far from being the triumph of cool reason, mechanism, or naturalism.

The crucial canto of a purely historical kind in getting us to the Restoration is the second of the third book. No one who has bothered to write about this canto seems to have felt anything but unalloyed irritation with it. It has, it seems, nothing at all to do with Hudibras, Ralpho, or the Lady. It departs from the poetic fable to versify the transition from Interregnum to Restoration. I agree that the shift from the fable is exasperating, but what in the poem is anything else? What surprises me is that those who have been most interested in the possibility of historical allegory in the poem have shown most hostility to its one canto that attacks historical individuals and ceases to sing, or cackle, about a worthy knight who may or may not exemplify some real Presbyterian knight. At all events, if we had missed the significance of Sidrophel's transformation, we should not fail to see that this canto shoves us into the Restoration, as may be easily shown. Lines 1557–1630 of the canto tell of the hated Rump Parliament. Although today that term usually designates only the Parliament sitting from 1648 to 1653, the term was used by Royalists to designate, and discredit, as the "Rump Songs" show, later pre-Restoration Parliaments as well. In lines 1625–30, Butler speaks of the Rump being recalled twice in 1659; it was at last dissolved for good in 1660:

> This said, A *near and louder shout*
> Put all th' Assembly to the Rout. (1665–66)

"Is that clear?" Butler seems to ask. The Restoration has come. The mad and perverted Rule of the Saints has been literally shouted away by Butler, whose theme thereafter certainly has no suggestions of *Astraea Redux*, of Justice returned, and the world's great age begun anew. If Butler had a French motto, it would be *Plus ça change, plus c'est la même chose.* The less insane Restoration settlement cannot alter the filthy nature of man. We shall see that the Restoration setting has importance for what the Lady represents in the poem, but it has even greater importance for Butler's view of man and history. One can get rid of a sanctimonious, avaricious, hypocritical tyranny, but one cannot escape the paltry limitations of man.

Of course unpitied Hudibras himself plays a historical role in representing the Presbyterian cause, as Ralph does the Independent, with whatever relation to historical individuals. The larger historical emphasis is the more important, and we must recognize the extent to which Butler and his contemporaries assumed that Presbyterianism and Independency were political as well as religious systems. From this larger historical theme, some fairly remarkable things emerge, and some equally remarkable things fail to emerge. Among the former must be reckoned what Butler does to the romance (was ever love so much ignored in wooing?) and the epic (was ever hero less heroic and more self-deceived?). Much of the poem kicks straight out of sight the romance and the epic elements in order to dwell upon acrimonious religious dispute. If any rational questions exist in all that haranguing, they are: What is true? What is right to be done?

Questions of knowledge and of ethics are central ones, occupying Milton in his two epics respectively, and ethics in a sense in his *Samson Agonistes.* Butler's conviction, founded on observation of men and women, and reiterated in his *Note-Books* as well as lesser poems, is that people debate what is true to gain advantage, not from any interest in truth. Truth so defined is power over someone else, not knowledge. Similarly, debate over what should be done has nothing to do except verbally with what is right or wrong. Words exist to substitute for action, enabling you to avoid doing what you wish not to do, to hope to deceive another person so that he will undo himself to your advantage.

In other words, *Hudibras* is less concerned with Calvin than with Ramus. Divine institutes may sleep on the shelf; dialectic is what counts. Something of import in Butler's view of man will be found not only in that fact but even more in the defeat of the learned Hudibras by the crafty ignorance of Ralph, whose "inner light" is no more than "a *dark-Lanthorn* of the Spirit" (I, i, 499). The description of Ralpho provides some of the most lyric and "poetic" moments of the poem, and people who remember little else remember them. As one much battered by the author of *Hudibras,* I warn all readers to watch out especially carefully for Butler when he is up to poetic touches. Those moments are either most profoundly ironic, as with Trulla and the Lady, or most expressive of rage and hatred, as with Ralph.

I have already touched on what does not emerge from the poem. If Zachary Grey in his assiduous fashion had made an index to *Hudibras,* the entries for "Church," "Kings," and "God" would read, "Not included." They existed, or were believed to exist, by the whole century, and the pressure the poem exerts to remind us of their existence would seem to be great, given the religious disputation along with the ecclesiastical and political allusions. But the overwhelming evidence proves that although Butler hated Puritans of all kinds, and their systems of government of all kinds, and religious quarrels always, *as a poet* his attitude toward the Church, the King, and God was that he just did not care.

Butler was after *man,* as the encounter (II, iii) by Hudibras and Ralpho with Sidrophel and his familiar, Whachum, well shows. Hudibras seeks out the astrologer to learn about the future of his suit of the Lady. Ironically Ralpho, who had professed to have oracular, even mystic, powers himself (I, i, 519 ff.), does not profess to be able to help his master in this. The irony doubles on itself, both because it is plain that he no more than Hudibras can predict what the Lady will do, and because he is so easily tricked by Whachum into revealing the details about Hudibras and his purpose that Sidrophel can talk pompously to Hudibras as if he knew all about a man he had never met. Butler's tone requires the context or environment for Sidrophel and Whachum, who lives in a bleak, solitary situation:

> Those two together long had liv'd,
> In *Mansion* prudently contriv'd;
> Where neither Tree, nor House could bar
> The free detection of a *Star*.
>
> (II, iii, 399–402)

The isolation has a rational enough explanation. But it also illustrates a central feature of the poem: whenever more than two people come together (and sometimes only two), violence results. By oneself, one merely suffers delusion, as is shown by Sidrophel's catching view in his telescope of a paper lantern at the tail of a boy's kite:

> *Bless* us! (quoth he)
> It is a *Planet* now I see;
> And if I err not, by his proper
> *Figure*, that's like *Tobacco-Stopper*,
> It should be *Saturn*; yes, 'tis clear,
> 'Tis *Saturn*, But what makes he there?
> He's got between the *Dragons* Tayl,
> And further leg behind, o' th' *Whale*;
> Pray *Heaven*, divert the fatal Omen,
> For 'tis a PRODIGIE not common,
> And can no less than the *World*'s end
> Or *Natures* funeral portend. (451–62)

The elephant is already in the moon, and Sidrophel is already the deceived Restoration virtuoso, or his prototype. Much of what he says must strike a reader today as gibberish. Butler's gibberish is always based on learned "knowledge," however, and it can be glossed out of William Lilly's *Christian Astrol-*

ogy (London, 1647). After naming the seven planets, Lilly adds (p. 25): "there is also the *Head of the Dragon*, thus noted ☊; and the Tayle ☋. ☊ and ☋ are not Planets but Nodes." Butler's *Whale* probably scoffs at Pisces, the last sign of the zodiac. The first planet, Saturn, gets caught in the Dragon's tail and then goes toward Pisces. The tobacco-stopper was a somewhat cork-like tool for stopping a pipe, and Butler fancifully uses that tool to express the astrological sign for Saturn: ♄.[7] Butler very well knows what he is talking about, detail by detail, every one of which he loathes.

At first impressed by the astrologer's detailed knowledge about his affairs, Hudibras subsequently finds it necessary as usual to argue. From argument things turn to insult, and insult leads to an action unique in the poem: a victory by Hudibras stemming from his superiority, which is of course purely physical. He thrashes Sidrophel, leaving him for dead. Ralpho has already escaped to tell the Lady that Hudibras has lied about his having whipped himself, the promise that led her to get him out of the stocks. What Sidrophel and Hudibras know does not deserve to be called knowledge but learned ignorance. That false *arcanum* leads to contention and violence. What men ignorantly know is all they know, and it divides them. What men do not know relates them to beasts.

Butler has no desire to spare us, himself, or the world. He envisions man as a creature wholly as mad or sick as ever Robert Burton feared, and he was no Democritus Tertius, no laughing philosopher. So profound was his pessimism that he believed that any change in the degenerate world would make it no better:

> The greatest extravagancys in the world are things that ever have been and ever wilbe, and to reforme them is but to

[7] See Lilly, I, viii, on Saturn. On the "further leg behind," see Wilders' note on II, i, 104 (p. 371).

> put them into another way, and perhaps a worse, and not to alter their Nature.[8]

It naturally follows that Butler suspects human designs for social, intellectual, and other grand ends. He attacks the Schoolmen along with the Presbyterians and Independents.[9] He of course hates anything tinged by mysticism or "fancy" (from "phantsy," meaning both phantasy and imagination) and in particular religious "enthusiasm," as he shows so mordantly in the depiction of Ralpho. Learned detail from "Pythagoreanism" and "Hermeticism" builds up the character, or tears down the character, of a religious fanatic. Butler acutely recognized with detestation and perhaps some nausea that the 1640's and 1650's had seen a burgeoning of "Neoplatonism," "magic," "Hermeticism," or whatever general name might be given to so many irrational but inspiring doctrines. To get Butler right, one must understand that his hatred of such cloudy symbolism does not prevent his rejecting a rationalist like Descartes and a scientific Epicurean like Lucretius.[10] Almost every seventeenth-century writer, perhaps all of them, would depreciate classical philosophies when such philosophies had to be compared to Christianity. Butler is happy, or rather angry, to reject them without any such damaging comparison. So Stoicism goes with the rest (I, iii, 1013–56).[11] His religious views are difficult to describe.[12] They

[8] *Characters and Passages from Note-Books*, ed. A. R. Waller (Cambridge, 1918), p. 345; hereafter *Note-Books*. Wilders' excellent introduction quotes this and certain other passages given in the ensuing pages.

[9] Ibid., pp. 283, 293; *Hudibras, passim.*

[10] *Note-Books*, p. 442; *Hudibras*, I, i, 523–62. The latter contains a sarcastic reference in 529–30 to the Neoplatonic "intelligible world," and in particular to Henry More's *Song of the Soul.*

[11] Wilders well points for illustration to the *Satire on the Abuse of Human Learning* in Butler, *Satires and Miscellaneous Poetry and Prose*, ed. René Lamar (Cambridge, 1928), pp. 73–75.

[12] Wilders has done so best, pp. xxii–xxviii.

include some very traditional concepts about Christian ontology and a Latitudinarian hope for at least limited toleration, perhaps Butler's one amiable conviction. But neither of these facts can be inferred from *Hudibras*, a world without God. If God has absconded in *Hudibras*, Butler seems not even to be aware of that, as far as it makes any explicit difference. His contempt for the world would have done credit to a medieval anchorite. But it led him to no expression of otherworldliness or transcendence.

Comfort will not be found in *Hudibras* by that familiar artful dodge whereby a critic justifies negativism or chaos in literature by positing affirmation in the poetic form itself. Butler anticipates that formalist in us who seeks to save something. He constantly rubs our faces in artistic muck. Who else would do what he does to the English tetrameter of *Il Penseroso* and Marvell's *Garden?* Who else would spoil rhyme so constantly and tiresomely? Butler *means* to debase art, his own included, lest we deceive ourselves that this one human accomplishment is uniquely free from pravity and folly. I do not present the formal depravity of *Hudibras* as a virtue mirroring the poem's great theme. *Hudibras* is, as I have said before, an altogether exasperating and terrible poem. When it starts to grow pretty, Butler is sure to be up to something. Otherwise, the formal art of the poem is as misshapen, grotesque, and filthy as the character from whom it takes its name. No, what makes *Hudibras* great in spite of itself is the overwhelming conviction it thrusts upon us that we and *our* lives are no better.

The downward inertia of degradation has great power in *Hudibras*. Butler models his two chief characters on the two chief in *Don Quixote*, degrading them both. Butler's example proved so impressive that even into the next century no English writer follows Cervantes in the second part of *Don Quixote*, where the hero greatly rises in our affection and esteem. Hudibras becomes more and more contemptible to us and less and less funny as in canto after wordy canto Butler allows us no relief.

One of the poem's greatest admirers, Dr. Johnson, complained over the mishandling of action and, worse still, the lack of action. There is, he said, too much talking and too little doing. We must understand clearly what we mean in all this if we are to know whether to agree. I am by no means certain that a précis of the "plot" of *Hudibras* would prove, length for length, scantier than a précis of *Paradise Regained*, of *Absalom and Achitophel*, or even of *Paradise Lost*. The important thing is what is done with action or talk or description or anything else, what we derive in the experience of reading. Hudibras mounts his horse. Hudibras falls from his horse. Someone hits someone. Argument. Violence. Hudibras falls on a bear. Stupidity. Action reduces itself very quickly to very few ingredients: hurt and words, words, words. *Hudibras* is not about the grotesque but about the grotesqueness in people, their bodies, minds, feelings. Above all the poem is talk. Each character argues as loudly, and Heaven knows as lengthily, as possible to claim that he alone has the truth. If one can be forever the sole talker in the universe perhaps one stands a chance of convincing someone. But all others have the same ambition. And so the harangue goes on until we, sitting willy-nilly in the poem's stocks every bit as much as Hudibras and Ralph, want to scream. When we are released, however, it is like waking from a nightmare, and we are ashamed of having been so disturbed at something so stupid. And so back we go into the stocks or, what is the same thing, off to a Skimmington, an astrologer, a Lady, a lawyer. Surely, we ask over and over, surely men are better than that? Only look, says Butler, and you will laugh at (or despair over) men without any sense of the humorous but because it is all so awful.

Men. The related words are all good: manliness, virility, humanity, humaneness. Butler puts, wholly secularly, to us the Psalmist's question praising God: "What is man that thou art mindful of him?" Man's highest capacity was traditionally thought his reason. Butler shares that view, affording us one of the many kinds of evidence to show the Restoration return to rationalism of the kind of Aquinas and Hooker.[13] Man's most glorious faculty proves his shame:

> Men without Reason are much worse than Beasts, Because they want the end of their Creation, and fall short of that which give's them their Being, which Beasts do not . . . a Fool is but Half Man, and Half beast, is depriv'd of the Advantages of both, and has the Benefit of Neither.[14]

In itself, this quotation would have been thought an innocent commonplace, at most a bit of theriophilic satire of man.[15] The whole of *Hudibras* shows Butler to have been a dedicated rationalist, and how pessimistic or how optimistic a passage such as that we have just seen should be thought depends entirely on whether we think the absence and misuse of reason something characteristic or uncharacteristic of man. The evidence in *Hudibras* admits no doubt, and the poem seems to represent Butler's settled opinion:

> They that layd the first Foundation of the Civill Life, did very well consider, that the Reason of Mankinde was generally so slight, and feeble, that it would not serve, for a Reine to hold them in from the Ruine of one another; and therefor they judg'd it best to make use of their Pas-

[13] See *Note-Books*, pp. 337–38: "The original of Reason proceedes from the Divine wisdome," etc.

[14] Ibid., p. 339.

[15] Ibid. See George Boas, *The Happy Beast in French Thought of the Seventeenth Century* (Baltimore, 1933) for excellent background; and my *Dryden's Poetry* (Bloomington and London, 1967), pp. 154–55 and 182 for some English uses of the tradition.

sions, which have always a greater Power over them, and by imposing necessary Cheats upon their hopes and Feares, keepe them within those limits, which no Principles of Reason or Nature could do.[16]

Hobbes has been unfairly criticized for views that Butler held. What Hobbes believed true of man in a state of nature, Butler held evident for civilized man. More than our civilized world was involved, however, because one should think on his immortal soul and the next world:

> If Reason be the only note of Distinction between the Immortality and Mortalitie of the Soules of Men, and Beasts [whose souls were "vegetal" and "animal" but not "intellectual"]; It is strange that this Reason should be of no use to men, in the Concernment of their eternall Being, but that *all* should be manag'd by the Imagination, with which Beasts are not unfurnish'd, and therefore may seem capable of Immortality, since they only want that, which man ha's no advantage by, Reason.[17]

Rational Butler presents the self-destruction of reason. As for the heroic, it is "Ridiculous" (*Characters*, p. 278). As for love, he does not trouble himself even to parody it in *Hudibras,* except in one brief passage. It should not be supposed that this leaves the poem devoid of feeling. Greed, envy, pride, suspicion, sloth, animate the poem, and above all two other passions: fear and hatred. No other English poem so infuriatingly, so messily, so wastefully of its own sordid means, but also so cogently, convinces us that those passions are indeed operative in our lives. "The stage is more beholden to love than the life of man," said Bacon. Butler would have agreed, adding that if we wanted other fine things we should go to the stage or the romance, but not to life, or to his poem.

[16] *Note-Books,* p. 339.
[17] Ibid., p. 340; I have added the stress.

Know yourself, indeed. What is to be done? Seek diversion. *Vive la bagatelle,* as Swift said. "I saw the famous old Mr. Butler," wrote a contemporary, "an old paralytick claret drinker, a morose surly man, except elevated with claret, when he becomes very brisk and incomparable company"—for a time.[18] As Butler said himself, "All the Business of this World is but *Diversion,* and all the *Happiness* in it, that Mankind is capable of—anything that will keep it from reflecting upon the Misery, Vanity, and Nonsence of it" (*Note-Books,* p. 271). Hate Butler and his ideas as we do, protest as we may against his studious degrading of art and ourselves, we consent to his integrity as much as we do to *The Tempest* or *Tom Jones. Hudibras* is a terrible, terrible great poem.

One more matter, Butler's most extraordinary diversion over man, has yet to be mentioned. If thoroughgoing misanthropes like Butler were rare in the seventeenth century, misogynists were not. Antifeminism runs straight through the Renaissance, diminishing only in the tepid waters of sentimentalism. Students who encounter Milton's attitude toward women erroneously think that he invented misogyny. Even critics fail to observe that his version is relatively mild, and that if he had not spoken about the matter he would have gone free. Women and love simply did not win approval in the seventeenth century.[19] Apparently Butler did marry, although we know almost nothing of his wife; and in his *Note-Books* he seldom troubles himself to observe that another sex exists. That omission obviously does not derive from prudery but from contempt or, from what is worse than contempt, indifference. Here is what he has to say in his rare female character, "A Proud Lady":

[18] Students of Butler like to cite this wonderful description of Butler by James Yonge in his *Journal,* ed. F.N.L. Poynter (London, 1963), p. 157.

[19] See the discussion of love in *The Cavalier Mode* (Princeton, 1971), ch. v.

> She sets so great a value upon her precious self, that she can allow nobody else any at all. She needs no flattery; for she can do her self that service without being beholden to any other. . . . She is a secular *Whore of Babylon,* and believes herself to be as good a woman as *Pope Joan.* . . . Her mind is swell'd with a tympany of vicious humours, that render her a monster of a kind, that Nature never purpos'd, nor design'd. She is cloath'd in jewels, but they all look upon her as if they were ill set, and were the very same with that which Aesop's cock found in a dunghill.[20]

That is what we would have expected. But the unexpected also awaits us, as in his definition of satire:

> . . . a kinde of Knight Errant that goe's upon Adventures, to Relieve the Distressed Damsel Virtue, and Redeeme Honor out of Inchanted Castles, And opprest Truth, and Reason out of the Captivity of Gyants and Magitians. (*Note-Books,* p. 469)

In this pure Butler the elephant is in the moon again. The "Gyants" are magnified pigmies, of course. Butler anticipates the nausea felt by Gulliver in seeing physical man enlarged in the Brobdingnagians. But there is no King of Brobdingnag in *Hudibras,* no person with so humane a nature.

Such being the case, Butler's most outrageous joke is the women of *Hudibras.* The misanthrope in a century of misogynists shows woman triumphant over man. The least impor-

[20] *Characters,* ed. Charles W. Daves (Cleveland and London, 1970), pp. 302–303. Other characters applicable to *Hudibras* may be grouped by topics: Art ("A Small Poet," "A Romance Writer," "A Play-writer," "A Modern Critic"); the Sects, etc. ("A Bumpkin," "A Fanatic," "A Rabble," "A Zealot," "A Silenc'd Presbyterian"); Science and the Occult ("A Philosopher," "An Astrologer," "A Mathematician," "An Hermetic Philosopher" [a very long character, Daves, pp. 139–59, showing Butler's ire]); the Skimmington ("The Henpect Man"); and Law ("A Lawyer").

tant of the thrice-repeated examples appears in the Skimmington episode. This folk procession ridicules a shrew and her henpecked husband. Butler is at it again. His great learning enables him to resurrect an obscure folk custom in order to degrade. The shrew hardly affords us any ideal to clasp, but she does prove stronger than the man. The episode is a Butlerian diversion in every sense. How terribly amusing. And how completely unconnected, irrelevant to the action before and after in the poem.

The two other women raise far more profound considerations. Trulla's role is confined to the two bearbaiting cantos (I, ii-iii), whereas the Lady ("A Proud Lady" if there ever was one) appears in the following canto (II, i) and has the last say in the poem. Butler refuses to fudge. Trulla is a trull, that lowest sort of prostitute or camp-follower, a slut. Nothing daunted, Butler twice compares her to Virgil's Camilla (I, iii, 104, 778). She is of course no such thing, but among the degrees of failure hers is the least. No one could think of Hudibras as *pius Aeneas* or of Ralph as *fidus Achates.* But Trulla is swift as Camilla, and in the end as much a figure of Victory.

Hudibras had stolen a triumph over the bearbaiters by accidentally falling with all his great bulk on the bear. The bear is put in such a fright that he routs the bearbaiters. Trulla and her friends return, and she bests Hudibras. More than that, she behaves toward him with great honor (something he never threatened to do), offering fair quarter, being altogether decent. It is astonishing. Such satire is a kind of Slut Errant going out to vanquish gross ignorance and self-inflated male vanity, in order to rescue oppressed Diversion out of the captivity of daily reality. With each canto and with each reading, one's wonder and one's sense of humorlessness grow steadily. Like Ralpho, Trulla evokes from Butler a certain lyricism manqué:

For *Trulla,* who was light of foot,
As shafts which long-field *Parthians* shoot,
(But not so slight as to be born[e]
Upon the ears of standing Corn,
Or trip it o're the Water quicker
Then Witches when their staves they liquor,
As some report) . . . (I, iii, 101–107)

A magic about Trulla rises from the images, but the learned detail of the images distracts our attention and the beauty is all but squandered, as if to say: Brave slut, how we love thee!

With her victory Trulla leaves the poem. Toward the beginning of "The Second Part" she is replaced by "th' unkind" Widow or Lady first shown racked with laughter over the news that Hudibras has been put in the stocks (II, i, 77–86). From that point she never loses control over our lunatic hero. In exacting from Hudibras a promise to whip himself as the price of release, the lady extracts a commitment modeled on that by Sancho Panza to whip himself that Dulcinea may be freed from enchantment. With typical ease, and debasement, Butler takes what had been applied to the servant and low-born heroine in *Don Quixote* for the hero of *Hudibras.* Of course a long harangue is required to get Hudibras to agree to *anything,* much less to whip himself.

The Lady scores some palpable hits during the verbal duel, but sometimes the reader wonders how safe he himself may be on the one hand, or the disputatious Widow on the other. In the following passage, for example, does the argument for female equality merely function as a rhetorical device?

Quoth she, What does a MATCH imply
But *likeness* and *equality?*
I know you cannot think mee fit,
To be the *Yoke-fellow* of your *Wit:*

Nor take one of so mean *Deserts,*
To be the *Partner* of your *Parts;*
A *Grace,* which if I could believe,
I've not the Conscience to receive.

(II, i, 669–76)

The irony should be apparent: she regards herself superior. The last two lines play on orthodox conceptions of faith necessary to receive divine grace. What she really says may be translated: I don't believe you, and so will not marry you, you fool. It may be possible to consider the argument for female equality as one designed to browbeat Hudibras. At least the Lady shows no compunction in doing that, as when she sets up the condition that Hudibras must (of all things!) grow a tail:

. . . though the *Vulgar* count them homely,
In *man* or *beast,* they are so comely,
So *Gentee, Allamode,* and handsom,
I'l never marry *man* that wants one.

(II, i, 745–48)

One scarcely knows whether to insist on, or deny, a sexual innuendo in this lunacy. But later, when Hudibras appears at her house after beating up Sidrophel, she takes great pleasure in having him abused physically and psychologically until he confesses to his perfidy and many lies (III, i). It is quite proper that her *Answer* concluding the poem argues that women should rule men and the state; in fact, she says, we do.

It is a cause for astonishment that critics have failed to grasp the central role of the Lady, and of her prototype, Trulla.[21] Surprising as it would be coming from any seven-

[21] Many valuable things have been said about *Hudibras,* however, including those in the following accessible studies: Ian Jack, *Augustan Satire* (Oxford, 1952), ch. II; James Sutherland, *English Satire* (Cambridge, 1958), pp. 41–44 especially; and W.O.S. Sutherland, *The Art of the Satirist* (Austin, Texas, 1965), pp. 55–71. I am particularly sym-

teenth-century author, the advocacy of female superiority by Butler is so extraordinary and so persistent in the poem that it must be considered a central theme. In one's bafflement over Butler's supreme irony, one wishes to regard the poem's feminism as a stick to beat a particular man. No one widely acquainted with Butler's writings, however, will be able to think that his mind thinks wholly in particulars: "all," that is, *all*, Butler says, are governed by delusion, "manag'd by the Imagination" (see above, p. 182), not only Hudibras. Of course that sordid anti-hero represents the Presbyterians in Church and politics. Of course he is also his own man, misshapen, gross, of tawny beard, and the rest. But in Butler's Parliament, Hudibras represents educated man. Ralpho, Sidrophel, Crowdero, Whachum—none of the other male characters provides the smallest relief; and the men in his other poems are no better. (Of course there is the ironic praise of the highwayman Duval.) Only in Trulla and the Lady does Butler give us any alternatives to the unrelieved squalor, folly, suffering, and constant defeat suffered by men. In all this joke, I suspect of Butler a yet worse misogyny. And I believe that farther beyond that very unfunny use of prejudice the pessimist has permitted the sickliest of ideals to take strength in transvestism.

The Lady may of course also represent something larger than the female sex. Hudibras represents something, so Ralpho, and Sidrophel. Perhaps she represents the state. It will be recalled that at the end of *The Last Instructions to a Painter* the King (Charles II) beholds "a sudden shape with Virgin's Face" (889). She being naked as Truth, the King follows his well known propensity and attempts to embrace

---

pathetic with the last, but must add a reference to a wider approach: Michael Wilding, "The Last of the Epics: The Rejection of the Heroic in *Paradise Lost* and *Hudibras*," in Harold Love, ed., *Restoration Literature: Critical Approaches* (London, 1972).

her, only to find himself frustrated: "And he Divin'd 'twas *England* or the *Peace*." I think that it must be said that although no reason excludes our regarding the Lady as Anglia, Britannia, or Respublica, no solid evidence exists to support it. Let us presume for the moment that she serves such a function. Widowed by the execution of Charles I, she is wooed by and rejects the Presbyterian faction. By itself that makes sense, but if the allegory is to be followed, history would require that after the execution of Charles the widow be wooed, not by Hudibras but by Ralpho, by Independency. That does not happen in the poem: What indeed would Trulla then represent? I conclude that doubt must govern any historical allegorizing of the Lady, and that she must be taken primarily as a widow and as a woman.

So striking a figure teases us to generalization, to some kind of more abstract principle, perhaps anything to get us out of the uncomfortable position of believing that Butler of all men in his time could possibly mean that the Widow is a widow, the Lady a lady. I confess to the temptation to regard her like Pharonnida, as a representative of that right reason (*recta ratio*, feminine in gender) that so eludes, Butler says, "all" men. Butler may have thought her rational compared to the other characters, but he does not oblige us with any evidence that he intended the representation. Again, since one of the Lady's chief functions is the exposure of Hudibras's lies, one could wish to see her as an embodiment of that common Renaissance trope, Truth the daughter of Time.[22] But again, we can honestly say only that there is a certain resemblance and that probably accidental.

It does seem that we must consider the Lady for what she

[22] See Morris Palmer Tilley, A *Dictionary of Proverbs in England* (Ann Arbor, 1950), T 580, "Truth is time's daughter"; cf. also T 324, T 329a, T 338, and T 591. The emblem writers used as their adage, "Veritas filia temporis."

obviously is and for what she says and does. *The Ladies Answer* presents the most sustained argument for feminism to appear in English poetry to that time. (Again, it staggers belief that Butler should be the one to write it.) Perhaps we can find some help in our problem itself. Butler seems at first to be arguing equality of the sexes, but more and more in what the Lady says, and in what the action has shown all along, we see that the real point concerns which of the sexes has greater power, which is superior in strength. The Lady accuses Hudibras and men generally of seeking "Dominion, / In *Grace,* and *Nature,* o're all Women" (*Answer,* 187–88). Her accusation is entirely just. It was believed that whether one consider the sexes in terms of God's providential order, or in terms of which sex is naturally the stronger, the smarter, etc., men were plainly and rightly possessed of "Dominion" or power over women. The argument from "Grace" is one that Butler troubles himself over no farther. But "Nature" of course also provides a subject worth exploring by any poet in the century.

The feminist cause twice refutes the allegation that men rule by natural right. The first, simplest, and easiest to miss is the poem's demonstration that women control men: Trulla with her arms and the Lady with her words and position. The second refutation comes more obliquely. Whatever may be true *in a state of nature,* art makes something else, as the Lady says:

> How fair and sweet, *the Planted Rose,*
> Beyond the *Wild* in Hedges grows!
> For without Art the Noblest Seeds
> Of Flow'rs, degenerate to Weeds:
> How Dul and Rugged, e're 'tis Ground,
> And Polish'd looks a Diamond!
> Though *Paradise* were ere so fair,
> It was not kept so, without Care.

The whole World without *Art*, and *Dress*,
Would be but one great *Wilderness.*
And Mankind but a Savage Heard,
For all that Nature has Conferd.
That do's but *Rough-hew*, and *Design*,
Leave *Art* to *Polish*, and *Refine.*

(Answer, 225–38)

The poem has once again grown suspiciously "poetic." In the first chapter of this book, something was made of the frequent attention shown to the art-nature polarity, and it must be said that Butler was far from alone in thinking such thoughts as the Lady expresses. But the fact that she speaks in a context of "Dominion," or rule, suggests a certain kinship between Butler and Thomas Hobbes.

The most famous passage in the *Leviathan* (London, 1651) comes in "The first Part, Of Man," ch. xiii, "Of the Naturall Condition of Mankind, as concerning their Felicity, and Misery." In the state of nature, men are equal, that is "without a common Power to keep them all in awe." They therefore live in a condition of "Warre; and such a warre, as is of every man, against every man." In nature, then, there can be no industry or agriculture; no science or history:

> no Arts; no Letters; no Society; and which is worst of all, continuall feare, and danger of violent death; And the life of man, solitary, poore, nasty, brutish, and short. (p. 62)

Also, as Hobbes had said in his "Introduction," it is "by Art [that] is created that great LEVIATHAN called a COMMONWEALTH, or STATE, (in latine CIVITAS) which is but an Artificiall Man; though of greater stature and strength than the Naturall, for whose protection and defence it was intended" (p. 1). Butler's passage corresponds well enough to these ideas, and these ideas make clear how art relates to rule and government. What Hobbes lacks is Butler's context of debased poetry. In that context, the Lady's words on art represent a sublime flight.

To recall Hobbes once more, we should think of ch. xx, "Of Dominion Paternall, and Despoticall." The matter relating to *Hudibras* concerns the origin of "Dominion":

> Dominion is acquired two wayes; By Generation, and by Conquest. The right of Dominion by Generation, is that, which the Parent hath over his Children; and is called PATERNALL. And is not so derived from the Generation, as if therefore the Parent had Dominion over his Child because he begat him; but from the Childs Consent, either expresse, or by other sufficient arguments declared. For as to the Generation, God hath ordained to man a helper; and there be alwayes two that are equally Parents: the Dominion therefore over the Child, should belong equally to both; which is impossible; for no man can obey two Masters. (p. 102)

The most surprising thing so far is the revolutionary attitude about the nature of parental dominion over children: by "Consent." Perhaps Hobbes saw farther into the truth than people could have imagined any time before the second half of this century. But what follows is equally revolutionary:

> And whereas some have attributed the Dominion to the Man onely, as being of the more excellent Sex; they misreckon in it. For there is not alwayes that difference of strength, or prudence between the man and the woman, as that the right can be determined without War. In Common-wealths, this controversie is decided by the Civill Law: and for the most part, (but not alwayes) the sentence is in favour of the Father; because for the most part Common-wealths have been erected by the Fathers, not by the Mothers of families. (pp. 102–103)

That also does not sound three hundred years old. What we can gain from Hobbes and Butler together is that during the larger Restoration from 1640 onwards men were thinking to the root, radically, about how the world does run, and how it might. Hobbes is animated by a vision. Butler is angered by what he sees.

The Lady makes clear that women not only possess the art of rule over would-be tyrannical men, but also that they exercise that ability:

> We make and Execute *all Laws,*
> Can *Judge the Judges,* and the *Cause.*
> Prescribe all Rules, of *Right,* or *Wrong,*
> To th' *Long-Robe,* and the *Longer Tongue:*
> 'Gainst which the world *has no Defence,*
> But our more *Pow'rful Eloquence.*
> We Manage things of Greatest weight,
> In all the world's *Affairs of State.*
> Are Ministers in War, and Peace,
> That sway *all Nations* how we Please,
> We rule *all Churches,* and *their Flocks,*
> *Heretical, and Orthodox.* (*Answer,* 289–300)

As the Lady expounds the power of women, she rises in eloquence and broadens her vision to include what she terms "all the *Mighty Powers,* / You vainly Boast" (367–68). She has been in something like an ecstasy, showing that all the many boasted physical and mental exploits of men are performed by them as puppets of women. Butler evidently thought enough of her vision to italicize the whole thing. Here is the major part of it:

> *While all the Favors we Afford*
> *Are but to Girt you with the Sword,*
> *To Fight our Battels, in our steads*
> *And have your Brains beat out o' your Heads,*

Incounter in despite of Nature,
And fight at once, with Fire, and Water,
With Pyrats, Rocks, and Storms, and Seas,
Our Pride, and vanity t'appease.
Kill one another, and cut throats,
For our Good Graces, and best Thoughts,
To do your Exercise for Honor
And have your Brains beat out, the sooner,
Or crackt, as Learnedly, upon
Things that are never to be known,
And still appear the more Industrious
The more your Projects, are Prepostrous.
To Square the Circle of the Arts,
And Run stark-mad, to shew your Parts.

(*Answer*, 345–62)

Woman's dominion is, in Hobbes's word, "Despoticall." And, the Lady says with a biting taunt, if men think themselves abused under such hard rule, let them be women!

Let Men usurp Th'unjust Dominion,
As if they were *The Better Women.*

(381–82)

Incredible as it may seem or be, *Hudibras* ends so, postulating a state made by the mothers rather than the fathers, in Hobbes's terms. The making of states was a popular occupation of the century. In John Fletcher's play, *A Sea-Voyage* (licensed 1622, published 1647), Rosellia sets up an Amazonian colony on a remote island. The Davenant-Dryden remodeling of *The Tempest* (1667) shows the effort to create a commonwealth. The drunken sailors receive material assistance from Sycorax, a sister supplied to Caliban in this version. In *The Isle of Pines* (1668), Henry Neville manages to depict a state of thousands born by virtue of one virile man and his poly-gams. Aphra Behn's *Oroonoko* (1688) looks ahead some decades by her depiction of noble savages living in a dignified state of nature until a corrupt Europe ruins the lives of the hero and his beautiful black princess Imoinda. Hobbes and Butler deserve credit for taking women more seriously than these other writers. The problem with Butler is that the whole context of the poem compromises any possible ideal.

Butler occasionally wrote about women elsewhere. Not just one or two characters but also some few observations in his notebooks touch on women:

> Virtue, as it is commonly understood in women, signify's nothing else but Chastity, and Honor only not being whores: As if that Sex were capable of no other morality, but a mere Negative Continence. (*Note-Books* p. 341)

The principle is right. The tone is not quite what we would like. He deals well with the faults in the way people "commonly" think, but he does not make his own view particularly plain. The same hesitation to show his hand fully will also be found in *Hudibras.* When we have conquered our astonishment over the role of his women and over the Lady's last answer, we still have room for questioning how far womankind is a vehicle for showing the pettiness and folly of all humankind, or how much womankind may actually be superior to mankind. What is rhetoric, and what is principle?

I confess that the Lady remains ultimately enigmatic to me. She and the other women of the poem are characters in their own rights, of course, and not merely or wholly women: they too represent humanity. Anything we deduce about the Lady as an ideal, must, moreover, be capable of including the two other women: the fair-dealing, victorious whore Trulla, and the shrew in the Skimmington. From beginning to end in *Hudibras* the women triumph. Sexual conflict was not discovered for the first time by the seventeenth century. But that it should be treated with seeming espousal of woman's power by a deeply pessimistic poet in so constantly degrading a poem, that is a wonder. That, moreover, the avatars of Victoria should be a whore, a shrew, and "A Proud Lady"—that is a greater wonder still. In the end I cannot explain it in a way citing chapter and verse. But in setting it before readers of *Hudibras* as a central theme and problem of the poem, I confess that to me the greatest wonder is that nobody seems to have seen what extraordinary things happen in *Hudibras.*

The bafflement with which *Hudibras* leaves us is ultimate. Its degrading messiness is, however, consistent and immediate. The mess provides Butler's conception of the world, a conception from which he will allow us no escape. We cannot escape to his art, which is as much a mess as anything else. I shall also argue that we cannot escape to the Lady either. After worrying over this problem for years, I have concluded that both sexes of readers participate in both sexes of his characters. After all, if the world is ruled by Trulla, the shrew, and the Lady, the men are relieved of responsibility for the very sorry world Butler shows ours to be. I think it is in Butler's spirit to say that we cannot blame the women, which would be to write *The Female Hudibras,* from which it would emerge that men rule and women have botched the world. I conclude that Butler believes that a *little* courage, lack of pretense, and common sense can be found in people. By taking women to exemplify these traits, he misogynistically emphasizes their rarity.

After all the noise of claim and counterclaim in *Hudibras,* after the long harangues have ended with the last, *The Ladies Answer* in 382 lines, we are finally left to silence and the relief of having got out of earshot of Samuel Butler, indisputably one of the worst as well as one of the great poets in the language. In lieu of that silence of infinite space that so terrified Pascal, Butler gives us noise. No one who has listened carefully to it for long hours will fail to recognize in its tinny cacaphony a real but ignominious meaningfulness. It would be altogether desolating if that were finally the real meaning and the true music of the spheres.

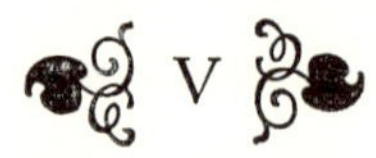

V

MILTON'S LAWS DIVINE AND HUMAN

Of Mans First Disobedience, and the Fruit
Of that Forbidden Tree, whose mortal tast
Brought Death into the World, and all our woe,
With loss of Eden, till one greater Man
Restore us . . .
. . . What in me is dark
Illumin, what is low raise and support;
That to the highth of this great Argument
I may assert Eternal Providence,
And justifie the wayes of God to men.
— *Paradise Lost*, I.

Lawes divine and humane.
— Dryden, *Don Sebastian*, V, i.

A READER OPENING his copy of *Paradise Lost* in its twelve-book form in 1674 would have found, before the Miltonic passages just quoted, the last known non-satiric verses by Andrew Marvell. Marvell commends in them those qualities that have always struck readers of *Paradise Lost* from those familiar opening lines:

That Majesty which through thy Work doth Reign
Draws the Devout, deterring the Profane.
And things divine thou treatst in such state
As them preserves, and thee, inviolate.
At once delight and horrour on us seise,
Thou singst with so much gravity and ease;

And above humane flight dost soar aloft
With Plume so strong, so equal, and so soft.[1]

"That Majesty" of *Paradise Lost* exceeds the height reached by any other English poet. We have now grown accustomed to think of Milton's lyric and other earlier poems in somewhat similar terms. To some critics, those poems "soar aloft" with strength of mind, borne by high Neoplatonic conceptions to another sphere. To other critics, when Milton rises "above humane flight" in the earlier poems he does so by infusing a heroic dimension into non-epic forms:

And all about the Courtly Stable,
Bright-harnest Angels sit in order serviceable.[2]

Cosmic issues, national struggle, superlative people, and the redoutable personality of John Milton give his earlier poems a sense of muscular movement in the bright harness of those angels attendant on the infant Jesus. The first to give the sonnet a public voice, and so anticipate by a decade or two developments culminating in the 1660's, Milton does use it, as Wordsworth said, as a trumpet in his hand. Sometimes he winds that horn more vigorously than it can stand. But the grand manner came early to Milton, even on such unlikely topics as "On the Death of a fair Infant dying of a Cough":

Then thou the mother of so sweet a child
Her false imagin'd loss cease to lament,
And wisely learn to curb thy sorrows wild;
Think what a present thou to God hast sent,
And render him with patience what he lent.

[1] "On Paradise Lost," 31–38. Somewhat satiric in these and other lines, Marvell's poem remarkably anticipates certain subsequent critical debates as well as here describing our responses to *Paradise Lost*.

[2] *On the Morning of Christ's Nativity*, 243–44.

This if thou do he will an off-spring give,
That till the Worlds last-end shall make thy name to live.[3]

Every sentiment is a commonplace of funereal poetry, but that active strength of Milton makes the poem seem to move, until that last line swings upward with doubt-free strength.

i. Our Prospect is Enlarged

Marvell could claim pride of discovery of "That Majesty" of Milton. But every reader rediscovers it for himself. What is known to be central to the experience of all readers deserves more attention than critics normally choose to devote to it. We have just had the example of *Hudibras* to show that narrative may insist on demeaning us. To Butler's mind few men show signs of reason, and the few like himself who use their reason end so depressed that diversion alone offers mollification, and that but temporarily. Butler constantly diverts himself by erecting a house of fiction in such manner that it may constantly fall. If we conceive of an aesthetic horizon between the poet and the reader, Butler's edifice falls farther and farther below it. We share in his condemnation, fear, and anger, even to some extent in the cruel laughter and contempt that he directs at his falling world. Our chief concern as we read Butler is to hold ourselves up, to keep above the Serbonian bog and all its filth. Within four years of the appearance of the first part of *Hudibras, Paradise Lost* was published. Milton's world rises above our horizon as if on angelic wing, just as Butler's sinks with hideous ruin and combustion down.

As we shall see in the next section, Milton responded as fully as Butler to the events following the outbreak of civil war in 1642. Milton also found successive frustrations in

[3] The concluding stanza, 71–77. Although first published in 1673, the poem was probably written about 1625.

those events. But *Paradise Lost* gives us characters, scenes, adventures, and language in which his early propensity for the heroic has been fully realized. Indeed, only on such scale could Milton justify the ways of God to man, and if he had not found a way to make the scale plausible to himself and us, life would have defeated Milton even more than it did Samuel Butler. What the eighteenth century called Milton's sublimity is not merely characteristic of *Paradise Lost:* it is a necessary element for the poet. As everyone knows, even those first voices we hear after the narrator's convince us that we are in the presence of titanic characters and momentous issues:

> O Prince, O Chief of many Throned Powers,
> That led th' imbattled Seraphim to Warr
> Under thy conduct, and in dreadful deeds
> Fearless, and endanger'd Heav'ns perpetual King;
> And put to proof his high Supremacy,
> Whether upheld by strength, or Chance, or Fate . . .
> (I, 128–33)

Beelzebub requires these six lines of apostrophe to Satan even before he embarks on what he has to say. Such tribute, such oratory, gives us a sense of Satan's sublime importance, and since the language employed proves more than adequate, we sense that "Majesty" that Marvell distinguished. Some readers fail to see in passages such as this, however, that the gradations rise to the very top. The orotund homage paid by Beelzebub proves him to be majestic. That he pays homage shows Satan to be yet greater. But the very terms of homage prove the ultimate height to be that of "Heav'ns perpetual King." He says it himself. The rebellious angels, like the heavens themselves, declare the glory of God.

Milton's capacity for eliciting our sense of the majestic shows through his evil characters, majestic though in ruin ("ruined" is a frequent Latinism for "fallen"), and equally certainly and literally fallen though majestic. Such splendor shines also in passages where Milton's attitudes about woman's subjection to man cross our own views:

> To whom thus *Eve* with perfet beauty adornd.
> My Author and Disposer, what thou bidst
> Unargu'd I obey; so God ordains,
> God is thy Law, thou mine: to know no more
> Is womans happiest knowledge and her praise.
> With thee conversing I forget all time,
> All seasons and thir change, all please alike.
> Sweet is the breath of morn, her rising sweet,
> With charm of earliest Birds; pleasant the Sun
> When first on this delightful Land he spreads
> His orient Beams, on herb, tree, fruit, and flour,
> Glistring with dew; fragrant the fertil earth
> After soft showers; and sweet the coming on
> Of grateful Eevning milde, then silent Night
> With this her solemn Bird and this fair Moon,
> And these the Gemms of Heav'n, her starrie train:
> But neither breath of Morn when she ascends
> With charm of earliest Birds, nor rising Sun
> On this delightful land, nor herb, fruit, floure,
> Glistring with dew, nor fragrance after showers,
> Nor grateful Eevning mild, nor silent Night
> With this her solemn Bird, nor walk by Moon,
> Or glittering Starr-light without thee is sweet.
>
> (IV, 634–56)

This is love poetry of a superior, timeless order, welcome in any age and to anybody, at least after those first five lines giving some small credence to what Dr. Johnson termed Milton's Turkish contempt of females. If simple honesty requires that we say that the opening lines trouble us today so does honesty require no less that we regard Eve's loveliest of love poems as an expression of the dependence we all feel on the person we truly love. That Eve does love truly cannot be questioned, and in that certainty—which is one of the most precious things we can ever know—we discover how Milton gives his heroic world reality.

Eve's speech excels Beelzebub's in the movement of its imagery. A whole day passes in her imagery and comparisons, even as Eve forgets "all time," devoting however all the time, the only kind of time she knows in paradise, the diurnal, to the person she loves. In what follows, our first parents walk on hand in hand, talking about the stars, to "thir blissful Bower" strewn and shaded with flowers. After prayers, they practice other rites, "the Rites / Mysterious of connubial Love" (IV, 742–43). We may return to Eve's phrase, "With thee conversing . . . ." We usually do not recall the central seventeenth-century meaning of "conversation" as we hear Eve: "living together; commerce; intercourse, society, intimacy" (first *Oxford English Dictionary* use *ca.* 1340). And before "conversation" came to mean "Interchange of thoughts and words; familiar discourse or talk" (first *OED* use 1580), it meant "sexual intercourse or intimacy" (first *OED* use 1511). Of course Eve's usage centers on the usual meaning in the century, includes the second, and proleptically involves the third.

Adam's own need of Eve (and the basis of the notion of his superiority over her) is given to us another third of the way through the poem (VIII, 379–97) when he asks God for one "fit to participate / All rational delight"; for with the brute creatures he can no more "participate" than can "Fish with Fowle / So well *converse*" (my stress). Whatever else may be said of their relations, Adam's behavior from the day of his creation to the moment of his eating the proffered fruit (and thereafter) definitely shows that he needs Eve at least as much as she him. And what Eve finds in her world,

Adam and the reader find in her, all that is "sweet," "pleasant," "delightful," "fragrant," "fertil," "orient," "glistring," "soft," "mild," "solemne," "fair," and "starrie." "Sweet" probably is the epithet most often repeated in connection with Eve, and that derives in considerable measure from the floral symbolism that the paradisal situation presents to Milton. But even such unlikely adjectives as "Glistring" describing the effects of the morning sun on a dewy earth prove remarkable and precious. This is the sequence: "pleasant . . . delightful . . . orient . . . Glistring . . . fragrant . . . fertil . . . soft." The masculine "Sun" (*sol*) and the feminine, "fertil" earth (*terra*) enact, as do the seasons of the day, the conversation of Eve. We, too, find deep feelings stirred, reasons for giving ourselves, responding, loving. We experience the surpassing beauty of full *conversing*, when nothing is hidden, all is given, all is possessed, and all time forgot.

Whether Beelzebub speaks, whether Eve, or whether that most intrusive of epic narrators, the perfecting art leaves us in no doubt of its magnificence. We need no explanation that evil may have "That Majesty," when we so evidently discover that it does, nor should we miss the evil in "That Majesty" of Satan. Our experience of reading leaves us with so large and essential a paradox of a positive "Paradise *Lost*," that the experience cannot be explained by intellectual or moral paradoxes. Satan is not the hero of the poem, as Beelzebub makes clear in his apostrophe; equally clearly, Satan is heroic, as few characters have ever been. Nor does the poem redeem loss by a doctrine of the Fortunate Fall, because Milton makes it perfectly clear that the Fall will be fortunate only for those very few who are saved and for them only at the Second Coming.[4] But in another sense the poet and the poem redeem the reader, who (however irreligious) comes

[4] As I have tried to show in "*Felix Culpa* in The Redemptive Order of *Paradise Lost*," *Philological Quarterly*, XLVII (1968), 43–54.

more and more to feel himself at one with three elect persons: Adam, Eve, and the narrator of the poem. Milton's assertion of providence claims assent, because his positive, affirmative assertion embraces sin and evil, even Chaos itself, in creating a universe essentially orderly and good.

If the positive element in Milton seems most striking after a consideration of Butler, a later poet attempted to give the same affirmative sense. Pope memorably concludes the first epistle of his *Essay on Man*, "Whatever IS, is RIGHT" (I, 294).[5] We do not condemn Pope by saying that what he so ardently asserts Milton has demonstrated in a narrative. Milton's great argument is just what he says it is, great, and even spirits as little akin to seventeenth-century Puritanism as William Blake found that Milton's majesty is not only majestic in itself but the cause of the majestic in others.[6] Dryden put it well in speaking of "Mr. Milton, whom we all so much *admire*," that is, both esteem and feel wonder over. The eighteenth century always gave Milton as its example of the sublime. One of the more important, although not very well known, of Milton's critics in the late eighteenth century, John Bayly, has a revealing comment on the "Manners" (that is, the habitual moral conduct) exhibited in *Paradise Lost*:

> Searching for manners in Milton, our eyes are not confined, as they were in Homer and Virgil, to virtues, forms, and customs merely social, and to exterior ceremonies; our prospect is enlarged, and our way made plain and short; uplifted, we are carried at once into the sublime doctrines

[5] As the Twickenham editor shows, the thought and some words are taken in part from Dryden (*Oedipus*, III, i: "Whatever is, is in its causes just") and Milton (*Samson Agonistes*, 1745 ff.: "All is best . . .").

[6] As in the illustrations by Blake for *Paradise Lost*. See Joseph Anthony Wittreich, Jr., *Calm of Mind* (Cleveland and London, 1971), pp. 93–132 and the Appendices.

> of faith and divine grace, into the origin of good and evil, and their final issue in another world: the Son of God, *nube candentes humeros amictus* [veiling his radiant shoulders in a cloud], hath appeared unto us, and opened the kingdom of heaven to all believers.[7]

Such is hardly the language of Milton criticism today, but that language (and our contemporary equivalents) has always been reserved for *Paradise Lost* alone among English poems. More people than undergraduates today have difficulty in recognizing Horatian phrases, and the very Christianity of Milton's poem sets some teeth on edge. And yet, whatever our difficulties with *Paradise Lost* may be, whether from pressing on us ideas not our own or from weaving so complex a design, the last effect of *Paradise Lost* is one of complete clarity: "our way made plain and short." As Adam and Eve, once again hand in hand, falter on their way out of the east of Eden into a world like ours, a hostile critic and an undergraduate thitherto fearful of Milton will feel that Bayly does not overstate: "our prospect is enlarged." The least common of all features of narrative is the most obvious thing about *Paradise Lost*: convincing grandeur.

ii. Heroic Celebration of One's Countrymen

One of the reasons why the majesty of *Paradise Lost* is so obvious and central is that Milton deliberately created it and next deliberately let us know that he did:

> What in me is dark
> Illumin, what is low raise and support;
> That to the highth of this great Argument
> I may assert Eternal Providence,
> And justifie the wayes of God to men.
>
> (I, 22–26)

[7] Bayly, *The Alliance of Musick, Poetry, and Oratory* (London, 1789), p. 304. The Latin line is from Horace, *Odes*, I, ii, 31.

The whole grand edifice of *Paradise Lost* rests on the two central features of his argument:

> assert Eternal Providence
>
> justifie the wayes of God to men.

What must be thought, after all, so evident has by no means brought a unanimity of view to Milton's critics. A prior question directs our attention to Milton's purpose in such an argument. A later question requires that we assess our response to such an argument.[8] Has there ever been another poet who starts off by saying that his role is to assert divine providence and to justify that providence? And what does "justify" mean? Milton's line is used to illustrate the meaning, "To show or maintain the justice or reasonableness of . . . ; to adduce adequate grounds for; to defend as right or proper" (*OED*). Milton's claim seems arrogant, and at those moments when we feel ourselves most uneasy in Milton we owe it to ourselves to examine our experience of the poem most carefully.[9]

Milton's claims to unparalleled poetic victory derive from the shocks and defeats of a lifetime. *Paradise Lost* is positive, an epic rather than a failure, only because Milton at last found the words to assert and the conviction to justify. The possibility of *not* asserting and of *not* being able to justify God's providence is precisely where *Paradise Lost* begins in more sense than one. No one of us at all, following Milton's writings in verse and prose up to 1667, could possibly have predicted that he could write *Paradise Lost* positively. That poem is, in terms of the author's experiences, the coun-

[8] The "later question" is raised in the last section of this chapter and in ch. IX.

[9] In his *Surprised by Sin* (London, 1967), Stanley E. Fish presents a lively account of the reader's "education" in the experience of *Paradise Lost*. Fish goes too far for me, but I think Milton would have included him among the few "fit" readers, and I find the rest of his book admirable.

terpart of *Hudibras*. The parallel in eighteen years of experience and the contrast in poetic result between the victorious royalist poet and the defeated Puritan poet defy anything other than wonder. *Paradise Lost* required the scale of majesty Milton managed if he was to retain his faith and count his life something other than a wreck. Incredible as it is, he wrote his epic in blindness and published it when otherwise discountenanced. Amid such handicaps he executed the epic that the whole Renaissance had been aspiring to achieve, and did so because he alone possessed not merely the capacity, but far more the need, to write it. To dismiss any possible doubts, he also wrote *Paradise Regained*.

Our record of Milton's experiences in religion and politics has been written by his own left hand, in prose. Some of Milton's prose works are turgid to the modern reader, some have been translated from Milton's Latin, many dispute with that embarrassing hatred shown by rival theologians in his time, and not all are consistently readable. In each, however, remarkable passages will be found, and even in dealing with very unpromising materials a mind as powerful as Milton's inevitably shaped them into forms recognizably his own. From these writings we can chart Milton's spiritual voyage. It seems to have begun within the then considerably Calvinist Anglican Church. It certainly next went on to Presbyterianism and, with some acrimony, to Independency (Congregationalism). That also failing, Milton ended in a Church of one, with *De Doctrina Christiana* its statement of belief. It cannot be said often enough that the best poets underwent grave spiritual crises early and late in the century. Donne left Roman Catholicism for Anglicanism, Crashaw and Dryden the reverse. Jonson, Marvell, and Wycherley moved to Rome and back to Canterbury. Religion was the focal point of enormous pressures exerted on thoughtful men in the century. It involved not only the salvation of one's eternal soul, as if that were not enough. It also entwined with politics, economics, social class and approval, and often with survival itself.

Milton worked in the thick of all this, devoting himself with complete dedication to the cause. In a word, the cause was God's cause, the only possible right one for a person of Milton's high character. But God's ways are not men's ways, and from 1641 to 1660 Milton repeatedly found himself in the position of rejecting part of his past. At each crisis, something central to the old has betrayed an ideal to which he has utterly devoted himself. Failure and rejection of the past lead to reorganization of the future, as it were, and to a new plan. Each new hope in turn becomes falsified by events, and on the eve of the Restoration everything that Milton had labored over for nearly two decades lies in ruins. England, which had been led out of prelatical and royal bondage, now (Milton thinks) is in the process of choosing a captain back for Egypt. The one thing that must have seemed to need explanation above all else was *God's* ways to man. And no one required explanation more than John Milton himself.

Milton's spiritual development, which is to say his biography, holds such importance for our understanding of *Paradise Lost* and *Paradise Regained* that attention must focus on what he says in his prose works. During the Protectorate, in 1654, Milton wrote in the *Second Defense of the English People* about his early life and training, his trip to Italy, and his return to England as the disputes between Charles I and Parliament were coming to a head:

> I saw that a way was opening for the establishment of real liberty; that the foundation was laying for the deliverance of man from the yoke of slavery and superstition; that the principles of religion, which were the first objects of our care, would exert a salutary influence on the manners and constitution of the republic; and as I had from my youth

> studied the distinctions between religious and civil rights, I perceived that if I ever wished to be of use, I ought at least not to be wanting to my country, to the Church, and to so many of my fellow-Christians, in a crisis of so much danger.[10]

The sense of full crisis and of an ideal order emerging from it kept Milton's mind attuned to the numerous millenarian and chiliastic schemes of the century.[11] Anyone can see profound idealism and hope in the passage. And yet it entails a number of problems that Milton and his contemporaries found difficult to answer. Milton's experience, in fact, well reflects the fate of the Puritan cause. Which is that "Church" he wished to serve? Milton adds, in a vein characteristic of writings after 1653, of "real and substantial liberty, which is rather to be sought from within than from without, and whose existence depends not so much on the terror of the sword as on sobriety of conduct and integrity of life." Such spiritualizing or, as we might say, psychologizing of politics is as alien to most modern minds as is the idea of the poet as defender of the state.

Milton then adds that he perceived there to be "three species of liberty which are essential to the happiness of social life—religious, domestic, and civil."[12] Because the last was being promoted by the "magistrates," and because he had already dealt with the first, he turned to "domestic" lib-

[10] *Complete Poems and Major Prose*, ed. Merritt Y. Hughes (New York, 1957), p. 830. Wherever possible I take prose quotations from this readily accessible edition. The nature of Milton's experience as sketched in these pages has been more fully described by Arthur E. Barker, *Milton and the Puritan Dilemma* (Toronto, 1942, 1964) and Michael Fixler, *Milton and the Kingdoms of God* (London, 1964).

[11] In *Millenium and Utopia* (Berkeley and Los Angeles, 1949), Ernest Lee Tuveson makes clear that chiliasm and ideal polity were not confined to any single group in the century.

[12] Hughes, pp. 830–31.

erty. The tracts involved include the essay "Of Education" (1644, but "Written above twenty Years since"), the divorce tracts (1643-45), and *Areopagitica* (1644). Only the last reminds us consistently of the poet Milton. But it was the divorce tracts that scandalized Milton's contemporaries, and the majestic *Areopagitica* seems to have been ignored in his time. Milton's arguments for divorce obviously involved special pleading, but what bothered his contemporaries was that he cut through religious ideals and the economic basis provided by the paternal family, two sanctions that could not be violated at the same time.

The divorce tracts, with those odd names that even Milton laughed at,[13] reveal a man who felt with Adam that one could not bear to be alone. This God-forsaken loneliness, as he called it, and his loss of self-esteem when Mary Powell absconded, explain why Adam and Eve are at the center of *Paradise Lost* and why Milton should show them hand in hand in a concord that he was vainly seeking in the mid-forties. It remains true, however, that Milton on religion, meaning also Milton on politics, brings us to more central matters in his epic poetry than do his efforts on behalf of "domestic" liberty. Milton entered the fray in May, 1641, with his first anti-episcopal (or anti-prelatical) tracts. His hopes for what was being termed a more godly and thorough Reformation were attached to the Presbyterians. At this early stage, he had a frightening notion of liberty. The civil magistrates were to deal with "the outward man" and a kind of Calvinist, local, inquisition with "the inward man." As the clouds of the First Civil War began to rumble, Milton maintained the belief, or the fiction, that the prelates rather than the King were to blame.

During the following years the divorce tracts and *Areo-*

[13] "*Tetrachordon* . . . bless us! what a word on / A title page is this" (Sonnet XI, 5–6).

pagitica comprise Milton's chief prose productions, and he found leisure to bring together his *Poems* of 1645. His next phase of religious and political controversy begins in 1649 and ends in 1655. Milton has by now given up on the Presbyterians, "revolters" from the principles of the revolution. Because people at the time distinguished both religious and political "Presbyterians," and because adherents of both often changed, the group is by no means easy to define. Simply put, however, their cause embraced property, Parliament, and presbytery. Like almost all parties in that great struggle, they sought revolution—down to themselves—and by this phase (1649), they were secretly bargaining with the King. Because Milton had turned his back on his former party, he seems to find it necessary to return to first principles that he might make a fresh start:

> . . . all men naturally were born free, being the image and resemblance of God himself, and were, by privilege above all the creatures, born to command, and not to obey; and that they lived so, till from the root of Adam's transgression falling among themselves to do wrong and violence, and foreseeing that such courses must needs tend to the destruction of them all, they agreed by common league to bind each other from mutual injury

and for self-defense.[14] Such doctrine is by no means new, and within two years Hobbes was to say similar things, although in a different tone and not adding what Milton does. That addition declares that kings and magistrates hold power only as derived from "the people to the common good of them all."[15] Partly by following that momentum that seems to take revolutions farther than first envisioned, and partly by reason of frustrated idealism, Milton has grown increasingly

[14] *The Tenure of Kings and of Magistrates* (1649); Hughes, p. 754.
[15] Ibid., p. 755.

radical. He now argues that powers that constrain us to do wrong need not be obeyed, and that "the principles of nature" in us can guide us how to respond to a tyrant.[16] Moreover, a king "is a name of dignity and office, not of person"—and so away with the Tudor and Stuart myths of kingship.[17]

In *Eikonoklastes* (also 1649), Milton renews his attack on the Scottish Presbyterians.[18] By now he has progressively cut himself off from prelates, the King, and Presbyterianism as being too conservative, too repressive of liberty. Yet in writing *Eikonoklastes* he faced the unpleasant dilemma that with *Eikon Basilike* the royalists had scored a great propaganda triumph. Where does the cause of liberty stand if popular sentiment moves toward the *ancien régime*? His answer will be familiar enough to students of the history of revolutionary movements. Popular sentiment is nothing but

> the worthless approbation of an inconstant, irrational, and image-doting rabble; that like a credulous and hapless herd, begotten to servility and enchanted with these popular institutes of tyranny . . . hold out both their ears with such delight and ravishment to be stigmatized and bored through in witness of their own voluntary and beloved baseness.[19]

The hysteria in this reminds us of *Hudibras*, and it is remarkable that we do not find Dryden, conservative as he is, saying such extreme things.[20] But we also find logic and principle, those motives of a man who hoped for the coming of an ideal state and who now finds himself cut off from all but

[16] Ibid., pp. 759–60.
[17] Ibid., p. 769.
[18] Ibid., p. 811 ff.
[19] Ibid., p. 815.
[20] In fact, in *Don Sebastian* Dryden shows the rabble or *mobile vulgus* assisting the restoration of justice, although he parodies the republican slogan in having a character say that "The voice of the Mobile is the voice of Heaven" (IV, ii).

that extraordinary, brilliant minority, the Independents under the leadership and genius of Cromwell.

Such allegiance, with a burst of new historical expectation, sustains Milton in his two defenses of the English people, written in Latin for a European audience. Cromwell became Lord Protector in December, 1653, and in his *Second Defence,* written the following year, Milton has a peroration on the new government: "For while you, O Cromwell, are left among us, he hardly shows a proper confidence in the Supreme, who distrusts the security of England, when he sees that you are in so special a manner the favored object of divine regard." [21] Nonetheless there follows a warning to Cromwell that if he "should hereafter invade that liberty which you have defended," all praise would vanish in a moment.[22] In fact Cromwell, who had his Secretary for Foreign Tongues to thank for such advice, found it necessary to take power more and more into his own hands. The crisis of the cause for liberty had arrived. Even the Barebones Parliament, selected so carefully for "saints," was unable to agree on anything useful, and so the major-generals were sent out to rule the land. Cromwell's dilemma was shared by Milton: who can be trusted to be good enough to rule under God? Milton disdainfully rejects the authority of even a Puritan vote:

> For who would vindicate your right of unrestrained suffrage or of choosing what representatives you liked best, merely that you might elect the creatures of your own faction, whoever they might be, or him, however small might be his worth, who would give you the most lavish feasts and enable you to drink to the greatest excess?

The small minority party then ruling England, and to which Milton gave allegiance, now ruled England in defiance of

[21] Hughes, p. 833.
[22] Ibid., p. 835.

royalty and Presbyterianism on the one side and in defiance of republicanism, democracy, and the populace on the other. At last the saints ruled.

Certainly Milton had a sense that with the genius of a government guided by Cromwell the revolution had reached its fulfillment. In that he could not have been more right. At this moment in the conclusion to the *Second Defence* epic aspirations receive what is in a double sense an epic simile:

> As the epic poet, who adheres at all to the rules of that species of composition, does not profess to describe the whole life of the hero whom he celebrates, but only some particular action of his life, as the resentment of Achilles at Troy, the return of Ulysses, or the coming of Aeneas into Italy, so it will be sufficient, either for my justification or apology, that I have heroically celebrated at least one exploit of my countrymen.[23]

Looking back over the distance traveled from 1641 to 1654, Milton treats the events themselves as well as his defense of them as a suitable, indeed a heroic "justification or apology" for themselves and himself.[24]

The national and personally celebrated epic in which Milton takes such pride obviously contradicts the whole conception of *Paradise Lost.* Yet like Cromwell's triumph, that of Milton's prose epic to this point was at last a reality. Both represented an astonishing triumph of mind, effort, and conviction by a few men previously unknown. In a series of

[23] The last two quotations will be found in Hughes, pp. 836 and 838.

[24] The Latin does not stretch quite to the "justification" of Robert Fellowes' translation, but it does seem to involve Milton more with the epics of the past: "ita mihi quoque vel ad officium [duty, rather than justification], vel ad excusationem satis fuerit . . ." (*The Works of John Milton,* ed. Frank Allen Patterson, *et al.,* 20 vols. [New York, 1931], VIII [1933], 252).

revolutions they had taken over the state and made England a power feared throughout Europe for the first time in centuries. It *was* an epic, but nothing like it was to be the subject of Milton's properly poetic epic, primarily because the prose account was tied to that other story, history on the move. The triumph was brief and the overthrow quick. A sensitive reader will observe that in celebrating the triumph of his epic, Milton vulgarizes his thoughts. Ten years earlier, he had set forth in *Areopagitica* (1644) his vision of what England was and might be, not a totalitarian oligarchy of a small group of saints, but a united people joined together for liberty:

> Behold now this vast city, a city of refuge, the mansion house of liberty, encompassed and surrounded with [God's] protection. The shop of war hath not there more anvils and hammers working, to fashion out the plates and instruments of armed justice in defense of beleagured Truth, than there be pens and heads there, sitting by their studious lamps, musing, searching, revolving new notions and ideas wherewith to present, as with their homage and their fealty, the approaching reformation; others as fast reading, trying all things, assenting to the force of reason and convincement.[25]

What hope there is in that vision of a city state humming with harmonious activities in the cause of liberty! If the vision be called utopian, the fault lies less with it than with the fractious nature of what ensued and the too hopeful mood of its heroic dreamer.

Such inclusive, generous hope vanishes at the moment of hard-bought triumph. In the *Second Defence* Milton enters indeed the claim that he has "not circumscribed my defense

[25] Hughes, p. 743.

of liberty within any petty circle around me," making the claim precisely because it is untrue.[26] His contempt for others outside that "petty circle" has grown pretty nearly complete. The voice that spoke so nobly in *Areopagitica* takes on an indescribable hauteur in addressing those who think they want elections or a voice in government. By a skillful begging of the question, he presumes that those outside the oligarchy of saints are at present free. The contempt in one of his rare short sentences quite takes one's breath: "You, therefore, who wish to remain free, instantly be wise or, as soon as possible, cease to be fools."[27] Again there comes to mind Milton's mirror-image, the pessimistic Samuel Butler.

In March, 1660, not much more than two months before Charles II returned from his travels, Milton published the last of his revolutionary tracts, *The Ready and Easy Way to Establish a Free Commonwealth.* The unconscious irony of that title deflates the triumph of the *Second Defence.* After Cromwell's death and the succession by his ineffectual son, Tumbledown Dick, Dryden's "foolish Ishbosheth," it was plain that the Protectorate was an experiment that could not be tried again. Unable to let his pen sleep in his hand, or his hopes die even in the demonstration of repeated failure of all that he had envisioned, John Milton tried yet again with a "Ready and Easy Way." The very phrase seems desperate, and talk of a "Commonwealth" already sounds like the Good Old Cause. The proposals were in fact useless to everybody except Milton, who still needed to assert that the *polis* must be founded on virtue. Men must be taught to be good, and the best men must be chosen to rule. In nineteen years of politics, Milton had not learned the art of the possible. He learned discouragement:

[26] Ibid., p. 838.
[27] Ibid., p. 837.

> Till this be done, I am in doubt whether our state will be ever certainly and throroughly settled; never likely till then to see an end of our troubles and continual changes, or at least never the true settlement and assurance of our liberty.

Pessimism delivers the revolutionary to the conservatives. Another burst of qualified hope follows in the tract, and gradually the thought takes on that eschatological hue that had scarcely tinged Milton's writings for fifteen years. If only his recommendations were followed, why should not the nation thrive, he asks,

> . . . with as much assurance as can be of human things that they shall so continue (if God favor us, and our willful sins provoke him not) even to the coming of our true and rightful and only to be expected King, only worthy as he is our only Savior, the Messiah, the Christ, the only heir of his eternal Father, the only by him anointed and ordained since the work of our redemption finished, universal Lord of all mankind.[28]

Milton has reached the dead end of any imaginable political design. If such millenarian political urgings were taken literally, England would have repeated the folly of the miserable visionaries of Münster, who committed all variety of excess while waiting for the Second Coming. But by being forced to regard England as something more than a state, Milton has grasped the central feature of *Paradise Lost.* Repeated frustration of constantly reviving hopes has shown that English history cannot possibly provide him with anything other than grounds for total despair. Again, one is struck by the close resemblance between Milton and Butler. I think it no accident that Cromwell's death should have

[28] These two quotations are from *The Ready and Easy Way,* in Hughes, pp. 891, 891–92.

produced a general sense of great loss, a sense that the spirit of the time itself had vanished, in men as different from Milton and Butler as Dryden, Waller, and Sprat. Unlike Butler, however, Milton possessed undying faith and hope. If the prose epic of England had turned sour, there would be no point in writing an Arthuriad. If one were to "assert eternal Providence" as one hoped, if one were to "justifie the wayes of God to men," as one needed to, nothing less than the whole span of providential history could make *Paradise Lost* that positive, affirmative thing that we have seen it is.

Nothing could be truer than that "before Milton could properly perform his role as poet, he had to become an historian of God's 'miraculous *ways*, and *works*, amongst men.' "[29] Of course history as we conceive it, even history as Milton had been conceiving it, had become meaningless to him, and in his *History of Britain* the tone becomes ever darker as he nears the end of his period, approaches most nearly modern history (William the Conqueror). Milton's experience of his own time denied what he required as a condition of the only history he wanted: an intelligible and moral order in which good was rewarded and evil punished. Without scope for that belief, all support would be gone for his conception of "Providence," "the wayes of God to men," God's "miraculous *ways* and *works* amongst men"; and all affirmation would have been gone from any poem he might write. This is not to say that after finishing the *Ready and Easy Way* Milton started to compose *Paradise Lost* from scratch. There is not a person in the world who *knows* exactly when Milton wrote *Paradise Lost, Paradise Regained,* and *Samson Agonistes*. But we know when the poems were published, when Milton had leisure to compose them as he

[29] French Fogle, "Introduction," *The History of Britain, The Complete Prose Works of John Milton,* v, pt. i (New Haven and London, 1971), xxix.

tells us, blind, and we know that the death of Cromwell finished the hopes on which years of political effort had been based. So it is that, whatever the exact chronology, the blind prose writer somehow escaped exemption from the Act of Oblivion and did what no Englishman had succeeded in doing, complete two epics. More than that, he *was* able to make *Paradise Lost* affirmative, majestic, and indeed heroic in a new way. At last he had found his scale, not in "The History of Britain" but in all time and in the total universe. Then and there only could his "great Argument" be true. And unless that argument was true, Milton would find his life and all of life meaningless. Unlike Butler, he could not settle for "Diversion." He had to take the world entire or not at all. If he could find a right way to take it, even the loss of paradise could give hope, affirmation, and resolved content.

iii. Parnassus and Sinai

We have been considering the dominant character of our experience of *Paradise Lost* and the relation of the poem to Milton's life and times. Plainly, literature must derive from felt needs in the poet if it is to continue through the years to arouse and satisfy similar needs in readers. The principle is really axiomatic, even when details cannot be provided. Yet there is a second axiom that we must now consider, that whatever enters into the poet's work does so on aesthetic terms. Both axioms will be presumed in what follows, which involves the classical and biblical elements in *Paradise Lost* and *Paradise Regained*. Of course we might also have pursued the aesthetic point with detailed autobiographical matter. But the autobiographical detail is really trivial compared to the larger motions in Milton's life, and it will do no harm to turn now to the two classes of writing that define a Christian humanist.

Everyone knows that *Paradise Lost* and *Paradise Regained* are epics, for if we are not sure whether we can give that name to *Troilus and Criseyde, The Faerie Queene, Absalom and Achitophel, The Dunciad,* or *The Prelude, Paradise Lost* leaves us secure. Each of us has been taught to expect certain things from the epic: grand subject and style; invocation and argument; a beginning *in medias res;* epic similes and catalogues; the heavenly visitor; the descent to the underworld; and the rest. Milton certainly satisfies such expectations. He honors them more than other poets, the classical poets included. In a real sense *Paradise Lost* goes to extreme lengths to define what the epic genre is, and in not a few respects it rejects the classical models by teleologically taking their features to their essential but extreme end. It is characteristic of this extraordinary poet that he should wish to write the most difficult species of poem, that he should make the difficult species yet more difficult, and that he should succeed. Compared to Dryden, Milton seems singularly uncreative of new forms, always going back with rigid conservativism or literary Protestantism, to what he considers the pristine conditions of his genres. His simile at the end of the *Second Defence* venerates the "rules." The brief prefaces to *Paradise Lost* on the verse and to *Samson Agonistes* on tragedy show Milton trying to return to primitive classicism as determinedly as he tried to return to primitive Christianity. In allowing no compromises, Milton intensifies and wholly transforms the classical epic. By insisting on the heroic element in the epic, Milton requires a definition of true heroism which brings him to contradict all previous epic writers. If grand characters, scenes, and issues are required, Milton provides the grandest that the human imagination can conceive, with the result that his poem is uncompromisingly Christian. If an epic usually has a descent to the underworld, even if brief and often perfunctory, Milton follows a hint from Cowley and radicalizes the convention by having his first two books situated there, an extraordinary and wholly unnecessary tribute to convention.

Milton's way of honoring the classical tradition effectively destroys it. Each symptom is honored and made into something other than what it was intended to be symptomatic of. Just as in politics Milton was so much the true royalist to the only King that he devoted himself to smashing the idols of the Stuart king,[30] so he devotes himself so much to the true epic spirit that nothing less will do. His scheme works marvelously well. For it does turn out after all that one can be Milton and also be a devout royalist: to Christ or God as king. Similarly, one can baptize the pagan form in that poetic as well as spiritual Jordan that Herbert wrote of:

> Sing Heav'nly Muse, that on the secret top
> Of *Oreb* or of *Sinai*, didst inspire
> That Shepherd, who first taught the chosen Seed,
> In the Beginning how the Heav'ns and Earth
> Rose out of *Chaos* . . . (I, 6–10)

Milton invokes the Holy Spirit in the proper place, at the beginning of his poem. The perfectly evident parallel is between Moses (author, it was believed, of the first five books of the Bible) and Milton, between the Bible and *Paradise Lost*, between "*the* Beginning" and Milton's beginning. I doubt that there could be any way of emphasizing more strongly than Milton has done that every classical feature of the epic tradition is going to be catechized into a new faith. Even so, Milton's presumption is almost as breathtaking as the ease with which he assumes the Mosaic role of setting down holy writ.

Milton is quite consistent, returning to the idea in later

[30] Cf. Dryden, *Absalom and Achitophel*, 63–66, surely recalling the iconoclast controversy.

addresses to his Muse. By the invocation to Book IV Milton has arrived at the other end of the Bible and now asks for the voice of John to declare an apocalypse. Whatever Milton's weaknesses, they never included shrinking from a comparison because it was grand or set himself in a positive light. And the attitude is epidemic, not just a pose reflected when the narrator speaks of himself. All readers of Milton will recognize the characteristic passage in which he describes the fallen angels marching in military order:

> For never [more] created man,
> Met such imbodied force, as nam'd with these
> Could merit more then that small infantry
> Warr'd on by Cranes: though all the Giant brood
> Of *Phlegra* with th' Heroic Race were joyn'd
> That fought at *Theb's* and *Ilium,* on each side
> Mixt with auxiliar Gods . . .
>
> (I, 573–79)

The classical epics, even the *Iliad,* provide some small basis for a comparison with my epic, Milton tells us. At least the *Iliad* (to which in the passage are shortly added other examples by Christian as well as pagan authors) will provide some small basis for Milton's fallen angels. He has yet to get to those still in Heaven! We shall repeatedly have reason to see how important such fine gradations of reality and truth are to Milton's two epics. Inattention to such matters may allow some readers to sleep more easily, but it also has often caused confusion. The metamorphosis of the classical into a Christian version makes very clear that distinctions and choices are being made, and that we shall fail to understand Milton if we fail to observe—and engage with—his distinctions and choices.

Milton's epic similes provide other prized examples of his art and also possibilities for us to understand his kinds of distinction. "Men call'd him *Mulciber*," he says of Mammon, echoing in particular one man, Homer, whose story *(Iliad*, I, 588–95) tells how the enraged and drunken Zeus threw Hephaestus from the sky to earth. But

> thus they relate
> Erring; for he with this rebellious rout
> Fell long before. (I, 740 . . . 748)

"And justifie the ways of God to men." Yet here "men . . . relate/Erring." They err by getting Mammon's name wrong, and by getting wrong as well all the details: when, where, and by what agency and on what occasion the event occurred. In fact the only point on which "men" are right is that someone Mammon-like was thrown out of Heaven. (We get the full true version some books later.) While correcting the pagan version, Milton extracts for his use the poetic essence (which also requires a few changes):

> from Morn
> To Noon he fell, from Noon to dewy Eve,
> A Summers day; and with the setting Sun
> Dropt from the Zenith like a falling Star
> On *Lemnos* th' *Aegean* Ile.

So loving does that seem, and certainly so perfectly cadenced, that we are brought up short then to read, "Thus they relate / Erring." What Milton is up to in such passages, and in similar features of the larger actions of his poem, has been the subject of considerable discussion in recent years. It seems to me that the best explanation is likeliest to be the simplest one commensurate with the most evidence. Because the pagan story of Mulciber as told by Milton affects us, I presume that it affected Milton. That it holds such interest makes it important, however, that we "men" get the truth right. Milton does not begin by saying that Mammon is

Mulciber, but only more doubtfully that "Men *call'd* him Mulciber." By improving on Homer, Milton earns the right to insist on earlier error and on our seeing that his version is true.

Milton's poetry turns out to be far more neoclassical in detail and other features than does the poetry of Dryden, although, as we have seen in Milton's effort to intensify the classical so far as to reach its ideal form, he transforms it completely. His classical lore is real, valuable, and indispensable. But his concern with reality and truth presents numerous claimants to relative or absolute status of the real and true. We shall be seeing in other contexts as well as in the present one that Milton endlessly juxtaposes or in some fashion plays on the false and the real, the partly and the wholly true, metaphoric vehicle and tenor, Old Testament type and Christian anti-type, and other such gradations. Milton sometimes seems himself to sigh, and at other times we wish that he did sigh, over the necessity ultimately to reject that which we know to be attractive but inferior. The most celebrated instance occurs in *Paradise Regained* (IV, 285–364) when Jesus rejects classical philosophy and literature. But as early as the Nativity Ode, the dismissal of the pagan gods has a flash of loveliness that tinges our dismissal with regret:

> And the yellow-skirted *Fayes*
> Fly after the Night-steeds, leaving their Moon-lov'd maze.
> (235–36)

In any other writer such canorous lines and those yellow skirts would defy rejection.

My purpose in what follows is to explore Milton's sense of reality and truth, and his means of creating them poetically. But I think it worth a moment's pause to consider that in posing to himself the question of the reality and the truth by which men must live, he once more proved most classical of them all. That question has been as basic to epic as the meaning and endurance of suffering is to tragedy. The *Iliad* abounds in some very simple but basic questions. Why gather all those men together and get so many of them killed over an adultery? Why revenge a friend when one had not obeyed a captain? And so on. Or again, Odysseus has strong inducements to settle with Calypso or with the Phaeacians, just as Aeneas has to stay with Dido. If we take the sirens as a motif from the *Odyssey* to *The Faerie Queene*, II, xii, or if we take the earthly paradise as made over into the bower of bliss by Tasso's Armida and Spenser's Acrasia, we can see how the epic had always concerned itself with seductive versions of reality, with lovely places or lovely women that had to be left, and particularly with a clash in the motives of a given hero. Since all this lore had been moralized and allegorized over the centuries by mythographers and classical scholars of a certain kind, the moral and epistemological aspects of attractions to be resisted had multiplied many times over.[31] Milton is himself both in seizing and in transforming this epic concern. One aspect of Milton's transformation has already been dwelt upon: his insistence on the truth of his version as opposed to others. There is a second change much more subtle. In the classical epics, as indeed in Tasso and Spenser, the division of mind belongs to the character, usually to the hero, although sometimes (as in the earthly paradise depicted by Camões) it seems that the poet has aroused his own longings as much as those of his hero. Milton places the conflict where the other writers seem to have meant all along to place it without knowing it: in the action or, rather, in the reader. If the yellow-skirted fays revealed

[31] For a mythographer contemporary with Milton, see Alexander Ross, *Mystagogus Poeticus;* for a recent scholarly study, see Don Cameron Allen, *Mysteriously Meant* (Baltimore, 1970), especially chs. VIII and X.

by moonlight make us regret for a moment that Milton presses us to dismiss them, and I at least find that I do so feel regret, then I think that Milton wished me to understand that distinctions of moral and epistemological kinds involve decisions, choice; and that neither distinction nor choice is an easy thing. The matter is worth raising in connection with Milton's handling of epic conventions, precisely because this is an instance of Milton's extracting a far from obvious characteristic from the epic. But the general point is so pervasive and so important in Milton that we shall return to it in other connections.

The Mulciber/Mammon simile also involves an element of great importance to Milton, time: "for he with this rebellious rout / Fell long before." Although men *called* him Mulciber, as having preceded John Milton in narrative art, in fact Mulciber himself is a later character, for the true Mulciber, Mammon, fell earlier in Milton's historical scheme. We are now getting into subtler distinctions, and the question we must ask is: Did Mulciber exist? He existed in the sense that those Ausonian "men" who "fabl'd" his story told a myth. Milton, however, is telling the truth shrouded in the mythic enigma. The relation between myth and truth may be thought of as a species of allegory, although it does have its resemblances to the type and its fulfillment or anti-type.[32] Milton's Mulciber/Mammon relation in fact more closely resembles religious typology (than do emblems and allegory) in one salient particular, time. It is of the essence of typology (as normally spoken of in England) that a historically real person or thing existing at one time represents another real person or thing at a later time that fulfills and makes perfect the former. Properly speaking the type is someone or some-

[32] See Barbara K. Lewalski, *Milton's Brief Epic* (Providence and London, 1966); and William G. Madsen, *From Shadowy Types to Truth* (New Haven, 1968).

thing from the Old Testament (e.g., Milton's Adam, line 1) fulfilled in the New Testament (e.g., Jesus, line 4). But especially among Protestants the custom grew of comparing princes and other great or good persons retrospectively, even to Christ.[33] In his treatment of Mammon/Mulciber, Milton combines the allegory of the mythographers with the temporal conflations of the typologists.

Another well known simile will show other features of Milton's temporal emphasis. Eden is described:

Not that faire field
Of *Enna*, where *Proserpin* gathering flours
Her self a fairer Floure by gloomie Dis
Was gatherd, which cost *Ceres* all that pain
To seek her through the world; nor that sweet Grove
Of *Daphne* by *Orontes*, and th' inspir'd
Castalian Spring, might with this Paradise
Of *Eden* strive; nor that *Nyseian* Ile
Girt with the River *Triton*, where old *Cham*,
Whom Gentiles *Ammon* call and *Lybian* Jove,
Hid *Amalthea* and her Florid Son
Young *Bacchus* from his Stepdame *Rhea's* eye;
Nor where *Abassin* Kings thir issue Guard,
Mount *Amara*, though this by som suppos'd
True Paradise under the *Ethiop* Line
By *Nilus* head, enclosed with shining Rock,
A whole days journy high, but wide remote
From this *Assyrian* Garden . . . (IV, 268–85)

Milton's grand roll-call of earthy paradises and *loci amoeni* can only specify places that came into being after the Fall. Once again, the recollection of what is so impressive offers

[33] Barbara K. Lewalski describes this method as "recapitulation"; I prefer "retrospection" and its easier adjectival form, "retrospective."

retrospective or recapitulative tribute to the one true paradisal garden. Certain elements in Milton's handling become clearer here than in the Mulciber/Mammon simile, and it would indeed be difficult to find a better example than this of that Miltonic language spoken of in Chapter III. The simile begins with classical detail treated in what seems standard mythographic fashion. With the mention of "old *Cham*," however, Milton explicitly assimilates Ammon and Lybian Jove into Noah's son (usually "Ham"). That is, we do not have now two or three elements being compared, with Eden emerging the zenith still; but rather the syntax for a time takes as its duty the absorbing of the pagan into the biblical. Then and only then are we permitted to resume the main track and add: Yes, Cham's isle, too, splendid as it is, does not equal Eden. The last place, Mount Amara, can scarcely be termed mythographic at all, since it derives from sources different entirely. In other words, Milton once again employs a method like recapitulative or retrospective typology to make his comparisons work. Mythography may be involved, but the temporal element certainly resembles typology better.

The functioning of Milton's catalogue involves yet other complicating factors. Milton does not *say* that these splendid places came after Eden, nor does he *say* that they are imperfect by comparison. The main predication is buried in the middle of the sentence: none of these places "might with this Paradise / Of *Eden* strive." The image is that of a race, a contest, an effort by places to compete; obviously Milton means that Eden comes in first, both temporally and qualitatively, but he does not say so. After the simile proper, he has another unusual expression. All these fine places are "wide remote / From this *Assyrian* Garden." That "remote" partly emphasizes Milton's conviction that the true earthly paradise was not in Africa but in the Near East. The difference in time and quality also has become one in space. And yet, as we might have expected, Milton puns on "remote," using the Latin meaning of distance to be sure, but also the Stoic concept *(remota;* cf. *promota)* of that which should be rejected, not preferred.

The temporal emphasis refers all these later places back to man's first home, the garden of Eden. Also, as has frequently been noticed, in each place Milton mentions there exists some sense of threat to a person, and consequently the simile is proleptic of the fall of man in Book IX, and in particular of Eve separated from Adam, as Satan had hoped for without expecting:

> Beyond his hope, *Eve* separate he spies,
> Veild in a Cloud of Fragrance, where she stood,
> Half spi'd, so thick the Roses bushing round
> About her glowd, oft stooping to support
> Each Flour of slender stalk, whose head though gay
> Carnation, Purple, Azure, or spect with Gold,
> Hung drooping unsustaind, them she upstaies
> Gently with Mirtle band, mindless the while,
> Her self, though fairest unsupported Flour,
> From her best prop so farr, and storm so nigh.
> Neerer he drew, and many a walk travers'd
> Of stateliest Covert, Cedar, Pine, or Palme,
> Then voluble and bold, now hid, now seen
> Among thick-wov'n Arborets and Flours
> Imborderd on each Bank, the hand of *Eve:*
> Spot more delicious then those Gardens feign'd
> Or of reviv'd *Adonis,* or renownd
> *Alcinous,* host of old *Laertes* Son,
> Or that, not Mystic, where the Sapient King
> Held dalliance with his faire *Egyptian* Spouse.
>
> (IX, 424–43)

The imagery here resembles that used for Eve in Book IV and elsewhere, but it is especially interesting that Milton returns to the garden of Eden again at the end, introducing another set of *loci amoeni*, again to be rejected in preference for the garden of Eden, but again enormously evocative. By the return to the strategy employed five books earlier, Milton confirms the threat implicit in the earlier comparisons, fulfilling the prospective or proleptic quality of the earlier simile.[34] The danger that existed later in time to Proserpina and Daphne is just now a present danger to Eve.

It does appear that such a temporal function of similes, whether prospective or retrospective and commonly (as we have seen) both at once, does not often occur otherwise in epic poetry, and we may almost consider that Milton's invention. The *Davideis* probably gave Milton the hint, because Cowley's similes occasionally refer to what *immediately* follows or precedes in the poem. In Book IV, for example, Cowley has some similes that look immediately ahead. Three of them begin as follows:

> As midst the Main a low small *Island* lyes . . .
>
> As when a wrathful *Dragons* dismal Light . . .
>
> And as a Spani'el when we'our aim direct . . .

And very rarely his similes function retrospectively, as in this from Book III of the *Davideis:*

> So a strong *Oak*, which many Years had stood
> With fair and flourishing Boughs, *it self a Wood,*
> Though it might long the *Axes* Violence bear,
> And play'd with *Winds* which other *Trees* did tear;

[34] In *Milton's Grand Style* (Oxford, 1963), Christopher Ricks discusses prolepsis in Milton's similes, augmenting the insights of eighteenth-century criticism of Milton.

Yet by the *Thunders* Stroak from th'Root 'tis rent;
So sure the Blows that from high heav'n are sent.[35]

Cowley is at his best in his epic similes, which alone must have meant something to Milton, and one marks as Miltonic that "strong *Oak . . . it self a Wood.*" We recall "*Proserpin* gathering flours / Her self a fairer Floure." Cowley does not often employ similes prospectively or retrospectively, however, and Milton's powers of gathering in detail, as well as deploying it in time and quality, surpass Cowley as well as other epic poets.

The highly admissive character of Milton's language and its syntax provides us with much that is very rich and stimulating, which is of course just what Milton desires and what an epic in part requires to give those feelings of majesty and affirmation that *Paradise Lost* so clearly possesses. But as we have been seeing, Milton does not merely wish to admit rich detail and stimulate responses, crucial and primary as those aims are. His language also finds ways of discriminating, ordering, and ranging the elements admitted. We are allowed the pleasure, indeed we are given it with great ceremony, of enjoying such things as

that sweet Grove
Of *Daphne* by *Orontes*, and th' inspir'd
Castalian Spring.

But by his temporal and qualitative comparisons with the garden of Eden, Milton makes quite clear that we do not linger like slaves of Circe, duped by pagan enchantresses. Eve alone in her garden is the true reality. Milton's most powerful linguistic control in assisting, or commanding, our responses is of course the use of negatives. The lines just quoted actually begin: "nor that sweet Grove . . . ." The

[35] *Poems*, ed. Waller, pp. 375, 379 (twice), 339.

iterative syntactic and semantic element in the "that fair field / Of *Enna*" simile is negation, as is signaled by the whole syntactic ordering and especially by the first word, "*Not* that faire field . . . ."

We may well pause to consider the grievous charge that Milton's verse is distinguished by a "sensuous poverty." Nonsense such as this often helps us understand what is true. It should be perfectly obvious that someone who does not find himself sensuously stirred by the depiction of Eve in the garden or by the simile we have been examining must have either very weak or very peculiar senses. Yet it is certainly true that Milton is no Imagist. All the sensuous details which are so lovingly admitted are arranged in qualitative order with no nonsense that one sensation is as good as another. Milton no more gives us a "sensuous wealth" than he suffers from a "sensuous poverty." His is ever an *economy* of the senses, almost in the original sense of the ordering of domestic affairs. How far this is so can be understood by just a moment's attention to the context of the simile in Book IV. The passage introduces Adam and Eve as present characters for the first time, and also describes Eden as a presence. But Milton narrates all this not merely to us. Adam and Eve in their garden are also being spied on by Satan in the guise of a cormorant. His reactions are described in passages preceding and following the introduction of Adam and Eve in their garden. We have to take in Satan's perspective and his career, even as we enjoy the loving depiction of Eden. In other words, just as within the syntax of the simile negatives discriminate and order, so outside the passage containing the simile there exists that threat embodied in the simile, a threat presented in what is a consciousness as intense as that of Adam and Eve, or of the reader. And yet above or beyond Satan's consciousness and his senses, we have those of the narrator and poet, the aesthetic and moral voice offering us endless riches provided we understand exactly how they must be valued.

Often Milton's negatives are very simply syntactic. At other times he avoids the use of negative terms but achieves the same effect semantically. Milton's recollection of Cowley can once again serve our purpose. It does not seem to be known that Cowley's description of the arms of Goliath lies behind Milton's description of the arms of Satan. Here is Cowley on Goliath's spear:

> His *Spear* the *Trunk* was of a lofty *Tree*,
> Which *Nature* meant some tall *Ship's Mast* should be.[36]

Cowley desires to communicate the irony that a giant so armed is defeated by a boy, and Milton's echo of Cowley for the villain's spear effectively places Satan. To compare great things to small, then, here is Milton on Satan's spear:

> His Spear, to equal which the tallest Pine
> Hewn on *Norwegian* hills, to be the Mast
> Of some great Ammiral, were but a wand,
> He walkt with. (I, 292–95)

The alliterative consonance assists Milton, and so too does the wonderfully ambiguous syntax ("were but a wand, / He walkt with"), in creating a whole of two elements resembling each other in being large, but the point of whose existence insistently remains the disparity of size.

A better example of such semantic negation can be found in another use of a tree for an image. In a passage preceding the "faire field / of *Enna*" simile, we discover Satan's entry into Paradise:

> Thence up he flew, and on the Tree of Life,
> The middle Tree and highest there that grew,

[36] Ibid., p. 334.

> Sat like a Cormorant; yet not true Life
> Thereby regain'd, but sat devising Death
> To them who liv'd. (IV, 194–98)

In this remarkable image, in itself no more than of a bird alighting on a tree, we find cause for great shock. It usually is discussed in terms of the process of Satan's degradation: here he is no longer the archangel with only the excess of glory removed, but an unattractive, rapacious bird. That hardly accounts wholly for our shock, and even the sense of threat from above, of a preying bird (animated by the satanic soul) staring intently down on his victims—not even this affects us most. One element surely is the perversion Satan represents. An angel housed in a brute is one thing. But more than that Milton makes explicit what is involved in the perversion of life into death, nothing less than Satan's *badness:*

> So little knows
> Any, but God alone, to value right
> The good before him. (IV, 201–203)

This would be a platitude were it not for the shocking fact that Satan as cormorant is perching in effect on the cross of Jesus, "the Tree of Life, / The middle Tree." The natural image of the bird on the tree is hard enough "to value right," although Milton takes pains that we shall understand that Satan is so evil that he cannot recognize good and regain "true Life." This passage is of a piece with the later Satan, exasperated in *Paradise Regained,* asking Jesus, "What dost thou in this world?" (IV, 372). Of course believers themselves can hardly explain the mystery of the incarnation and Christ's sufficient sacrifice. For Satan, sacrifice of oneself for others is totally incomprehensible.

The cormorant on the tree is not unlike the vision of

other gardens invoked at the end of the passage in Book IX describing Satan's coming upon Eve alone. By arranging details so carefully, Milton exercises us in a mental process distinguishing best from the less, "true Life" from seeming life, garden from garden, and purpose from purpose in such a way that perception and cognition wholly dominate sensation. We *must* take in what Milton affords the senses, but places and emotions raise questions of faith, reason, and will and so must be dealt with by such large faculties. Rudely put, places like all else belong to the mind, and the mind must order them properly. Nothing could be more crucial to understanding this aspect of Milton's poetry than getting right what Satan had got wrong in declaring "The mind is its own place, and in it self / Can make a Heav'n of Hell, a Hell of Heav'n" (I, 254–55). Milton is very well aware of man's ability to present place as well as anything to the mind in terms of some "reality" the mind wishes to discover. In fact, Milton's psychology and epistemology are remarkably acute. Both serve the ends of faith (getting our minds directed toward their proper object) and ethics (choosing what is right). In a sense completely unallegorical, *Paradise Lost* and *Paradise Regained* are alive with thought. Put differently, the poems excite in us a powerful exercise of mind in following Milton's rich provision and in ordering the provision rightly.

In further considering the means of Milton's ordering, we ought now to turn to larger matters, one of the most familiar of which is Milton's repetition of motifs, images, and so on. Some iterations come to us affirmatively, some parodically. Almost all we see in Books I and II functions like a gigantic proleptic simile in parodying what is to follow. The example commonly given is that of the "infernal trinity," Satan, Sin, and Death as parody of the heavenly. In view of Milton's Socinian, or at any rate his non-Trinitarian, concept of the

Son of God and in view of his all but completely omitting the Holy Spirit from the *dramatis personae,* I am inclined to doubt the usual example. Rather, let us say that the sexual relations of Satan and Sin hideously (and proleptically) parody the "wedded love" of Adam and Eve. To commit incest with your daughter must be terrible enough, but to do it with an abstraction like Sin must take away whatever perverted pleasure might be there! The Fall does not derive from sex, although the Fall includes concupiscence and all other sins. At any rate the relations between the members of each of the two couples produce death. Since Eve is not Sin but a sinner, and Adam not Satan the "adversary" but one temporarily averse to God, the deaths brought about in the two cases are greatly different, as God makes clear (III, 129–34). God Himself enters into comparison, as do the angels, because love is one of those primary experiences Milton draws upon to give his epic that centrality to experience on which alone grandeur may be based. God is the only sufficient unity, the only being able to create by Himself. His love for His creatures, especially for the Son and Adam and Eve, contrasts with Satan's hatred, and His strength with the weaknesses of Adam and Eve. Such larger parallels will be familiar enough, and we may turn again to details and large concerns less often considered. These will take us from the Christian poet's Sinai to his Parnassus.

Of all poetic forms, the epic was the one Renaissance critics treated most in terms of rules and precedent. Milton, who speaks of the rules at the end of the *Second Defence,* obviously knew them and made typically free use of them by intensifying them. But the number of epics to choose from is not many, even if we add to them variant forms. It seems altogether natural that Milton should have chosen the *Aeneid* as a model, since that work had for centuries been regarded as the most spiritual or even proto-Christian epic by allegorical interpreters.[37] My purpose leads me chiefly to discuss larger matters, but it surely will not be amiss to demonstrate the importance of the *Aeneid* in one very specific detail.

Milton's editors record that he is echoing Virgil in these lines (432–33) of the second book of *Paradise Lost:*

> long is the way
> And hard, that out of Hell leads up to light.

Milton of course echoes one of the most famous passages of the sixth Aeneid, in which the Sibyl comments to Aeneas about his desire to visit the underworld. In Dryden's translation, the *Aeneis,* we read:

> The Gates of Hell are open Night and Day;
> Smooth the Descent, and easie is the Way:
> But, to return, and view the chearful Skies;
> In this the Task, and mighty Labour lies.
> To few great *Jupiter* imparts this Grace:
> And those of shining Worth, and Heav'nly Race.
> (VI, 192–97)

Virgil differs in some small details.

> facilis descensus Averno;
> noctes atque dies patet atri ianua Ditis;
> sed revocare gradum superasque evadere ad auras,
> hoc opus, hic labor est. pauci, quos aequus amavit
> Iuppiter aut ardens evexit ad aethera virtus,
> dis geniti potuere. (VI, 126–31)

Dryden's change of Avernus to "Hell" and his introduction of "Grace" show him Christianizing details. That is very common in his translations and so no cause for surprise, but

[37] See Allen, *Mysteriously Meant,* ch. VI; and Ross, *Mystagogus Poeticus.*

it does show how readers like Dryden would have instantly recognized what Milton was up to in having a character exclaim, "long is the way . . ."

The character Milton has speaking is Satan, and what precedes and follows the lines quoted assists us in placing him, or in practicing the ceaseless Miltonic art of judging how far Satan is right (it *is* hard to ascend, as the Sibyl had said), and how far he is wrong (he looks forward to trying himself, and he is not one of the few beloved by the Christian Jupiter). What the editors seem to have missed is that Satan is echoing and answering Mammon, whose "sentence is for open warr." No laggard he:

> But perhaps
> The way seems difficult and steep to scale
> With upright wing against a higher foe.
> Let such bethink them, if the sleepy drench
> Of that forgetful Lake benumm not still,
> That in our proper motion we ascend . . .
> Th'ascent is easie then;
> Th' event is feared. (II, 70 . . . 82)

Mammon betrays himself (no part of him is any longer "upright"), but the Virgilian resonance makes very clear how wrong he is. Any doubts can be dispelled by recollection of Satan's erroneous anticipation, "The mind is its own place . . ." (I, 254–55), or by attention to the narrator's decisive version (III, 17–21).

Belial in effect replies with what seems another Virgilian query. What is meant by this mad longing for the light? This smooth-tongued orator is especially good in the sibylline art of wrapping truth in darkness, as Milton makes clear before and after he speaks. Mammon then counsels the civil engineering of Hell, an unmilitant proposal quickly embraced by the angels, and equally quickly killed in this People's

Democracy of Hell. Beelzebub diverts attention to earth and man and revenge. Having at last had a lead on the party line, the lesser angels agree and next receive an empty commendation from Beelzebub. He praises them. You have, he says,

> Great things resolv'd; which from the lowest deep
> Will once more lift us up, in spight of Fate,
> Neerer [on earth] our ancient Seat; perhaps in view
> Of those bright confines, whence with neighbouring Arms
> And opportune excursion we may chance
> Re-enter Heav'n . . .
>   But first whom shall we send
> In search of this new world, whom shall we find
> Sufficient? who shall tempt with wandring feet
> The dark unbottom'd infinite Abyss [?] . . .
>   What strength, what art can then
> Suffice, or what evasion bear him safe
> Through the strict Sentries and Stations thick
> Of Angels watching round? (II, 392 . . . 413)

The Virgilian passage and its context are echoed by the entirety of Books I and II. The difficulty of ascending without Dryden's "Grace" is shown in Satan's effort after it has been recalled in allusion. In more than one sense an *infelix Ulixes*, Satan's struggle parodies the voyage of the Argonauts in search of rich treasure (II, 1015), the voyage of Odysseus in search of home (II, 1019), and the voyage of Aeneas to found a new country. In Book III, the Son of God offers to descend, not indeed to Avernus but to earth and human flesh. In Book VI Raphael concludes his story of Satan's rebellion and the war in Heaven by narrating the way in which the Son drives the rebellious angels into Hell with his chariot and then, effortlessly, returns from Avernus to the light of Heaven (824–92). Joining a specific Virgilian passage to its context, then, Milton shapes his own story and renews the epic convention of descent to the underworld. Numerous enriching parallels are the result, as is also his astonishing placing of the descent at the poem's very beginning.

We have all been taught that Milton's beginning is *in medias res* and that that is one of the central epic conventions. It is and it is not. The beginning of the *Odyssey* is in middle things in that instead of starting with Odysseus' departure for Troy or from Troy, the poem begins with Telemachus looking for his father, who is on his wanderings home. Or again, the *Iliad* begins with two books on the bickering in the Greek camp (and a catalogue of warriors). It is only with the third book that battle starts, and in any event the beginning of this action would need to be thought of as Paris's seduction of Helen, or perhaps even the Judgment of Paris. But what is usually meant by students of Milton by the "beginning *in medias res*" is a forestalling of a long action that must be retrospectively narrated, as by Raphael, for example. Retrospective relation of this kind definitely is not a feature of either of the Homeric poems. Of course various things are so reported: but not by altering the whole chronological structure at the beginning of the poem. In that radical sense, the *Aeneid* is unique among classical epics. Virgil's "convention" is not followed in the *Metamorphoses* by Ovid, the *Pharsalia* by Lucan, the *Thebiad* or *Achilleid* by Statius, the *Punica* by Silius Italicus, the *Mosella* by Ausonius, or the *Apotheosis, Hamartigenia,* or *Psychomachia* by Prudentius. For that matter the technique is not used in the epics of Ariosto, Tasso, or Camões. Dante does not use it, and although Spenser seems to have had some such plan, *The Faerie Queene* as we have it does not follow it. It cannot be a very essential convention of a genre that is observed only twice by principal epics. Even *Paradise Regained* begins in the usual way. To emphasize what Virgil's really radical method entails, one must say that it begins at some point relatively far along in a total sequence of action, and after that point various characters or the narrator may look back in retrospection or forward in anticipation. But the *Aeneid*-model deliberately and obviously begins so far along the chronological sequence actually *included* in the poem that subsequently it will be necessary to delay the action and recount the past. No feature of *Paradise Lost* better shows Milton's decision to write a Christian *Aeneid* than this supposedly simple matter of epic convention.

In choosing the *Aeneid* as his model, Milton chose that classical epic most familiar to his readers. He also chose as model the poem technically most difficult to follow. We have seen how characteristic such a choice was. By following the *Aeneid* he committed himself to starting his poem at a point subsequent to the first action that would be included in the poem and therefore to the necessity of relating the action that had been skipped over. By the end of the third book of the *Aeneid*, Virgil completes his relation of prior events, most of which have been told to Dido. At last the two orders of time have become one. An astonishing two-thirds of the twelve-book version of *Paradise Lost* are required to bring Milton's two orders of time together. Only at the beginning of Book IX have we unequivocally arrived in the present, and then but for two books. The present exists importantly in Books XI and XII, but its function entails Michael's relation of the future of humanity after Adam and until the predicted (not narrated) Second Coming.

I have given one reason why it is a mistake to think that Milton follows convention, when in reality he follows Virgil. In a much more fundamental sense, however, great poems do not follow convention but create it. Virgil had many reasons for proceeding as he did, and most of them come down to his inclusion of the sack of Troy, Aeneas's flight, and his early difficult voyages. Because he wished to tell the story of the founding of the New Troy, Rome, he clearly felt the desirability of relating the end of the old. Aeneas's initial actions, especially that of carrying his father, help establish the character of *pius Aeneas*. As that distinguishes the "man" of the poem's opening line, so does the reminder of his valor at Troy distinguish him in the "arms" of the same line. The narration of his voyages established the theme of fate, of Aeneas as one *fato profugus*. And his affecting story helps motivate Dido credibly to fall in love with her Trojan guest. It may also be true that the relation of the voyages fitted in with what has long been thought Virgil's purpose: re-creation of an *Odyssey* in Books I–VI of the *Aeneid* and of an *Iliad* in Books VII–XII.[38]

Milton's reasons for his so much lengthier retrospection were also compelling. His scheme allowed him to make something far more impressive even than Virgil of the descent to the underworld (I–II), of the heavenly convocation (III), of the earthly paradise (IV–VIII), of the descent from Heaven (IV–VIII), of war (V–VI), and of something new to the epic, creation (VII). Yet to put thus what he does suggests ornamentation or pleasure more than anything very necessary. Necessity can be found perhaps in the very brief biblical account of the Fall (Genesis 3). The rapidity of movement in the first book of the Bible is quite breathtaking, and no doubt Milton needed much more action to sustain an epic. Quite beyond all such considerations, however, were the needs of the poet choosing as his great argument the assertion of divine Providence and the justification of God's ways to men.

As we have seen, Milton's ideal hopes rose repeatedly and were frustrated equally often. To assert divine Providence in

[38] See Dryden, ed. Watson, II, 275, one of the commonplaces in criticism of Virgil. On another occasion, I hope to enter farther than is proper here into Milton's use of Virgil.

the affairs of men, he simply required the total universe, not merely England, and all of human history as he understood it. The problems of England in the seventeenth century required far larger than usual explanation if one was to understand why such great enterprizes had come to nothing. To explain what had gone wrong, Milton had to go back to the first human wrongdoing, the Fall of Man. To explain how things would yet come right, Milton had to deal with God's purposes in creation of angels and man, and to take his story to the prediction of the Second Coming. Nothing less would do. Having committed himself to that grand task, no common form, no mere sequence of episodes was required. The model of the *Aeneid* and the model of the *Divine Comedy* were the only two likely to be usable. Dante had the advantage of being Christian, but the disadvantage for a seventeenth-century English Puritan of being at once less familiar and of being given to vision rather than action. Dante chose to use the figure of Virgil. Milton chose to use Virgil's poem as the convenient basis for that epic that he needed to write after his prose epic had turned sour. The allegorists had assisted in making the *Aeneid* into a poem about human life from its beginning in childhood to youth, to maturity, and to adult triumph over adversity. With *Paradise Lost* Milton transcended by christianizing Virgil's *Aeneid* in a way far more radical than the allegorists had ever envisioned.

Milton's decisions had the results that we know, and those results must now concern us. To put it as simply as possible, Milton's decisions and execution coil ever more tightly, for eight books, a magnificent past that bears on the reader's experience of the Fall in Books IX and X. When we read of Eve and Adam sinning, we have in us the results of Satan's sin in Books I and II; we have knowledge of divine intent from Book III. We have the loving description of the garden of Eden and of man's place in it during the five books devoted to it (IV–VIII). We have the rebellion of the angels, and the creation; we have man's easy relation to that sociable archangel, Raphael. We have, in order of our experience, Hell, Heaven, and earth "and all that in them is." All this bears on "Mans First Disobedience, and the Fruit / Of that Forbidden Tree." The multivalent or polysemous (as the allegorists put it) word, "Fruit," foretells not only Books IX and X but also XI and XII. Adam and Eve's disobedience and contrition occupy only two books of *Paradise Lost*. But the weight given their action by what precedes is that which can only be judged in terms of two-thirds of the poem and by the last one-sixth prophesying result. Providing us in his close with the expulsion and yet another of his quiet endings, Milton invests a single action with *all* the past and *all* the future as he understood it. Past and future; court, city, and country; good and evil; creation and dissolution—all bear on the surpassingly beautiful image of husband and wife hand in hand seeking their home under the guidance of Providence.

Milton's christianizing of the *Aeneid*-form is merely another way of terming his use of it, since the providential history and its scope led him to Virgil in the first place. Yet other elements are also involved by Milton's christianized Sinai. The remarkable opening of the action in Hell bespeaks Milton's knowledge of Dante as well as Cowley.[39] Another feature of the christianizing is Milton's very frequent allusion to the two Testaments. Because he knew them in at least four languages, his echoes do not always sound as distinctly to the ears as do Bunyan's, who not only used the language of the Authorized Version but also cited chapter and verse in the marginal notes. One student of Milton's use of the Bible has said that the first thirteen lines of *Paradise Lost* allude "to

[39] See Irene Samuel, *Dante and Milton* (Ithaca, N.Y., 1966).

no less than fifteen familiar biblical passages."[40] I find it somewhat difficult to decide in this our time just what constitutes a "familiar" biblical passage, but an example from another day may serve our purpose. In *Milton's Paradise Lost Illustrated with Texts of Scripture,* John Gillies ("One of the Ministers in Glasgow") demonstrates for us what a late-eighteenth-century Scots divine saw of the scriptures in Milton's epic.[41] He saw eleven biblical allusions in the first thirteen lines. We probably ought to think that the reason for Gillies' effort was to draw attention to Milton's use of scripture from those readers likely to hear far fewer echoes than he, or a desire to label with chapter and verse what would have been familiar enough but not necessarily at one's fingertips.

Gillies' usefulness is not confined to telling us what readers of another day might find in Milton (of course we have no such edition from the seventeenth century). One of the surprises, if it really is a surprise, given by his glosses is the frequency with which Milton alludes to the New Testament in a poem whose ostensible subject was related in Genesis 3. The fact that the New Testament allusions are so frequent emphasizes Milton's specific Christian end and his Christian sense of the "Providence" in his great argument and emphasized in the last line but two in the poem. Both the frequent New Testament allusions and the most frequently called-upon books of the Old Testament—Psalms, prophets, and Job—relate Milton and his poem to the central English Protestant tradition of meditation and typology. The Psalms and Job are preeminently the "literary" books of the Old

[40] James H. Sims, *The Bible in Milton's Epics* (Gainesville, Fla., 1962), p. 11.

[41] My copy of Gillies is labeled the second edition (London, 1793), and the prefatory matter claims augmentation of the first edition. Biblical echoes are quoted and cited at the foot of the page; classical echoes are merely cited at the end of each book.

Testament (along with the Canticles), and they are the most often levied on by poets (again with Canticles) for literary application to the life of the individual Christian.[42] In Christian interpretation, the prophetic books foretell Christ's coming, as well as the sufferings and eventual triumph, in the Second Coming, of the Church, or believers, represented as Israel. The use of the prophetic books along with the New Testament ensures the functioning of typology in *Paradise Lost* and heightens Milton's christianizing of his Roman model.

Milton's frequent, even constant, allusion to the Bible or use of biblical language and figures serves another purpose. Such appropriation plays down his sometimes unusual religious views and even his Protestantism. By the latter part of the seventeenth century, Catholics were reading their Bible much more assiduously. The Vulgate was being printed more frequently in smaller sizes suitable for private study and devotion, and from 1635 English Catholics had the Rhemes and Douay Version of both Testaments in their own language. Given Milton's approach, no Catholic would need to think that the epic violated his own faith, and all evidence shows that the poem was enthusiastically read by Protestants regardless of denomination. All the same, and without touching on Milton's radical beliefs, we can discern a specific Protestant emphasis. His epic's announced topic, original sin, was of course no news to Christendom, but to make it and redemption through faith and by grace alone the two central features of the poem was to recognize the claims of the Reformers, especially of Luther and Calvin. The medieval attitude *de contemptu mundi*, by contrast, could be read into the last two books of the poem, although only as a lesser topic:

[42] See *The Metaphysical Mode* (Princeton, 1969), pp. 236–46. Further study is needed, since what is meant by "the Bible" depends crucially on what in it is used, and how.

"Of Mans First Disobedience . . ." The third word of the poem emphasizes *original* sin, and the fourth a Protestant concept of its nature. Man ought to have obeyed (in faith) the will of God. For the same Protestant reason, one will not find much talk of good works in *Paradise Lost*. Here are passages from Adam's last speech.

> Henceforth I learne, that to obey is best,
> And love with fear the onely God, to walk
> As in his presence, ever to observe
> His providence, and on him sole depend . . .
> that suffering for Truths sake
> Is fortitude to highest victorie,
> And to the faithful Death the Gate of Life;
> Taught this by his example whom I now
> Acknowledge my Redeemer ever blest.[43]

The soul of the *Aeneid* is fate: the destiny of Troy and the new Troy, along with its founder, whose vicissitudes and triumph parallel the history of Rome till the founding of empire under Augustus. By attention to Virgil's emphasis, one can more readily understand Milton's. Virgil's conception of fate is eclectic but richly developed in the poem. The central problem in a fatal metaphysics is the role of the individual, just as to those who believe in freedom, the necessitarian character of the world poses a problem. In two of the most often cited passages of the *Aeneid*, Virgil emphasizes that the world is as it is, and that the individual must bear up and adjust to it:

> sunt hic etiam sua praemia laudi,
> sunt lacrimae rerum et mentem mortalia tangunt.
> solve metus. (I, 461–63)

[43] XII, 561 . . . 73. Gillies glosses the whole passage as having one allusion to Genesis, two to 1 Samuel, four to Psalms, and three to the New Testament.

(Here, too, virtue has its due rewards; here, too, there are tears for misfortune and mortal sorrows touch the heart. Dismiss thy fears.—Loeb ed.)

Dismiss weakness. Fate and empire call you to be yourself. Virgil combines Stoicism with full acknowledgement of human feeling: "mens immota manet, lacrimae volvuntur inanes" (IV, 449: His will stands unshaken; the tears fall in vain.) To Milton, as to most other English poets in the century, Stoicism was the most admirable of the pagan ethics but no code for a Christian. Milton conveniently assigns the figure of Aeneas in these passages to Satan. How far that is so can be judged by yet another passage from the *Aeneid* and a couple of passages from *Paradise Lost.* In the first book of the *Aeneid,* the hero seeks to instill courage in his men after the storm has buffeted them on an unknown coast:

> Talia voce refert, curisque ingentibus aeger
> spem voltu simulat, premit altum corde dolorem.
> (I, 208–209)

(So spake his tongue; while sick with weighty cares he feigns hope on his face, and deep in his heart stifles the anguish.—Loeb ed.)

It quickly becomes apparent that Satan resembles the pagan hero, except that the evil in the angel is brought out by Milton's alterations. Here is Satan exhorting his followers to Stoic fortitude of will:

> All is not lost; the unconquerable Will,
> And study of revenge . . . (I, 106 ff.)

And here is the narrator's comment adapted out of Virgil.

> So spake th' Apostate Angel, though in pain,
> Vaunting aloud, but rackt with deep despare.
> (125–26)

Aeneas is *fato profugus*, harried, tried, and finally justified by fate. Milton replaces that pagan order with the Christian: law, sin, mercy, grace, faith, and restoration. In the Christian order the believer sanctified by grace becomes "heir to the promises" of the christianized Old Testament covenants and prophecies. All this and more comes under the head of Providence, the explicit topic of the poem and, for Adam and Eve, the end of the poem as well:

> Som natural tears they drop'd, but wip'd them soon;
> The World was all before them, where to choose
> Thir place of rest, and Providence thir guide:
> They hand in hand with wandring steps and slow,
> Through *Eden* took thir solitarie way.
>
> (XII, 645–49)

Once again Virgilian tears and Virgilian reconciliation, but now wholly christianized. As they leave the court, city, and garden of paradise, they walk hand in hand, guided to a new world and a new "place of rest." As Aeneas had borne his father Anchises toward a new world, taking his son Ascanius by the hand, leaving behind the flame and wrack of Troy, Adam and Eve similarly but differently go to their new world with flames behind:

> They looking back, all th' Eastern side beheld
> Of Paradise, so late thir happie seat,
> Wav'd over by that flaming Brand, the Gate
> With dreadful Faces throng'd and fierie Armes:
> Som natural tears they drop'd . . . (641–45)

Providence is the subject of an early chapter (I, viii) of Milton's *Christian Doctrine*, which he *may* have been writing about the same time that he was writing his epic. That chapter concerns "God's Providence or General Government of the Universe," precisely the explicit concern or argument of his poem. He distinguishes the general or ordinary providence of God as that which ordains, preserves, and governs the universe by divine wisdom and will, in an order at once natural and moral in causation. Milton also distinguishes God's special or extraordinary providence by which His wisdom and will effect results contrary to nature and usual causation. With fluctuating hope and question, Milton and his like-minded contemporaries had believed during Puritan times in the special providence of God being vouchsafed to England, the elect nation, the saving remnant before the impending Second Coming. Milton's hopes for special providence were among the casualties of the Civil Wars.

The last two books of *Paradise Lost* confirm how the dashing of Milton's hopes had affected him. The record of history was acrid with the flavor of the "Fruit / Of that Forbidden Tree." Milton did not lose hope, however, as did the fallen angels when Satan returned in a triumph shortly turning into ashes. Of them it was true, as Virgil said, that the cry attempted mocked their gaping mouths.[44] In blindness and in a kind of exile, Milton enlarged his terms. The achieved totality could be sustained not by any immediate expectation of special providence but by faith in "God's Providence or General Government of the Universe." Like the early Christians whom Puritans chose as their model (when the choice was not some Old Testament model typologically conceived), Milton had hoped, for a time, that he lived within the hour of the promised return of the Messiah. He came to realize that God's wisdom and will did not depend on human desires, and instead he found cause for optimism in the same source that had buoyed earlier stages of English Protestantism: divine providence. Could poetry be more public?

[44] Cf. *Aeneid*, VI, 493, "inceptus clamor frustratur hiantis."

Admitting, then, all that Butler did about the vain expectations of the Interregnum, Milton found it possible to transcend his frustrations and make *Paradise Lost* the poem of affirmation that it is. Both the sense of failure and the sense of triumph would have led Milton to recall the words of the Apostle (1 Corinthians 13: 12–13): "For now we see through a glass, darkly; but then face to face: now I know in part; but then shall I know even as also I am known. And now abideth faith, hope, and charity, these three; but the greatest is charity." Michael's last words before telling Adam it is time to leave recall Paul's words on "Love / By name to come call'd Charitie."[45] It must have cost Milton a great deal to admit that he was blind when he saw. But that Michael with his stern duty should emphasize love above all else well fits with the very last lines of the poem, where there is much for tears but also love and providence divine.

iv. Making Whole

The ending of *Paradise Lost* gives a profound sense of beginning. Looking back over the ground we have traversed in this consideration of the poem, we see Milton's concern with his affirmation, the scale and historical motivation of his enterprise, his choice of epic alternatives, and his christianizing of that choice. What now requires some stress is the unusual wholeness, the narrative integrity of *Paradise Lost* and *Paradise Regained*. Because that integrity eluded for the most part the other poets of his time, we ought to find, if we can, symptoms helping us to explain it. One of the best symptoms is the inseparability of myth and reality. Adam talks not only

[45] XII, 581–87. If we accept Gary D. Hamilton's novel thesis that God's remarks in Book III are wholly Arminian in implying sufficient grace for all rather than Calvinist election of but few, Milton is yet more optimistic than I regard him. See "Milton's Defensive God: A Reappraisal," *Studies in Philology*, LXI (1972), 87–100.

with Eve, but also with Raphael, God, the Son, and Michael. Eve herself talks with Satan in the serpent and (briefly) with the Son. The Son talks with them and with God. Satan talks not only to his followers but also to unfallen angels, to Eve, Chaos, Sin, and Death. It does not seem to me so much a triumph that Milton created Satan as that he could have him speak to an abstraction, Sin, as his daughter, or within the toad or serpent—and yet seem credible. The one strain readers have noticed in this glorious fabric is God's speech. Numerous explanations have been given to justify the speeches by God, or indeed His appearance as a character in the poem. These justifications seem to me to testify to a need for justification, rather than to sheer perversity in the adverse critics. Of course the standard by which we judge that portion of Book III is the standard of most of the poem. One could compare the speeches with those Cowley has God deliver in the *Davideis*.[46] But the question is not so much why God talks as He does as why He talks at all, why Milton troubles himself to undertake a project sure to entail loss. Milton knew how far Dante had gone to represent the Godhead in symbolism and he might have done so if he wished, especially given his special view of the created nature of the Son. But God in Book III is a character, not a symbol. Milton wished to have God a character in the poem so much that he was willing to suffer loss in doing so. That loss is immediate and unquestionable, I feel. But the gain is greater if less tangible. For one thing, God's first speech (III, 80 ff.) suddenly makes clear that He alone rules; Books I and II now appear indeed in a new light. For another thing, Milton's poem includes the Creator as well as the creation, an ontology that stretches, as does his history, from beginning to end. What Milton loses by way of what might be termed dramatic satisfaction, he

[46] Waller, pp. 252 and 373 (*Davideis*, I and IV). The latter is in hexameters jutting into the left-hand margin.

gains in narrative integrity: all that Milton can conceive of exists *in the same literary terms* in one poem, ruling Creator and ruled creatures.

The achievement is remarkable and would not have been possible unless Milton believed in what he was doing, that is, in the reality of his characters and their world. Of course as Chaos, Sin, and Death show, such belief does not have to be so literal as to imagine that God always speaks seventeenth-century English. Nor can God and Milton's other characters be dramatized. *Paradise Lost* realizes not only many important potentialities of narrative but also many of its conveniences. We do not speak entirely loosely when we speak about a dramatic episode or conflict in *Paradise Lost*, but as Dryden found—and Milton before him, for that matter—one might begin a drama based on Milton's subject, but one could not finish it. Epic narrative was Milton's only possible medium.

Milton's ontology also plays a special role in giving us a sense of the poem's wholeness. Some features of that articulated system of life would have been familiar to Chaucer earlier and Pope later. There exists only one Being, God, the Creator. All else are creatures. Milton's heresy holds that the Son and the Holy Spirit are also creatures (however exalted) rather than of the same essence as the Father and coeternal with Him, as in trinitarian belief.[47] Milton distinguishes the angels by function rather dimly: "Thrones, Dominations, Princedoms, Vertues, Powers," etc. (V, 601). They are subject to the Son, who was however "begot" after them (V, 600–607). Man comes next beneath the angels (and with this we are back to orthodoxy), being also a rational creature, although man's reason is usually discursive, requiring time to operate, rather than, like the angels', intuitive (V, 487–90). Beneath men with their immortal rational souls are the brute

[47] *Christian Doctrine*, I, v (the Son) and vi (the Holy Spirit).

beasts possessed only of vegetal and animal souls. There follow vegetables with their single soul and the inanimate (literally, unsouled) creatures. Milton does not stop there but goes on beyond nature to Chaos, a personification of a kind.

Milton's version of the scale of nature, or the great chain of being, has libertarian features not found in the versions we find in (for example) such more conservative writers as Shakespeare and Dryden. For one thing, man can talk with angels and God, which is no doubt a special condition suitable to man's prelapsarian state, but still has no precedent on such scale. For another, Milton insists much less on hierarchies within each order. The so-called Dionysius the Areopagite had written of the hierarchy of the blessed angels, and Milton does borrow some of the traditional terminology. He also seems to rank some angels higher than others. But no one has ever been able to derive a hierarchy from his account, and he seems to conceive of the angels more in terms of their functions, with a kind of angelic civil service of ranks. Another feature emerges from comparison, again, with Shakespeare and Dryden. Milton makes less of hierarchical correspondences between the orders of the creation. In particular he does not insist on correspondences between the heavenly King, kings among men, the king of beasts (the lion), the king of birds (the eagle), the royal planet (the sun), and the royal metal (gold). His hierarchy of the creatures involves only goodness or function, and in this he is quite radical. In *Paradise Lost*, there is but one true king, God; in *Paradise Regained*, a second, "*Israel's* true king," Jesus. Men are equal, at least when there is but one before the Fall! But woman is inferior, having been created from man, whereas man was created in God's image.

It does not seem likely that Milton will be thought very libertarian by modern readers. They do not encounter "degree" or what Dr. Johnson termed "subordination" so markedly in their own lives. That "great chain of being" so much sentimentalized over as a kind of sacrament in Elizabethan thought was a rationale for order with despotism, arrogance, and benefit for a few, along with submission and misery for all the rest. If we need to see Shakespeare and Dryden in their time and culture out of a hope that we shall one day be judged on the same terms, then we must also understand that Milton really was more libertarian than they or than any major poet before the eighteenth or nineteenth century. Milton seems to posit a kind of equality for all adult males of consequence. He was no Leveller or Digger, and holiness of life enfranchised his citizens in a way that has not been true since the American colonies.

The relative equality that we discover in *Paradise Lost* certainly tends to make the poem into a whole by the freedom between individuals in a class and by the possibility of rising above one's class. Adam and Eve have the promise of rising to angelic status if they do not sin, and even well after they have fallen, Christian liberty is thought to give man a dignity he did not have before Christ. Moreover, after the Second Coming, those who are saved will enjoy the promise held out to Adam and Eve. Milton's prose shows how impatient he was with the privileges of prelates and princes. He followed Aristotle in defining tyranny as rule by an equal or an inferior, and he defined equality, inferiority, or superiority in human affairs largely in ethical terms, although with Milton intellectual considerations could hardly have been omitted. None of this makes Milton into a republican in the strict sense, much less a democrat. But it does testify to two principles that give *Paradise Lost* the special wholeness and order it possesses. The libertarian principle has been stressed: any group of creatures in their order live in harmony. Milton shows that in paradise all the beasts live in amity. Raphael discourses on subjects that in any other context would have been thought scandalous. The second principle, however, is very different and provides the basis for Milton's otherwise libertarian views. He believed in an absolute inequality between the Creator and His creatures. God's essence and attributes are reflected, though imperfectly, in man, ensuring that man is rational and free. But the relation of Creator to creatures, of infinite to finite, of omniscient to rational, and so forth is such as to call for *obedience* to God. This central principle supports Milton's moral order through all its ramifications and thereby gives coherence to his entire ontology.

Milton believed in God. He premised the whole universe not just on the existence of God, but also on God's benign providence. The order that gives *Paradise Lost* its wholeness is then unsurprisingly, but first and last, religious. God rules by total right a universe that is His. He created it. He chooses to rule mildly, to love His creatures, to offer them mercy and grace. But there should be no mistake about obedience—or, more properly, justice—as the basis of moral causation in the poem. No act is unknown, and every act constitutes a decision of value, of spiritual and moral choice for good or for evil. Each act has therefore its consequences. Pleas as to chance, ignorance, or necessity get one nowhere. *Paradise Lost* is so fully organized on these terms that each act, however trivial it may seem (eating a bit of fruit being merely the most obvious), is a clear, total moral choice, with moral and total consequences.

No reader of *Paradise Lost* can evade that order of moral causation by praise of the style or by attention to Satan's grandeur though in ruin. In another sense, readers can of course evade as much as they wish, but that means making a poem that Milton did not write. By the same token, it will not do that Milton's apologists should consign such matters to myth. Milton believes totally in what he writes, and he forces his knowledge on us. Nothing else in *Paradise Lost* or

Paradise Regained can be thought more overwhelming, both in terms of the acceptance it entails and the grandeur it affords. None of us is likely to be totally at ease in such a milieu. It is very unfashionable. It is also very meaningful and hopeful. We owe it to Milton and ourselves to ask what the alternatives may be. Milton's view gives life meaning, constant and total meaning.

The clear inference is that, like Adam and Eve, we are free to choose. Even postlapsarian men and women have roles to make such momentous choices. Milton has often been said to have based most of his major works on temptation. That is another way of saying that they center on decision or choice: reason is but choosing. *Paradise Lost* shows mankind in Eve and Adam in a grand capacity for choice—and in peril over each action undertaken. With so much bearing on each act, it is a wonder that *Paradise Lost* does not resort to the mode of *The Divine Comedy, The Faerie Queene,* and *The Pilgrim's Progress*: allegory. The authors of those works were equally obsessed with choice and its meaning. But in this we have incontrovertible testimony to the wholeness and integrity of *Paradise Lost,* to its single rather than double focus. In a fundamental Protestant sense the poem is *literal.* Like the Protestant conception of the Bible, *Paradise Lost* means one thing at each moment, and it means everything.

Such literalism really designates a wholeness, an ability to sustain a single if complex vision of reality. By admitting as much as possible, and by holding that combination of action, figuralism, imagery, myth, and reality as a single combination, Milton gives us that powerful sense at the end of the poem that it has all been clear and simple and profoundly meaningful. But of course we do not read all the poem at a glance or even, as Poe complained, at a sitting. In the temporal process of reading, the *Erzählzeit,* there are numerous orders as well of *erzählte Zeit,* of narrated or described time.[48] The intensification of the *Aeneid*-form brings one special form of temporal focus: on the act of sin. But along with this extraordinary elongation of time or one sustained moment (drawn out at unexpected length from the sin of Eve to that of Adam, as if suddenly a new order of time were emerging by a slow shift), our reading constantly gives us elements resembling something else, parodying something else, anticipating or recalling something else. Spiritual figuralism, or typology, provides the readiest example and begins, as we have seen, with the two Adams in the first four lines of the poem. Raphael is a good typologist and so gives Eve that angelic salutation, Hail:

> the holy salutation us'd
> Long after to blest *Marie*, second *Eve*.
> (V, 386–87)

To the modern mind there may be something strange in a wife and her husband (Eve, Adam) being types of a mother and her son (Mary, Jesus). For this Milton had an answer: "why is it necessary that things which are analogous should coincide in all points?"[49] In other words, the typology has the double effect of resembling and relating (and so giving the poem coherence of one kind) and at the same time of discriminating (and so giving a qualitative order to the poem). Adam remains sinful Adam in whom we have all sinned, whereas "one greater Man," Jesus, remains wholly virtuous, our Savior. The central facts of figuralism are the time span between the type and its fulfillment, and the reality of both type and antitype. Resemblances and differences together make up the comparison, allowing us reason and choice.

Discrimination of likeness and difference was thought

[48] See Günther Müller, "Erzählzeit und erzählte Zeit," *Festschrift . . . Kluckhohn und . . . Schneider* (Tübingen, 1948), pp. 195–212.

[49] *Christian Doctrine*, I, xxviii.

basic to the operation of the mind by most people in the seventeenth century and, to a poet continually setting his characters choices, such discrimination is only less crucial than the inner state of goodness that choice ought to imply. Such discrimination also applies to that single truth or wholeness of the poem as a means of shaping our experience through constant processes of clarification. To take a very simple example, the invocation to Book VII calls to Urania; however, we must get clear that "The meaning, not the Name I call" (VII, 5). There is something fundamentally bizarre about Raphael's news that angels require food and possess some exquisite metabolism that can "corporeal to incorporeal turn" (V, 404–13). And one would have thought that Milton rather than Raphael might be the blusher over the news that angels enjoy sexual relations (VIII, 618–29). None of this allows us to confuse angels with men, in spite of the fact that Adam and Eve might one day "participate" with angels. Part of Raphael's speech, and a very long part to be sure, really must be quoted for the way in which it encapsulates Milton's discriminating process leading to wholeness. Apart from an omission of temporal matters, the passage (V, 469–505) otherwise says very nearly everything necessary to be known about the ontology of *Paradise Lost*:

> O *Adam*, one Almightie is, from whom
> All things proceed, and up to him return,
> If not deprav'd from good, created all
> Such to perfection, one first matter all,
> Indu'd with various forms, various degrees
> Of substance, and in things that live, of life;
> But more refin'd, more spiritous, and pure,
> As neerer to him plac't or neerer tending
> Each in thir several active Sphears assignd,
> Till body up to spirit work, in bounds
> Proportiond to each kind. So from the root

Springs lighter the green stalk, from thence the leaves
More aerie, last the bright consummate floure
Spirits odorous breathes: flours and thir fruit
Mans nourishment, by gradual scale sublim'd
To vital Spirits aspire, to animal,
To intellectual, give both life and sense,
Fansie and understanding, whence the Soule
Reason receives, and reason is her being,
Discursive, or Intuitive; discourse
Is oftest yours, the latter most is ours,
Differing but in degree, of kind the same.
Wonder not then, what God for you saw good
If I refuse not, but convert, as you,
To proper substance, time may come when men
With Angels may participate, and find
No inconvenient Diet, nor too light Fare:
And from these corporal nutriments perhaps
Your bodies may at last turn all to Spirit,
Improv'd by tract of time, and wingd ascend
Ethereal, as wee, or may at choice
Here or in Heav'nly Paradises dwell;
If ye be found obedient, and retain
Unalterably firm his love entire
Whose progenie you are. Mean while enjoy
Your fill what happiness this happie state
Can comprehend, incapable of more.

In a subsequent passage, one much discussed in recent years, Raphael stresses the necessity of accommodating what he has to say to the capacities of man:

what surmounts the reach
Of human sense, I shall delineate so,
By lik'ning spiritual to corporal forms
As may express them best—

and then comes a question—

though what if Earth
Be but the shaddow of Heav'n, and things therein
Each to other like, more then on earth is thought?
(V, 571–76)

This is undeniably set forth as merely a question. It seems to me equally evident that Milton is daydreaming through Raphael (who "on earth" besides Adam and Eve could be meant, unless Milton is thinking aloud?). But even in this unusual instance, when we have deduced something without a hint from the poet, we find that question bestows great hope and confers on human life a dignity otherwise lacking. Such shadowing here takes the form not of "shadowy types" that forecast a greater truth at a later historical time when the antitype appears. In this passage Milton uses what has been termed "Platonic" typology, by which an inferior ("corporal") world instantaneously designates a superior ("spiritual") world.[50] It will also be clear that both kinds of typology differ from usual allegorist and materialist views of the world in being double and spiritual like allegory but also in holding to the reality of *both* terms. David is as real as Christ; earth is real, if not perhaps as real as Heaven. We make the distinction not by asking what is real and what is illusory, and not even by saying that David only foreshadows Christ. The necessary distinctions are evaluative: to the good man or woman, two things resembling each other can still be distinguished (and of course must be) on the basis of their quality. The use of "real" things gives *Paradise Lost* the unusual sense it possesses: the poem is real and true.

That is a miracle in itself, considering the kind of subject and the characters Milton has to deal with. Yet again we see

[50] See Madsen, who includes the salutary warning that "Milton charges the key Neoplatonic symbols with Christian significance and thus reverses their polarity" (p. 83). Lewalski's discussion (see above, n. 32) of typology seems to me the fullest we have, although Dryden's use of figuralism will require additional consideration in my next chapter.

the advantage above all else of having God speak in the poem, although the immediate loss is great. The constant necessity of discrimination, on the other hand, makes our experience ceaselessly one of judgment, the counterpart for Milton's readers of the choices and decisions he sets his characters. Because that process of evaluation or judgment is constant in Milton's major works, and because it also is a major aspect of the fables of those works, we come away from his poems with the sense that we do in fact know, that the many complexities have all been clarified, and that the design of the whole is perfectly clear in our memories. Students find to their joy that they feel they really understand *Paradise Lost* very well, and Milton assists all of us in coming to that feeling by his ending the poem, and most of his best poems, on a subdued note. By discriminating his realities Milton achieves that extraordinary wholeness in which matter turns into angelic spirit and a real David foreshadows a real Christ.

Milton's habit of presenting in his narrative systematic, or at least constant, sets of graded, real resemblances would give us merely binary opposites or pairs if it were not for a major import of the qualitative differences between the things that so resemble each other. He requires that his characters and his reader exercise choice between many things that greatly resemble each other. Allegorists such as Spenser and Bunyan create worlds fraught with meaning and requiring choice. But their usual method entails two postulates: either what we see is but seeming (the pious looking hermit is really Archimago), or what is not truly real represents something else that is importantly real. Milton uses the former device in one of his most crucial scenes, the temptation of Eve: what seems to be a serpent given speech by eating the forbidden fruit is really the beast with Satan's intellectual soul taking over its brutish faculties. But we have satanic pretense, not allegory. Such pretense is a species of reality, like that yet more urgent one, Adam's dilemma in seeing fallen Eve and needing to choose between her and God. With so much attending decisions like Adam's, it is essential that a character, and we readers, not confuse corporal with spiritual forms (though the one may develop into the other). Above all, *nothing* must be confused with the expressed will of the Creator by any creature. Milton seems rigid to very many readers, for the good reason that he allows us no escape from the issues posed by his method and his Christianity—other than not reading the poem attentively. It is particularly true that the attentive reader is engaged by Milton's resemblances of realities, because they offer so valuable a sense of grand possibility, even while they demand stern choice.

A particularly good example of this aspect of Milton arises again and again in his ability to make sin attractive. Many a reader and many a critic has been misled, or, in Milton's terms, has made a reprehensible choice, on encountering attractive sin. (Of course Sin herself has long since grown hideous, a general point that Milton emphasizes in other contexts as well.) Nothing could illustrate Milton's respect for real human experience better than this. If sin were not attractive, who would be so foolish as to choose it in preference to virtue? To take the signal instance, from his first appearance Satan is clearly a defeated bully ready to blame anyone but himself, eager to get revenge by attacking those weaker than himself rather than to risk the humiliation of a second defeat by divine omnipotence. But Milton does not endow him with a cloven hoof, a tail, and horns. Milton gives him attractions. In fallen Eve the reader has yet more reason to err than readers who cry up Satan. When Adam in distress gives first consideration to his "Bond of Nature" (IX, 956) with Eve, the reader knows that the hero bound by nature is wrong not to prefer nature's Creator, but he also feels the reality of Adam's tie to Eve. So Adam sins, and so readers participate in the completion of the mortal sin original by giving their sympathy to Adam rather than to God. (The narrator also falls and does not again intrude his own concerns into the poem.) If we did not feel much of what Adam feels, we would not think that a real choice was involved, and the poem would lose its point. Moreover the essence of original sin—that we share in it—would be lost. Milton tirelessly sets us alternatives, each commanding some degree of attraction. Equally insistently, he always makes clear the costs of wrong choice.

Through nine books he presents us with such choices, and in the last three he shows us the consequences. In Book II, a sufficiently early point to assist our weak judgment, he goes out of his way to give us a cautionary example that is unique in his major works. For once, instead of presenting us with his usual sequence of attraction-consequence, Milton chooses a prosopopoeia of Sin and Death that shows the true form of the consequences of wrong choice. Satan finds both Sin and Death remarkably disgusting. So do we. He and Death are about to attack each other when Sin cries out to stop the spectacle of father and son battling to kill each other. (Such is the wholeness of the poem, such the sense of real character and even of family relationship, that we ignore that a fallen archangel confronts a personification.) The moment possesses macabre interest. Sin of all characters shows compunction, and Satan speaks a kind of truth we have not heard from his lips. He tells Sin flatly:

> I know thee not, nor ever saw till now
> Sight more detestable then him and thee.
> (II, 744–45)

Like every rejected lover, Sin recalls the intimate past. In a nice humanistic parody of Minerva born from the head of Jove, Sin tells how she was so born, and how

> I pleas'd, and with attractive graces won
> The most averse, thee chiefly, who full oft

> Thy self in me thy perfect image viewing
> Becam'st enamour'd, and such joy thou took'st
> With me in secret, that my womb conceiv'd
> A growing burden. (II, 762–67)

I cannot emphasize sufficiently the credibility of this happening between an angelic, even anthropomorphic, character and an abstraction, or our concurrence that this could somehow happen in heaven. That we consent to such strange happenings derives from the fact, among others, that Sin's speech just given presents so accurate a psychology of sin, crime, psychosis, or whatever modern label we might choose to give. The dynamism of that psychology continues in the prosopopoeia. Father-daughter incest yields to the rape of Sin by their son, Death. In more than one disgusting sense, the wages of Sin is Death. And he, monstrous son, engenders in her "The yelling Monsters" that crawl into her womb, gnaw on her, barking such noises as can be heard outside. Such was the good evidence on which Satan had found her "detestable." In the most ironic moment of the poem, "the suttle Fiend," now reminded of his parental role, speaks in a new tone: "Dear Daughter, since thou claim'st me for thy Sire, / And my fair Son . . . " (II, 817–18).

Milton shows how much we are attracted to that which is our own thought, and how we indulge ourselves in it. The sexual fable dramatizes both attraction and indulgence, also showing the consequences. The instance is rare in presenting some part of the consequences before the attractions, but in other parts of *Paradise Lost* the consequences are not ignored. One cannot do wrong (or good) without appropriate results following, ever. That Dante-like "ever" on Milton's total, universal scheme recaptured the ideal Milton lost in the failure of his prose epic. On this scale at least, Milton discovered with a greater happiness than that of Aeneas that virtue has its due rewards, and also sin its consequences.

Because the poem is *Paradise Lost* rather than *Paradise Regained* the consequences are very much more in evidence than the rewards. And Milton presses the lesson home with condign punishment of Satan. The tempter had deceived Eve by infusing himself into the serpent. He returns to Hell gloating for congratulations. His followers' obeisance issues as a mocking hiss. And Satan finds thereupon that his shape is constrained into "A monstrous Serpent on his Belly prone" (X, 514). All that follows is appropriate to all that has gone before. Moral order, moral cause and effect, prove to be ineluctable.

And yet, any conclusion about *Paradise Lost* must return us to the point where we began, the affirmative, positive nature of the poem. No small part of that affirmation derives from moral clarity. Milton and we share in the sense of justice. However much evil may prosper and virtue may suffer in Milton's century and ours, by viewing the whole Milton has found a satisfying moral order, an intelligibility of cause and effect. Milton buttresses such hopeful clarity with other normative elements: family, love, and "conversation" of many kinds. His style and scale speak the same affirmative language. Although it is notorious that any theodicy faces the problem of explaining how evil can exist in a world ruled over by a benign God, poetically, humanly the problem is more one of overcoming confusion and mess. The philosophical problem may sleep when the poetic problem has achieved such clarity. Of course God makes all as clear as Milton can make it by his speeches in Book III. But I have already stated my views of Milton's losses and profits in that celestial scene. In the rest of the poem we do not need philosophical explanation when the same truths appear so real in the action.

Paradise Lost also seems positive on balance because its moral order holds such happy escape clauses as mercy and grace. Such men and women at least (and we number ourselves among them as we read) have a hope beyond the undeniable rigor of Milton's strict order of justice. Since we have sympathized knowingly with Adam's conscious sin in love for Eve, we participate with Adam and Eve as creatures less than angelic in being heir to the grace and mercy allotted to them. In Adam we have sinned, and in the second Adam we also find lasting hope. Even in Michael's sorry depiction of the evils following Adam's sin (and our own partial concurrence in it) we observe that we do not need to wait for Adam's and our full instruction for images of comfort. Book XI ends with Noah and God's covenant that the earth will not again be enveloped in a flood destroying us. As Michael says of God,

when he brings
Over the Earth a Cloud, [there] will therein [be] set
His triple-colour'd Bow, whereon to look
And call to mind his Cov'nant: Day and Night,
Seed time and Harvest, Heat and hoary Frost
Shall hold thir course, till fire purge all things new,
Both Heav'n and Earth, wherein the just shall dwell.
(XI, 895–901)

That rainbow in its arc "Betwixt the world destroy'd and world restor'd" (XII, 3) gives us a vision of future salvation. For Noah as well as Adam was a type of Christ. From darkness visible, we have moved to the rainbow. And at the end of the last book, we too take hands with Adam and Eve, with Providence our guide.

v. Recovered Paradise

Paradise Regained strikes every reader as something quite distinct in experience from *Paradise Lost*, and although the admirers of the brief epic have been distinguished, not many have troubled themselves to present with "reason and convincement," as Milton says, the virtues of that poem.[51] Any other writer would have achieved fame with Milton's brief epic, but since he had already written a longer and richer one, he fails to get the credit he might have for *Paradise Regained.* The first thing that strikes a reader moving from the longer to the shorter epic is a spareness of style that at first seems deficient in interest but that, on better acquaintance, becomes as hard and clear as one would wish for in a debate between two formidable antagonists. The complete lucidity of the style answers perfectly to the minds of the narrator and of Jesus in challenging the falsehoods of Satan. *Paradise Regained* is a poem of related (sometimes joined, sometimes conflicting) perspectives, those of Satan, of the Son, of the narrator, and of the reader. Certain lesser perspectives also contribute to the first and part of the second books of the poem: the proto-Christians, Mary, and the fallen angels. In my view, these other perspectives help establish the situation and the scene but otherwise exist only to be subtracted in that gradual process of taking away that reduces the four other perspectives to two clear and crucially focused choices.

In writing his brief epic Milton seems less interested than he had been in writing *Paradise Lost* to observe and renovate the pagan epic conventions, or even their modern counterparts. He does begin, however, in very characteristic fashion: "I who e're while the happy Garden sung . . ." *Paradise Lost* was a pastoral? We shake our heads. Of course Milton knows what he is doing. The four prefatory lines to the *Aeneid* (beginning, "Ille ego, qui quondam gracili modu-

[51] Dr. Johnson greatly admired the poem. In our time we have had: Elizabeth Marie Pope, *Paradise Regained: The Tradition and the Poem* (Baltimore, 1947); Arnold Stein, *Heroic Knowledge* (Minneapolis, 1957); and most fully and helpfully, Lewalski, as above, n. 32.

latus avena / carmen," whose first four words Milton closely follows) spoke of Virgil's changing from the pastoral and georgic worlds to that of war for his epic. Before Milton, Spenser had begun *The Faerie Queene* with an echo of the same Virgilian preface:

> Lo I the man, whose Muse whilome did maske,
> As time her taught in lowly Shepheards weeds,
> Am now enforst a far unfitter taske,
> For trumpets sterne to chaunge mine Oaten reeds,
> And sing of Knights and Ladies gentle deeds;
> Whose prayses having slept in silence long,
> Me, all too meane, the sacred Muse areeds
> To blazon broad emongst her learned throng:
> Fierce warres and faithfull loves shall moralize my song.

Numerous matters emerge from this. Milton's strength and lucidity are apparent at once in the contrast with Spenser's leisurely style. We observe once again the hold that the *Aeneid* has on Milton's imagination. More important, we do *not* infer from what is said that Milton will now essay a larger form than hitherto, or one more martial. No, what Milton is saying is that *Paradise Lost* ought to have been a pastoral, and in some sense was in Books IV to VIII. With the pastoral as it were totally lost as a world-genre, a new genre (again in a universal, typological sense a pastoral) is necessary.

> I who e're while the happy Garden sung,
> By one man's disobedience lost, now sing
> Recover'd Paradise to all mankind
> By one man's firm obedience fully tri'd
> Through all temptation, and the Tempter foil'd
> In all his wiles, defeated and repuls't,
> And *Eden* rais'd in the wast Wilderness.

Five of the first seven lines of the poem end with verbs, a highly unusual procedure for any seventeenth-century poet, especially since the first two lines thereby suggest a couplet, and the fourth, fifth, and sixth a Drydenian triplet. The activity of most of the verbs also heightens the sense of action or movement. When Blake declared that we would not cease from *mental* fight (I take it that the sword in his hand was his pen) until Jerusalem had been rebuilt in England, he caught something of the temper of Milton's beginning. Milton himself stresses contrast and transformation. As "one man's disobedience" had turned a pastoral into a tragic epic, so now "one man's firm obedience" will make out of that the new pastoral ("*Eden* rais'd in the wast Wilderness"). "For as by one man's disobedience many were made sinners, so by the obedience of one shall many be made righteous." [52] The opening lines of *Paradise Lost* have been recalled and transformed.

"By one man's firm obedience": experienced readers of Milton know that the problem-word of the phrase is "man's." Setting aside the christological considerations,[53] and deferring other problems, we must ask why, having chosen Jesus as his hero, Milton takes that "man's" heroism to be exemplified in the temptations in the desert? The question has often been raised in one way or another, and perhaps the best answer is another question: what alternatives were there? Two, really: the Passion and Resurrection or the Second Coming. Apart from the difficulties involved in narrating both of those subjects (the one too familiar and the other, as Milton had learned, not familiar enough), only the temptation in the wilderness answered symbolically and logically to that in Eden. "By one man's firm obedience":

[52] Romans 5:19. I agree with Lewalski (and certain others) that the Christian element predominates over the classical and others in the poem.

[53] See Lewalski, ch. VI.

we can now see the kind of elaborate interlingual and typological pun that had existed, or that is now brought into existence, in the opening lines of *Paradise Lost*. "Mans First Disobedience" and "one greater Man" obviously refer to the two Adams in a kind of reverse typology, because after all in Hebrew "Adam" means "man."

In the epic trying the obedience of the new Adam, Milton once again isolates the scene of temptation and again presents one-to-one confrontation. We have very simple and momentous confrontation and choice. And yet the surprise *Paradise Regained* reimposes on one in each reading is the extraordinary degree of uncertainty in most of the poem. The fallen angels meeting twice in the "gloomy consistory" of the air have not the faintest notion of their problem or what to do about it (except Satan, to whose problems we shall return). The newly baptized have a chorus of anxiety at the absence of Jesus, and Mary's brief appearance conveys her fearful trust in her mysterious son. Even the brief scene in Heaven makes us long for the School Divine of *Paradise Lost* whose plain-speaking now seems a most valuable virtue, especially in a deity. God addresses Gabriel (traditionally the angel of the Annunciation) about the fulfillment of the promise to Mary "that she should bear a Son . . . call'd the Son of God" (I, 135–36). Particularly in the context of *Paradise Regained* that simple "call'd" carries something of the dubiety of a Spenserian "seem'd": "Men call'd him Mulciber . . . Thus they relate erring." Why, in an account so familiar and, one would have thought, so well established, is Jesus merely "call'd the Son of God"? We learn indeed about Mary's conception: "on her should come / The Holy Ghost" (I, 138–39), engendering a son, "This man . . . of birth divine." (I, 140–41).

In the *Christian Doctrine* Milton denies trinitarian orthodoxy (I, v). He accepts of course the existence of the Son of God as Messiah, and also the existence of the Holy Spirit (I, vi), but as we have seen he treats them both as "posterior" creatures rather than as beings coeternal and coessential with God. As for the Holy Spirit, who acts for God ("the power of the highest," I, 139) in visiting Mary (I, 139), he was "created . . . later than the Son, and far inferior to him" (*Christian Doctrine*, I, vi). Now no one can pretend that orthodox trinitarianism proves any clearer than Milton's idea, or that the mystery of the Incarnation is less difficult. But by giving us an Incarnation without trinitarianism, Milton presents the Son of God created after the angels but superior to all other creatures, and one "call'd the Son of God" who was conceived by Mary when visited by that Holy Spirit (acting God's mission) who was created after the Son of God and far inferior to him. A "man" of "birth divine" is indeed a man of mystery, and the working-out of that mystery constitutes the action of *Paradise Regained.*

After Satan's second consistory (i.e., after II, 234) we find the scene reduced in effect to only two characters, the Son and Satan. With such simplification the air of uncertainty thickens. Jesus tells of God's voice at his baptism, calling him "his beloved Son." That baptismal appellation is rehearsed three times, growing less certain with repetition. Indeed the whole central point of Jesus's being in the wilderness is in one sense his ignorance:

> And now by some strong motion I am led
> Into this Wilderness, to what intent
> I learn not yet, perhaps I need not know;
> For what concerns my knowledge God reveals.
>
> (I, 290–93)

Again we observe the extraordinarily verbal character of the style at a crucial moment, with three of the four lines ending with verbs, with the sequence from "led" to "learn," and from "not know" *via* "knowledge" to "God reveals." Jesus trusts divine revelation, and whatever "Son of God" may mean, Jesus plays the role that Christians must emulate, trusting God's revelation. Jesus has made the central Protestant and Miltonic point about the supreme importance of faith: "Now faith is the substance of things hoped for, the evidence of things not seen" (Hebrews 11:1). In *Paradise Regained*, faith is also acquiescence in the divine will although unknown; it is patience; it is obedience. Like reason, faith is heroic choice. The faithful Jesus, *deo profugus*, does not know why he is in the wilderness, and he does not speculate on *who* he is.

That speculation which I found difficult to sort through is the chief business of Satan in the poem, and he too speaks about the baptismal pronouncement:

> Who this is we must learn, for man he seems
> In all his lineaments, though in his face
> The glimpses of his Fathers glory shine.
>
> (I, 91–93)

The metrical agitation of the first line quoted well expresses Satan's concern. Satan seems to possess the answer to his implied question, since he says that although Jesus looks like a man his Father's—surely only "God's" can be meant? —glory shines in his face. But as we have been seeing all along, knowing is virtually impossible in this poem. More than that, knowing is not the *essential* thing. Faith is essential, *sola fides*, as the Reformers insisted. Satan lacks faith and declares: "we must learn." He lacks knowledge of just what "Son of God" means in reference to Jesus (all angelic creatures as well as human creatures deserve the phrase, as with the "sons of God" in Job and elsewhere). He has something more than suspicion from the outset that this is *the*

Son of God who will spell the end of his reign over the sinful world. To the extent that the poem is, like *Paradise Lost*, something of a Sataniad, the irony directed toward Satan is enormous and grows with each action he takes. Increasingly frustrated by the ease with which Jesus rejects his temptations and by Jesus's calm refusal to say who he is, Satan employs "All his wiles" for an essential but profoundly ironic reason. He cannot afford not to know what will undo him. To accept not knowing would be faith in God, and Satan just will not believe. He would rather *know*, which, as this poem points out again and yet again, and more clearly than anything else written by Milton, without faith is perverse. To Satan knowing means defeat, destruction, the fulfillment of the prophecy made to Eve that her seed would avenge her on the serpent. And yet he must know.

Amid uncertainty at least as great as that in our own lives, and meant by Milton to answer to our own lives, the two antagonists meet. Satan, deceiver that he is, appears as a hungry old man, he the "great Dictator" as he is now styled, the magician. Jesus, the hero, is the man of pure faith, one of "the rarest and most hopeful of images, wisdom without bodily decrepitude, early, with the hero young, at the flower, unbruised." [54] As the two interact, Satan becomes more and more desperate, the Son more and more in control. We can regard the course of the action in the poem in an easy way. Following Milton's invitation, we can compare this with the earlier epic. Let us consider part of the first book of *Paradise Regained.*

1–7: Epic proposition and forecast.

8–17: Epic invocation; talk of style.

[54] Stein, pp. 132–33.

18–32: John the Baptist, line 20, "Heavens Kingdom nigh at hand" (the kingdom and time motifs); first version of the baptism.

33–125: Satan's gloomy consistory *(Par. Lost,* I–II); second version of baptism ("A perfect Dove," rather than the Holy Spirit); question of sonhood; play on time and timelessness; the kingdom motif in Satan's view of dictatorship; his thoughts on the Son's nature.

126–81: God's conversation with Gabriel; angelic hymns (*Par. Lost,* III).

182–293: Jesus in meditation (actual soliloquy is employed) on events precedent (like Raphael and Adam, *Par. Lost,* IV–VIII); the Son's knowledge that he is the Messiah; his lack of assurance of how to act, except that his faith and will are unshaken.

Following the invited parallel, we see that Milton has used up as it were the first eight books of *Paradise Lost* in as few as 293 lines of the first book of *Paradise Regained.*

Most of what follows is concerned with direct encounter between Satan and the Son. All of us refer to those encounters as temptations, as choices between good and evil, but it proves no easy thing to say what in Jesus is being tested or how many temptations he endures. One view that is particularly appropriate to the central question of Jesus's identity as one "call'd Son of God," is that in each approach Satan seeks out a different one of the "natures of the Son of God." [55] The initial temptation, to turn stones into bread, tests the manhood of Jesus insofar as he hungers at last after forty days of fasting. But to perform that miracle, Jesus would have to enter on his role as Messiah before God's will

[55] Lewalski, p. 330. For example, she takes the last temptation on the pinnacle as that of "the suffering Priest."

had been revealed to him. As is well known, the three traditional roles of Christ are those of prophet, priest, and king.[56] The long temptation (or temptations) of the kingdoms obviously plays on the Son's nature as king. His rejection of the kingdoms offered by Satan points to his role as "*Israels* true King," as also king of the (typologically) true Israel, his Christian Church. But more than anything else, the temptations show Jesus in his role of prophet. In writing "Of the Office of the Mediator" in the *Christian Doctrine* (I, xv), Milton says that as prophet the Son has an internal "manner of administering," the "illumination of the understanding"; and an external manner, "the promulgation of divine truth." The internal clearly predominates in the Son himself until his last utterance to Satan on the pinnacle of the temple. Satan fears that he has not only a man but also a king to deal with, and his temptations drive at those two natures of the Son. He is defeated by those two natures in that they rebuff him constantly. But the defeat is made whole by Jesus's taking on the role of prophet at the moment he accepts his ministry as priest.

It is possible to consider the poem under one or three aspects, then—or four, or two, or six.[57] A major function of the lucidity of *Paradise Regained* is the clarification less of our ignorance than that we *are* ignorant and will continue to be until in faith we accept our ignorance. Milton does not help us to number the temptations, nor does he aid us in

[56] Milton uses the word "Christ" only once in his poems, and that in a poem of the 1640's, "On the new forcers of Conscience," line 6. Milton accepts the traditional three roles for the Son (*Christian Doctrine,* I, v). His avoidance of "Christ" in his poetry suggests his own unusual views and therefore I follow his example when referring to his poems.

[57] Lewalski gives reasons for considering "various structural patterns," pp. 329–31. She also points out how each temptation derives from the preceding (p. 331).

distinguishing whether there is one or more temptations of the kingdoms. The real point is that one choice is like another, that no matter what Satan does he does and fails at the same thing, and that as long as the Son maintains faith until God reveals some new larger matter, his every reply is essentially the same. Some simplification of Milton's clarity, and some ordering of his constants, can assist us in understanding what happens as it were in the poem after it reaches its equivalent of Book IX of *Paradise Lost*. The distinctions are based on episodes involving either a different time or locale or a different object of view:

I, 294–502: Tempted action: to turn stones into bread
II, 1–235: Interlude: the "new baptiz'd"; Mary; Satan in consistory
II, 235–406: The Banquet
III, 1–IV, 194: The Kingdoms (power)
IV, 195–393: The Kingdoms (wisdom)
IV, 394–450: The Storm
IV, 451–580: The Pinnacle
IV, 581–631: Denouement

It should be stressed that these divisions are offered only as convenience. Fewer or further divisions make perfect sense: perhaps one should distinguish in the section I have termed the temptation of the Kingdoms (power) a further temptation. After suffering various rebuffs over Rome and Parthia (each of which is worth being termed a separate temptation), Satan suddenly utters his price: Jesus must bow down and serve him (IV, 155–69). How very crude that seems. But the complete shift of front and its very crudity are well calculated to arouse the unguided anger and self-betrayal that Satan has all along been looking for. As a master psychological stroke, the sub-episode deserves to be set apart. But once again we see that, far from being crucial, the difference in Satan's approach makes no difference whatsoever as long as the Son's faith and choice remain unshaken. The Son has but one way of defeating his opponent, faith, but Satan has numerous ways of losing. The opposition between those two facts sustains the tension of the poem.

The opposition of those two perspectives on common experience leaves the narrator and the reader somewhere between. We think that we can distinguish various temptations, but it turns out that they may be very many or very few and that they all seem in succession to repeat their predecessors.[58] In creating such perspectives of choice, Milton in general gives us another version of that discriminating whole, *Paradise Lost*. But his brief epic is more original than the earlier (not that that means better), more independent of earlier epics. The recapitulative *Aeneid*-form is ignored; there is none of the descent to the underworld, the epic shield, the epic catalogue, or of those things so carefully renovated for *Paradise Lost*. Instead we discover a series of episodes basically all one, as if *Paradise Lost* in its central ten books dealt with the temptation of Adam and Eve. Another related characteristic is the amount of talk in the poem. *Paradise Lost* had obviously included more talk than any previous epic, because of its exaggeration of the *Aeneid*-form. But that unusual structure also makes most of the talk seem to be the action that the talk relates. In *Paradise Regained*, speech follows speech so persistently that one might wish to follow an interpretation of the poem as a drama.[59] What is acceptable in such speech-making in narrative, however, would be precisely the thing that would be thought non-dramatic, because tediously extended, on the

[58] See Stanley E. Fish on Milton's "jumping up and down in one place" in the prose style of *Reason of Church-Government*, in *Seventeenth-Century Imagery*, ed. Miner (Berkeley and Los Angeles, 1971), ch. v.

[59] This is Stein's approach.

stage. Allowing that, however, we must also allow that Milton's climax shares a great deal with drama in that it involves a reversal and recognition of enormous impact. The placing of that climax so near the end of the poem, and the nature of the climax, both make the poem a novelty in the epic tradition. At that moment, all perspectives become one. And it happens so quickly. When Satan suddenly sweeps the Son to the pinnacle of the Temple in Jerusalem, he leaves him on the perilous footing, scoffing that he stand or fall:

> To whom thus Jesus: also it is written,
> Tempt not the Lord thy God, he said and stood.
> But Satan smitten with amazement fell
> As when Earths Son *Antaeus* (to compare
> Small things with greatest) in *Irassa* strove
> With *Joves Alcides,* and oft foil'd still rose,
> Receiving from his mother Earth new strength,
> Fresh from his fall, and fiercer grapple joyn'd,
> Throttl'd at length in the Air, expir'd and fell;
> So after many a foil the Tempter proud,
> Renewing fresh assaults, amidst his pride
> Fell whence he stood to see his Victor fall.
> And as that *Theban* Monster that propos'd
> Her riddle, and him, who solv'd it not, devour'd;
> That once found out and solv'd, for grief and spight
> Cast her self headlong from th' *Ismenian* steep,
> So strook with dread and anguish fell the Fiend,
> And to his crew, that sat consulting, brought
> Joyless triumphals of his hop't success,
> Ruin, and desperation, and dismay,
> Who durst so proudly tempt the Son of God.
>
> (IV, 560–80)

Having made so much of falling and its Latinate variants, "ruined," etc. in *Paradise Lost,* Milton dwells on the opposite here, standing when standing is difficult. The metaphorical play about the image of those two figures on the perilous pinnacle, one of them standing, one falling, unfolds suddenly in our minds. The éclaircissement contradicts itself in some sense by being that manifestly paradoxical thing, a religious epiphany without an apotheosis. What, after all, is the Son of God? He is, as the poem started by saying, that man who can overcome all temptation, who can obey in faith. At the end of the poem, we are at one with Milton. We have discovered what each episode of the poem has taught us again and again, and which we have simply not learned and so had to be taught again and again. The answer to our quest or disposition to know is that we need not know. We need only believe and understand.

The coming of the grandest climactic episode at the very end of *Paradise Regained* resembles no other work of Milton's so much as *Samson Agonistes*. Likewise the "strong motion" leading Jesus to the wilderness is reminiscent of Samson's "rousing motions" once Dalila leaves.[60] It also resembles in that the detective story. As in that genre, so here we also have the investigator, the search for clues in a series of episodes, and the revelations of the last few pages. Of course Milton "renovates" a genre as yet unborn by reversing the guilt and putting it in the investigator, as also by making something profound out of such a form of plot. *Paradise Lost* also anticipates a later genre, science fiction, by combining two human creatures at the center and supernatural ones from places other than the earth converging on the human pair. We also find battles in space, strange weapons, magic, and a controller of the universe. The interest of the detective story and of science fiction in them-

[60] No one knows when *Samson Agonistes* was written. My likenings imply only that the traditional late date is formally useful. See note 62.

selves is as legitimate as such other conventions as the blazon or the epic itself. Our minds are well exercised in reaching out into space, in rattling through chaos, and above all in our concern for threatened humanity. Similarly, the mystery-story atmosphere of *Paradise Regained* creates a genuine compulsion and suspense. Satan's irresistible and fatal curiosity arouses both a similar response and a counter-response in us. The divergence of perspectives sometimes puts our own in peril. There are those who criticize Milton for having run a risk that he failed. But after all, he does not write detective stories or science fiction, and we can trust what happens as we read his brief epic.

vi. Trusting Milton and Ourselves

A question often asked of *Paradise Regained* turns on the success of Milton's unusual narrative pattern and unusual hero. Truly, there is something odd about a narrative of decision in which the decisions repeatedly frustrate action. Yet if that seems odd, it is odder still that the brief epic creates a genuine sense of conflict in a lucid relation of character and scene. Milton succeeds in his old art of getting to us by getting at us. In entering now into vexed matters, my only hope of getting them right is to trust my own responses and to trust Milton in them. I hope that others exercising the same trust will find agreement possible.

If the narrative of decision or choice does not issue in action as ordinarily understood but instead raises a sense of momentous opposition, we may assume that Milton wished it so. He has found not only a way of treating something important but a way of making us share his sense of the important. I have already given the simplest example I know of in the poem: Satan's suddenly telling Jesus to bow down and worship him. We are shocked by the terrible grossness, the stupidity, and the effrontery of Satan. Our instinct to react so emotionally to that crude gesture shows that Milton has made Satan get at us in a way he does not get at the Son. In other words, *Paradise Regained* has its equivalent of the Satan problem, of the yellow-skirted Fays, and of Comus on natural plenitude. In a word, if the temptations are to be real, they must be important and some at least must in fact be felt by the reader.

The crucial example is of course the Son's impatient rejection of our classical inheritance. It is notorious that in this scene readers do not enjoy the same perspective as does the Son. I shall present something of that episode, beginning with excerpts from Satan's presentation:

> Be famous then
> By wisdom. . . .
> All knowledge is not couch't in *Moses* law.
> Look once more e're we leave this specular Mount
> Westward, much nearer by Southwest, behold
> Where on the *Aegean* shore a City stands
> Built nobly, pure the air, and light the soil,
> *Athens* the eye of *Greece*, Mother of Arts
> And Eloquence, native to famous wits
> Or hospitable, in her sweet recess,
> City or Suburban, studious walks and shades . . .

The entire speech (IV, 195–284) possesses that magnificence which we know to be one of Milton's greatest characteristics. We are genuinely moved. And now we must consider how "our Savior sagely thus repli'd":

> Think not but that I know these things, or think
> I know them not . . .
> he who receives
> Light from above, from the fountain of light,

No other doctrine needs, though granted true . . .
  Who therefore seeks in these
True wisdom, finds her not, or by delusion
Far worse, her false resemblance only meets,
An empty cloud. . . .
  All our Law and Story strew'd
With Hymns, our Psalms with artful terms inscrib'd,
Our Hebrew Songs and Harps in *Babylon*,
That pleas'd so well our Victors ear, declare
That rather *Greece* from us these Arts deriv'd;
Ill imitated, while they loudest sing
The vices of their Deities, and thir own
In Fable, Hymn, or Song, so personating
Their Gods ridiculous, and themselves past shame.
(IV, 286 . . . 342)

And so with much else in like vein of rejection of the glory that was Greece as "varnish on a Harlots cheek" (344). Of course the passage has brought out brave efforts to defend Milton. Scholars say that Satan displays a sophistry counter to Plato's true spirit, that the seventeenth century still believed that the Greeks got what truth they had from Moses and the rest of the Bible, or that Milton always carefully distinguishes between essential and nonessential wisdom. All those points are no doubt true, and we can remind ourselves that we have accorded with the Son at the other major temptations. But I must say that I find myself on the one hand attracted by what Satan says and on the other repelled by the coldness of the Son's reply. From what I observe in others, I infer that they feel the same.

Can we not trust ourselves and Milton in this? Trusting ourselves means acknowledging, or rather hazarding, ourselves in the literary experience. Trusting Milton means believing that he knew what he was doing, and that something right is going on when we find ourselves wishing what we should obviously not wish. At this juncture in the poem, in this temptation to take up pagan classicism and give up our religion, Milton catches us in our humanity. (I believe that he caught himself out, too, as over Adam's willingness to sin with his beloved Eve.) He catches us out by getting us to respond differently from "our Savior." Even to an infidel that comes as great shock, used as we all are to identify hero and villain with assurance. We have not liked the manner of our Savior, of the hero of the poem, with whom we had agreed all that while, and in short we have fallen for Satan. Precisely. If we did not do so, we should have no need for a Savior, and Milton is mightily concerned that we not forget we do.

That episode is one of Milton's greatest literary triumphs. We *know* we should respond as Jesus does, and we *know* to our depths that we do not. In a highly unobtrusive way, Milton reveals to us something not yet revealed to Satan: Jesus is truly "our Savior," and he is truly Son of God in a way quite unlike Satan and ourselves. We reveal our humanity and sinfulness in our reaction, in our emotionalism and lack of faith, in our response to surfaces and names, rather than our desire for that one true wisdom founded on a faith that does not require knowledge. Milton has gone beyond *Paradise Lost,* in which an over-favorable response to Satan will merely reveal our tie with Adam and Eve. In *Paradise Regained,* he makes us face up to the fact that Jesus differs from us and that that difference is crucial to us if paradise is to be regained.

Of all the perspectives of the poem, Milton's finest success involves our turning our own perspective successively on Satan, Jesus, and then ourselves, and again on Jesus. Such is the equivalent in this poem of the multiple voices of *Paradise Lost*. After the reader's crisis in *Paradise Regained,* every perspective outward on other things in the poem retains a lasting inwardness, a kind of conscience in both the ordinary and the root Latin senses. From that crisis, we recognize that the epic itself is especially inward, both because and in spite of its having, as its biblical model, the Book of Job.[61] Milton gradually reduces the characters of his poem to two, but the temptation to make the wrong choice is grounded in his lasting conception of the centrality of faith in God. For the voice in the whirlwind in Job, Milton substitutes two crises: one for the reader, as we have just been seeing, and one for Satan, as we saw earlier. Like Job, we learn that our knowledge is limited and that in some areas, and those the most important, only affirmation is possible. And like Job also, we are doubly rewarded for our pains. Job's faith was expressed in his assertion, "I know that my redeemer liveth, and that he shall stand at the latter day upon the earth." But "the Lord answered Job out of the whirlwind, and said, who is this that darkeneth counsel by words without knowledge?" Job can finally say only, "I uttered that I understood not; things too wonderful for me, which I knew not. . . . Wherefore I abhor myself, and repent in dust and ashes" (Job 19:25, 38:1–2, 42:3, 6).

Milton's whirlwind turns not to reveal the voice of God but to reveal the two different failures of ourselves and Satan. The ending of *Paradise Regained* therefore provides greater assurance than does the climax of Job, which in its present state is a much vexed work and by no means so lucid as Milton's poem. The final assurance Milton gives us is precisely the knowledge, however, that our Redeemer lives or, in more purely literary terms, that although we have erred in knowledge we now understand in faith—literary if not religious. The last seven lines are divided between the angels praising Jesus and the narrator concluding the poem:

[61] Lewalski magistrally canvasses this relation, perhaps overstressing it.

Hail Son of the most High, heir of both worlds,
Queller of Satan, on thy glorious work
Now enter, and begin to save mankind.
   Thus they the Son of God our Savior meek
Sung Victor, and from Heavenly Feast refresht
Brought on his way with joy; hee unobserv'd
Home to his Mothers house private return'd.

That quiet ending marks Milton's finest longer works. The details associate with those in *Paradise Lost* and *Samson Agonistes.* If Jesus goes "Home to his Mothers house," Samson is taken "Home to his Fathers house."[62] And "to thir place of rest" go Adam and Eve (XII, 647). Jesus has been "Brought on his way with joy." The "servants" of God at the end of *Samson Agonistes* receive from him a similar benediction: they "With peace and consolation [He] hath dismist, / And calm of mind all passion spent" (1757–58). Adam and Eve in like wise have

Providence thir guide:
They hand in hand with wandring steps and slow,
Through *Eden* took thir solitarie way.
(XII, 647–49)

In a profound sense, Milton's great narratives take us through heaven and hell and a kind of purgatory. But at the end they take us home. The emphasis and the workings of our emotions vary. But I think it just to say that in *Paradise Regained,* after leading us to humiliate ourselves over Athens, Milton arranges things so that each reader discovers that, like Jesus, he is finally "Brought on his way with joy."

[62] The remarkable verbal parallels do not prove that the two poems were composed at about the same time. But with others (see n. 60, above) they assist the hypothesis of the traditional late dating.

VI

DRYDEN'S HEROIC IDEA

A Heroick Poem, truly such, is undoubtedly the greatest Work which the Soul of Man is capable to perform.

— Dedication of the *Aeneis*

the same images serve equally for the Epique Poesie, and for the Historique and Panegyrique.

— "Account" of *Annus Mirabilis*

Now let the few belov'd by Jove, and they,
Whom infus'd Titan form'd of better Clay,
On equal terms with ancient Wit ingage,
Nor mighty Homer fear, nor sacred Virgil's page:
Our English Palace opens wide in state;
And without stooping they may pass the Gate.

— *To the Earl of Roscomon*

A QUARTER CENTURY junior to Milton, Dryden nonetheless preceded his elder in publishing a narrative poem of length. *Annus Mirabilis* follows *Hudibras* (the first part) by four years and precedes *Paradise Lost* by about the same number of months. Like Butler and Milton, Dryden is a poet whose vision of the world and of himself in it was shaped by experience before 1660. The fact is not as blatant as in *Hudibras*, nor as documented as is Milton's career by prose. And it must be added that Dryden had a capacity for steady development in poetry that leaves us no such hiatus of time and quality as that between Milton's *Poems* of 1645 and *Paradise Lost* twenty-two years and a prose epic later. Everything about Dryden's earlier life can be characterized as a move from uncertainty to certainty, whether we consider our sources of information or the development of his work as a poet. One could wish that he had fulfilled his promise to Aubrey to supply a memoir of himself. Whether Dryden was the "Draydon" who served the Protectorate in some capacity is not certainly known. There were too many John Drydens, Dridens, Draydons, and Dreydens about for us to be sure, and yet the example of Pepys makes it seem quite possible. As a schoolboy, the diarist was a professed Presbyterian in Church and politics, cheering the execution of Charles I. As a man Pepys was, like Dryden, devoted to the royalist, naval cause that made them "Yorkists," men loyal to James, for all his faults. Whatever Dryden's earlier participation in the Protectorate may or may not have been, he first revealed poetic vision in the *Heroique Stanzas* on Cromwell's death. Cromwell stirred in Dryden as in others a sense of English triumph, a sense that men were rising to larger achievements than before: "For he was great e're Fortune made him so" (22). As he recounts the Protector's achievements, Dryden shows that he has grasped a potential of the public mode never fully exploited in England: the possibility of making recent or present history into poetic reality.

i. The Great Idea

During the Interregnum the "Puritans" were obsessed by the belief that God's finger was writing before their eyes. The supernatural expressed itself in other ways: through astrologers like Sidrophel, through portents and signs (armies in the sky, the great wind blowing as Cromwell died), and through God's vouchsafing intimations of His will to the Saints (so Cromwell wrestled in prayer until he gained unshakable certainty that he knew God's will). Moreover, the widespread Puritan habit of keeping diaries, and sometimes of writing spiritual autobiographies based on their journals, lent great importance to the intersection of individual personality, events of the time, and divine purpose. Such tendencies brought a result that no one could have anticipated and of which Dryden became the chief poetic exponent: the historical present, historical events, and historical process acquired an importance they had not held. Men had at last come to see that their own time was historically as real as the ages of Moses or David, of Alexander the Great or Augustus Caesar.

That Dryden is the heir to such promises will be understood at once by those conversant with his poetry. But there is another form of evidence of high interest: it is he who gave to English criticism the very concept of a literary age, the very basis for a historical conception of literature and literary process.[1] Dryden unquestionably found the present to occupy him more, and certainly more favorably, than did Butler or Milton. But he also maintained a providential view of history that emphasized creation, divine and human purpose, and last things, and this view distinguishes him from many of his younger contemporaries and from his important successors. Both of these historical attitudes were fertile for narrative poetry. Other historical attitudes held by him greatly modified the effect, however. He also held to the idea that human nature was a constant thing (with whatever local variation), so that predictive historical comparisons could be made between ages and nations when in like (i.e., cyclical) postures of events. This view, along with Dryden's driving, clarifying intelligence, had the effect both of adding meaningfulness to the events he related and of diminishing the pressure of narrative. His most fully narrative poems come to us from the beginning and end of his career which, as that of a narrative poet or almost a poet of any major kind,

[1] As I seek to show in "Renaissance Contexts of Dryden's Criticism," *Michigan Quarterly Review*, XII (1973), 97–115.

begins with *Annus Mirabilis* (1667) and ends with *Fables Ancient and Modern* (1700).

Dryden undertook to write a history of important events of 1665–66, the year of wonders: the Great Plague, the Great Fire, and the early stages of the second Anglo-Dutch Naval War. Why not do so? And yet Dryden was the first to do so in a way uniting history and narrative. Anniversary poems like Marvell's on Cromwell's first year, character poems like Marvell's of Holland, or ballads like those that rallied both sides during the Interregnum simply do not qualify for what Dryden had in mind. Dr. Johnson unerringly recognized that the one English poet who gave a start to *Annus Mirabilis* was Edmund Waller, whose poem *Of a war with Spain* Dryden uses as a model for his opening.[2] For that matter, Dryden's poem can seem scarcely less novel today, when anybody writing about the present is required by modern custom to be critical or humorous, and when there seems to be a gulf between what seems crucial in the actual transactions of people and the poetry written. Every year has its wonders, but every year does not have its *Annus Mirabilis*. Nor does our poetry about our time always bring the events to narrative life, as Dryden does in telling of battle in days of sail and cannon: "Silent in smoke of Canons they come on" (329). The visual evidence comes of course before the aural, and the sense of the great Dutch fleet bearing upon the English comes to us with no doubt but that the world of three centuries ago is real.

The usual concern of critics in dealing with *Annus Mirabilis* has lain very little with the poem's reality, however, and very much with the poem's unity. How successful, they ask, is Dryden in uniting the story of naval war with that of the fire? (The plague is largely left out.) The usual answer is,

[2] Johnson, "Dryden," *Lives of the English Poets*, ed. G. B. Hill (Oxford, 1905), I, 431.

Not very. And that answer is too true. What we discover reading *Annus Mirabilis* afresh, however, is almost a dialectic between very unlike events and a driving sense of relation on a higher level. What I mean can be understood in part by a supposition. Suppose the reader of these sentences asks himself what were the two major events in the world in the year before he reads these words, and that he then considers the degree of possibility that they could be made one in a narrative poem. Such a supposition shows that, contrary to our usual critical decrees, Dryden has very much overstated the connection between the Second Dutch War and the Great Fire. To put it another way, he sought to relate too closely events that paradoxically were too close to allow for easy relation. The comparison of England and Holland to Rome and Carthage works altogether more easily than does the relation of two events occurring in the same year.

In the "Account" he prefixed to the poem—one of his briefest and most significant critical pieces—Dryden talks of the nature of his poem:

> I have call'd my Poem *Historical*, not *Epick*, though both the Actions and Actors are as much Heroick, as any Poem can contain. But since the Action is not properly one, nor that accomplish'd [completed] in the last successes, I have judg'd it too bold a Title for a few *Stanza's*, which are little more in number than a single *Iliad*, or the longest of the *Aeneids*.[3]

Dryden says that his action "is not properly one," plainly meaning not that it is improperly unified but that it is not unified as it ought to be for epic purposes. Moreover, one of

[3] Where possible, I shall be using the "old spelling" texts for Dryden's prose as they are found in the California edition (I [1961], 50), or in James Kinsley's edition (see the Bibliography). Hereafter I shall not remark, as I do now, on my having changed italic or roman usage in prose quotations.

his two subjects, the naval war, was still in progress and so the narrative has as it were no ending. For these reasons, and these alone, he determines that his poem is historical rather than epic. His reasoning becomes clearer with a fuller discussion of the kinds of images suitable to certain genres and of the relation between those genres:

> Such descriptions or images, well wrought, which I promise not for mine, are, as I have said, the adequate delight of heroick Poesie, for they beget admiration, which is its proper object; as the images of the Burlesque, which is contrary to this, by the same reason beget laughter; for the one shows Nature beautified, as in the picture of a fair Woman, which we all admire; the other shows her deformed, as in that of a Lazar, or of a fool with distorted face and antique gestures, at which we cannot forbear to laugh, because it is a deviation from Nature. But though the same images serve equally for the Epique Poesie, and for the Historique and Panegyrique, which are branches of it, yet a several sort of Sculpture is to be used in them.[4]

The passage reveals two things of first importance in understanding Dryden's major nondramatic poetry. To begin with, his conception of poetic mimesis is at once rhetorical and affective. The affective function is evident in this passage. The rhetorical is more clearly expressed in a passage written later in which he declares that art takes a better or worse "likeness" while remaining within the compass of truth.[5] Such a view allows him to associate epic, historical, and panegyric poetry, as well as the obverse of praise, satire.

[4] Ibid., I, 56.

[5] See A *Parallel Betwixt Poetry and Painting*, ed. George Watson, *Of Dramatic Poesy and Other Critical Essays* (London, 1962), 2 vols., II, 202. The passage is quoted below, p. 350.

At the center of that group, affecting all other members and defining the whole, is the "heroic" or epic. As the epigraphs to this chapter show, Dryden defined his poetic aims by reference to the heroic.[6] The epic itself was a genre and a form with certain principal exemplars. The intellectual, moral, imaginative, and affective qualities of the epic were those that could be separated from the genre and designated the heroic. That heroic conception of the world he was celebrating as a historical process often comes to replace action as the basis for treating events. It is such a heroic treatment of a double history that gives *Annus Mirabilis* the second dialectical character of unity. Without that heroic conception, there would have been no need for Dryden to connect the war and the fire. Even in *Annus Mirabilis* the conception of present English history as heroic endeavor (an idea shared, with a difference, by Butler and by Milton in his prose) often intrudes into the action. But it does not dominate the action as it does in *Mac Flecknoe* and subsequent poems in the 1680's. The heroic conception of history may mean many things, but to Dryden it is centrally a vision of man's rising by his own efforts in a providential world to achieve immortal accomplishments. Dryden devotes his attention again and again to three components of that heroic idea: the great individual, the great achievement in some specific action or art, and the glory of one nation, England.

We have come upon the fourth historical strand in Dryden's thought: a belief in the possibility of human progress distinguishing him from his "decay"-minded predecessors. Here at length is his, and the English, first clear celebration of a faith in human progress, an evident heroic idea expressed in the history of navigation and the apostrophe to the Royal Society:

[6] See H. T. Swedenberg, Jr., "Dryden's Obsessive Concern with the Heroic," *Studies in Philology*, extra series, no. 4 (1967), pp. 12–26.

Digression Concerning Shipping and Navigation

155

By viewing Nature, Natures Hand-maid, Art,
  Makes mighty things from small beginnings grow:
Thus fishes first to shipping did impart
  Their tail the Rudder, and their head the Prow.

156

Some Log, perhaps, upon the waters swam
  An useless drift, which, rudely cut within,
And hollow'd, first a floating trough became,
  And cross some Riv'let passage did begin.

157

In shipping such as this the *Irish Kern*,
  And untaught *Indian*, on the stream did glide:
Ere sharp-keel'd Boats to stem the floud did learn,
  Or fin-like Oars did spread from either side.

158

Adde but a Sail, and *Saturn* so appear'd,
  When, from lost Empire, he to Exile went,
And with the Golden age to *Tyber* steer'd,
  Where Coin & first Commerce he did invent.

159

Rude as their Ships was Navigation, then;
  No useful Compass or Meridian known:
Coasting, they kept the Land within their ken,
  And knew no North but when the Pole-star shone.

160

Of all who since have us'd the open Sea,
  Then the bold *English* none more fame have won:

Beyond the Year, and out of Heav'ns high-way,
They make discoveries where they see no Sun.

161

But what so long in vain, and yet unknown,
By poor man-kinds benighted wit is sought,
Shall in this Age to *Britain* first be shown,
And hence be to admiring Nations taught.

162

The Ebbs of Tydes, and their mysterious flow,
We, as Arts Elements shall understand:
And as by Line upon the Ocean go,
Whose paths shall be familiar as the Land.

163

Instructed ships shall sail to quick Commerce;
By which remotest Regions are alli'd:
Which makes one City of the Universe,
Where some may gain, and all may be suppli'd.

164

Then, we upon our Globes last verge shall go,
And view the Ocean leaning on the sky:
From thence our rolling Neighbours we shall know,
And on the Lunar world securely pry.

Apostrophe to the Royal Society

165

This I fore-tel, from your auspicious care,
Who great in search of God and Nature grow:
Who best your wise Creator's praise declare,
Since best to praise his works is best to know.

166

O truly Royal! who behold the Law,
And rule of beings in your Makers mind,

And thence, like Limbecks, rich Idea's draw,
To fit the levell'd use of humane kind.
(617–64)

Man explores space, creates a peaceful and prosperous world, and uses human capacities to the greater glory of God, whose wisdom rather than will Dryden emphasizes. The elephant is *not* in the moon.

We must admit, however, that what might be termed the purest narrative in the poem comes in this digression. (Also that the early, expletive "did's" bother us until Dryden's imagination kindles from the 159th stanza.) The progress-piece digression affords a total heroic "history" or narrative of an art, from its rude beginnings long ago to a triumph whose first stage alone can be glimpsed. This vision of achievement by man, in England, for the world, and under God represents a digression from the story of naval war. The important thing, however, is that it also provides the narrative model and the heroic idea for the whole poem. The hope, the conception, give direction to the naval action and the fire. That is, by evident analogy Dryden predicts similar triumph in the war and a new London rising glorious from the flames. The naval prediction came almost ludicrously early, in view of the protracted struggle with Holland, but in fact Dryden saw before most others that future of English imperialism triumphant in the following two centuries. James Duke of York and Pepys in their ways shared the view, but neither used it to understand contemporary history or human life. As early as the poem's fifth stanza, Dryden had detailed a triumphant analogy for the war with Holland, in which the Dutch become Carthaginians and the English Romans: "And this may prove our second Punick War" (20). The picture of the Dutch echoes Virgil (*Aeneid,* I), "Stout for the War, and studious of their Trade," as Dryden later rendered Virgil (*Aeneis,* I, 22). England's first "Punick" war was of course the Anglo-Dutch naval war of 1652–54. Curious as it is, it would take England a third war, as it had Rome, to displace her rival.

The triumph envisioned for English heroism is commercial as well as intellectual, and it focuses more heroically on the City than does any other English poem. Here again, we sense Roman overtones, the city-as-empire. Toward the close of the poem Dryden refers to London as "More great then humane, now, and more *August*," noting that Augusta was "the old name of *London*" (1177). In *Mac Flecknoe* London has become "The fair *Augusta* much to fears inclin'd" (65) for another set of actions and characters. In so switching in *Annus Mirabilis* from the Roman Republic to the Empire under Augustus, Dryden gives expression to a new analogy for English poets, and brings the *Aeneid* as a model equally for his own poem and his age. And so *Annus Mirabilis* ends with a vision of London transformed:

297

Now, like a Maiden Queen, she will behold,
From her high Turrets, hourly Sutors come:
The East with Incense, and the West with Gold,
Will stand, like Suppliants, to receive her doom.

298

The silver *Thames*, her own domestick Floud,
Shall bear her Vessels, like a sweeping Train;
And often wind (as of his Mistress proud)
With longing eyes to meet her face again.

299

The wealthy *Tagus*, and the wealthier *Rhine*,
The glory of their Towns no more shall boast:
And *Sein*, That would with *Belgian* Rivers joyn,
Shall find her lustre stain'd, and Traffick lost.

300

The vent'rous Merchant, who design'd more far,
And touches on our hospitable shore:
Charm'd with the splendour of this Northern Star,
Shall here unlade him, and depart no more. . . .

304

Thus to the Eastern wealth through storms we go;
But now, the Cape once doubled, fear no more:
A constant Trade-wind will securely blow,
And gently lay us on the Spicy shore.

(1185–1200; 1213–16)

The real occasion of the poem proved to be less the year of wonders than Dryden's attaining a conception of England's future earned in present effort and trial. In the almost contemporary *Essay of Dramatic Poesy*, the patriotic discussion of English and other dramatic traditions begins with the thought (and shortly the sounds) of naval warfare:

> It was that memorable day, in the first Summer of the late War, when our Navy ingag'd the *Dutch*: a day wherein the two most mighty and best appointed Fleets which any age had ever seen, disputed the command of the greater half of the Globe, the commerce of Nations, and the riches of the Universe.[7]

Here, too, Dryden has grasped England's imperial destiny, along with its imperialist cost, the defeat of Holland. And here, too, the naval war provides but one incident in a larger historical concern, dramatic art from ancient to present periods or "ages." The concept of historical periods of literature emerges here for the first time in English criticism, along with a sense of historical movement or development—and of

[7] California edition, XVII (1971), 8.

a period of literature as something related to the other events of the time. In Dryden's sense, the *Essay* on drama gives us heroic criticism.

Dryden's heroic idea dominates his best known poetry, and his conception of historical periods and their implications dominates conceptions of literature since. He had used the word "age" six times merely in opposition to "youth" in his early poetry. The seventh time was significantly enough the poem celebrating the meaning of the Restoration of Charles II, *Astraea Redux,* which concludes in address to the King:

> Oh Happy Age! Oh times like those alone
> By Fate reserv'd for Great *Augustus* Throne!
> When the joint growth of Armes and Arts forshew
> The World a Monarch, and that Monarch *You.*
>
> (320–23)

Here as later in *Annus Mirabilis* and in *An Essay of Dramatic Poesy* the heroic idea governs the actions and meanings of history. Poetry and the other arts play central roles in the new *imperium,* for the epic requires "the joint growth of Armes and Arts." The same spirit animates the Epilogue to *The Second Part of the Conquest of Granada,* in which Dryden declares that his age has improved upon the language of the Elizabethan playwrights. In the "Defence of the Epilogue," he professes to "no other ambition in this essay than that poetry may not go backward, when all other arts and sciences are advancing."[8] Like Milton and the Puritans, Dryden had a sense of his own age as one appointed for mighty achievements.

Most of Dryden's nondramatic poetry entails the heroic conception of history on an axis centering in Dryden's own day. His profoundly conservative temperament matches with

[8] Watson, I, 169. Watson prints the Epilogue on the preceding two pages.

an unusually liberal counterpart of faith in human potential and in progress. He ridiculed those who falsely thought themselves part of the heroic scheme. He castigated the evil ones seeking self-interest. And he praised those who deserved to be thought immortal for their achievements. Now no one could say that his choices coincided with those of all his contemporaries, but his verdict on Elkanah Settle or Thomas Shadwell and his different verdict on Thomas Southerne and on William Congreve resemble our own. If Shaftesbury was a great politician, and he was, that fact was as well concealed from the England of the Protectorate as from the England of Charles II. Dryden could praise the Ormonde family with clear conscience, and he could join his poetry to the valor of old Barzillai's son, for the Duke of Ormonde

> well the noblest Objects knew to choose,
> The Fighting Warriour, and Recording Muse.[9]

Reviewing the career of his honored kinsman, John Driden of Chesterton, the poet joined their achievements in a double triumph at the close of the poem:

> Two of a House, few Ages can afford;
> One to perform, another to record.
> Praise-worthy Actions are by thee embrac'd;
> And 'tis my Praise, to make thy Praises last.
> For ev'n when Death dissolves our Humane Frame,
> The Soul returns to Heav'n, whence it came;
> Earth keeps the Body, Verse preserves the Fame.[10]

In "Alexander's Feast" Dryden goes yet farther, showing that the bard Timotheus manipulates the world's greatest military figure. Or again, following good iconographical tradition, in "A Song for St. Cecilia's Day," God at the beginning, and the angels at the end, are presented as musicians. It was faith

[9] *Absalom and Achitophel*, 827–28.
[10] *To My Honour'd Kinsman, John Driden of Chesterton*, 203–209.

in his art that gave Dryden faith in his heroic conception of his own age, just as the lack of faith in both so darkens the world of *Hudibras*. And Dryden was right. The epic of his lifetime made possible the georgic of the next century. Historically authentic in spirit, Dryden's poetry in turn authenticates history by rendering it heroic. This is that "great idea" necessary to give any vision the title of epic.[11]

Dryden's conception that London in his time was an epic place at a heroic hour of course reminds us of Milton's vision in *Areopagitica* and other prose passages. When *Paradise Lost* appeared, Milton showed that the whole of time and history was required, "And ever best found in the close." To Dryden, Homer and Virgil could be translated in more than one sense into the palace of English poetry, not needing to stoop as had Aeneas in entering Evander's dwelling, because

> Our *English* Palace opens wide in state;
> And without stooping they may pass the Gate.[12]

He is reported to have said on reading *Paradise Lost*: "This man cuts us all out, and the ancients, too." Which says the same thing in another way. The opening lines of *To My Dear Friend Mr. Congreve* say it in yet another:

> Well then; the promis'd hour is come at last;
> The present Age of Wit obscures the past:
> Strong were our Syres; and as they Fought they Writ,
> Conqu'ring with force of Arms, and dint of Wit . . .

Again, if but in metaphor, the heroic combination of arms and wit sanctions the ideal. Again, Dryden understands that "The present Age" provides the definition—our day, our lives, our times. And with faith in his own powers to recog-

[11] By way of parallel, see the excellent essay by Sheldon Wolin, "Hobbes and the Epic Tradition of Political Theory" (Los Angeles, 1970; a Clark Library booklet); also note 6, above.

[12] *To the Earl of Roscomon*, 77–78.

nize the classic, immortal achievement in his own time, Dryden praises the younger Congreve as he had the older Milton. With such individuals and their devoted effort, we have epic triumph, heroic achievement. I know of no poet so rich in hope for so much in his own day, of no poet to whom history as present epic so mattered.

The poetic implications of Dryden's affirmative vision of history as present epic are profound for our understanding of his peculiar genius for narrative. Of narrative pure or proper there is astonishingly little, except in *Annus Mirabilis*, the *Aeneis*, and *Fables*. On the other hand, narrative emphasis appears anywhere—in songs for plays, for example, or in a prologue:

> After a four Months Fast we hope at length
> Your queasie Stomachs have recover'd strength
> That You can taste a Play (your old coarse Messe)
> As honest and as plain as an Address.[13]

By the same token, however, one must search with difficulty to find grounds to term longer poems proper narratives. I believe that every reader of *Mac Flecknoe*, *Absalom and Achitophel*, and *The Hind and the Panther* feels doubt on this score. We feel that we lack justification to call such poems narratives when they offer little in the way of plot, and yet the poems insist on behaving as if they were narratives none the less.

Such a response seems to me obviously right and inescapable. In the poems mentioned, it will be found repeatedly that the most "natural" narrative (plot, or a "story") will come at a point where it would usually be forgiven for laps-

[13] Prologue to Lee's *Mithidrates*, revived in 1681, lines 1–4. The revival coincided with the late stage of the Popish Plot: "an address" was a loyal or Tory paper presented to the king. "Seditious," or Whig, papers were termed "petitions."

ing: in a digression, in a set speech (which in the Thucydidean model alternates with, rather than includes, action), in a lyric section, or in a description. The "natural" narrative of *The Hind and the Panther* can be put into a few dozen words of précis. Not very much more space would be required, however, for a précis of *Paradise Regained.* Narrative achieves significance in large measure by counter-narrative means harmonized to a "story" in such ways as to modify the natural narrative. *Annus Mirabilis* and *Fables,* not to mention Dryden's plays, show that he could enjoy creating plots. But most of his poems make much more of the significance of his heroic idea than they do of a story of epic action. In many of his best known poems Dryden solves the problem of deriving significance from narrative movement that so troubled earlier poets by very nearly taking away altogether that most obvious symptom of narrative, a plot or a story. The fact of the absence, on the whole, of sustained, detailed natural narrative must be stressed at the outset. It is that which first strikes us.

Yet we are also struck in reading by there being some kind of narrative *presumption* made by a poem like *Mac Flecknoe.* We feel that the natural narrative itself exists as a slim, subordinate element in the poem, but also that it seems to be at once assisted by, and thwarted by, something much larger and more central to the whole poetic experience. Leaving lesser matters again out of consideration, the larger presumption seems to me to be nothing else than Dryden's great idea in satiric inversion. From Augustus to anti-Augustus in Flecknoe, from Aeneas to anti-Ascanius in Shadwell, from John the Baptist to Flecknoe, from Christ to anti-Christ in Shadwell, from Jonson to anti-Jonson in both Flecknoes—and so the whole scheme of heroic conception and epic hope seems to have gone hideously awry, except that the poet and we can retransform, set the world on its feet again. That ideal action engaged in by the poet and the reader is made possible by the small natural narrative, but in some sense runs counter to the poem's actual plot. We seem to lack associations in English for the implications of Dryden's "idea." He was clearly aware of the Greek sense of εἶδος, which may mean not only "idea" but "design" or "pattern" as well;[14] and like everyone else in the century he was aware of the Platonic conception of the ἰδέα, or ideal form. Dryden's heroic idea was such an ideal form to be embodied in a narrative, or to give a poem a narrative presumption; and his historical, temporal, chronological bent as well as his use of analogies (Ascanius, Shadwell) gave his idea a patterning that also had quasi-narrative status. More simply put, his informing heroic idea gave him an ideal narrative of human events that provides the narrative presumption of poems as different as *Mac Flecknoe* and *The Medall, Absalom and Achitophel* and *The Hind and the Panther*. Such a meta-narrative, however, has as its main role the life of the idea, and as *Religio Laici* shows, it can also drive the poem so far toward realization of thought that narrative is wholly excluded in the large and is re-admitted only in the part.

The provision of narrative in the part (for example, the account of the growth of obscurantism in Roman Catholicism in *Religio Laici*, 370–97) is symptomatic both of Dryden's basic narrative affiliations and also of the way in which expression of his heroic idea takes both counter-narrative and narrative forms. But perhaps the point is more evident in poems where narrative is not to be expected at all. Dryden's pindaric odes, for example, turn out to be more narrative in nature than *Religio Laici*. Anne Killigrew clearly represents for Dryden an ideal of the artist which transforms a minor but attractive painter and a small poet into what the ideal

[14] Epistle dedicatory to *Eleonora*, California edition, III (1969), 233; see also n. 22, below.

human potential must have. To do so, it must give her a history within history. The ode begins with a time before she was born, then her birth, and subsequently Mistress Killigrew is taken through her dual career, death, stellification, and on to the Day of Judgment. "The Grand Chorus" of "A Song for St. Cecilia's Day" in fact gives the world's whole narrative in nine lines:

As from the pow'r of sacred Lays
The Spheres began to move,
And sung the great Creator's praise
To all the bless'd above;
So when the last and dreadful hour
This crumbling Pageant shall devour,
The TRUMPET shall be heard on high,
The Dead shall live, the Living die,
And MUSICK shall untune the Sky. (55–63)

Such remarkable narrative pressure does not exclude lyricism but only defines its emphasis. It is difficult to say why that metanarrative expression of the heroic idea should emerge so much more explicitly as natural narrative in lyric than in more discursive poems, satire, and forms of heroic poetry itself, but it does appear that the reason is that it has in an ode no natural narrative to which it might adapt itself.

As we have been seeing all along, Dryden's idea addresses itself to a heroically conceived present (or recent past). The presence of the present order of time is as intense in his public poetry as it is in Donne's private. Dryden differs from Donne in using that present so consistently as the axis for past and future: with a sequence between. Even in *Eleonora,* where he, like Donne, deals with the *idea* of a woman in a Neoplatonic sense, he emphasizes time, generations, and heroic analogues. Examples as different as *Mac Flecknoe, Religio Laici,* the Anne Killigrew Ode, and *Eleonora* emphasize how variously Dryden proceeded in the encounter with his present world. They also show, however, how consistently the variety expresses his conception of the high destiny of human individuals and the age in which they lived. We have, then, in these poems sometimes an element of what I have termed natural narrative, story or plot, and sometimes not. But until late in his career we always have that great idea clearly expressing itself either as a form of signifying counter-narrative or as a narrative force in poetic forms not requiring narrative. Such an unusual combination of literary elements is the one we all have encountered in Dryden. It can only be said that an ordinary narrative in his poems is assisted or fought against insofar as it might express that which is most important to the poet, what I have been terming his heroic idea. Since that is most important to him, it is also so to us. After getting to know Dryden, we share the sense that one's own day may be meaningful. It is no accident that he taught people whose language is English to think of the present and of other "ages."

Such features as have been discussed provide as it were the radical, characteristic elements of much of Dryden's finest poetry. They do not provide all, however, and in Dryden's poems of the early Restoration, few if any of which achieve total success, we can discover how he gradually appropriated certain means that would later come together as a creative whole. The last four lines of *Astraea Redux* are worth another glance:

> Oh Happy Age! Oh times like those alone
> By Fate reserv'd for Great *Augustus* Throne!
> When the joint growth of Armes and Arts foreshew
> The World a Monarch, and that Monarch *You*.
>
> (320–23)

Something there is not yet right. The *Heroique Stanzas* on Cromwell had done much better in realizing a great man and what he stood for. Dryden here seems to have donned a toga and turned orator. The first line quoted seems almost to turn into Latin: "O album saeculum, O tempora . . . ."[15] Dryden summons, but his world has not yet come. Recognizing that, we can consider what he ambitiously seeks. The conclusion and the very title show that Dryden seeks enlargement of the present by other ages and values. The title resounds with royalist legends of strong government under that earlier Astraea, Elizabeth I, as well of the new golden age and return of the goddess of justice that Virgil forecast in his Pollio eclogue (IV). The last four lines harmonize with that conception, like all else in the poem, but they do not bring it into being. Everything is there but the animating principle itself. *Astraea Redux* adds as it were the classical inheritance to Dryden's store. But a poem must also give readers with little Latin and no Greek, and the learned as well, the sound of a music that carries words of whatever kind, a general harmony that sings the meaning and tells us that it belongs to Dryden and to us.

Dryden's next poem, "To His Sacred Majesty," likewise seeks to increase the poetic range, to make the total harmony more encompassing. Again the result seems to me both interesting and deficient. The element that now enters Dryden's poetry fully for the first time holds profound import for his understanding of man:

> In that wild Deluge where the World was drownd,
> When life and sin one common tombe had found,
> The first small prospect of a rising hill
> With various notes of Joy the Ark did fill. (1–4)

The key words show how different a scheme of historical and evaluative reference has been invoked: "drownd . . . life and

[15] Cf. the earlier lines (292–93): "And now times whiter Series is begun / Which in soft Centuries shall smoothly run."

sin . . . tombe . . . prospect . . . rising . . . notes of Joy the Ark." Henceforth the Christian conception would control the terms on which other elements could enter to make their claims, and since Dryden believed that his was a revealed religion, the Book provided him with much of a narrative nature as well. The first four lines here do possess an advantage lacking in the last four of *Astraea Redux*: syntactically, intellectually, stylistically they move in a narrative fashion.

The passages from these two early poems suggest something more about Dryden's use of the present. Again and again that present is located in a context of threat, loss, death, confusion, revolution, or madness. That context relates to an individual, an institution, an art, or a civilization. And out of that threat Dryden brings free the present to recovery, life, meaning, restoration, and triumph. Perhaps such a triumphant conception of the present (or near future) is merely the realized aspect of his heroic treatment of the present (or near past). But its centrality to his idea of life can be best understood by reference to his plays. In them, we find little of that present so crucial to most of his nondramatic poetry. But we do find in most of his comic plots an impulse to folly, license, and sin that in the end receives a kind of social redemption, a putting to rights by reintegration of individuals with their customary world. His heroic plays, tragicomedies, and tragedies show threat and subsequent triumph as the plot works itself out. It is very telling that the central figure in such "serious" (comedy merits the word, too) plays normally is a king. Whether the king is restored by having a good prince like Aureng-Zebe attain rule, or whether like Antony in *All for Love* the prince loses half of mankind to rule with Cleopatra the other half, the restoration or triumph proves central to the experience.

If there is any one human need satisfied by such a recurrent motif, it is the need for hope. That such is Dryden's motive rather than any purely conservative desire to see things return to the way they were can be shown very clearly by Dryden's rejection of the materialism of Lucretius in the Preface to *Sylvae*:

> I think a future state demonstrable even by natural Arguments; at least to take away rewards and punishments, is only a pleasing prospect to a Man, who resolves before hand not to live morally. But on the other side, the thought of being nothing after death is a burden unsupportable to a vertuous Man, even though a Heathen. We naturally aim at happiness, and cannot bear to have it confin'd to the shortness of our present Being, especially when we consider that vertue is generally unhappy in this World, and vice fortunate. So that 'tis hope of Futurity alone, that makes this Life tolerable, in expectation of a better. Who wou'd not commit all the excesses to which he is prompted by his natural inclinations, if he may do them with security while he is alive, and be uncapable of punishment after he is dead? If he be cunning and secret enough to avoid the Laws, there is no band of morality to restrain him: For Fame and Reputation are weak ties; many men have not the least sence of them: Powerful men are only aw'd by them, as they conduce to their interest, and that not always when a passion is predominant; and no Man will be contain'd within the bounds of duty, when he may safely transgress them. These are my thoughts abstractedly, and without entring into the Notions of our Christian Faith, which is the proper business of Divines.[16]

The need for hope does not distinguish Dryden from other people or other writers. It is his growing ability to expose

[16] California edition, III, 11.

that need to hazard and to redeem it with triumph that matters. That is what distinguishes, say, *Absalom and Achitophel* from the two poems just considered. But it also distinguishes *Annus Mirabilis* and provides the end, or the purpose, toward which his major lyrics and *The Hind and the Panther* aspire. "Well then; the promis'd hour is come at last. . . ." So the poem to Congreve begins, offering great hope. And it begins in the present. But like hope itself, Dryden's heroic idea cannot exist outside a present that possesses a past from which it derives and a future toward which it aspires. For this reason also, his heroic conception carries with it a metanarrative energy.

Dr. Johnson admired *Annus Mirabilis* in spite of its unevenness, but had a complaint against what might be termed the contranarrative tendencies of the poem: "The general fault is that he affords more sentiment than description, and does not so much impress scenes upon the fancy as deduce consequences and make comparisons." [17] That characteristic puts into another set of terms the complaint Johnson had with *Hudibras* or even his praise of Richardson, that although a man reading him for the story would hang himself, one should read for the sentiments, or thoughts. In fact almost all narratives, at least poetic narratives, after a certain stage in the development of a culture, find natural or simple narrative deficient in meaning, and the finest seventeenth-century narrative is distinguished by its preoccupation with speech, dialogue. Sir Francis Kynaston showed with his *Leoline and Sydanis* that he could tell an absorbing but superficial story, and after the Glorious Revolution Sir Richard Blackmore turned out narratives as organ-grinders do tunes. In a fundamental sense those stories are meaningless. It is Milton's great praise that by his extraordinary renovation of the *Aeneid*-form he could make the very plot of *Paradise Lost*

[17] Johnson, ed. Hill, I, 431.

meaningful to himself and us. Dryden could not make that last reach, nor has anyone else. But he certainly could "deduce consequences and make comparisons," for as we have seen his poetic "language" is distinguished by its perpetual assimilation of likenesses as well as by its celerity.

The ending of *Astraea Redux* discovers that Charles II is the new Augustus Caesar, and the beginning of "To His Sacred Majesty" that Charles is the new Noah. In one case England becomes the new empire, in the other a covenanted people. In one case the poet is a new Virgil, in the other a prophet and priest. Such "comparisons" do not interfere with narrative at the beginning or the end of the poem, and sometimes they do not interfere with the plot. For example, the simile in the following quatrain from *Annus Mirabilis* may give no real assistance to the plot as such, but it also does not threaten the action:

> The chearful Souldiers, with new stores suppli'd,
> Now long to execute their spleenful will;
> And, in revenge for those three days they tri'd,
> Wish one, like *Joshuah*'s when the Sun stood still.
> (469–72)

We feel the movement continue and find the "comparison" made part of the action. Sometimes, however, as the same poem shows, the plot suffers, as in this account of the new warship, *The Loyal London*, going grandly to sea:

> The goodly *London* in her gallant trim,
> (The *Phoenix* daughter of the vanish'd old:)
> Like a rich Bride does to the Ocean swim,
> And on her shadow rides in floating gold.
> (601–604)

The image of a rich bride swimming down the Thames to sea is Metaphysical and bizarre, although we shall come to see in a moment what Dryden is up to. Clearly Dryden is *not* getting the *London* into the Channel.

If what I have been saying about Dryden's heroic idea is right, we should be able to relate the *London* to it and to that metanarrative tendency that has been discussed. *London* was the name of a series of ships (all of which ended disastrously), the one previous to Dryden's having blown up in a fire two years before. That helps explain the Phoenix image, and it certainly relates to the City of London and that fire which Dryden will be narrating subsequently. The other associations of richness, gold, and wedding had entered the poem at an early stage. The king had resolved "t'assert the watry Ball" or rule the sea (53). A bit later we read:

> But since it was decreed, Auspicious King,
>   In *Britain*'s right that thou should'st wed the Main,
> Heav'n, as a gage, would cast some precious thing
>   And therefore doom'd that *Lawson* should be slain.
>
> (77–80)

We can see that here the actual narrative is greatly assisted and heightened by the metanarrative that gathers into itself and the narrative proper the later bride simile about the *London*. At the earlier stage, we have sea, King, wedding, precious thing, sacrifice. In the subsequent interlude in the war, subtitled in part "His Majesty Repairs the Fleet" (stanzas 142–54), there appears the passage on the *London*. That adds the Phoenix and her restoration as well as gold. Lawson has symbolically revived, and the City of London has returned the King's love by offering itself, the *London*, to its "best-lov'd King" (614).

To render a lengthy process short, the triumph of the poem begins of course in the fire that will enable the City as well as the ship named the *London* to rise like a Phoenix:

Yet, *London*, Empress of the Northern Clime,
By an high fate thou greatly didst expire;
Great as the worlds, which at the death of time
Must fall, and rise a nobler frame by fire.
(845–49)

The City, now an empress, as befits the wife of a king, endured the fate of the Phoenix and enjoys her rebirth by a transformation into something finer. Or so she will, after the "King's Prayer" saves her (1045 ff.) and she asks him not to leave her (1149 ff.).The transformation also entails an alchemy that suits the image of royal gold as well as fire:

Me-thinks already, from this Chymick flame,
I see a City of more precious mold:
Rich as the Town which gives the *Indies* name,
With silver pav'd, and all divine with Gold.[18]

Before, Dryden adds, "she like some Shepherdess did show,/ Who sate to bathe her by a River's side" (1181–82), so recalling for us the swimming bride, who is now herself transformed into that Maiden Queen of the concluding passage previously quoted. Dryden's great idea issues here, as so often, in prophecy. The Queen who is wooed, London, the Queen of Gold, the Queen of the Main, will fulfill her high destiny, the love of the King; she will fulfill Dryden's heroic idea. The poet we know to be conservative has provided the century and us with the first glorification—not of the Court alone or the Country—but that third region, the City; and, in peace, Hobbes, its version is the heroic. The intrusion into narrative in *Annus Mirabilis* hardly compares with the fuller intrusion in *The Hind and the Panther*. But the early poem

[18] Lines 1169–72. The alchemical emphasis of the poem has been well discussed by Bruce A. Rosenberg, "*Annus Mirabilis* Distilled," *Publications of the Modern Language Association of America*, LXXIX (June, 1964), 254–58.

shows that the metanarrative takes on its own sequence as well as enriching the narrative sequence. Because it is unquestionably a narrative poem, *Annus Mirabilis* is the more useful to make such points.

The precise relation between such elements in Dryden's poetry has proved difficult to define. Dr. Johnson was unquestionably the first to try, with his "comparisons." T. S. Eliot muddled things by remarking that Dryden's was a poetry of statement (however immense), and only in recent years have critics been able to return to Johnson's insight by investigating what has been variously termed imagery, analogy, and metaphor.[19] "There is, in other words, a kind of action in the imagery. . . ."[20] Such is one valuable formulation, and since *Absalom and Achitophel* relies on a relation between two historical orders, we certainly find the explanation illuminating. Since "a kind of action in the imagery" occurs in poems by Donne and Milton as well, we require some means of discriminating what is distinctive about Dryden's "action." I think it fair to conclude that Dryden's "action" differs in that it originates in his heroic idea. It also differs from Donne's in seeking a narrative context and in taking form in public poetry. It differs also from Milton's by the creation of a metanarrative that counters as well as assists the natural narrative of a given poem, sometimes to the point of excluding narrative from the whole and allowing it only in the part, or of entering and enriching lyric pieces.

For Dryden to call Charles II Augustus, Noah, or David is itself no wondrous thing. But to do so as part of a conception of the dignity of man is another. So also is looking

[19] The three terms have been respectively favored by Arthur W. Hoffman, *John Dryden's Imagery* (Gainesville, Fla., 1962); by Alan Roper, *Dryden's Poetic Kingdoms* (London, 1965); and by myself, *Dryden's Poetry* (Bloomington and London, 1967).

[20] Hoffman, p. 46.

upon one's age and its actions so constantly, so characteristically, as if present reality holds such hope when it can be understood by past and future realities. In any instance action or non-action, image or idea, may seem to exercise claim as the best representative of Dryden's heroic idea. Experienced readers of Dryden will recognize that his poetry offers a dynamic configuration of experience. It is dynamic because it is so constantly on the move in both narrative and metanarrative ways; it possesses a configuration because figurative elements are formed into a whole; and it recreates experience because Dryden is concerned with a vision of life, not merely with "comparisons."

ii. Configuring the Whole

Reading Dryden's nondramatic poems clearly proves that he created whole experiences, not leaving us with incomplete works, trailed-off endings, or such studied squandering of means as in *Hudibras*. Reading also shows that the kind of wholeness we discover in his poems differs from Milton's. After all the complexity, discrimination, and resemblance, Milton's poetry seems to have clarified all, to have become one, and in that sense impresses us as something powerfully simple or pure. Dryden does not reach that degree of purity, such as one also finds in Homer and Dante. If in Milton we find it impossible and unnecessary to distinguish between reality and myth, in *Absalom and Achitophel* one must understand two histories and their relations.

One thing in Dryden perpetually suggests another like it, may dissolve into it, and then emerge as itself or as something else quite different. Given his royalism, Dryden much favors using the figure of the king, kingship, succession, royalty, coronation, restoration, fatherhood, vice-gerency under God, emblems of the king, and exemplary princes. The individual details enter, reenter, relate, and are distinguished in innumerable ways; however, seemingly very numerous and dispersed elements fit into a predication governed less by the narrative or other procedure than by the heroic idea. *Mac Flecknoe* and *To . . . Congreve* are astonishingly alike in dealing with drama, with king figures, with succession, with father and son artists, and with some of the same allusions. Here is Flecknoe:

> The hoary Prince in Majesty appear'd,
> High on a Throne of his own Labours rear'd.
> (106–107)

That obviously is picked up as a "High on a Throne" trope by Dryden out of the opening of *Paradise Lost*, Book II, describing Satan. Given Dryden's belief that panegyric and satiric topics can both take a likeness of nature and remain true, it is no wonder that years later he should prophesy of Congreve's success in the same terms:

> Yet this I Prophesy; Thou shalt be seen,
> (Tho' with some short Parenthesis between:)
> High on the Throne of Wit. (51–53)

(Recognizing the principle, Pope satirically reversed the trope again at the beginning of the second book of the *Dunciad.*)

The single trope tends to relate with others, and both in *Mac Flecknoe* and *To . . . Congreve*, we discover that the kingly detail and the images of art fall into relation with each other, producing what has been finely termed "Dryden's Poetic Kingdoms."[21] Any age tends to identify to some extent its systems of values. Nationalism may be related to agrarianism, capitalism, or socialism. That relatedness of values becomes to Dryden a systematic way of making his poems whole. The images of value cohere in themselves and

[21] By Roper as the title of his book; see note 19, above.

relate to each other. Because Dryden believed so deeply in art and in monarchy, the relation of the two carried full conviction in his time and does still today. But it would not have carried conviction for an anti-monarchist like Milton or for a poet with a mind as divided as Marvell's. On the other hand, an earlier royalist, Thomas Carew, could anticipate Dryden in the epitaph concluding *An Elegie . . . upon Dr. John Donne.* I shall quote all four lines (changing to Roman letters):

> Here lies a King, that rul'd as hee thought fit
> The universall Monarchy of wit;
> Here lie two Flamens, and both those, the best,
> Apollo's first, at last, the true Gods Priest.
>
> (95–98)

Poetry and wit are honored by becoming a kingdom. The "kingdom of letters" also implies its complement, the art of kingship ("rul'd as hee thought fit," a true Stuart absolute monarch). And Carew's kingdom of letters yields at the end to another system of values, religion, giving us a religion of letters. Dryden does the same in *Mac Flecknoe.* Flecknoe prepares the anointing oil for his successor, playing the role both of Samuel the priest and Saul the king:

> The King himself the sacred Unction made,
> As King by Office, and as Priest by Trade.
>
> (118–19)

Dryden differs from Carew in moving beyond the use of superior values (monarchy, religion) for lesser ("wit") to the interchangeability of values. Flecknoe now offers his successor the regalia:

> *Love's Kingdom* to his right he did convey,
> At once his Sceptre and his rule of Sway;

Whose righteous Lore the Prince had practis'd young,
And from whose Loyns recorded *Psyche* sprung.

(122–25).

The passage is not as obvious as may seem. Shadwell's opera, *Psyche,* is "recorded" both in the sense of having been "musically rendered" and "preserved in writing" (*Oxford English Dictionary*). That Psyche or soul came from the "Loyns" of *Love's Kingdom,* a play by Flecknoe. Since "Loyns" was pronounced like "lines," the literary descent works as well as the physical in the ambiguity of "Love's Kingdom." Sexual activity or practice of "Love's Kingdom" is in this context "righteous." Unhappily for those hasty Freudians who have recently discovered Dryden, the sceptre (a book) is not a phallic symbol, if anything a female symbol, but also part of the regalia, a Bible for the depraved, and a play, *Love's Kingdom.* In such fashion, Dryden's schemes of value relate and exchange functions: who could say finally what are the vehicles and what the tenors of the images here? The point really comes down to Dryden's values supporting each other by taking each other's roles.

Mac Flecknoe primarily concerns art, but the publisher, or whoever it was who supplied the subtitle for the surreptitious first edition, certainly understood what was going on; it was, he said, a satire on the true-blue Protestant Poet, Shadwell. The poem is about poetry (and other arts), particularly drama, but Dryden does not write of poetry in the abstract. There are particular plays produced in his own time, and the tinsel-and-cardboard romance of the poem is set in that present. Moreover, one can only understand the sense in which Shadwell is bad by attention not just to the good, but to the good in politics and religion as well as in art:

Heywood and *Shirley* were but Types of thee,
Thou last great Prophet of Tautology:

Even I, a dunce of more renown than they,
Was sent before but to prepare thy way.

(29–32)

Flecknoe ("I") compares Shadwell (or Mac Flecknoe) to Christ (the "last great Prophet"), the fulfillment or antitype of such earlier types as Thomas Heywood and John Shirley. Shadwell can be termed the last prophet because he will fulfill the promises, and because he is the Messiah announced by Flecknoe as John the Baptist. A believing Christian cannot introduce references of this kind without expecting that they will take over what they are aligned with (literature) and totally evaluate it. Which is of course Dryden's aim: Flecknoe and Shadwell are respectively anti-Baptists and anti-Christs of wit.

Dryden's well known poems of the 1680's offer a number of variations on the technique of *Mac Flecknoe*. *Absalom and Achitophel* runs two histories, divine and present, concurrently and although anyone can see some discrepancies between the two, for the good reason that Dryden wishes us to do so, the relation or allegory between them is not merely closed more tightly than in any other English poem one can think of, but each also means the other. The King is David and Charles—and God, because David was a type of Christ, and Charles is treated as the same retrospectively, especially by virtue of his mercy. But as kings, David and Charles are vicegerents of God the Father, the role that the "king" of the poem comes more and more to fill in both segments of the histories Dryden deals with.

Dryden's one angry poem, *The Medall*, uses his normal comparisons of religion, monarchy, art, and creativity, but in a way putting the synthesis of *Mac Flecknoe* into extreme tension. So angry is Dryden, or so angry he pretends to be, that the resemblance of his value systems, which is his great source of confidence and strength, undergoes the trial of having their terms constantly set at the greatest possible distance from each other. Anyone so *artful* as the "Chief" (Shaftesbury) puts art in bad repute, and so the poem has as its examples of art a counterfeit coin and a bagpipe. Similarly, the irreligion of the villain makes true religion seem almost impossible. Creativity becomes venereal disease, monarchy Shaftesbury's absurd ambition to be elected King of Poland—as if, in Dryden's view, a true king could possibly be elected. The last five lines suddenly veer into optimism in a prophecy using the past prophetic tense:

> Thus inborn Broyles the Factions wou'd ingage;
> Or Wars of Exil'd Heirs, or Foreign Rage,
> Till halting Vengeance overtook our Age:
> And our wild Labours, wearied into Rest,
> Reclin'd us on a rightfull Monarch's Breast.
>
> (318–22)

That convinces one reader as Dryden's view of what had happened between 1642 and 1660, but not that he believed—in the context of this poem—that it was shortly to happen again.

It is possible to argue that in *The Medall* Dryden strikes a more anxious pose than represents his true feelings, and that he does so to warn his countrymen against a dangerous but remote possibility of civil war. Here is the central ironic passage on the treatment by England of the two Charleses:

> Crowds err not, though to both extremes they run;
> To kill the Father, and recall the Son.
> Some think the Fools were most, as times went then;
> But now the World's o'r stock'd with prudent men.
> The common Cry is ev'n Religion's Test;
> The *Turk*'s is, at *Constantinople*, best;

Idols in *India*, Popery at *Rome*;
And our own Worship onely true at home.

(99–106)

The prospect of civil war and of a religion's being untrue seem to me too fearsome for John Dryden to wish to risk. For much of the poem he cannot leave the subject alone, although today the Exclusion Crisis could certainly be talked about without reference to the Civil Wars, divine Providence, and the nature of man, the subjects of the following passage:

God try'd us once; our Rebel-fathers fought,
He glutted 'em with all the pow'r they sought:
Till, master'd by their own usurping Brave,
The free-born Subject sunk into a Slave.
We loath our Manna, and we long for Quails;
Ah, what is man, when his own wish prevails!
How rash, how swift to plunge himself in ill;
Proud of his Pow'r, and boundless in his Will!

(127–34)

I think that Dryden the monarchist is shaken, and that his prophecy of all coming right at the end is not much more than wishful thinking. I believe this from reading the poem and from some circumstantial evidence.

His next major piece, *Religio Laici*, is a religious confession. Once one set of values, monarchy, had been so sorely tried, it was inevitable that the other values exchangeable with it in his scheme should also come into question. Although Dryden would detest the characterization, *Religio Laici* is a Trimmer's poem, cool, accommodating, but principled in holding to what the confessor thinks is the middle way, and even inclined to think that the virtuous heathen will be saved. (Cf. *The Medall*, 91–98, and *Religio Laici*, 206–11, opposing Socrates and the crowd.) So much does Dryden seem to shrink from his usual exuberance and vision that he simply drops two of his systems of value, monarchy and art, in making up *Religio Laici*. More strikingly still, they disappear not only as values but also as images, leaving the poem almost completely a Lucretian discourse by its end. Yet more strikingly still, Dryden's great idea seems to have been put away for safe keeping. Far from having any great hopes for man in the world ("Ah, what is man!"), it will be enough for now to survive, turn inward, and get the one essential thing right:

> For *MY* Salvation must its Doom receive
> Not from what *OTHERS*, but what *I* believe.
> (303-304)

So bare a statement testifies indirectly and negatively to the importance of narrative in Dryden's poetry. The shock to his political values not only excluded for 1682 the interrelation of his central values but also led him to drop imagery and to abandon narrative almost completely, and metanarrative altogether. There is no reason *a priori* that *Religio Laici* should be any different from what it is. But the absence of characteristics central to his poetry before and afterwards testifies to the fact that *Religio Laici* reflects, as does *The Medall* more explicitly, a time of crisis that can be spoken of in terms of Dryden's political and religious beliefs, in terms of his straining the imagery of *The Medall* and losing it in *Religio Laici*, and in terms of his loss of narrative power. Dryden seems to pause and think. And yet the cool temper and basic generosity of *Religio Laici* seem so much healthier than the disturbance and anger of *The Medall*. It is as though the crisis has just been weathered. And I believe that there is a major symptom of that also: Dryden has written a poem. He might not have written a poem. He might have written simply in prose and let it go at that. Indeed the Preface to *Religio Laici* covers exactly the same points as the poem. When all has been said about what is missing in *Religio Laici*, one must reserve poetry, the poet, and control. Cast in on himself for belief, Dryden had, as he was to have to the end of his life, the resources of the poet.

By 1684, Dryden had recovered composure, and his system of values again seemed secure, if altered by the challenge. They are back in good form in the poem to Roscommon and the poem on Oldham. The former begins with a progress piece of poetry treated in terms of nations and concludes with the palace of the best kingdom, English poetry. The poem to Oldham treats art and the artist's life as an epic, and as in *Mac Flecknoe* and the poem to Congreve, the problem is that of succession in the kingdom of letters. Narrative on a larger scale than a progress piece or allusion to Virgil awaited the second Dryden-Tonson miscellany, *Sylvae,* in 1685, in which Dryden's excerpts from Lucretius make a coherent story not intended by the great Epicurean poet. About the same time, Dryden's first two English "pindaric" odes, *Threnodia Augustalis* and the Anne Killigrew Ode, show that Dryden is in fact wholly recovered. The Anne Killigrew Ode is no less a celebration of the poetic art and the poet than it is a narration of the career of one exemplar.

Before undertaking to discuss *The Hind and the Panther,* Dryden's longest poem not a translation, and his most difficult, it seems advisable to consider means of achieving configuration in his poetry, means distinct from, but not unrelated to, those features we have been considering. Some things are marginal, others essential. Dryden's use of emblems, for example, proves to be of something less than crucial importance, not because he fails to use them but because they are subservient to the three recurrent values of his mid-career: religion, monarchy, and art. Other emblems, such as the circle or sphere for perfection, can easily be found in his work, but they lack a temporal, historical dimension and hence do not really fit in with his kind of poetry as centrally as they do with that of many earlier poets. A somewhat more important procedure suffers from the same limitation. The kind of Neoplatonic typology previously distinguished [22] marks *Eleonora.* Its chief function in Dryden's poetry is rather to provide the basis for other procedures than to constitute a procedure itself. The presumption that the present, earthly, and mortal may be spoken of in terms of the timeless, celestial, and immortal, or eternal, certainly is central as a procedure of praise in *Eleonora.* Otherwise, however, it enables Dryden to work out his analogies, metaphors, and images. The characterization of Anne Killigrew may be said to draw upon the instantaneous character of Neoplatonic typology to represent the "Sacred Poets," just as at her birth the omens showed that she would have the eloquence of Plato. Clearly, Dryden expected no one to make him go on oath as to literal truth. He uses a figural method to relate two realities of great importance to him: a poet who was a good woman and the heroic idea of what a poet may be. Dryden almost always wishes to depict things historically, however, and so the Neoplatonic, instant shadowing of the supernal by the diurnal usually must adapt itself to some kind of historical and quasi-narrative scheme. One might say that the basis of his analogies rests on Neoplatonic typology adapted to secular as well as religious purpose, but that the function of the analogies necessarily entails history and a movement like that of narrative. Of course his last poems do not use such analogies, and we shall need to consider them as a subsequent development.

The configurative process of Dryden's poetry consists of a figuralism [23] involving not only typology, but also processes

[22] See above, n. 14; and see William G. Madsen, "Neoplatonic and Christian Symbols in *Paradise Lost*," ch. IV of *From Shadowy Types to Truth* (New Haven and London, 1968).

[23] On figuralism, see Erich Auerbach, *Mimesis* (Princeton, 1953). Among books dealing with writers treated in this volume there is Madsen's book, just mentioned. Barbara K. Lewalski canvasses the matter at

regulating or directing typology. Given the confusion that seems to exist as to the meaning of typology, however, and the dangers of being too doubtful or permissive in speaking of it, we may start with a few simple observations as introduction to Dryden's special uses. When the Christian Church took over the scriptures of the Jews as the Christian Old Testament, the prophecies, covenants, and much other Jewish lore were Christianized. David was a type of Christ, or Christ was the "antitype" or "ectype" (two ugly words), or the fulfillment of David. As Jewish scholars had interpreted Solomon's song as an expression of God's love for Israel, Christians read it as an expression of Christ's love for His Church. Such is the original basis and strict usage of typology.

Figuralism includes numerous other elements, however, and some of these came to be associated with typology. To take a major instance, the spiritual glosses and interpretations of the Bible (for example, the allegorical, moral, and anagogical) led to application of things in the Bible (or in ecclesiastical tradition) to the priesthood or individual believers in the present (moral glosses) and to the Church Triumphant in the future (anagogical glosses). Catholic and Protestant forms of figuralism differ from each other and within their own histories of development. But once "moral" applications are made, the strict sense of typology becomes greatly extended or distorted. In England, as we have seen, it becomes common to compare an important person to Christ, so reversing the central direction of time in strictly defined typology.[24]

---

length in *Milton's Brief Epic* (Providence, 1966). Stephen N. Zwicker has been the first to discuss very fully the typology of Dryden's secular poems: "The King and Christ: Figural Imagery in Dryden's Restoration Panegyrics," *Philological Quarterly*, L (1971), 582–98; and *Dryden's Political Poetry: The Typology of King and Nation* (Providence, 1972).

[24] See also Barbara K. Lewalski, "Donne's Poetry of Compliment," *Seventeenth-Century Imagery*, ed. Miner (Berkeley and Los Angeles, 1971), ch. III.

Moral edification may lead a poet or a preacher to show an individual as an example of someone whose faith and effort helped make him or her into some resemblance of Christ, offering us hope in our attempt at the *imitatio Christi.* That Virgin Queen, Elizabeth, knew the mentality of her Members of Parliament very well and so promised them to be a father to Israel. That means that they are Christian believers, the new Israel.

Such ideas were not new. The conception of a Christian congregation as Israel is beautifully set forth by the *Nunc Dimittis* in Anglican Evening Prayer. The Canticle comes from that of Simeon (Luke 2:29–32):

> Lord, now letest thou thy servant depart in peace, according to thy word; For mine eyes have seen thy Salvation, . . . A light unto the Gentiles, and the glory of thy people Israel.

The Anglican priest and his fellow worshipers make up the new Israel, and the passage in Luke itself recognizably embodies Old Testament echoes.[25] That canny queen Elizabeth also had another purpose in mind, for if she was father to that new Israel, her Lords and Commons, she was playing the role of God (as in Jeremiah 31:9). The Stuart kings somewhat altered the Tudor myth and its despotism by substituting replacements, in the case of the myth an emphasis on a Davidic figuralism so successful that Marvell tried to appropriate it for Cromwell. David was especially useful to poets like Dryden because, in the first place, he was considered to be a poet himself (having, it was thought, written the Psalter), and so allowing for the relation of poetry and kingship. David was also a type of Christ and, as a king, a vicegerent of God the Father. For such reasons, Dryden could write "To His Sacred Majesty," not impiously thinking that another person

[25] They include Psalm 98:2, Isaiah 52:10, 49:6, etc.

had been added to the Godhead, but figurally showing the King's participation, as a king, in the function of rule in the universe. Dryden could of course apply the same thing to the King's subjects, giving a happy escape clause or enlargement to the Tudor-Stuart despotism that regal figuralism supported.

Ideas of typology became freer in the middle of the century. In his *Madagascar,* for example, Davenant speaks of some lovers: "Of these the God-like *Sidney* was a Type."[26] That does not make much sense in the usual operative meanings of typology. He seems to mean that Sidney is the antitype or perfect embodiment. Or perhaps all he means is that Sidney is the perfect exemplar of a male lover. Usage could grow freer still. To remain with Davenant, he writes in *Gondibert* of

Cypresse Boughs;
From ancient Lore, of Man's mortalitie
The Type, for where 'tis lopp'd it never grows.
(II, iv, 57)

What Davenant calls a type would have been termed an emblem twenty years before, and probably twenty years later as well. Whether his "ancient Lore" introduces the usual temporal element of typology I rather doubt. I think his usage simply libertine.

Another form of figuralism originated long before the seventeenth century and revived in popularity during that renewal of the "spiritual" and the occult in mid-century.[27] I mention this revival again simply because it has been so

[26] Davenant, *The Shorter Poems,* ed. A. M. Gibbs (Oxford, 1972), p. 14.

[27] In *Mysteriously Meant* (Baltimore, 1970), D. C. Allen presumes that the Age of Reason or some other inhospitable *Zeitgeist* killed off spiritual readings of pagan lore. However, the great popularity of the occult and related forms of spiritualism from 1640 to 1660 strongly affected people like Milton, Dryden, and Newton, as has been said before.

seldom acknowledged. Unlike those who extol the marvels of a culture excited by such things in the air during the 1580's, I regard the undoubted recurrence in the 1640's and 1650's as something less than a cultural apogee. The question must always be not what ideas thickened at a given time, but what was made of them in the literature and in the lives of the people who entertained the ideas. One quickly sees that Davenant's loose talk of "types" is simply another way of speaking of old emblems. One sees almost as quickly how abhorrent such illumination by inner light, or inner shadows, was to Butler. His terrible great poem found its motive in deep anger over what other people were thinking, saying, and doing. Milton and Dryden in their different fashions benefited from the resurgence of old ways of thinking, because those old ways developed into new outlooks on life and literature generated by what they knew to be of profound importance to themselves.

Dryden has been so often appropriated into the eighteenth century that it seems axiomatic to many critics that he belongs to some day other than his own. Of all axioms, that can be least acceptable. He was eighteen when Charles I was executed, twenty-two when Cromwell became Lord Protector, and twenty-nine when Charles II was once more firmly at home in England. We can only guess what his responses were to the first two of those events and the currents of the times that produced them. It seems most unlikely that he was ever cousin to Ralpho, and in spite of his practicing judicial astrology, at least to the extent of casting nativities, we do know that his outlook was far wider than Sidrophel's, and that he did not believe that astrology could foretell public events.[28]

The senses in which Dryden should be thought conserva-

[28] See, in context, Dryden's *Hind and the Panther*, III, 471–72; also III, 511–22.

tive, and they are many, as well as the senses in which he is progressive, and they are also numerous, have seldom been carefully considered. Twenty-seven years after the Restoration, his *Hind and the Panther* showed that he entertained many kinds of thought that our intellectual historians seem to think died with the chartering of the Royal Society in 1662, or at Bosworth Field. Perhaps such thoughts should have died, and perhaps the members of the Royal Society should have ministered the intellectual euthanasia. But—in spite of numerous changes—neither did. Typology of numerous kinds enters into Dryden's second religious confession. The figurative and intellectual aspects of the poem depend for its extraordinary fable on Aesop as modified to rather more narrative ends in the previous two or three decades, on sacred zoögraphy and its uses of beasts for religious symbolism, and on spiritual glosses of scripture. The fable employs a species of allegory nearly opposite to that closed, parallel system used in *Absalom and Achitophel.* Now the allegory is open, intermittent, and various. At times the vehicles are beastly, at times religious, and at times humanistic. The tenors of those vehicles vary from the immediately historical, to the typological, the religious in other terms, the emblematic, the personal, and the purely literary. Having discussed such matters more than once before, and in terms of philosophical, religious, and historical emphases, I should like now to concern myself with their literary and particularly narrative emphases.

Dryden's use of the humanist tradition to serve the purposes of a semi-narrative gives us an opportunity to begin with stress on the conservative element in his thought. That seems appropriate to a poem confessing changed religious adherence to an older Church. A line fairly early in *The Hind and the Panther* (I, 284) contrasts the tyrannical ways of Nimrod, that symbol of the tyrant, with a more merciful personage: "Not so [like Nimrod] the blessed *Pan* his flock encreas'd." The line occurs in a narrative or progress piece of persecution and toleration from Creation and the Fall of Man (one of Dryden's very few references to the mortal sin original) to Christ and Dryden's own time. "Pan" is of course Christ in that humanist identification that seems to have originated in the story told by Plutarch of a voice shouting from the Italian shore, "Pan is dead!" That was just at the time when Jesus was born, and hence Christ fulfills the pagan type.

The example glances and Dryden moves quickly on. He could not have done so without its seeming to him an easy instance, for him and his readers. But perhaps a later passage will show that Dryden's thinking in that narrative of persecution—the ugly legacy of the Reformation and counter-Reformation—really shows one aspect of his way of thought and writing. Having led the Panther to her poor hermitage, the Hind urges her guest not to condemn so poor a seat:

> This peacefull Seat my poverty secures,
> War seldom enters but where wealth allures;
> Nor yet despise it, for this poor aboad
> Has oft receiv'd, and yet receives a god;
> A god victorious of [over] the Stygian race
> Has laid his sacred limbs, and sanctified the place.
> This mean retreat did mighty *Pan* contain . . .
> (II, 705–11)

In the *Aeneid* (VIII, 362–65; *Aeneis*, VIII, 477–82), Evander invites Aeneas in such terms, saying that Hercules (Dryden's "god victorious" over the infernal regions) had stayed there, and preceding the lines alluded to in the *Aeneid* Virgil gives a hymn to Hercules. Hercules parallels and foreshadows Christ in that his last and greatest deed was to overcome Cerberus, so foreshadowing Christ's harrowing of Hell. The passage also tells us that the hermitage repeatedly receives a god, or in other words that celebration of the mass involves the so-called Real Presence of Christ whenever enacted. The Hind's invitation is nothing other than an offer to the Panther to "reconcile" herself, or the Anglican Church, to Rome. Dryden's beast fable and his humanistic (or medieval) christianizing of Virgil's Hercules leads the poet in a fashion characteristic of such writings to introduce a second figure, Pan, also representative of Christ. After establishing Dryden's connection with the mythographic tradition in this passage, we can consider the narrative implications of the passage.

The fullest if not the best gloss on the passage can be found in comments by that irascible Scot, Alexander Ross. Inveterate scribbler, he was without charity, a sounding brass and tinkling cymbal attended to by many, as Butler testified in exasperation. Ross attacked Sir Kenelm Digby (1645), Sir Thomas Browne (1651), Hobbes (1653) and, not to mention others, the "Galileans" with their heliocentric notions about the universe (1646). He also completed Sir Walter Ralegh's *History of the World* to 1640 and moralized fictions in *Mel Heliconicum* (1642). But his best-seller was *Mystagogus Poeticus* (1647), which had reached the sixth of its sporadically extended editions by 1675. This compilation of pagan typology and such other forms of figuralism as moral interpretation affords students of seventeenth-century literature with readiest access into ways of thinking not our own. Ross often gives the bad sides of the pagan deities, because they were after all pagan. But he also concerns himself with their "true," that is, their Christian or mythographic, significance. One section (19) of the entry on Hercules will show how our ancestors once thought (1647, pp. 119–20; 1648, as here, pp. 169–70):

> Our blessed Saviour is the true *Hercules*, who was the true and only Son of God, and of the virgin *Mary*; who was

persecuted out of malice, and exposed to all dangers, which he overcame: hee subdued the roaring Lion, that red Dragon, that tyrant and devourer of mankind, the Devill; he subdued the *Hydra* of Sin, the *Antaeus* of earthly affections: hee by his Word supporteth the world; Satan is that *Cacus* [ὁ χάχος] that Sea-monster, from whom by Christ we are delivered; it is hee only that went down to hell, and delivered us from thence; hee alone travelled through the Torrid Zone of his fathers wrath; hee purged the *Augean* stable of Jewish superstition, and heathenish profanation; hee overcame the world, and all his enemies, and hath killed the Eagle of an evill conscience, which continually fed upon the heart of man: he was the only true ἀλεξίχαχος, the expeller of all evill from us; who with the club of his power, and chains of his eloquence hath subdued and drawn all men after him; who at last was burned but not consumed by the fire of his Fathers wrath: who having subdued principalities and powers, was received up into glory, and exalted above all heavens, where now he sits at the right hand of God, being adored by the Angels in heaven, by men on earth, and by the spirits under the earth, to whom be glory and dominion, and power for ever and ever, *Amen.*

A telling example is worth a dozen instances. Surely this remarkable paraphrase of the Creed speaks for itself. But we shall not understand how men could think that way unless we are aware of what immediately follows in Ross' account:

20. Let me complain with *Lactantius, de falsa. rel. l.* I. *c.* 9 of the pravitie and madnesse of the Gentiles, who would make a god of *Hercules,* who scarce deserved the name of a man, if we consider his adulterous birth, his whoredomes, oppressions, murthers, gluttony, and other sins . . . .

But had Ross himself not sinned with the Gentiles in the preceding section? No, because there he was not writing of a mere Hercules but about the "true *Hercules*" in the same sense of "true" as Milton's in speaking of Jesus as "*Israels* true King." Ross, like Milton and Dryden, was concerned mythographically with "The meaning, not the Name" (*Paradise Lost,* VII, 5).

Another gloss on Hercules given by the Scottish mystagogue will return us to Dryden's figurative use of mythology. Ross offers an interpretation of the story of Hercules' relieving Atlas of his duty to hold up the world:

> 4. *Hercules* may be the type of a good king, who ought to subdue all monsters, cruelty, disorder, and oppression in his kingdom, who should support the Heaven of the Church with the shoulders of authoritie, who should purge the *Augean* stable of superstition and profanation; who should relieve the oppressed, and set at liberty the captives.

Hercules, says Ross, is the *type* of a Christian king. This use of "type" is not loose as was Davenant's. Rather it is a secular, "classical" version of religious typology: a classical figure has achievements that foreshadow in moral allegory the quite different order of achievements in modern, Christian times. Hercules represents, then, Christ, a murderer and whoremaster, and a Christian king (as well as other things). It all depends on what kind of truth a mystagogue or a poet wishes to allegorize out of ancient legend. In *Threnodia Augustalis,* Dryden uses classical myth in secular terms that Ross has well explained:

> As if great *Atlas* from his Height
> Shou'd sink beneath his heavenly Weight,
> And, with a mighty Flaw, the flaming Wall
> (As once it shall)

Shou'd gape immense and rushing down, o'erwhelm this
neather Ball;
So swift and so surprizing was our Fear:
Our *Atlas* fell indeed; But *Hercules* was near.

II

His Pious Brother, sure the best . . . (29–36)

Obviously Dryden expected his readers to consider Atlas a type of Charles II and Hercules of "His Pious Brother," James II.

The examples given from *Threnodia Augustalis* and *The Hind and the Panther* differ in that the former uses a secular typology, the latter a religious, notwithstanding that Hercules is involved in both instances. But the two usages resemble each other in a fundamental matter of poetic form. Both use narrative in a mythographic or allegorical fashion to relate something about the Atlas-Hercules, Charles-James succession, or about Hercules-Christ visiting the hermitage-church. Beginning with the nearly contemporaneous *Threnodia Augustalis* and Anne Killigrew Ode, Dryden began to bring back into his poetry more and more of the narrative elements that had gradually been excluded by crisis and his unusual procedures in *The Medall* and *Religio Laici.* It may seem strange that narrative begins to occupy a prominent place again when Dryden turns to the lyric, the major ode form in loose pindarics. Perhaps it is strange, but one can observe that as narrative had been a casualty of crisis, its return coincides with the revival of Dryden's confidence. The Anne Killigrew ode celebrates Dryden's faith in the artist and her (that is, his) art. *The Hind and the Panther* affirms a settled faith. Immediately following, "A Song for St. Cecilia's Day" narrates a providential history of art and the artist (music and the musicians) from creation to the Day of Judgment. Dryden has recovered his great idea, but we must observe that its terms have altered from the specifically English and secular to the more widely human, mythopoeic, and religious. The course of Dryden's development astonishingly resembles Milton's. Political and personal crises were endured and survived by both, and both gained an enlarged conception of the world and man by broadening the terms of the conception. Both had to, if the idea was to survive. Differences of course exist. Milton's agony was longer and found expression in prose. Dryden uses poetry, prose (*The History of the League*, "Postscript") and even drama (*The Duke of Guise*). The change in religion took Dryden into an older orthodoxy and Milton to a greater heterodoxy. The differences are more obvious, however, than the fundamental similarity: religious and political crisis met all thinking men in the century, and only those poets of the greatest powers could survive such challenges to reaffirm their hopes without falling into the pessimism of a Butler or the cruder satiric strain of the later Marvell.

The affirmation after crisis notably expresses itself in narrative. Equally notably, both for Milton and Dryden what might be termed the new narrative (after the simpler forms of the Nativity Ode and *Annus Mirabilis*) turns out to be a far more complex and highly adapted species. *The Hind and the Panther* does not so much abound in narrative as abound in narratives. Whether Dryden gives a character of one of his ecclesiastical beasts, writes a *confiteor*, describes Christ's reception of His spouse the Church, or offers fables of birds, he all but constantly moves by narrative means. So various are the narratives themselves, both as to episode and to the class of actor in the episode (beast, poet, Christ, or bird, for example), that the result proves far more complicated than in Milton's epics. Without depreciating the richness of *The Hind and the Panther*, one must say that there is a simpler and higher art in making what is complex possess the clarity and purity of *Paradise Lost.* Only with the *Fables* would Dryden achieve something like that last step.

The linking of numerous narratives in *The Hind and the Panther* looks forward to *Fables Ancient and Modern,* but the religious poem also has its governing fable of the Hind's encounter and talk with the Panther. All the successive subnarratives fill in this natural narrative, or rather deprive the natural narrative of any very complicated development. What is in a sense too complex in the succession of small subnarratives has as counterpart a too simple narrative in the dominant fable. No other poem of Dryden's has quite the dazzling variety of *The Hind and the Panther,* and none the personal and religious magnificence. To have created so much in a poem too simple in the large and too complex in the small implies that as poet and narrator Dryden had to employ some powerful controls in adjusting the entire narrative movement and in working out terms on which the simple larger fable might be served by the heterogeneous smaller narratives. We have been concerned with one such control: various figuralist methods that are held in common by the main plot and by its numerous subforms. Two others now claim some mention: interruptive procedures that control the larger narrative, and a transference by which the values of the small are taken to the large.

A milk-white Hind, immortal and unchanged, finds herself among many other beasts of the forest. One evening she meets the Panther who, like her, has problems. She invites the Panther to her hermitage (end of the First Part). The two dine very simply and fall to talking about recent and present conflicts and problems in matters religious, and the Hind more than once offers the Panther "reconciliation" but is refused (end of the Second Part). They then turn to further debate about the present religious situation in two major sequences, each of which is concluded by a bird fable which foretells the religious future of England. The Panther foretells the destruction of Swallows (Catholics), and the Hind a general toleration for birds of every feather.

It is remarkable that so slight a story can sustain a poem of 2,592 lines. True, the story of the Fall that Milton inherited from Genesis 3 is just as sparse, and the temptation of Christ also is no extensive story in the New Testament. Milton's brief epic is about a fifth shorter than Dryden's poem (2,070 to 2,592 lines).[29] What Milton sustains by repetition until finally the reader and Satan find themselves caught, Dryden sustains not by repeated but by all manner of episodes. These episodes or subnarratives sustain by the principle of interruption. The story of Hercules visiting the Hind's hermitage comes at the end of the First Part in one of the few strongly felt narrative energies of the chief plot. We observed that Dryden intervenes with the little narrative of Hercules, just as most of the First Part constitutes an intervention between the introduction of the Hind (lines 1–26) and the introduction of the Panther (lines 392 ff.). Even after the introduction of the Panther, a considerable amount of the narrator's attention goes into talk of sacraments (with intervening demi-demi-narratives involving allusions to three Aesopian fables) and into talk of her plight among other beasts (which serves partly to motivate her willingness to talk with the Hind, but hardly seems to the reader to be part of a main plot that has yet to begin). At last, 511 lines on in the poem, the two meet, and the narrative goes on for all of 62 lines before the First Part ends. In the conversation that follows in the Second Part, we discover that again a succession of intervening smaller narratives takes

[29] A fair range of length for the "brief epic" (Milton's conception, revived by Lewalski) extends from the 983 lines of the *Psychomachia* by Prudentius to the 5,835 lines of the *Argonautica* by Apollonius of Rhodes.

from the main plot its *de facto* powers, leaving it a *de jure* ruler, a monarch herself governed by the strange constitution of the poem, until, again, the close of the part.

The principle of intervention seems nearly constant, and yet it works by a reciprocal principle of constant transference from the little narratives to the *de jure* narrative. This can be seen best where the threat of intervention is greatest, that is, in the lengthy stories told by the Panther and by the Hind about the Swallows and the Pigeons. In each case, the narrative continues much longer and more plainly as narrative than in other sections of the poem. Such being the case, they should in theory depose the main fable entirely. In fact, however, all readers have found these two narratives the most engrossing in the poem and have considered them inseparable from the poem. Dryden has effected a transference to the main narrative. He can do so because both the main narrative and these nominally subordinate parts are figural. The Panther tells about Swallows or Catholics whose stupidities lead them to their destruction. Dryden allows the Panther to voice his own fears over the rash policies of Sunderland and Father Petres, which James showed increasing willingness to adopt as his own. But the poet also has the Panther betray her cruelty in describing the deaths of the Swallows. In the sacred zoögraphies, the Panther was termed beautiful in body although deformed in face, cruel, sexual, and of a double nature (being identified with the leo-pard). Dryden's Panther is all these things, and she does not realize that in representing Catholics as Swallows she has chosen a bird which, on the basis of Psalm 74:3, was a figure of the faithful or the true Church. Since the Panther's listener, the Hind, also represents that Church, we discover a kind of mutual parabolic procedure that shares in method and meaning while differing in details. By different figurative means, such intervention and transference also sustain *Absalom and Achitophel*.

The Hind's fable of the Pigeons works yet more wholly in terms of a double figuralism effecting a transference from the Pigeons to the world of the Hind and the Panther. The Pigeons are Anglican birds, and on the estate of a plain good man (James II, with an adaptation of Chaucer's Nun's Priest's tale as well as a basic Aesopian story) many other birds exist. The avaricious Pigeons are disgruntled over having been given only the most on the estate and in an effort to get everything, they call in the Buzzard (William of Orange merged with Gilbert Burnet). They are stopped just in time by the plain good man from ruining themselves as well as the other birds.

Dryden makes clear that the Anglican birds are Pigeons, not doves, because the dove is an emblem of the true Church. But in the Hind's fable, the Catholic bird is the domestic fowl, the poultry, chiefly represented by Chanticleer and Partlet, the cock being an emblem (even before Christian times) of the priest, and the hen, for Dryden, of the nun. The Hind's fable tells about the Panther and herself by moving one step lower in the scale of nature than had the narrator with what he terms his "mysterious writ" (II, 2). The degree of sharing and transference exceeds anything that might have been thought feasible since monkish times. There is a remarkable simile at the end of a passage telling how the prospect of the Buzzard's coming over leads all manner of bird to attend religious services:

> The House of Pray'r is stock'd with large encrease;
> Nor Doors, nor Windows can contain the Press:
> For Birds of ev'ry feather fill th' abode;
> Ev'n Atheists out of envy own a God:
> And reeking from the Stews, Adult'rers come,
> Like *Goths* and *Vandals* to demolish *Rome*.
>
> (III, 1209–14)

Dryden speaks of "The House of Pray'r" because he is talking about Anglican buildings that he is not wholly prepared to call churches, at least not in terms of worship and sacraments. In the passage as a whole, the fable seems to disappear, for "Birds of ev'ry feather" superbly begs the question, and we move to atheists and adulterers who, like Goths and Vandals, come to destroy. The agents are vile, and their object in this simile suddenly turns out to be entirely literal, papal "*Rome*," just as the lines immediately preceding the simile had seemed to talk of men rather than birds. In this instance, the transference from the fable to the main narrative moves from a simile for the birds of the fable to the ecclesiastical tenor of the main narrative. Men at last provide a simile: for birds. And when they do so, they reveal most fully how birds and beasts mean Churches.

The result of this extraordinary manner of narrating is scarcely a story at all. Or rather, there are so many stories that we are left with a sense of character rather than of plot. As the title of the poem suggests, its aim is to characterize the Hind and the Panther, and in this Dryden succeeds in ways seldom acknowledged explicitly but always felt in reading. Those who think the beast allegory absurd acknowledge how vivid and almost palpable the two central characters are. Both as a beast and as a Church that had been persecuting Catholics and (especially) Dissenters rigorously since 1662, the Panther is a cruel character. But talking with the Hind on the night of July 6–7, 1685 (see II, 654–62), the Panther finds it necessary to restrain her cruelty for a later occasion. She

> watch'd the time her vengeance to compleat,
> When all her furry sons in frequent Senate met.
> Mean while she quench'd her fury at the floud,
> And with a Lenten sallad cool'd her blood.
>
> (III, 24–27)

"Furry" and "frequent" are both ambivalent, since "furry" refers both to the hides of panthers and also to ecclesiastics in the furred robes of an Anglican convocation. "Frequent" uses both the English and the Latinate senses. Both bear on "furry." And all bears on that grand absurdity of a panther dining on a salad. Of course no one could possibly expect a panther to do that, she being a carnivore. Exactly. Say it was all a mistake for the Anglican Church: who could expect it to observe a true Lent? To repress its cruelty very long? The poem is absurd, and the absurdity is entirely given over to "The Lady of the spotted-muff" (I, 572). Lines like that have a wonderful baroque charm, as does, "The *Panther* grin'd at this, and thus reply'd" (II, 60). She grins, she yawns, her eyeballs glisten, she pacifies her tail, and she licks her frothy jaws. In short she, and the Hind as well, not to mention the stupid Martin and brazen Buzzard, are not just emblems or types but also free characters.

Of all the characters in the poem, the Panther certainly best testifies to the art of her author. She is giddy and cruel, witty, and immoral sexually in certain late scandals with the (Presbyterian) Wolf. The Hind, on the other hand, has little sense of humor at all. She is stern and dignified, although her language at times is very broad. She also is not averse to pointing to herself as an agency by which the Panther may be saved. Few people today seem to realize that a widespread view of the sixteenth and seventeenth centuries held that the Catholics were austere, the Puritans (or Dissenters) sensually indulgent, and the Anglicans somewhere between, enjoying, as one example of Christian liberty, a married clergy. Such an outlook informs Dryden's poem, and although the passage describing the Hind as bride of Christ (II, 499–525) is magnificent, the Panther is Dryden's finest creation in the poem. It may be doubtful whether he was very certain what an actual panther looked like, but he knew the Panther of the sacred zoögraphies and the Anglican Church intimately, and he drew on long-tried talents for characterization to make her the elegant ecclesiastical slut that she is. There is in her not a little of Charles's mistresses, just as there is in the Hind something of James's queen, Mary of Este and Modena. As has often happened before, the lady no better than she ought to be interests us more than the lady of stern virtue. Absurd she is, the Panther, but, like the strange narrative landscape in which she finds herself, she is also real by literary means and to significant end.

iii. The Higher Mimesis

The turning of something absurd into a vehicle of meaning testifies to Dryden's faith in the reality of experience, both as we conceive that from our conscious selves and as we conceive it from external reality. His belief in the correspondence of those inner and outer worlds assisted him in acquiring the confidence that he maintained for all but a short period of his life, and the belief also permitted him to think of art in terms of a higher mimesis. Dryden's mimesis is "higher" not only because of its role in his heroic idea, but even more because of the evident reality he discovers to be shared by the subjective and objective worlds, by ancient and modern times, by religion and art, by pagan and Christian lore. At the center of all those things in *The Hind and the Panther* we discovered, perhaps to our surprise, that character was the important thing. Some two decades before, Dryden had defined drama (or rather art):

> A just and lively Image of Humane Nature, representing its Passions and Humours, and the Changes of Fortune to which it is subject; for the Delight and Instruction of Mankind.[30]

[30] California edition, XVII (1971), 15.

The sense of what men and women are, the knowledge of what life is like, was as important to Dryden's art as his great idea, which told him what people and life might be. By enriching the real with the possible, Dryden heightens realism and makes life seem more valuable. Both his sense of "Humane Nature" and his hopes for it lead him into the preserves of narrative in most of his career, but both also lead him to swear a higher allegiance to matters that qualify—and make meaningful—the narrative he employs.

Mac Flecknoe offers us a useful early example, and a glance at the *Aeneis* will give us later evidence. Since I have found myself surprised on making a précis of *Mac Flecknoe*, I shall offer one here. The reigning emperor of the realm of Nonsense, Flecknoe, has grown old. He debates with himself as to which of his sons (in the Turkish fashion) ought to succeed him. He decides that it must be Shadwell, who most resembles his father in dullness. Flecknoe then (29) begins his first speech, the Thucydidean *logos* interruptive of historical narration. He tells how earlier dunces were only types of Shadwell, how even he himself merely prepared the way by making songs in Portugal, foretelling Shadwell's own recent lute-songs for water-music. His own raptures over his son lead him to weep for joy and to conclude that every reason, but chiefly Shadwell's plays, argue that he was destined to be prince of dullness.

The narrator then describes the locale where the succession ceremony is to take place: by the ruins of a Tower of the wall of the City, where now there thrive brothels, a school for stage-players, and other disreputably suburban activities. A prophecy by Thomas Dekker is recalled, naming a prince like Shadwell, a man prolific in the creation of characters. Now, hearing the call of Fame, unread authors appear, with a publisher leading the guard. Old Flecknoe appears on a throne made from his own books, and on his right hand sits

Shadwell, his brows heavy in fog. When he swears the coronation oath, his father passes to him the regalia, a mug of ale and Flecknoe's own play, *Love's Kingdom.* Just then twelve owls hoot, and the crowd shouts three times.

At this Flecknoe delivers a prophetic exhortation. Beginning with a blessing on the prince, he evokes an Amen from the crowd. He urges his son to new depths of ignorance and impudence, to continuous nonproductive effort. Anything interesting should be left to others, and the fools in the plays should take their author as model. Above all, he should rely on his own talents for dullness, avoiding any claim to kinship with Jonson, life, or art. Jonson never reached such ideal stupidities as Shadwell, whose latest work is always more of the same dullness. The praise continues, mentioning Shadwell's grossness, his risible tragedy, soporific comedy, and toothless satires. The old prince particularly recommends leaving playwriting for acrostics, shaped poems, and torture of words. His last charge is muffled, however, for he is unceremoniously sent down a stage trap by two characters of Shadwell's dramatic creation. As the old man sinks, his prophetic mantle blows upward on a subterranean draft to Shadwell with the promise that he will be twice as dull as his father.

With omissions of detail not essential to the simple narrative line, that represents the plot of *Mac Flecknoe,* as anyone would recognize. The actual amount of plot surprises us, and I think that that helps account for the fact that we always remember the poem to be longer than it is, 217 lines. I take it of great importance that the poem in fact possesses a considerable measure of plot, and of equal importance that our impression runs quite contrary to the fact. If Dryden has provided us with more plot than we sense exists, that can only mean that his concern lies less with simple narrative than with other matters. As we have seen, Dryden's interest lies particularly in the evocation of a system of values interrelating the three principal ones: art, religion, and monarchy. Two other particularly Drydenian emphases fall on speech and place. Of course what is said carries the constant irony of praise for the wrong reasons. When so systematic, irony tends to take on some degree of unreality or of allegory: Pope's Sylphs, Swift's Lilliputians breaking eggs, or the Romantics designating the breach between symbol and reality. Dryden's irony creates no Baudelairean unreal city. It is the Thames that flows, well fed by the sewer ditches. A real place, the Barbican, provides the scene. Scholars have always assumed that Aston Hall must exist somewhere in London, although they have not identified it. So strong is the sense of London, or at least of suburban, extramural London.

The sense of reality, of the just and lively image of the known world, constitutes that higher mimesis of a truer, stable reality on which Dryden's poems are founded. His irony lacks what might be termed the metaphysical import of Swift's irony, because Dryden's metaphysics confirms the reality we feel. His irony is rhetorical in that it is rooted primarily in speech, the means by which individuals establish their relations with each other and express their understanding of people in their world. From *Mac Flecknoe* through the poems of the 1680's, skipping the period of crisis, Dryden's major poems use speech at great length. His trust in this capacity distinguishing men from beasts resembles his trust in those two other characteristics similarly distinguishing man: reason and laughter. Of course this satire orders things in gradations and contrasts. Shadwell is not quoted for a single word, and so becomes an inarticulate poet, whereas his reputed father seems garrulous to more people than the eager heir. Perhaps Dryden's higher mimesis can best be represented by his pretense to take as (unpleasant) realities the characters in Shadwell's own plays. Shadwell took great pride in them as humours creations in the tradition of Ben Jonson, and Dryden says in effect, yes, they are real: look what they do.

We must carefully consider Dryden's command of reality. It has long been assumed that Flecknoe was an Irish priest. In fact the only evidence for that assumption is provided by *Mac Flecknoe,* and a close reading of the poem does not support the assumption at all. Dryden symbolically equates Ireland with illiteracy and barbarism, dubs Shadwell "Mac" Flecknoe, and that is as real to the world as is the portrait of Shadwell in this poem. Dryden of course develops essential facts about Shadwell and uses traits of personality and character that can be verified. But Dryden also makes of Shadwell a literary character who varies considerably from the historical dramatist. One need only compare another "Shadwell," the Og of the second part of *Absalom and Achitophel,* or compare the "Shaftesbury" that is Achitophel and that who is the "Chief" of *The Medall* to see that Dryden's art creates the reality we presume so readily.

Numerous other examples exist. For example, in *Absalom and Achitophel* there occurs a well-known crux. Absalom is said to have "Some warm excesses, which the Law forbore." There follows an example:

> *Amnon*'s Murther, by a specious Name,
> Was call'd a Just Revenge for injur'd Fame.
>
> (39–40)

So powerfully does Dryden persuade us that what he says in his poems is real, historical, that for years readers have assumed that Monmouth murdered someone, and scholars have vainly sought to identify the victim. Similarly, the twelve lines added to the character of Achitophel have established Shaftesbury's career as a judge wholly honest and efficient. The excellent modern biography of Shaftesbury sifts the evidence (which is meager and contradictory, as from friend or foe), and concludes that he was an able and upright judge: with Dryden's lines there for proof.[31] Or again, in *The Hind and the Panther* (II, 654–62) Dryden speaks out in a passage marked *Poëta loquitur,* testifying to his seeing a celestial and testimonial "fireworks" on the night of Monmouth's defeat at the Battle of Sedgemoor (July 6–7, 1685). Various modern historians, notably Macaulay, no friend of Dryden, tell how there was fog on the battlefield (that from accounts written in the West Country) but also how there came an aurora borealis or some other play of heavenly light. The evidence? Dryden's lines. What real evidence exists shows that London was closed in by rain during this time.[32]

I know of no parallel to such creation of "real" people, places, and events. Since the Romantic poets, we have come to expect that writers may reveal themselves, the dye in their works betraying the dyer's hand. But we do not read even Shakespeare for evidence of what was actually happening in his time. Dryden has created in us the presumption that certain kinds of poetry convey to us actual historical reality, even when the historical detail may be present merely to illuminate the poet's fictional narrative. As we have seen in earlier chapters, such a presumption has led many interpreters of Denham, Chamberlayne, Butler, and other poets mentioned in this volume to read their glancing allusions as systematic historical reality. Whatever critical theory we espouse, such an effect on readers must be thought extraordinary. But it is not accidental. Dryden's remarks on Spenser make it clear that he so interpreted his great predecessor in narrative; and his plans for his own epic show that he would have written

[31] K.H.D. Haley, *The First Earl of Shaftesbury* (Oxford, 1968), p. 309. Haley well remarks that W. D. Christie's earlier and very pro-Shaftesbury biography "struggled largely in vain" against Dryden's characterization. But many of Haley's chapter titles and much else comes from Dryden, so that he too shows signs of such struggle.

[32] See the California edition, III, 405–406.

something like historical allegory on a subject like the achievements of the Edward the Black Prince. His heroic idea and historical emphasis undoubtedly led him to look more carefully at the people and events of his own time than poets usually do. At least he made such a regard a central feature of his art. The fact that we read *Mac Flecknoe* to learn about Shadwell, and other poems to learn about Shaftesbury, Congreve, the Duchess of Ormonde, the Fire of London, the Popish Plot, or a celestial display on the night of the Battle of Sedgemoor—all this means that we assume that Dryden sets forth what is real. It is truly a higher mimesis that elicits such consent from us. No more than any other poet could he create that literary integrity of Milton's, in which myth and reality are finally indistinguishable. Yet he could create the next thing, a poetry in which historical reality and historical fiction are finally indistinguishable, as also along with that, the presumption that his kind of poetry, his kind of vision represent for us the ways of understanding used by poets of quite different art.

It is little short of amazing. And it also gives some pause as we consider his success in "creating reality," a phrase that entails a sense of contradiction for the philosopher or the plain man in us all. How real can that reality be when, as with the instances given, it is the product of art and when the proof is derived from that which requires the proof? What shall we think of art's mimetic mirror of reality, when the mirror replaces reality as the source of the real? Be what they may, our answers must recognize that what *lives* in Dryden's poetry takes life in his art, not from the reality "imitated." He made this clear late in life when he set forth his mimetic theory in greater detail than he had before. He differs from Aristotle on the central question of why imitation pleases us. Dryden disagrees that we take pleasure in comparing the imitation with the original. If that were true,

> every speculation in nature whose truth falls under the inquiry of a philosopher [in particular, a scientist], must produce the same delight, which is not true. I should rather assign another reason. Truth is the object of our understanding, as good is of our will; and the understanding can no more be delighted with a lie than the will can choose an apparent [i.e., obvious or glaring] evil. As truth is the end of all our speculations, so the discovery of it is the pleasure of them; and since a true knowledge of nature gives us pleasure, a *lively imitation* [my stress] of it, either in poetry or painting, must of necessity produce a much greater.[33]

That is finely said, and such is Dryden's faith in reality. But we ought not presume from it that Dryden has in mind any photographic literalism in his idea either of what nature should be imitated or of what latitude is allowed in the imitation. On the latter issue, he takes a very clear stand:

> In the character of an hero, as well as in an inferior figure, there is a better or worse likeness to be taken: the better is a panegyric, if it be not false, and the worse is a libel [or personal satire].[34]

The passage shows that Dryden allowed the poet considerable if unspecifiable latitude in taking a "likeness" of truth. His context includes painting as well as poetry, and in both arts he esteemed character-drawing as the most interesting art, as a notable passage in the Anne Killigrew Ode shows.[35]

Plainly, Dryden did allow himself latitude, and the evident reality so convincing in his poetry must be considered always to be an artistic version of the truth, requiring other evidence to determine the degree of likeness or of latitude. In the end

[33] "The Parallel Betwixt Poetry and Painting," in Watson, II, 193–94.
[34] Ibid., II, 202.
[35] See the Anne Killigrew Ode, 88–141; and the California edition, III, 321–22 for a gloss.

each of us must feel a certain degree of embarrassment in attempting verification, in imagining ourselves sitting down, for example, to read Dryden with the many volumes of Ranke's history of seventeenth-century England beside us. Dryden's poetry sufficiently creates its own world, its own people, its own laws, customs, and belief. That is the whole point of our belief in the reality. That world is altogether logical in the sense that it answers to our sense of what the world and people are like: again, the higher mimesis. But is it true? Does Dryden describe something, as Ranke put it in a famous phrase, "wie es eigentlich gewesen?" The short answer is, No. The long answer would take us through such nice questions as that of the knowability of the world outside the consciousness of each of us, as also of the reality of that world, and of such others as methods of verification. The medium-length answer must be, Yes, Dryden gives us as true a picture of reality as poets and historians give, and not only one as true but even more real, in the sense that our own psychological "sets" based on previous experience accord his depiction an unusually high degree of assent. Shaftesbury's learned biographer shows that Dryden allowed considerable latitude in taking the likeness in Achitophel. And yet even he takes the praise of Shaftesbury as judge to be proof positive, and the absence of charges of fiscal corruption by Dryden (unlike other contemporaries) to be proof negative. Dryden's power to create conviction of what is real, of what exists, of what a person is like, is nothing short of remarkable.

If no adequate answer can be given to the question of the degree of truth in that evident reality, we can content ourselves with raising another, related, matter, Dryden's mental outlook. *Absalom and Achitophel* has been discussed from the viewpoint of a "conservative myth." [36] Perhaps it might

[36] Bernard N. Schilling, *Dryden and the Conservative Myth* (New Haven, 1961).

better be described as the conservative epic, at least in the sense that its task and labor do not build a new Troy so much as save an old Jerusalem. Dryden is a conservative all right, and his outlook is one to which we must come to terms if we are to be honest with him and ourselves. T. S. Eliot said many fine and many foolish things about Dryden, and one of the most amusing came in his description of himself as a classicist, monarchist, and Anglo-Catholic. After denying that Dryden had ideas, he took Dryden's very stance. Of all the three kinds of principle, that of monarchy seems to me as far removed from our lives as anything in Dryden. Yet it is not just that we can get wound up very little over the issues of the Succession Crisis, but that Dryden's whole political outlook was simply repressive and inegalitarian by our standards today. But so were those of all sides who held the remotest chance to rule. We have seen that the Puritan Revolution followed the logic of widespread support dwindling to a small ruling clique supported by major-generals in the counties.

Dr. Johnson betrayed the secret that our political soul is governed no little by a Whig who wishes to bring our superiors to our level and a Tory who insists on the inferiority of our inferiors. But Dryden does not deal with social classes. There is nothing startling in that, since Marxism emerged two centuries later, and the very word "economics" in its modern sense is the child of the first third of the last century. Dryden is concerned with the conditions that will foster the realizing of his heroic idea, and that concern focuses on two central matters: institutions and human agency. The Stuart legitimacy was restored in 1660 along with the so-called Clarendon Settlement, a rather uncertain constitution including the king, Parliament, and "our laws." Dryden resembled Marvell and others in supporting that settlement, but questions of emphasis and interpretation repeatedly came to a head in the heated atmosphere of the century. At times of crisis, Dryden turned to the throne as the prime source of legitimate power. That provides a clear example of his conservatism. Dryden did not need modern political theorists to tell him that legitimacy without power was an unstable situation likely to bring the revolution it had under Charles I; or that power without legitimacy is tyranny, and for that his example was the Interregnum. Clearly Dryden was conservative on the question of institutions, and on the side of his choice lay law, history, and the emphasis of civilization. On the other side lay revolution, certain kinds of justice, and the future.

Dryden's conservative respect for institutions could hardly be shown more clearly than he does himself in *Absalom and Achitophel*:

> All other Errors but disturb a State;
> But Innovation is the Blow of Fate.
> If ancient Fabricks nod, and threat to fall,
> To Patch the Flaws, and Buttress up the Wall,
> Thus far 'tis Duty; but here fix the Mark:
> For all beyond it is to touch our Ark.
> To change Foundations, cast the Frame anew,
> Is work for Rebels who base Ends pursue:
> At once Divine and Humane Laws controul;
> And mend the Parts by ruine of the Whole.
> The Tampering World is subject to this Curse,
> To Physick their Disease into a worse.
>
> (799–810)

The temper of mind in that passage does not admit dispute, and if it cannot be called conservative, nothing can. Dryden clearly finds strength in institutions, fears that the effort to change them will make things worse, invests the past with a power almost to render what is inherited sacred, and thinks that something of divinity has been shed by God the King on the human king.

What many readers have missed is that Dryden does not

adopt the corollary, for men, of those beliefs about institutions. His trust in institutions does not imply suspicion of individuals. His fear of change does not make him think that the direction of history is downward. The veneration of the past does not depress him over the future. And the divine aura about kings does not lead him to offer his reason in sacrifice. But in positive terms, whereas Dryden is so conservative about institutions, he is unusually optimistic about individuals. Indeed on the question of institutions and individuals Dryden and Milton take opposite sides. The rarity of Dryden's references to the Fall of Man and the centrality of that topic to Milton give one kind of evidence. Another comes in Dryden's common temporal order from past to future, with a prophesied triumph and new order at the end of time. If Dryden on institutions is past-oriented, Dryden on individuals is future-oriented. For that reason he was incapable of writing a normal funeral elegy. He could mourn over institutions needing rescue, but he could only treat people in triumph. With the exception of *The Medall*, Dryden's poems treat great people as great people. The Shaftesbury of *Absalom and Achitophel* is truly great and called so; even Shadwell is ironically great. One need only compare his Shaftesbury and Zimri to Pope's Atticus and Sporus, or his London to that of Donne in his satires and elegies to see the difference at once. In dealing with men and women, Dryden is the great liberal of the century, just as he is the great conservative among poets in his depiction of institutions. (I leave Butler to a pessimistic category all his own.) It deserves to be asked how such a seeming contradiction can give us that sense of reality to which we assent in his poems. Could it be because the view is a particularly realistic one?

An explanation more susceptible of proof lies in Dryden's heroic idea of England and its implications. His belief in the epic character of experience in his age involved as it were both a genre of conservatism and a progressive, indeed radical story of human achievement. The security of the inheritance seemed to him a counterpart of the security of England. Like James and Pepys, he hoped to the end of his life for a defensive navy rather than an offensive army. England must be preserved and protected, but not just out of motives of conserving, strong though such instincts certainly were with him. Rather, by holding fast to that which is good, or at least workable, man might achieve that which is better, and in doing so win immortality. Both Charles II and James II were staunch supporters of trade, as was Dryden. They were enthusiastic about science and the arts, at least when Charles II could find moments free from his spaniels and mistresses and James II from his autocratic designs. Looking about him, Dryden had some reason to fear the recurrence of the civil strife he had known as a young man. During the reign of the second Charles, there were ominous signs to one of Dryden's concern with institutions: the revolt of the miserable and savagely repressed Fifth Monarchy Men early in the reign; later the Popish Plot, the Rye House Plot, the Meal-tub or Catholic counterplot, and Monmouth's aborted invasion. Other Englishmen worried constantly about Catholics, particularly as symbolized by France and the Jesuits; and for a time Shaftesbury's "brisk boys" harassed London in what was termed their street capacity. But Dryden could also see in his time such achievements as that of Blake's navy and the desperate but brilliant Protectorate; he could see a Royal Society with ornaments like Boyle, Hooke, and Newton. In music there were Blow and the two Purcells, in art Lely and Kneller. An architect like Wren (one of the few of his great contemporaries that Dryden did not honor with a poem) was answered in philosophy by so various a trio as Hobbes, Dr. Charleton, and Locke. Such great men and their actions deserve all the stress that emphasis or repetition can give them. And there were also Milton and, Dryden knew, himself, as well as two generations of dramatists. The world was alive with men of genius, and Dryden reacted to them with hope or, when they threatened institutions and his heroic idea, with a vigorous attack turning "reality" on his victims. Dryden must have known himself to be more creative in numerous realms of poetry, drama, prose, and translation than any English writer before him, never repeating himself except in such minor forms as prologue and song.

Dryden was, then, conservative to an almost militant degree. But if he harkened to the past so strongly in the institutional Church militant, he looked forward with eagerness to that Church triumphant of individual worth. An establishment man where the establishment was involved, he welcomed the life of speech and action as a beckoning sphere of hope for novel and indeed radical achievement. As with all people, his own example proves more telling than any precept. If one were a Marxist, Dryden would provide a fascinating paradox of a man in whom the "feudal" order claimed sentiment and allegiance, but also a man in whom the dawn of the bourgeoisie was heralded with joy. Not being a Marxist, one may still see a paradox but find it resolved in poem after poem in which the human spirit finds full liberation in a world secured by being firmly stable. Such was the dream, and such the cause that he fought for.

It seems a dream, and it seems a cause, particularly English. Preserve; but change by individual effort and the power of the word. In his life of Dryden and in his life of Pope, Dr. Johnson stresses Dryden's innovations, showing himself to be a conservative two or three generations after Dryden. He could appreciate Dryden's revolution in literature, and could even make too much of the new and disregard Dryden's deep attachment to the old. Like all great and prolific writers, Dryden teaches more than one lesson, and his achievement as well as his life offer the two faces of conservatism and radicalism. Rymer and Eliot could respond to those differently, and so can people today. But seeing Dryden steadily and seeing him whole requires that we see a man, a writer, at once reactionary and radical, or at least conservative and liberal. And in reverse terms, the same is true of Milton.

As the three greatest poets of the Restoration showed, one cannot live as long as Butler, Milton, and Dryden did without undergoing test and ordeal. If it is typical of Milton that his liberal hopes were challenged and led to a necessarily wider view in which both liberalism and conservatism would require merging for eventual triumph, it seems equally typical of Dryden that his conservative principles should be tested and that he should also come to a wider view of men in which his liberalism and conservatism found a new adjustment. Both poets found themselves in the last decade and more of their lives in a society in which major changes rendered them aliens after the closest participation in events before their trials. And both found—in the epic redefined, retranslated one might say—their last and in many ways their finest achievements. Dryden's works comparable to *Paradise Lost* and *Paradise Regained* include not only the verse addresses, not just *Don Sebastian* and *Amphitryon*, but also the *Virgil* of 1697 and the *Fables* of 1700. I shall leave the *Fables* to the last chapter and say only a very little about the former. The translation of Virgil's *Eclogues* shows Dryden at the height of his powers but in an uncongenial genre. All considered, his translation of the *Georgics* probably achieves perfection more nearly than he or anyone else in English has ever reached in its fidelity and imaginative re-creation. But his *Aeneis* must be the test case, given its preeminence in the Virgilian canon and for Dryden's own heroic ideal.

Classical scholarship was only developing in the seventeenth century, and almost all important work was done by Continental scholars. England continued to lag as far behind in scholarship as it did in printing. With many grudging and unworthy strictures on Dutch humanists, Dryden benefited from them and their French counterparts. By now his own scholarship has been shown to be abreast of what was then known. Like all poets from the Middle Ages to his own time, he found special interest in the story of Dido and Aeneas (*Aeneid*, IV). One of the truly great stories, its heroine has been described as "the first woman in love in whose case we know why she loved." [37] A widow and a queen, she meets a widower and king. She had had to wander and establish her city before Aeneas, and with so much in common with him she yet is so feminine that she falls in love when his wanderings from Troy bring him to Carthage and he tells his heroic story. The love between them seems wholly natural, given their characters and strong personalities. Dido is prompted by her sister Anna; and Aeneas, lonely in his eminence, naturally finds her attractive. Each has a tragic flaw in the Aristotelian sense. She is torn between the memory of her husband, Sychaeus, along with her duty as queen and on the other side by her love for the hero. He deviates from the task imposed on him by fate. Their union joins contrasts: her Epicureanism with his Stoicism; her submission of a nation's interests to love with his submission of his emotions to the interest of family and nation. Although the Dido story is the most personal thing in the *Aeneid*, in Virgil's handling there are strong suggestions of the origin of Roman and Carthaginian strife, as also in Dido some recollections of Cleopatra. Along with such larger historical implications, book IV possesses "a considerable symmetry":

> the very middle of the book is formed by a speech of Aeneas lying between two short bits of framework of nearly equal size, outside which come two nearly equal speeches by Dido, framing which, in turn, are two narrative portions

[37] Quoted by Arthur Stanley Pease, ed., *Publii Vergili Maronis Aeneidos Liber Quartus* (Darmstadt, 1967), p. 33. In what follows I am indebted to this splendid edition.

> each of 28 lines. Midway between the beginning of the book and its centre and again between the centre and the end are found the narrative portions containing the story of Fama and the magical scene, respectively. Mercury's speech in the first half of the book approximately corresponds in length to that in the second. Near the beginning of the book are two speeches by Dido and Anna and near the end two others by the same speakers.[38]

Dryden's translation observes the spirit of this order and of the characters Virgil depicts. His changes are small but steady and in the end not inconsiderable.

One kind of alteration is difficult to show in words, since it involves the conception of Dido. Dryden borrows to some extent from Ovid's characterization in the *Heroides*.[39] In that letter Dido's passion is no greater than it is shown to be in the *Aeneid,* but we seem to observe it from a closer distance and to sense its physicality more. From Ovid's depiction of a character more a woman than a queen Dryden adapts Virgil to emphasize her outraged femininity. For example, Dido at once sees through Aeneas' furtive efforts to ready his ships: "What Arts can blind a jealous Woman's Eyes!" To Virgil, Dido is simply "amantem." Later, realizing that in her anguish she is losing control of her mind, Dryden's Dido expostulates:

> What have I said? where am I? Fury turns
> My Brain; and my distemper'd Bosom burns.
> (853–54)

He follows Virgil with great closeness, except that the last clause is an addition emphasizing the psychosomatic torture.

[38] Ibid., p. 30. Those familiar with current classical scholarship will recognize my choice of the mildest authority for "mathematical symmetry."

[39] Ovid, *Heroides,* VII. For the collection of *Ovid's Epistles* translated by various hands and brought out by Dryden in 1680, he himself translated "Dido to Aeneas."

In view of the long literary tradition developed about Book IV, it is not surprising that Dryden somewhat alters Aeneas by making Dido's perspective on his character more prominent. From Dido's characterization of Aeneas in the second half of the book, "perfidus ille" (*Aeneid*, IV, 421; *Aeneis*, IV, 608), Dryden takes the idea of treachery in love, and in an earlier passage has Dido call Aeneas (without Virgilian authorization) a traitor. Her sense of being wronged is dwelt upon by Dryden, so as to stress both her feminine anger and certain philosophical emphases that are new. Dryden gives Dido some lines of resentment against her fate that much expand on Virgil. Only the last line but one quoted below is fully authorized by Virgil ("nusquam tuta fides," 373). The rest, with its sad accusation against Jupiter and against her celestial supporter, Juno, show Dryden's full recognition of her tragedy as an individual in an inimical world:

> The Gods, and *Jove* himself behold in vain
> Triumphant Treason, yet no Thunder flyes:
> Nor *Juno* views my Wrongs with equal Eyes;
> Faithless is Earth, and Faithless are the Skies!
> Justice is fled, and Truth is now no more.
>
> (532–36)

"Triumphant Treason." Something of the language of Dryden's early heroic plays echoes in the phrase. But the context differs in lacking the sallies of argument and salvoes of reasoning; a new conception of man's lesser place in the state of things has emerged forcibly. Dido's dignity and her tragic plight are heightened by Dryden's insistence on her being a timeless woman when Virgil has her a queen, and a queen when Virgil has her a Carthaginian woman. Like Aeneas, but far more tragically, her division of mind between duty and passion is enhanced by the queenly dignity of the person suffering. Aeneas is the one well known to be driven or pursued by fate ("fato profugus"), and Dryden takes a hint from Virgil to characterize Dido in similar terms. For Virgil's "infelix fatis exterrita Dido" (450), Dryden gives, "The wretched Queen, pursu'd by cruel Fate" (653). A common superhuman agency drives them both, him to epic achievement, and her to tragedy. And for "infelix . . . Dido," Dryden gives us that oxymoron of humiliated dignity, "The wretched Queen." The sympathy he extends to Dido as a tragic queen owes less to Lee's play of a similar title than to a Jacobite recollection of the sufferings of James II, for whom, we recall, Dryden had held up his translation of Virgil in hopes that he might lay it at his misguided master's feet.

"The Gods." From his translation of excerpts from Lucretius for *Sylvae* in 1685 to his play *Amphitryon* in 1690, to his translation of Ovid's *Metamorphoses*, I, for *Examen Poeticum* in 1693, and on to the many poems in the *Fables* in 1700, Dryden had to deal with the pagan deities in instances when they could not be humanistically or typologically absorbed with much ease into the Christian dispensation. From 1685 he found his method in a complex treatment of the gods. On the one hand, like his Dido he criticizes them. (Except when he can extract a humanistic equivalent of God the Father, he never has a kind word for Jupiter any more than for Louis XIV.) On the other hand, he increases their presence. He describes Aeneas resolute to leave Dido adding three words to Virgil: "Fate, *and the God*, had stop'd his Ears to Love" (637, the italics showing the addition). In other words, Dryden brings his Christian awareness to bear in such a way that it evokes that of the reader. The result is "to expose the destitution of pagan philosophies." [40] At the

[40] See the excellent article by the classicist Norman Austin, "Translation as Baptism: A Study of Dryden's Lucretius," *Arion*, VII (1968), 576–602.

end of Book IV, Dryden must follow Virgil in detailing the end of Dido and her agonies. He heightens or dwells upon Virgil's own sense of a noble, deceived, self-deceived creature of fate:

> Then *Juno*, grieving that she shou'd sustain
> A Death so ling'ring, and so full of Pain;
> Sent *Iris* down, to free her from the Strife
> Of lab'ring Nature, and dissolve her Life.
> For since she dy'd, not doom'd by Heav'ns Decree,
> Or her own Crime; but Human Casualty;
> And rage of Love, that plung'd her in Despair;
> The Sisters had not cut the topmost Hair;
> Which *Proserpine*, and they can only know;
> Nor made her sacred to the Shades below.
> Downward the various Goddess took her flight;
> And Drew a thousand Colours from the Light:
> Then stood above the dying Lover's Head,
> And said, I thus devote thee to the dead.
> This Off'ring to th' Infernal Gods I bear:
> Thus while she spoke, she cut the fatal Hair;
> The strugling Soul was loos'd; and Life dissolv'd in Air.
>
> (993–1009)

Dryden no more than Milton (or their contemporaries) shared our idea of the equality of the sexes. If Dryden escapes the censure earned by Milton, it is only because he had the good judgment not to make explicit in his mature work the assumptions held so widely during the seventeenth century. And like Ben Jonson, he honored good women: the Duchess of Monmouth, Anne Killigrew, the Duchess of Ormonde, and others. More than that, however, in the last decade and a half of his life he came to see that the role of *women* in a male world presented to all people an especially appropriate version of mankind's sorry experience in the world. In his comedy, *Amphitryon,* Molière had kept Alcmena offstage after the revelation that Jupiter had assumed the guise of her husband, entering her bed and life, lest the comedy turn into tragedy. Dryden's version, which borrows a great deal from Molière and something from Plautus, deliberately brings her on stage for the last scene. The result verges on tragedy. Admittedly, *Amphitryon* has a pagan milieu, and Dryden continues to find hope in Christianity. More than that, Aeneas does find the new Troy, and great individuals continue to achieve great things. Yet Dryden inescapably concerns himself in his last fifteen years with more than the pagan element in stories as timeless as that of Dido. The human story, narrative's higher mimesis, is involved as it had so preeminently been involved in *Paradise Lost.*

The fullest version of these many concerns was reserved for the *Fables,* which make so fitting a close to this book that discussion of that collection is reserved to the last chapter. They show what is revealed by the story of Dido and of Aeneas and what is revealed by the other late works by Dryden. We discover a ripeness of style and tone, a mellowness of attitude toward the lives of women and men that proves to be in the highest, but also the most complex, degree affirmative. In the last years of his life a change occurs in Dryden's heroic idea. Hope remains, but with grave qualification and with an almost Miltonic deferment to the last historical adjustments by Providence. Dryden's position after the Revolution of 1688 was strangely like Milton's after the Restoration of 1660. Both were in danger of their lives. It was by statute a treasonable act to be "reconciled" to Roman Catholicism, and the punishment for treason remained death by hanging, drawing, and quartering. In the confused early years after the Revolution, many Catholics were being arrested, and the resolute assertion of Catholicism by the first poet of the age could only embarrass a government some of whose Anglican bishops were refusing to take the Oath of Allegiance. It is remarkable that in those years of trial Dryden returned to narrative, protecting himself by translating (often with criticism or gibes against the order of William III). It is not remarkable that he, like Milton, found it necessary somewhat to change his notes to tragic. Or that, also like Milton, his heroic idea suffered fundamental challenge. Undeniably that idea suffered loss of hope and deferment of the hope that remained. But for both poets and their art there was abundant recompense in the still, sad music of humanity. What Dryden's heroic idea lost in hope it gained in affection for a Dido or an Alcmena. As the scope of humankind lessened, as its aspirations required deferment, its attractions increased for a now old man who had seen so much and in whose hopes the human comedy and the divine found their last adjustment.

PART THREE
COLORS OF GOOD AND EVIL

VII

THE SONS OF BELIAL

In Courts and Palaces [Belial] also Reigns
And in luxurious Cities, where the noyse
Of riot ascends above their loftiest Towrs,
And injury and outrage: And when Night
Darkens the Streets, then wander forth the Sons
Of Belial, flown with insolence and wine.
— *Paradise Lost*, I

The Sons of Belial had a glorious Time.
— *Absalom and Achitophel*

The examples Milton gives of the riotous behavior of the Sons of Belial are situated in Sodom and Gibeah, but to many readers it has seemed as if Milton is commenting on the sins of the Restoration court. I do not know (nor does anyone else) just when Milton wrote the lines or whether he had London in mind. Dryden thought of Belial as a rebel whose uncontrolled life was a symptom of a larger disease. His line therefore occurs in the character of Shimei, the Whig sheriff, Slingsby Bethel:

During his Office, Treason was no Crime.
The Sons of *Belial* had a glorious Time:
For *Shimei*, though not prodigal of pelf,
Yet lov'd his wicked Neighbour as himself.[1]

There is no question, however, that what we may label the profligate Sons of Belial offended the sober in the Restoration as much as their counterparts had the sober during the

[1] *Absalom and Achitophel*, 597–600; see also 1016.

reign of Elizabeth I. The rakes received notoriety for their pursuit of pleasure, their excessive indulgence, and their disorderliness even at court. They derived their designation from "rakehell," and "rake" came to imply some degree of position in society. The height of the dissipation came about 1669, although even later there were disgraceful incidents like that at Epsom in 1676. Rochester, Etherege, and others brawled with the watch, lost one of their fellows, and had to lie low for a time. It was for such behavior that the word "Cavalier" had been used as an insult by the "Puritans," another name of insult. Profane and erotic works were no longer burned by a bishop's orders, but there were still among the Sons of Belial those who, like Marlowe and Marston, were gifted writers. Besides Rochester and Etherege, there were notably Sedley and Buckhurst, who were notorious for three public escapades in 1662, 1668, and 1669, as well as for much that was darkly suspected.

It is almost as difficult to judge fairly the misconduct of others as it is the misconduct of ourselves. For some reason, probably because of the King's profligacy (profligacy is what "Belial" means), the Restoration is commonly regarded by some admirers and detractors alike as a low tide in sexual morality, with other aspects of morality largely forgot. Drink, sexual license, and rowdyism are said to have existed and did exist. And how shall we judge the behavior with women of Charles II next to that of Henry VIII? What was the morality of Clarendon or Danby in comparison with Thomas Cromwell? For degrading endings, one might compare that of Lee with that of Marlowe. While we consider the many lies of Elizabeth I, excusing them and her hatred of Puritans as examples of statesmanship; and when we consider the constant betrayal by her courtiers of her and each other—then we can take the same moral satisfaction that we get from clucking our tongues over the Restoration. It seems pretty evident that cooler and more judicious examination is desirable.

One can contradict the mistakes of custom by pretending that they had no basis, however, and that would get us nowhere. The particular nature of folly and evil that flourished during the Restoration and found literary expression requires that we use the same interpretive standards that we employ on subjects less lush. The traditional explanation for what occurred holds that after the excessive puritanical rigor of the Commonwealth and Protectorate, the nation swung to the other extreme. There may be something in that, although Butler's Hudibras and Bunyan's Christian do upset the idea at both ends. We must consider individuals when we lack information about a whole society. We do not know the year of Etherege's birth, but it was probably near 1635. Buckhurst and Sedley were born within a year of each other (1638, 1639), and Rochester was born in 1647. It is a generation that came of age about 1660, and consequently it seems unlikely that those gentlemen had long memories of Puritan rigor. Whatever the causes impelling these four to behave differently from other writers, we can find in what they wrote evidence of what they were up to and why.

One small part of the social milieu of the early Restoration, the time being talked about, has been especially well described by Etherege in his first play, *The Comical Revenge; Or, Love in a Tub* (1664).[2] The name of the hero, Sir Frederick Follick, suggests the kind of "frolic" or wenching and brawling favored by the rakes. Another character and one of the first of the fops, Sir Nicholas Cully, seeks vainly to imitate Sir Frederick. According to the *dramatis personae*, Sir

[2] I owe to my friend Tetsuo Kishi the sense of the particular social relevance of the play. See "George Etherege and the Destiny of Restoration Comedy," in *English Criticism in Japan*, edited by me (Tokyo, 1972), pp. 156–69.

Nicholas was "Knighted by *Oliver*," and a character later says that "his Mother was my Grand-mother's Dairy maid" (V, iii, 26). To some of us the snobbery and utter lack of charity in the rakes are far worse than the frolics. From Sir Nicholas the social scale descends yet farther to London gamesters, to whores, and to the "saucy impertinent French-man, Servant to Sir *Frederick*," Dufoy, who contracts the venereal disease to which those of higher orders in the play possess social immunity. The comedy also has a high-flown "serious" plot of love and honor among the aristocracy and an intrigue plot involving that Widow who is Sir Frederick's target as a means to improve his fortune. It usually proves possible to recall Butler as a base of comparison, and often, as with the widow here, it is instructive.

The action of the play effectively starts with Etherege's favorite opening scene, the rake awakening after a "frolic" or "ramble." Sir Frederick and his companions had visited late at night the dwelling of Mrs. Grace, the "Wench kept" by the gamester Wheadle; as Grace's maid Jenny says, Sir Frederick and his "rude ranting Companions hoop'd and hollow'd like Mad-men, and roar'd out in the streets, *A whore, a whore, a whore*" (I, ii, 78–80). She adds for Sir Frederick other details of the wholly unedifying escapade:

> *Maid*. These were not all your Heroick actions; pray tell the Consequence, how you march'd bravely at the rere of an Army of Link-boys; upon the sudden, how you gave defiance, and then wag'd a bloody war with the Constable; and having vanquish'd that dreadful enemy, how you committed a general massacre on the glass-windows: Are not these most honourable atchievements, such as will be registred to your eternal Fame, by the most learn'd Historians of *Hicks's-Hall*? (I, ii, 117–25)

Jenny is properly ironic about such "Heroick actions" as marching "bravely" at the rear of a gang, attacking a grossly outnumbered constable, and smashing windows. For our part we should not feel anger so much in judging Sir Frederick as think that there is something approaching mental, emotional, and moral deficiency in such actions. When Shadwell's Don John (in *The Libertine,* which is of course a version of the Don Juan story) burns a convent so that he and his companions in evil may rape the nuns as they flee, that deficiency has gone lurid beyond belief. But then we recall that Shadwell never possessed the intelligence or ambivalence of Etherege, who is the one, after all, who first created and first judged Sir Frederick. Whatever one may say about the morality and the normality of Etherege, and it is not too much, he did happen to possess an intelligent and creative mind.

The great threat to the world of Etherege and the other rakes is the haunting thought that there may be nothing more that is new, that life has no more sensation and meaning for them. Judging others by themselves, they suspected the same motives in even the most straitlaced, so presuming that if others behaved with the propriety of custom they merely concealed their motives in hypocrisy. The rakes wished to recognize what one feels and thinks, to act on one's real motives without cant, and to set what was "natural" as a code. They interested themselves accordingly in a variety of Epicureanism, in classical naturalism, and in French *libertinisme.*[3] The easy answer to the question of what a person wants is always gratification, and it takes little effort to laugh out of the room such notions as love, duty, modesty, and self-respect. Of course we need not pull the long face. Sometimes we should ask of the moralist the question raised by Shakespeare's Pompey: "Will your Worship geld and splay all the boys

[3] See Dale Underwood, *Etherege and the Seventeenth-Century Comedy of Manners* (New Haven, 1957), chs. I and II on the intellectual backgrounds. The description wholly fits only Etherege among the dramatists, but it applies well to our Sons of Belial.

and girls of the town?" But the pursuit of gratification is one like that engaged in by Dr. Johnson's Rasselas in having a conclusion in which nothing is concluded. At least not in the terms posited. After so much in the way of ramble, the sense grows that the world is really empty, and the fear rises that one's own life may be hollow. The couplet tagging the end of Etherege's play suggests more than idle George thought:

> On what small accidents depends our Fate,
> Whilst Chance, not prudence makes us fortunate.
>
> (V, v, 157–58)

Butler might have thought so, too, but the idea made him furious. Idle George has the proper Anacreontic shrug, even if he detested drinking.

The patron saint of the rakes, and of some others, was clearly Sir John Suckling. The evidence is various, and includes the third stanza of Etherege's poem "To a Lady, Asking Him How Long He Would Love Her":

> Then since we mortal lovers are,
> Let's question not how long 'twill last,
> But while we love let us take care
> Each minute be with pleasure [passed];
> It were a madness to deny
> To live because we're sure to die.
>
> (13–18)

This lesson read to Cloris gives a psychological version of the old "persuasion to enjoy." It has the semi-pastoral, semi-elegiac (that is, love elegy) aura of many Restoration songs, again a Cavalier inheritance.[4] Something has happened, however. The pastoral-elegiac weave had once combined good manners with euphemism. Now, for a small group of rather gifted rakes, that pastoral-elegiac covering constitutes the lace

[4] See *The Cavalier Mode* (Princeton, 1971), pp. 232–37.

and wig for the human animal. I see no need to go out of my way either to choose or avoid the obscene and the scatological. My point is that the poets involved did retain the manners, such as they are, of gentlemen, even while (to misapply Donne) their bodies thought. A hierarchy of poems, beginning and ending with those by the best poet of the group, Rochester, will suggest something of the limits, as well as of the power within the limits, of the rake poets.

One of Rochester's finest love poems, "The Mistress," has an opening well known by readers of Restoration poetry:

> An age in her embraces passed
>   Would seem a winter's day,
> Where life and light with envious haste
>   Are torn and snatched away.

The fours and threes of English song still have their magic, giving a sense of possible lasting happiness from a source seldom so reliable, a love almost wholly physical. I know that some biographical readings would like to suggest far more, but I do not think that the poem, or Rochester's other poems, supports any degree of "spiritual love." To take a fairly mild example, "The Advice" to Celia will have none of her insistence on that "gewgaw" reputation, and so dismisses her with a curse:

> Live upon modesty and empty fame,
> Foregoing sense for a fantastic name.
>
> (49–50)

From plays in the period, we might expect a father sarcastically to tell his errant daughter to go off with her unsanctioned husband and live on love. But to consider virtue a barren diet is a novel tenet of the libertine catechism. Insofar as love is considered to be physical, like food and drink it must satisfy "sense." [5]

"Sense" requires not only steady fare, however, but also constant stimulation. And in the lesser known stanzas of "The Mistress" that follow the first, the rake shows how his satisfaction has been attained. His love flourishes with the hunger brought by absence, with the arousal by beauty, and with the pique by jealousy. The last two stanzas must be read with some care and in the context of the intervening stanzas. Once more the "fantastic" (modesty, empty fame, customary notions about love) is rejected:

Fantastic fancies fondly move
  And in frail joys believe,
Taking false pleasure for true love;
  But pain can ne'er deceive.

Kind jealous doubts, tormenting fears,
  And anxious cares, when past,
Prove our hearts' treasure fixed and clear,
  And make us blest at last. (29–36)

The first three lines quoted here can easily be misread (especially because "fondly" now does not mean "dotingly" or "foolishly"), but the fourth line makes all clear. If the "pain" is sufficiently constant, so will the love be. Rochester's view of experience has a clear-sightedness that brings the reader no more comfort than do Hobbes and Butler in telling us what they believe we are really like.

One means of keeping sensation atingle was to treat sex in those semi-pastoral terms that could gauze nakedness.

[5] Some people might wish to read "sense" here as "Natural understanding . . . practical soundness of judgment." The first *Oxford English Dictionary* usage (1684) does not support such a reading. The overwhelming linguistic evidence and the evidence from Rochester's writing is that he means sensation.

Many songs using the device can be found in the period (Dryden often uses such semi-pastoralism in lyrics). Rochester's semi-pastorals range from the conventional to the disturbing:

> As Chloris full of harmless thought
> Beneath the willows lay,
> Kind love a comely shepherd brought
> To pass the time away. (1–4)

After some parley she yields, out of "A sudden passion" (9). If we take the poem at all seriously, its point is psychological. When "a comely shepherd" can catch the nymph "in the lucky minute" (23), she will yield. It is a matter of luck, and of inexplicable swells of passion. Of course Rochester's skill with the fours and threes also lends assistance. He uses the same measure (adding the yet more lyric touch of trochaic or feminine rhymes) for another "Song" that I find disturbing:

> Fair Chloris in a pigsty lay;
> Her tender herd lay by her.
> She slept; in murmuring gruntlings they,
> Complaining of the scorching day,
> Her slumbers thus inspire. (1–5)

That remarkable first line sets a paradox capable of rousing the most lethargic sense. In what follows, she dreams that one of her swains comes running to her with the ill news that a pig of hers has been caught "in the gate / That leads to Flora's cave." The swain follows her as she runs off, catches her in the cave, and rapes her. "Frighted she wakes." Reassured that it was only a dream, she masturbates and so, after all, "She's innocent and pleased." She has it both ways, so satisfying our "Fair Chloris" and our "pigsty" expectations. The pastoral is an astonishingly capacious genre or convention, and although it had long concealed some grand social injustices in tributes to the great, it had never made us wallow among English pigs.

Other kinds of poems added to the stock of libertine conventions. Among those inherited from the Cavaliers is that of the "imperfect enjoyment." [6] Etherege's version (with that title) treats of senses so stimulated by love play that

> The action which we should have jointly done,
> Each has unluckily performed alone.
>
> (33–34)

Rochester's version (same title) really begins where Etherege's ends. The woman is more and more forgot as the man fusses and berates his unperforming member. He is thinking of other occasions.

> Stiffly resolved, 'twould carelessly invade
> Woman or man, nor ought its fury stayed . . .
> When vice, disease, and scandal lead the way,
> With what officious haste dost thou obey! . . .
> But when great Love the onset does command,
> Base recreant to thy prince, thou dar'st not stand.
>
> (41–42, 52–53, 60–61)

Rochester sees, and is driven, much more intensely than Etherege. He would rather be foul-mouthed with words never polite than leave a possibility of euphemism in word or thought.

The search for conventions, like the search for originality, represents the constant business of poets, but those who espoused libertinism perhaps had a greater need in that their subject matter was restricted. One of the new conventions

[6] See Richard E. Quaintance, "French Sources of the Restoration 'Imperfect Enjoyment' Poem," *Philological Quarterly*, XLII (1963), 190–99, who traces the motif in Ovid, *Amores*, III, vii, and Petronius, *Satyricon*, chs. 128–40, and so forward in time.

was given the name of the "ramble." Its cousin in plays, the "frolic," chiefly involves banging about and "roaring," but in the poems the usual version involves waking up after debauchery, either once more aroused or, more usually, surfeited and sick, and then going out on the town to agitate the "sense" again. The form seems to originate with Etherege, as indeed the analogy between its opening and those of his plays suggests. The "Letter from Lord Buckhurst to Mr. George Etherege" uses a tetrameter like neither Marvell's nor Butler's, a new medium affecting a downright maleness and bluff plainspeaking. Buckhurst starts off by telling of his state of morning arousal and imagines that he might have improved the time of "the fair Egyptian slattern" (7). But "Let us discourse of modern bitching" (24).

The call for information about the wenches led to "Mr. Etherege's Answer." He tells of waking in his friend's bed after their night of debauch, of sleeping out the day, and then going after wenches. The four-letter words and their longer counterparts sprinkle the lines of these poems, and like the verse form they seem calculated to give a brusque male sense that is as much a fiction as the simpering sentimentality of another day. Like the semi- or anti-pastoral, the obscene and the scatological provide a fiction to keep sensation in business. Etherege shows as much with a new dodge, a "Song" by a woman on the ramble: "To little or no purpose I spent many days." Over some decades the convention rattled on its way, culminating if not ending in Alexander Radcliffe's volume, *The Ramble: an Anti-Heroick Poem* (1682), in which the ramble continues for a considerable length. The form shares some characteristics and aims with the satiric prospect, as we shall see in the next chapter. But its sensational and sexual pretense to autobiography distinguishes it from the prospect. The ramble also is related to the "itinerary" poem. Richard Braithwaite's *Barnabee Itin-*

erarium; Or Barnabee's Journal held considerable popularity from its appearance (1638) into the eighteenth century. It is second- or third-grade Butler and (like so many of these ephemeral novelties) soon becomes tiresome.[7]

Found in the underwoods of the Restoration forest, such various forms and conventions, including versions of pastoral and obscenity, must be judged for poetic quality like any other poetry. Etherege's verse letters from his post at Ratisbon illuminate the libertine world better than most others. He sent them to his chief, the Earl of Middleton, Secretary of State. Their dominant themes, like those of his prose letters, are loneliness, longing for England, and sexual bravado. The poems seem rather woefully to attempt re-creation of the libertine world he had known and sauntered through, and they use the ramble measure. Being no poet but sensing a need to send a reply in verse, Middleton asked Dryden to draft a reply in his name after Etherege's second poem had arrived. Once the superior hand was in, Etherege wrote no more. So far was the libertine life fed and indeed created by fictions.

It should not be thought that the conventional bluffness of Dorset (at this time Lord Buckhurst), Etherege, and Rochester excluded other conventions from the practice of the mob of gentlemen that wrote (and lived) with feverish ease. Dorset managed to give the sophistication of the semi-pastoral one more turn in a "Song":

> Methinks the poor town has been troubled too long
> With Phillis and Chloris in every song. (1–2)

For his part, he will speak "The truth that I know of bonny Black Bess," who is the toast, and lover, of many in the town.

[7] Lesser but interesting poets like Radcliffe appear in the excellent anthology edited by Harold Love, *The Penguin Book of Restoration Verse* (Harmondsworth, Mddx., 1968).

A somewhat more familiar piece, another "Song," "Dorinda's sparkling wit, and eyes, / United, cast too fierce a light," manages a satiric creation of character seldom found in lyrics. It seems unlikely to have been possible in any century save that in which Donne's poems first appeared in print.[8] Yet Dorset and Sir Charles Sedley—Charles II's "Little Sid"—really do not match Rochester or Etherege in the creation of a libertine style. Dorset's poem sent off from a quiet moment during a sea-battle, "To All You Ladies," passed even the Victorian double standard. Sedley also seeks a purer, what Rochester would have thought a "fantastic," fiction. Sedley lives almost wholly for two songs: "Not *Celia* that I juster am," in which he gives credit for his fidelity to her unusual attractions; and "Love still has something of the sea / From which his Mother rose." This lovely opening is not sustained, and perhaps could not have been, but what follows does not really betray it.

Very different conventions of experience as well as of style govern such poems. We can see from them that those people who followed the libertine code meant different things by it, just as various motives have always led different people to membership in the same political cause. Dorset gradually grew more serious in the conventional sense, and Sedley became more sober in the 1670's. Playing tennis indoors with Etherege in 1680, Sedley was almost killed when the roof collapsed upon them. In what was still a highly superstitious age, he took it as a sign. Along with the affecting death of Rochester, the warning put him into a track of sobriety.

The contemporaries of Etherege and Rochester were mostly people who attended church twice on Sundays and who felt that numerous proprieties had to be observed in the name of morality and public order. Many women feared to

[8] The whole poem has at last been restored by William J. Cameron, *Poems on Affairs of State*, v (New Haven and London, 1971), pp. 384–85.

be in the very presence of our "profane wits," as Lady Woodvil described such as Dorimant in *The Man of Mode*. Many people who feared them were enchanted, however, by their brilliance and were fascinated, as if by witchcraft, by their charm. Like the memory of Cromwell and the thought of Hobbes, the images of Etherege and Rochester represented a challenge to the age and could neither be ignored nor forgot. In many ways their code of libertinism made up a counter-Restoration opposed to that offered by Butler, Milton, and Dryden—along with Marvell, Bunyan, Pepys, Otway, and the rest. But libertinism did not exist simply in isolation. It affected, and was itself increasingly affected by, the Restoration mainstream. Only Etherege seems to have held to the code throughout his life. Born we do not know when, dead equally uncertainly, in his pose of idleness he holds something of himself in reserve. Charming he was, teetotaling, but gamester and wencher to a frantic degree. His version of idleness or the Horatian *otium* held a negligent frenzy for sensation that makes him difficult to puzzle out. There is in him none of the tragic air that hangs over Rochester's filthy observations on others and shocking revelations of himself:

> Bawdy in thought, precise in words,
> Ill-natured though a whore,
> Her belly is a bag of turds,
> And her cunt a common shore.[9]

Once a poet reaches such a point, lyricism has been spoilt entirely, and, as with the growing frenzy of De Sade, ever stronger and more repulsive measures may be required to keep in business. Wreck cannot be far off.

Three of Rochester's finest poems depict the descent. The

[9] Rochester, "On Mrs. Willis," 17–20. "Precise" means hypocritically, puritanically pretending to be pure; the "shore" is an open sewer (cf. Shoreditch).

first, "To the Postboy," is a kind of perverted couplet-sonnet and is therefore short enough to be given entire:

Rochester. Son of a whore, God damn you! can you tell
A peerless peer the readiest way to Hell?
I've outswilled Bacchus, sworn of my own make
Oaths would fright Furies, and make Pluto
quake;
I've swived more whores more ways than
Sodom's walls
E'er knew, or the College of Rome's Cardinals.
Witness heroic scars—Look here, ne'er go!—
Cerecloths and ulcers from the top to toe!
Frighted at my own mischiefs, I have fled
And bravely left my life's defender dead;
Broke houses to break chastity, and dyed
That floor with murder which my lust denied.
Pox on't, why do I speak of these poor things?
I have blasphemed my God, and libeled Kings!
The readiest way to Hell—Come, quick!
Boy. Ne'er stir:
The readiest way, my Lord, 's by Rochester.

Conjectured to be a comment on that escapade at Epsom in June, 1676, Rochester in any event generalizes on many experiences. His frantic, filthy push for sensation carries with it a calm, clear awareness of it all. In that combination, or tension, lies the power of Rochester's poetry. Few of us will ever have to endure his fever, but all of us must admit, as he seeks to make us admit, that we do share things with that unhappy young nobleman.

One of Rochester's last known efforts at poetry, perhaps his very last, was his translation of the conclusion of a chorus from Seneca's *Troades* (lines 397–408, "post mortem nihil est ipsaque mors nihil"). Once again the brevity allows us to quote entire one of his finest poems:

After death nothing is, and nothing, death:
The utmost limit of a gasp of breath.
Let the ambitious zealot lay aside
His hopes of heaven, whose faith is but his pride;
  Let slavish souls lay by their fear,
  Nor be concerned which way nor where
  After this life they shall be hurled.
Dead, we become the lumber of the world,
And to that mass of matter shall be swept
Where things destroyed with things unborn are kept.
  Devouring time swallows us whole;
Impartial death confounds body and soul.
  For Hell and the foul fiend that rules
  God's everlasting fiery jails
  (Devised by rogues, dreaded by fools),
With his grim, grisly dog that keeps the door,
  Are senseless stories, idle tales,
  Dreams, whimseys, and no more.

A distinction can be drawn between Rochester and most other writers of the second half of the century by virtue of his choosing that chorus rather than the much more popular one in *Thyestes* (lines 391–403, "stet quicumque volet potens," etc.) which Cowley had popularized in his Essays.[10] Rochester's phrasing, especially in lines 3–4 and 13–18, takes specifically Christian ideas for targets, and the age would have

[10] On the *Thyestes* choral motif, see the excellent study by Maren-Sofie Røstvig, *The Happy Man*, vol. I of two (Oslo and Oxford, 1954, 1962), pp. 21–22. Although the second edition of the first volume is almost a new book, the discussion of this matter will be found in both, along with the comment that after the Restoration the *Troades* chorus was entertained by "many serious men" (2nd ed., p. 230). I doubt the number, but Rochester was certainly serious.

seen so at once with a shudder. The fine translation reminds one of an even finer one, Dryden's of Lucretius "Against the Fear of Death."[11] Dryden heightens Lucretius so much as to expose the limits of Epicureanism and make the Christian explanation essential.[12] Both Lucretius and Seneca in the vein of the *Troades* present a pagan challenge to Christianity, unless some means of subversion like Dryden's could be found. The Deist Charles Blount acknowledged receipt of the translation by a letter to Rochester:

> I . . . must confess, with your Lordship's Pardon, that I cannot but esteem the Translation to be, in some measure, a confutation of the Original; since what less than a divine and immortal Mind could have produced what you have here written? Indeed the Hand that wrote it may become *Lumber*, but sure, the Spirit that dictated it, can never be so.[13]

A translation of a Stoic challenge to Christianity is taken by a Deist as proof of the immortality of the soul. I must confess that I have difficulty in judging whether in the last year of his life Rochester was becoming steadily more Christian or whether a variety of moods led to various responses. No absolute contrast need exist between the alternatives, perhaps, and there exists some evidence for both. The Senecan poem affords some of the best evidence, but more must be considered.

In 1680 there was published in folio a two-page *Letter to*

[11] Printed in *Sylvae*, the California edition, III (Berkeley and Los Angeles, 1969), 48–56. It should be observed that Seneca's soft Stoicism and Lucretius' hard Epicureanism have much in common.

[12] See the article by Austin cited above, p. 361.

[13] The letter is very aptly quoted by David Vieth in his edition, *The Complete Poems of John Wilmot, Earl of Rochester* (New Haven and London, 1968), p. 150, citing Blount's *Miscellaneous Works* (London, 1695), p. 1/117.

Dr. Burnet, From the Right Honourable the Earl of Rochester, As he Lay on His Death-Bed. Rochester wrote in great appreciation of Burnet's ministry to him, saying that he hoped

> to be exalted to that degree of Piety, that the World may see how much I abhor what I so long lov'd, and how much glory in Repentance in God's Service. Bestow Your Prayers upon me, That God would spare me (if it be his good will) to shew me a true Repentance, and amendment of Life for the time to come.

Even today, when deathbed repentances have become almost totally inexplicable, one can understand the excitement and even the thrill felt by Rochester's pious contemporaries in reading such words. The *Letter* opens with words very flattering of Burnet, who had later to insist that he had nothing to do with its publication.[14] Burnet then went on to describe at length his earlier conversations with Rochester. He professes to give the story he was told with but few "reserves," and he specifies the three chief topics of their series of talks in London: "*Mortality, Natural Religion and Revealed Religion, Christianity* in particular." [15] The discussion appears to have been very lively and at times to have involved considerable disagreement. It would not be far wrong to say that the result of those London talks was a standstill. That is, Rochester was still not sure about religion but "firmly resolved to change the whole method of his Life." [16] In the last week of his life, it was evident to Rochester that he was dying. He professed repentance and belief, amending even his language, except "calling any damned, which . . . was not decent," Burnet says.[17] In "The Conclusion," Burnet skillfully (being

[14] *Some Passages of the Life and Death of the Right Honourable John Earl of Rochester* (London, 1680), "Preface," sigs. A5ᵛ–A6ʳ.

[15] Ibid., pp. 28, 35.

[16] Ibid., p. 125.

[17] Ibid., 153.

one of the best preachers of the century) draws out the moral for others, particularly for "our Libertines." [18]

It is a haunting thought that, after exploring every other sensation and finding each successively more hollow, Rochester found his last sensation in Christian repentance. But if we believe in our own sincerity, we should grant the same capacity to a person who had long sought to be ostentatiously honest with himself. From beginning to end Rochester appeals to us, and often appalls us, by the sheer fire of his experience. In the paradoxical spirit of Blount we can close this consideration of the Sons of Belial by the observation that Rochester wrote *something* "Upon Nothing." Roughly the first half of the poem (1–27) deals with the paradox that "primitive Nothing Something straight begot" (5) and foretells that the agency of time will drive all back into Nothing's "hungry womb." The latter half of the poem (28–51) takes another direction, into satire of politicians and others, concluding with an apostrophe.

> Nothing! who dwellst with fools in grave disguise,
> For whom they reverend shapes and forms devise,
> Lawn sleeves and furs and gowns, when they like thee
>   look wise:
>
> French truth, Dutch prowess, British policy,
> Hibernian learning, Scotch civility,
> Spaniards' dispatch, Danes' wit are mainly seen in thee;
>
> The great man's gratitude to his best friend,
> Kings' promises, whores' vows—towards thee they bend,
> Flow swiftly into thee, and in thee ever end.
>
> (43–51)

There is in such Attic salt some mirth of a wry kind and a genuine moral base. But the poem very much suggests that

[18] Ibid., p. 161.

within about two years of his death Rochester held little in the way of Christian belief. His life, like King Lear's, had spiritually to come to nothing before anything positive could result.

Finest poet among the Libertines, greatest wastrel, John Wilmot, Earl of Rochester, was the last born and soonest dead. The expense of spirit in a waste of shame was such lust in action. Yet as "Upon Nothing" shows, there was in him another poetic vein. Burnet said that Rochester "often defended" satire "by saying there were some people that could not be kept in Order, or admonished but in this way." Burnet cautioned him that malice might be excessive and hurt the innocent:

> To this he answered, A man could not write with life, unless he were heated by Revenge: For to write a *Satyre* without Resentments, upon the cold Notions of *Phylosophy*, was as if a man would in cold blood, cut mens throats who had never offended him: And he said, The Lyes in these Libels come often in as Ornaments that could not be spared without spoiling the beauty of the *Poem*.[19]

Rochester directs us to such "Resentments," "Ornaments," and keeping "in Order" of the malignant. To the extent that the "Resentments" find their way into his lyrics, they possess that mingling of satire and song begun long before by Donne.[20] Indeed, the scatology and obscenity were never altogether remote in his writing: "pain can ne'er deceive." The total world of satire in the Restoration, however, lies between the role of Rochester's discovery of pleasure in plain and of knowledge in nothing, and the other role of Christian epic. The satiric dish of the time held many familiar and some strange fruits. For it was, we learn, a fruitful age for satire.

[19] Ibid., pp. 25, 26.

[20] See *The Metaphysical Mode* (Princeton, 1969), ch. IV.

VIII

A FRUITFUL AGE FOR SATIRE

difficile est saturam non scribere.
— Juvenal, *Satires*, I, 30

Nor needs there Art, or Genius here to use,
Where Indignation can create a muse.
— Oldham, *Satyrs Upon the Jesuits*, "Prologue"

Heroique Poetry . . . of which this Satire is undoubtedly a Species.
— Dryden, "Discourse" of Satire

THE SONS OF BELIAL and "our dreaming Platonists" (as Dryden once called them) held in common something more than the frail human estate. They shared satire, and they shared it with the whole century, although certainly not with all poets on all occasions. Henry More, with whom this book almost begins, has in his *Platonick Song of the Soul* (1642, 1647) "satirical sketches . . . of erroneous types of religion." [1] Those sketches afford the most interesting stretch in that preposterous allegory, as even More seemed to have recognized, since he enlarged them for the second edition. Kynaston's *Leoline and Sydanis* probably has more naughtiness than satire, but the two elements march under the same head of wit. The satiric element grows to be prominent in Davenant's *Gondibert*, which in fact directs criticism at so many quarters

[1] Douglas Bush, *English Literature in the Earlier Seventeenth Century*, 2nd ed. (Oxford, 1967), p. 92. See also *The Metaphysical Mode* (Princeton, 1969), ch. IV.

that one wonders what is left to support the poet's values. Chamberlayne's *Pharonnida* controls the fire better, usually directing it against the unbridling of will and passion by a mob, a city, villains, and others possessed of pride or self-interest. But Chamberlayne also had, like Kynaston, the ability to relax, and on one of those occasions that would be a digression in any other poem, he gives us a delightful exposé of "Phantastick Love" (II, v, "Argument"):

> That new Platonnick Malady, the way
> By which imperfect Eunuchs do betray
> Natures Diseases to contempt, whilst by
> Such slight repast, they strive to satisfie
> Loves full desires, which pines, or else must crave
> More then thin Souls in separation have.
>
> (II, v, 17–22)

It may seem strange that in a poem whose plot surrounds the main lovers with mystic symbolism Chamberlayne should satirize these "amorous Humorists" (II, v, 181).[2] Apart from the evident possibility of anything's happening in *Pharonnida*, the explanation involves, I believe, the persistence of satire from Donne, Marston, and Joseph Hall to Pope and Dr. Johnson.

i. The Right Vein of English Satire

Satire, and especially seventeenth-century English satire, need not arise necessarily from the object of formal attack. It sometimes seems just to spill out when, as Juvenal puts it, the poet finds it difficult *not* to write satire. Moreover, like any kind of literature, satire creates its own energies, independently fashioning those "Ornaments" that Rochester told

[2] Apart from the reasons given below, there are those given on the score of "Platonick Love" in *The Cavalier Mode* (Princeton, 1971), pp. 214–25.

Burnet could not be dispensed with merely because they were untrue. Satirists no more than panegyrists are on oath. The important thing is that satire, like panegyric or any poetic kind, should respond to, and re-create, important features of human experience. Rochester said that satire keeps in order those who cannot be ruled by other means. That nice way of putting it does not come very near the truth. Rather, satire testifies to a sense that things have gone wrong, that society or literature or morals are degenerating, and frequently the satirist shows an order ending or the very edifice of civilization crumbling into ruin.[3] Donne had used satire to protect his private sphere from the "World." In the greater arena of public poetry developed in mid-century, English satire found its fullest capacity.

Our premise is that satire identifies a specific or general sense of something's having gone wrong. Butler's *Hudibras* shows his lively faith in the complete applicability of that premise. The only one approaching him in the belief in what one might call satire as the realistic norm was Rochester, whom Andrew Marvell regarded (according to his friend, John Aubrey) as "the best English Satyrist and had the right veine." [4] The other satirists of the century did not lack all satiric conviction, and they sometimes wrote with passionate intensity. Where satire represents a central truth to Butler and Rochester, however, it was to other poets one of many means for expressing truth, or a means of expressing one kind of truth. Satire seems to have fulfilled one or more of three functions. It could give satisfaction in itself, as is shown by such noisy writers as Marston, Hall, and Oldham. Even Roch-

[3] For the image, and for my thoughts about the nature of satire, I may refer to "In Satire's Falling City," in *The Satirist's Art*, ed. H. James Jensen and Malvin R. Zirker, Jr. (Bloomington and London, 1972), pp. 3–27.

[4] *Aubrey's Brief Lives*, ed. Oliver Lawson Dick (Harmondsworth, Mddx., 1962), p. 370.

ester took relish in satire as if it were a sharp sauce for the diet of the senses, and Butler found it an essential diversion from the meaninglessness of life. Satire could also be, however, a means of making moral discriminations and judgments. And it could provide a rhetoric for dealing with poetic problems requiring moral, tonal, or other control.

In my view, the moral purpose of satire seldom finds very satisfactory realization in poems totally satiric or wholly lacking in other elements. The satiric moralist elects himself as judge in Israel and of course provokes response. It seems most unlikely that from even so overwhelming and in some sense sincere a satire as *Hudibras* one could derive any ethical code. Both before and after the Restoration the Horatian model served to give satirists means of engagement and detachment. The focus is personal—on the poet himself or his friends—and the satire avoids irritation by taking up the stance of the defense. Jonson summed it up with his usual cogency in defining his art as one of moral discrimination: "Against the bad, but of, and to the good." [5] What all the poets shared was a sense of the rhetorical utility of satire. Jonson uses satire to set off praise, as do Milton, Marvell, Dryden, and others.

Until recently rhetoric has had a bad name, and even now we have not recaptured anything like the need for it that existed in a century much taken with decorums and occasions. And yet something of the rhetorical bent of the age can be well appreciated in a wonderfully satiric attack on satire: *Raillerie à la Mode Consider'd: or The Supercilious Detractor* (1673).[6] The anonymous author directs to satirists the ancient charge of a "lecherous itch to write slanders and lampoons," and his image shows that he attacks the satirists with their own weapons. Do they think that they have some

[5] "To William Earl of Pembroke," 3.

[6] My quotations are taken from Ruth Nevo's excellent study, *The Dial of Virtue* (Princeton, 1963), pp. 209–10.

precious new way of writing? He criticizes them coming and going, coming by telling them that their novelties are "no more than the old Mad Humor of the *Cobler* of *Gloucester*," and going by denying them their language and instead telling them they follow a "*New Canting Drolling* Way . . . Frenchifi'd into Raillerie à la Mode." Worst of all, they write without art or dignity but with

> a Sort of Natural Rhetorick . . . [for] though they do not distinguish or use them Grammatically, by the Names of *Sarcasmus, Asteismus, Micterismus, Antiphrasis, Charientismus,* or *Ironia,* yet they have their Dry *Bobs,* their Broad *Flouts,* Bitter *Taunts,* their Fleering *Frumps,* and privy *Nips.*

Instead of using as they ought the terms of the true *ars rhetoricae,* they have their modish "Natural Rhetorick." Now in fact it comes to the same thing, since the English terms used are taken or adapted out of that respectable source, George Puttenham, in order to explicate these very Latin terms.[7]

Our literary generalizations find their most adequate tests in the works of authors of high quality and large canons, and consequently a consideration of satire in the Restoration may begin with Milton and end with Dryden. There is a tendency to deny that Milton's singing robes have any satiric wrinkles and to assume that Dryden's are entirely so rumpled, but the notion is in error. For one thing, Milton came to subscribe to (and later to transcend) the satiric premise that things had basically gone wrong. Apart from such a general matter, there are details. One of the most appealing comes from Aubrey, who has the following among much else on Milton, with Dryden apparently a main source:

[7] Puttenham writes, for example, of the "bitter tawnt called *Sarcasmus*" (G. G. Smith, ed., *Elizabethan Critical Essays,* 2 vols. [Oxford, 1904], II, 160.

> Temperate man, rarely dranke between meales. Extreme pleasant in his conversation, and at dinner, supper, etc.; but Satyricall. (He pronounced the letter R (*littera canina*) very hard—a certaine sign of a Satyricall Witt—*from John Dreyden.*) [8]

The thought of Dryden enjoying pleasant talk with Milton and remarking especially on the blind poet's "Satyricall" bent has an unexpected charm. I am very much of the opinion that Dryden could recognize satire and a satirist when he saw them even if, given the date of Milton's death, Dryden was speaking from his observations of Milton before he himself wrote a satire. Milton never wrote a thoroughgoing satire, unless those sophomoric poems on the University Carrier be so dignified. But in a profound sense, Milton is a satirist, as has lately been shown again by an authoritative scholar.[9] And it is not difficult to find examples of Milton's use of a natural rhetoric of satire, even in his last published poems. In *Paradise Regained,* after the tremendous storm he has got up, Satan has a privy nip and a dry mock at Jesus, whom he addresses "in a careless mood."

> Fair morning yet betides thee Son of God,
> After a dismal night; I heard the rack
> As Earth and Skie would mingle, but my self
> Was distant. (IV, 451–54)

Jesus replies with the "bitter tawnt called *Sarcasmus*": "Mee worse then wet thou find'st not" (IV, 486). Or, if one desires a copybook example of meiosis, there is Manoa's remark to Samson: "I cannot praise thy Marriage choises, Son" (420).

[8] Aubrey, ed. Dick, p. 274. "R" was the dog's letter because it was used to represent a dog's growl.

[9] Irene Samuel, "Milton on Comedy and Satire," *Huntington Library Quarterly,* xxxv (1972), 107–30. Other Milton scholars have dealt with aspects of the matter.

Such details are as nothing, however, in the light of the grand parodic function of *Paradise Lost*, whose model is not the sacred one that serves for *Paradise Regained* but rather the pagan *Aeneid*. Here is Dryden on some of Milton's unusual divagations from epic practice:

> As for Mr. *Milton*, whom we all admire with so much Justice, his Subject is not that of an Heroique Poem, properly so call'd: His Design is the Losing of our Happiness; his Event [outcome] is not prosperous, like that of all other *Epique* Works: His Heavenly Machines are many, and his Humane persons are but two.[10]

Plainly, the more one knows about epics—and Milton and Dryden knew far more than we—the more unexpected *Paradise Lost* seems and was meant to seem. Milton himself insists unequivocally on the difference between his poems and previous epics (e.g., IX, 25–47). What he does in the whole can be seen most readily in his similes. After squeezing the pagan tradition for all it is worth, he flings away the pulp, gives the juice a Christian blessing, and declares it alone the true wine. *Paradise Lost* takes as its business a conscious parody, a sacred parody of the pagan and Renaissance epic, whether we consider its form or its treatment of the usual epic subjects and motifs.[11] John Gillies' edition of Milton's *Paradise Lost* once again comes to my assistance. When a

[10] "Discourse" prefixed to *Satires* in *The Poems*, ed. James Kinsley, 4 vols. (Oxford, 1958), II, 610. As Dryden's ensuing sentences show, his aim was to anticipate an attack on Milton by Thomas Rymer and, by getting in a few criticisms, to establish Milton's greatness. Rymer never did publish the promised critique.

[11] In *Milton and the Renaissance Hero* (Oxford, 1967), John M. Steadman well details the senses in which Milton has radically altered the notion of heroism. Michael Wilding provides an arresting comparison of Milton and Butler in "The Last of the Epics: The Rejection of the Epic in *Paradise Lost* and *Hudibras*," in *Restoration Literature: Critical Approaches*, ed. Harold Love (London, 1972), pp. 91–120.

second edition seemed called for, he added some new "Texts of Scripture" to his notes at the bottom of the page. As his "Advertisement" also shows, he now had an afterthought:

> And as Milton owns *he did not sometimes forget the celebrated heathen poets,* it was thought an improvement of this Edition, to point to such passages as seem to have been in his mind, when he composed Paradise Lost. They are therefore selected from Bishop Newton's notes, and *placed at the end of each book.*[12]

Gillies found in Newton's edition 33 "allusions to the Classics" in the 798 lines of Book I, and he prints them at the end without more than a phrase of quotation. For only the first hundred lines of the book, however, he finds forty-two allusions to passages of Scripture, which he quotes fully at the foot of the page. Such appropriation and exploitation of the pagan has a long history in the use of non-Christian literatures, and it is as old as Moses in the practice referred to as spoiling the Egyptians, or appropriating things to God's use (and one's own: see Exodus 3:22).[13] It does not need to be emphasized that *Paradise Lost* is an epic rather than a satire, but it does need to be emphasized that satiric technique enabled Milton to appropriate what he desired in justifying the ways of God to man. He was a man of his age even in transcending it.

Satire proper had taken a new direction in England on the appearance of John Cleveland, who made "state poetry" of it. His most recent editors have cleared the canon of a large number of poems long associated with him, and some of those are far from contemptible. But enough is left to preserve a latter-day *Clievelandi Vindiciae* such as was printed in 1669. Thirty-two collections alone were printed between

[12] I have reversed italic to roman usage; the italics are my stress.

[13] See R. R. Bolgar, *The Classical Heritage* (Cambridge, 1954).

1647 and 1699, and some in more than one issue.[14] Cleveland and Clevelandism have been charged with many literary misdemeanors by Dryden and others since. Yet he is the only English poet quoted in *An Essay of Dramatic Poesy*, and he is twice quoted approvingly, once from a satire.[15] Whatever one's final judgment may be, Cleveland must be granted to have been fertile in the invention of motifs that one will discover throughout mid-century public poetry. The satiric dialogue between two scoundrels seems to begin with his "Dialogue between two Zealots." After his, there appear a number of other poems on "The Kings Disguise," "Upon an Hermophrodite," and on such paradoxical occasions as "A Young Man to an old Woman Courting him," "A Faire Nimph scorning a Black Boy Courting her," and a "Miser that made a great Feast." Above all, he enjoyed the gift of a superior "character" writer, finding an instant audience with his "Smectymnuus," "The Mixt Assembly," and "The Rebel Scot." Such poems were widely appreciated, as they deserved to be, and were flattered by imitation. He had a knack for fastening on what had gone wrong (in the view of one of his fervent royalism) and of setting it forth rather luridly but in effective and characterizing detail. His "Smectymnuus, or the Club-Divines" begins by gibing at the name:

> SMECTYMNUUS? The Goblin makes me start:
> I' th' Name of Rabbi Abraham, what art?
> *Syriac*? or *Arabick*? or *Welsh*? what skilt?
> Ap all the Bricklayers that *Babell* built.

[14] *The Poems of John Cleveland*, ed. Brian Morris and Eleanor Withington (Oxford, 1967), pp. ix–x. See Nevo (as in n. 6, above) on Cleveland's role in poems on affairs of state.

[15] See *The Works of John Dryden*, the California edition, XVII (Berkeley and Los Angeles, 1971), ed. Samuel Holt Monk *et al.*, 30. The point about Cleveland was made by Paul J. Korshin in his very useful study, "The Evolution of Neoclassical Poetics," *Eighteenth-Century Studies*, II (1968), 102–37.

Some Conjurer translate, and let me know it:
Till then 'tis fit for a West-Saxon Poet.
But doe the Brother-hood then play their prizes,
Like Mummers in Religion with disguises?
Out-brave us with a name in Rank and File,
A Name which if 'twere train'd would spread a mile?

(1–10)

Later he conceives of a strange marriage (such bizarrie being a particular talent) "Betwixt Smectymnuus and *Et caetera*": [16]

The Banes are askt, would but the times give way,
Betwixt *Smectymnuus* and *Et caetera.*
The Guests invited by a friendly Summons,
Should be the Convocation and the Commons.
The Priest to tie the Foxes tailes together,
Moseley, or *Sancta Clara,* chuse you whether.
See, what an off-spring every one expects!
What strange Plurality of Men and Sects!
One sayes hee'l get a Vestery; another
Is for a Synod: Bet upon the Mother.
Faith cry *St. George,* let them go to't, and stickle,
Whether a Conclave, or a Conventicle.
Thus might Religions caterwaule, and spight,
Which uses to divorce, might once unite.
But their crosse fortunes interdict their trade;
The Groome is Rampant, but the Bride is Spade.

(75–90)

Such lines are effective in a topical way, but the things that made them seem so very much up-to-date, or to constitute raillerie à la mode, now deprive them of much of the old appeal. And yet Cleveland better than any other satiric poet

[16] The so-called bride, "*Et caetera,*" had appeared in an equivocal public oath required by Convocation in 1640. It seemed as difficult to parse as "Smectymnuus."

marks the transition to public poetry and to the belief that what was happening in England was historically and poetically real. It is comforting that even his new editors seem willing to allow him the "Epitaph on the Earl of Strafford," one of the most penetrating epitaphs ever put into verse, and indeed verse for all time:

> Here lies Wise and Valiant Dust,
> Huddled up 'twixt Fit and Just:
> STRAFFORD, who was hurried hence
> 'Twixt Treason and Convenience.
> He spent his Time here in a Mist;
> A *Papist*, yet a *Calvinist*.
> His Prince's nearest Joy, and Grief.
> He had, yet wanted all Reliefe.
> The Prop and Ruine of the State;
> The People's violent Love, and Hate:
> One in extreames lov'd and abhor'd.
> Riddles lie here; or in a word,
> Here lies Blood; and let it lie
> Speechlesse still, and never crie.

Apart from such an achievement, Cleveland also anticipated the concerns of later poets. "Upon the Kings return from Scotland" effectively foreshadows the myth of Restoration that Dryden was to make so much of. Before the developing satiric tradition was taken up by Dryden's hands, however, it had gone through others that put it to uses sometimes familiar and sometimes novel.

The satires by Andrew Marvell (and those others by him with some degree of assurance as to authorship) vary considerably in tone, method, and experience depending on whether Marvell belongs, as it were, to the party in power or out. Since the detached Horatian figure did not seem suited to satire fully engaged with public events, poetic strategies usually took their cue from one's relation to power. Of course all the satirists show how something has gone wrong. But given the hierarchical ideas of the seventeenth century, one praised (if one was Marvell) that heroic figure Cromwell and that group of God's chosen, those people who followed Cromwell; but one satirized the tyrant and the mob on the other side (whose partisans were busy doing the same in return).

Marvell's first satire of consequence, *Fleckno, an English Priest at Rome* (ca. 1645), "is an extravaganza in the manner of Donne." [17] It derives either from Donne's first satire, or from Donne's own model, Horace, *Satires*, I, ix. Horace tells of being accosted by a bore as he walks one morning along the Via Sacra. The pest keeps boasting and asking questions of a leading but obscene kind until, finally, it emerges that he wants Horace to get Maecenas' favor for him. Apollo saves his poet at last when the plaintiff in a lawsuit hales the bore off to court. Donne typically shows his troubled speaker already accosted, and he uses the device of walking to the royal court in order for him to introduce something of the satiric perspective or gallery. Marvell has his speaker go to Flecknoe's tiny room by social obligation. To escape Flecknoe's lute-playing, the speaker invites the half-starved lutanist to dinner. As they leave the room, they encounter a youth on the stairs. After some words pass, he joins them. Flecknoe pulls out his poems after they have eaten. The young man reads them aloud, but so badly that Flecknoe rushes home to write a satire on "the waxen Youth." Dismissing the young man, the speaker is free at last.

Fleckno does not measure up to Donne's satires, because it lacks Donne's dramatic power, and it has not made the experience matter very much in any other way. The kind of wit—and the general lack of focus and intensity—are evident at the poem's beginning:

[17] George deF. Lord in his edition, *Andrew Marvell: The Complete Poetry* (New York, 1968), p. 207.

Oblig'd by frequent visits of this man,
Whom as Priest, Poet, and Musician,
I for some branch of *Melchizedeck* took,
(Though he derives himself from *my Lord Brooke)*
I sought his Lodging; which is at the Sign
Of the sad *Pelican;* Subject divine
For Poetry . . . (1–7)

Melchizedek (Genesis 14:18 ff.) was considered a type of Christ for having been a prophet, priest, and king. Similarly, the pelican was an emblem of Christ, because of the legend that she sustained her young with the blood from her breast. Another cluster of religious allusions occurs in Marvell's description of the exceptionally narrow stairs:

there can no Body pass
Except by penetration hither, where
Two make a crowd, nor can Three Persons here
Consist but in one substance. (98–101)

"Penetration" concerns simultaneous occupation by two bodies of the same space, a point of dispute between Catholics and Protestants on the issue of the Eucharist. The Protestants denied the possibility, whereas the Catholics cited John 20:19, 26, on Christ's "penetration" or appearance through a closed door.[18] Marvell's "Three Persons . . . in one substance" of course refers to the Trinity. Such religious detail comes in the true seventeenth-century vein: learnedly, wittily. But it comes to no adequate end and, having no function, it is debased by its context, unlike Dryden's use of religious detail in *Mac Flecknoe.* Of course, debasement constitutes Marvell's purpose in the satire. Flecknoe is called "the Tyrant" (35; Dryden had obviously read the poem when he wrote *Mac Flecknoe*), but he possesses no power, except

[18] See Dryden, *The Hind and the Panther,* I, 93–105, and the notes in the California edition, III (1969), for a fuller account.

to show how his own intestines can respond harmoniously to the plucked gut-strings of his lute:

> So while he with his gouty Fingers craules
> Over the Lute, his murmuring Belly calls,
> Whose hungry Guts to the same streightness twin'd
> In Echo to the trembling Strings repin'd.
>
> (41–44)

Marvell needed a more important subject, a public subject.

His *Character of Holland* (ca. 1653) and *The First Anniversary of the Government Under His Highness the Lord Protector* (late 1654 or early 1655) have the common purpose of extolling the greatness of the Protectorate and its triumphs, present and future, over its enemies. The *Character* is a satire concluding with a panegyric on "our *State*" and its navy; *The First Anniversary* is a panegyric on Cromwell with satire on his opposition. That opposition is made up of the "Princes" of other countries (103–24), who earn both Marvell's satiric attention and promise of further treatment. Marvell also does not forget to expose the naked villainy of Cromwell's domestic enemies (293–320). In such mixtures of the panegyric and the satirical Marvell achieved his best public style (apart from his splendid *Horatian Ode*), and *The First Anniversary* is a notable if wordy poem. He fashioned such art in *The Character of Holland*, although the poem itself is, in spite of some high spirits, a low-minded, chauvinistic ridicule of the Dutch such as commonly gets written against the enemy in time of war.

Marvell's masterpiece in satire (if it is by him) is *The last Instructions to a Painter*.[19] The poem is not as unified as

[19] My remarks here are drawn from my essay, "The 'Poetic Picture, Painted Poetry' of *The last Instructions to a Painter*," reprinted by George deF. Lord in *Andrew Marvell: A Collection of Critical Essays* (Englewood Cliffs, N.J., 1968), pp. 165–74, along with John M. Wallace's fine essay on *The First Anniversary* (pp. 143–64), which bears on my considerations here.

Clarindon's House-warming and some of the other shorter pieces attributed to him, but it is the product of a superior mind and an ability to make detailed knowledge about the times come to life. The poem has energy, stance, focus, and purpose, and with these it does not matter whether a satire has an orderly narrative. Marvell's stance was one that could only have won the sympathy of his readers. He is a patriot outraged by the venality and corruption of the "Court-party" and the ignominy of the navy. (The Dutch had recently sailed up the Thames and the Medway with impunity, firing ships.) That stance in itself conceals for the most part the extent to which Marvell has been frustrated by the experience of being politically "out." But one need only compare the tone of this poem with the panegyric of *The First Anniversary* to see how Marvell's shift in relation to power has required a shift in strategy.

The last Instructions directs its satire first on prominent members of the court, who are castigated for numerous debaucheries and political corruptions (1–104). The charges against Anne Hyde, Duchess of York (49–78) are, as Marvell knew, simply untrue. Although a mixture of a lie doth ever add pleasure, as Bacon observed, Marvell appears to be stigmatizing in the Duchess her father, Clarendon, who was resented for his rapid rise in the nobility and for his power early in the Restoration. Marvell (or at any rate the poet) also uses her to discredit her husband, James, whose ultra-royalist views could only have aroused the fears of someone of Marvell's convictions. The next two episodes come from one who knew Parliament and events very well. After describing the tumultuous sitting of Parliament in the autumn session of 1666 (105–396), the poet details with sardonic humor the court's frantic and foolish efforts to obtain peace with the Dutch (397–520). What follows (521–884) must have surprised early readers even more than it does us. The Dutch under the great admiral De Ruyter are depicted sailing up the Thames. Instead of storming and howling, the poet narrates the event in a lyric tableau, almost as if it were an idyll. Marvell very well understood that an event that so outraged English nationalism could be given with the greatest effect if told as a pastoral:

> *Ruyter* the while, that had our Ocean curb'd,
> Sail'd now among our Rivers undisturb'd:
> Survey'd their chrystall Streams and Banks so green
> And Beauties ere this never naked seen.
> Through the vain Sedge, the bashfull Nymphs he eyd
> Bosomes and all which from themselves they hide.
> The Sun much brighter, and the Skyes more clear,
> He finds the Aire and all things sweeter here.
> The sudden change and such a tempting Sight
> Swells his old Veins with fresh Blood, fresh Delight.
> Like am'rous Victors he begins to shave,
> And his new Face looks in the *English* wave.
>
> (521–32)

The pastoral tale seems to imply a rape of the goddesses of that countryside which the Cavalier poets had made the sweet norm of England. This section also contains a panegyric on "brave *Douglas*" (647–94), the intrepid Scot who fell trying to defend an English ship from a Dutch firing party.

What makes the poem seem to have been written by Marvell (at least to one reader who recognizes the absence of proof) is found in the use of those oblique and even contrary perspectives that often provide his lyric poems with their richest assessments of experience. Those passages, along with the concluding section, possess a quality so superior to the rest of the poem, and to most of the satiric poems "on affairs of state," that they make it difficult to believe that Marvell was not the author. The last section of the poem (883–946) presents an audacious picture of the King, who has a vision of "a sudden shape with Virgin's Face":

> Naked as born, and her round Arms behind
> With her own tresses interwove and twin'd;
> Her mouth lockt up, a blind before her Eyes.
> (889 . . . 893)

We seem to be back to De Ruyter and "the bashfull Nymphs" and a possibility of sexual approach not diminished by the fact that the prince is Charles II. The King "wonder'd first, then pity'd, then he lov'd" (898). The tone is perfect. But as he touches her, the vision disappears, "And he divin'd, 'twas *England* or the *Peace*" (904). It is a brilliant tableau of a king and his party about to ravish *Respublica Anglicana* or to demand the favors of a vanishing *Pax Britannica.*

Prynne and his Elizabethan counterparts would have lost their lives rather than their ears for such lèse-majesté. Charles could not have been pleased, although only he among English princes is likely to have admired the daring wit. He would not have enjoyed the last section, "To the King," one of those petitions that he abhorred. ("God save me from my petitioners," he sighed.) Marvell obliquely and perhaps sincerely blames the "Courtiers" rather than the King: we seem to be back in the early 1640's. The conclusion expresses the ideals of "Presbyterian" politics, showing the poet a parliamentary royalist:

> But they whom, born to Virtue and to Wealth,
> Nor Guilt to Flatt'ry binds, nor Want to Stealth;
> Whose gen'rous Conscience and whose Courage high
> Does with clear Counsells their Large Soules supply;
> That serve the *King* with their Estates and Care,
> And as in Love on *Parliments* can stare,

(Where few the Number, Choice is there lesse hard):
Give us this *Court* and rule without a Guard.

(981–88)

Here is no constitutional radical. The thoughts (if not the style) could be imagined in *Absalom and Achitophel.* The King remains surrounded by a court of the noble and the rich, working harmoniously with Parliament. Charles II would certainly have wished it so, and yet more certainly Dryden.[20] As the crucial word, "Virtue," shows, however, Marvell splits on the same rock as Milton and Dryden. The lack of coincidence between good institutions and good men had bedeviled the Tudors, then Cromwell, and Charles II, as it had his father and grandfather. Only when William III brought Dutch efficiency did England become the great power that the vain search for "Virtue" had failed to bring about. All of us, whatever our political beliefs, are apt to sigh over the loss of so vain an ideal.

It has always been thought a dilemma irresolvable that the fine, delicate, much considering mind creative of Marvell's lyrics should also have written such noisy satire. Any of us can imagine that satiric decorum, especially for verse meant to be circulated widely, was likely to call for cruder expression. But Milton and Dryden show that such is not necessarily the case, and the dilemma remains. Once again [21] I shall postulate that Marvell's emotions led him to fear excess, in himself and others, as I believe his last lines show. What was small, what could be encompassed in "Those short but admirable lines," put him at ease. What was large, what

[20] John M. Wallace has argued in *Destiny His Choice: The Loyalism of Andrew Marvell* (Cambridge, 1968), pp. 179–83, that the poem's conclusion reveals a loyal poet and subject. I think this very true, but I also think that Charles II and Dryden had a very different concept of what loyalty entailed.

[21] As in *The Metaphysical Mode,* pp. 211–12.

seemed uncontrollable or excessive, seems to have put him ill at ease, and he was no happier with the rough measures designed to correct excess. In *The Rehearsal Transpros'd* (1672; "The Second Part," 1673), Marvell wrote one of the most successful of prose satires in his or any age, at least if the achieving of a political end constitutes success. He set out to discredit Samuel Parker, the chief apologist of Anglican persecution of Dissenters and Catholics. Siding throughout with Charles II, even to an extent beyond what he himself believed, Marvell aimed to divide the rigorous Anglican persecutors from a king they needed but who was proposing toleration for Dissenters and (no doubt particularly) for Catholics. Marvell would have nothing to do with persecution and absolute power, fearing even the rigors of law:

> But, I say, Princes, so far as I can take the height of things so far above me, must needs have other thoughts, and are past such boyes-play to stake their Crowns against your Pins. They do not think fit to command things unnecessary, and where the profit cannot countervail the hazard. But above all they consider, that God has instated them in the Government of Mankind, with that incumbrance (if it may so be called) of Reason, and that incumbrance upon Reason of Conscience. That he might have given them as large an extent of ground and other kind of cattle for their Subjects: but it had been a melancholy Empire to have been only Supreme Grasiers and Soveraign Shepherds. And therefore, though the laziness of that brutal magistracy might have been more secure, yet the difficulty of this does make it more honourable. That men therefore are to be dealt with reasonably: and conscientious men by Conscience. That even Law is force, and the execution of that Law a greater Violence; and therefore with rational creatures not to be used but upon the utmost extremity. That the Body is in

the power of the mind; so that corporal punishments do never reach the offender, but the innocent suffers for the guilty. That the Mind is in the hand of God, and cannot correct those perswasions which upon the best of its natural capacity it hath collected: So that it too, though erroneous, is so farr innocent. That the Prince therefore, by how much God hath indued him with a clearer reason, and by consequence with a more enlightned judgment, ought the rather to take heed lest by punishing Conscience, he violate not only his own, but the Divine Majesty.[22]

Some of this is satiric rhetoric, but I believe that force genuinely frightened Marvell, excited him, and led him to respond in ways that seem crude by comparison with his non-satiric poetry or even with the best satire by his contemporaries. Yet we assent to the essential truth of Marvell's prose. A nervously intense man will be found in Aubrey's depiction of Marvell and in the painting hanging in the National Portrait Gallery. But in his political stance—as a"Presbyterian" Cavalier, a "Presbyterian" royalist, an M. P. of the "Country" party—Marvell "misdoubted" much of what he saw about him. After he left Nun Appleton House, there was never again to be a Mary Fairfax to give an unforced beauty and order to his world. For as all of us discover, children will grow up and make choice of their own destinies:

Mary Fairfax had been promised to the Earl of Chesterfield, and the banns had been twice published at St. Martin's, Westminster; but Buckingham was irresistible, the lady fell deeply in love with him, and the proposed match was broken off.[23]

[22] *The Rehearsal Transpros'd* (both parts), ed. D.I.B. Smith (Oxford, 1971), pp. 111–12.

[23] Quoted from the *Dictionary of National Biography*, the entry on George Villiers, 2nd Duke of Buckingham.

In 1657, Marvell's Maria permanently left the garden world to marry that man whom Dryden was to dub Zimri, a man who became involved in a double adultery with the Countess of Shrewsbury, with whom he had openly lived for a time, and whose husband he mortally wounded in a duel. Marvell might have recalled wanly that Memory was mother of the Muses, and that satire has no Muse, unless, in Oldham's phrase, "where *Indignation* can create a muse."

ii. Humanity's Our Worst Disease

Marvell's satire shares with *Hudibras* a lowness of style that constitutes one satiric decorum and that also suggests the moral degeneration of the world depicted. The comparison also suggests the more radical pessimism of Butler's great poem. Marvell aimed at the particular object in a particular cause. Butler's particularities do not suffice for themselves, because they merely illustrate the general failure of man to be wise, decent, and good. The seeming exception will be found in Butler's seeming ode, "To the Happy Memory of the Most Renown'd Du-Val." As we might anticipate, all Butler's pindarics are satires, but this has a lightness of touch and an amused detachment that make it his one thoroughly humorous poem. Claude Duval was born in France, came to England at the Restoration, turned into a highwayman famous for his ostentatious gallantry to ladies and notorious for his daring. Notwithstanding the pleas of women, many of them of "quality," he was executed at Tyburn on January 21, 1670, in his twenty-seventh year.

Butler adumbrates the ironic "great man" such as was to be developed in Fielding's *Jonathan Wild* and in other such inversions of low into high as Gay's *Beggar's Opera*. He does tell, after a fashion, the story of his mock hero's life, but he concerns himself (as might be expected) with more general matters, and he uses many old panegyric topics.

'Tis true, to compliment the Dead
Is as impertinent and vain
As 'twas of old to call them back again.

(1–3)

Here is Butler's version of the inexpressibility topos that Donne and others had made so much of earlier in the century. The conclusion of the first stanza has the general application of his usual satire, but less anger than mock and real sorrow:

For as those Times the Golden Age we call,
In which there was no Gold in Use at all,
So we plant Glory and Renown,
Where it was ne'er deserv'd, nor known
But to worse Purpose many Times,
To flourish o'er nefarious Crimes,
And cheat the World, that never seems to mind,
How good, or bad Men die, but what they leave behind.

(st.i)

The witty paradox gives the poem the energy that sustains *Hudibras* and that brightens some of Butler's other poems. With characteristic wit he tells of Duval's being put in prison:

As Jewels of high Value are
Kept under Locks with greater Care,
Than those of meaner Rates,
So he was in Stone Walls, and Chains, and Iron Grates.

(st. viii.)

The inversion has grown complete by the end of the poem when Butler describes the response of the "*Ladies*" who "Strove who should have the Honour to lay down" their lives as also to "Yield up *Love* and *Honour* too" (sts. ix, x). Duval is "doom'd to die," however much they weep and attend him to his last "action." Hudibras's strong Widow is forgot, for these ladies

Came swell'd with Sighs, and drown'd in Tears,
To yield themselves his Fellow-sufferers;
And follow'd him, like Prisoners of War
Chain'd to the lofty Wheels of his triumphant Car.
(st. x)

The world stands on its head, *mundus inversus,* and we are amused.

Amusement does not survive inspection of Butler's other satires, where he shoots at such familiar targets as the Saints (*Upon an hypocritical Nonconformist*) or the Royal Society and vain learning (*Satyr upon the Royal Society, Satyr upon the Imperfection and Abuse of Learning*). The third topic (or satire) spirits us some distance toward the milieu of Rochester's poems. From what was said of *Hudibras* it should be clear that Butler and the noble Earl possess different ideas about the practice of life. If we doubted that, we would only need read Butler's *Satyr upon the licentious age of Charles the 2d., contrasted with the puritanical one that preceded it.* (That title accords with usual explanations of what happened in 1660, but if anyone is happy in Butler's hands, we should wish him luck.) The poem does not have Jonson's wonderful concentration of language, but it does recapture the Jonsonian vision of the times:

For Men have now made Vice so great an Art,
The matter of Fact's become the slightest Part;
And the debauchd'st Actions they can do,
Mere Trifles, to the Circumstance and Show.[24]

Such lines have the Sons of Belial in view, and Rochester could hardly have written them. Nor is John Wilmot given to reflection on a better past, so absorbed is he in the feverish

[24] Lines 53–56. For Jonson, see *The Cavalier Mode,* pp. 169 ff.

pursuit of the moment. Here we discover Butler using another topos much loved by the satirists, the virtuous past that condemns a vicious present. (Of course Butler puts the usual askew.)

> So simple were those Times, when a grave *Sage*
> Could with an Oldwive's-Tale instruct the Age;
> Teach Virtue, more fantastick Ways and nice,
> Than ours will now endure t' improve in vice.
>
> (153–56)

Where Butler and Rochester agree is on "the nature of man." [25] Few phrases could be more appropriate for both poets than Butler's *Satyr upon the weakness and misery of Man.* Employing his hudibrastics, Butler again postulates a better past and, surprising to say, a better half of men, although the worse half "devours" the better, and we degenerate:

> Far from the ancient nobler Place
> Of all our high paternal Race,
> We now degenerate, and grow
> As barbarous, and mean, and low
> As modern *Grecians* are, and worse,
> To their brave nobler Ancestors.
>
> (59–64)

The sense of an idyllic past will not be found in Rochester, but the two satiric boundaries overlap when Butler complains, "Our *Pains* are real Things, and all / Our *Pleasures* but fantastical" (81–82). Butler's satiric vision has far greater power than his style seems to allow because for all his wit he shows evident conviction that he merely sets down the truth. In a sense he is not so much a satirist at all as a realist of the same uncomfortable stripe as Hobbes and Mandeville. Like

[25] W.O.S. Sutherland, Jr., makes this the basis of his perceptive discussion of *Hudibras* in *The Art of the Satirist* (Austin, 1965).

Hobbes, he also gets inside man, not blaming the miserable human state of things on exterior "*Plagues*" alone:

> But all these *Plagues* are nothing near
> Those far more cruel and severe,
> Unhappy Man takes Pains to find
> T' inflict himself upon his Mind.
>
> (169–72)

Man's two highest faculties, his reason and will, conspire to torture and curse themselves:

> So *Man*, that thinks to force and strain
> Beyond its natural Sphere his *Brain*,
> In vain torments it on the Rack,
> And, for improving, sets it back;
> Is ign'rant of his own Extent,
> And that to which his Aims are bent,
> Is lost in both, and breaks his *Blade*
> Upon the *Anvil*, where 'twas made.
>
> (215–22)

Butler's satires other than *Hudibras* possess his distinctive touch: "How witty's ruin," as Donne put it. They do not, however, exhibit the terrible imaginative power and exasperating penetration of his great poem. Some of them are little more than fragments, and none adheres to very adequate formal canons. Yet they do show the same intelligence, the same conviction, and the same intense disappointment with man that make Butler the serious artist he is. I have observed before how much Butler's world was one likely to have been inherited by Milton and Dryden as their hopes went down, had they not found means to revive their great argument and great idea. In Butler we find the counter-epic that exists within an epic age and, *mutatis mutandis*, within the poems of Milton and Dryden themselves.[26] It is difficult not to in-

[26] See n. 11, above.

clude the thoroughgoing satirist like Butler or Juvenal in the world he creates, and I do think we feel an unwashable vulgarity in both of them. But for Butler at least, it is the vulgarity of a highly intelligent man who will permit nothing to clothe or perfume man's simian resemblances. The terrible thing, the great thing, about his poetry surely is its capacity to convince us that we share that vulgarity, that tawdriness, stupidity, and moral depravity. The search for "Diversion" does not in any way detract from the seriousness of the morose old man.

Rochester has a considerable range of poems worthy of being termed satiric or satires proper. His impromptus and bitter epigrams show how near allied were the profane wit and the satirist in him, and many Belialean poses also display the satirist's ragged sleeves. Apart from the generally satiric tone, he essayed a number of purely satiric forms, motifs, and objects. In *Timon* he presents yet another example of the Horatian motif of accosting by a bore, taking Horace in the light of Boileau's third satire. The poem begins with a questioner, something akin to the satiric *adversarius*, "A," asking Timon what is the matter with him. What follows is lively enough, but since no single aim is sufficiently realized, the poem seems more an exercise than a satire. *Tunbridge Wells* represents a very considerable improvement. The choice of a fashionable spa for the satiric scene provides an excellent opportunity to blend the Horatian motif of accosting with satiric perspective. The satirist, and we, encounter in succession a Sir Nicholas Cully (a fop and fool: 6–24), next "a tall stiff fool" whose gravity lacks sense (25–40), then a "tribe" of clergymen in "a new scene of foppery" (41–69). The satirist next evades some Irishmen (70–75), enters a crowd (76–85), and observes a rendezvous of stupid lovers. The two final groups encountered include women who have left their husbands behind so that they can get children by the young sparks at the spa (114–48) and a rowdy group of cadets (149–65). Neither in such a list nor in the verses themselves does the satire thus far rise above the ordinary. One could shuffle the episodes with no loss of sense or satiric effect. All this while the satirist and we have, however, been dissociating ourselves from one satiric object after another. That self-satisfaction ends at last, because Rochester has been leading himself and us to the collapse of our dignity in the final ten lines:

> Bless me! thought I, what thing is man, that thus
> In all his shapes, he is ridiculous?
> Ourselves with noise of reason we do please
> In vain: humanity's our worst disease.
> Thrice happy beasts are, who, because they be
> Of reason void, are so of foppery.
> Faith, I was so ashamed that with remorse
> I used the insolence to mount my horse;
> For he, doing only things fit for his nature,
> Did seem to me by much the wiser creature.
>
> (166–75)

Women emerge as speakers in two of Rochester's satires, reminding us again of his tie to Butler. One of those poems, an untitled fragment, effectively wields a misanthropic attitude in a misogynous age: "What vain, unnecessary things are men!" (1). The Amazonian attitude is not enough to constitute a complete poem, however. A finer poem, *A letter from Artemisia in the Town to Chloe in the Country,* of course uses such a title to set forth credentials as a verse epistle. Because about a third of Horace's epistles are satiric, Rochester has ancient sanction. Artemisia rattles on, developing what seems to be another satiric perspective (1–72). There then appears a termagant who seems to have been designed at first as just another satiric object. But she takes over the poem, her voice displacing that of the satirist. A brazen woman of the world, her first act on entering London and the poem is to send her submissive husband off to drink. Running upstairs to Artemisia, she bursts at once into a dissertation on woman's rightful mistreatment of men and on the great preferability of a fool to a man of wit as a lover. When she speaks of "The perfect joy of being well deceived" (115), we sense that something of Swift has entered the world. But Rochester's satiric flow disappears like a desert stream into the sand when the harridan catches her breath. The poem recovers from time to time, but it can hardly be said to make us feel that we move into a new sphere when it returns to her saying once again how necessary it is that women use male fools (169–255). Many of these rather unformed poems are redeemed by striking passages, and midway through this verse letter we hear not the termagant's voice or Artemisia's but Rochester's:

> God never made a coxcomb worth a groat.
> We owe that name to industry and arts:
> An eminent fool must be a fool of parts.
> And such a one was she, who had turned o'er
> As many books as men; loved much, read more;
> Had a discerning wit; to her was known
> Everyone's fault and merit, but her own.
> All the good qualities that ever blessed
> A woman so distinguished from the rest,
> Except discretion only, she possessed.
>
> (159–68)

A Letter from Artemisia is successful only by fits, and its best ordered, most powerful passage (189–251) gives a whore's progress told by our virago. Corinna (the name of Ovid's girlfriend) begins as the toast of the town and degenerates into a half-crown prostitute. Managing to entice "my young master's worship" when that new heir and looby first comes to the town, she gets him to keep her on so lavish a scale that his family suffers. When she has got all from him that she can, she poisons him. Except for the more rigid morality that Hogarth was to bring, one could almost imagine a series of pictures like his being made of Corinna's progress.

The largest group of Rochester's satires, four of some length, concern literary matters. I find these consistently more interesting for what they represent than for themselves. Rochester again had models. Marvell's *Fleckno* sketched somewhat fuzzily the possibilities of literary satire, and Horace had given clear examples (*Satires,* I, iv; vi). But an attack "On Poet Ninny" (Sir Car Scroope, whom Rochester belabors in other poems as well) testifies less to any tradition than to the fact that in the Restoration literature has come to matter as it had not done before. Rival poets did not need to concern Rochester for the reason they had Elizabethan poets: as rivals for patronage. Their only possible danger to him lay in their being poets. Even that much emerges from the coarse attack on John Sheffield, Earl of Mulgrave, *My Lord All-Pride.* Rochester was to tell Burnet that he could not esteem "a *Satyre* without Resentments, upon the cold Notions of *Philosophy,*" and it is quite clear that his personal hatred of Mulgrave was founded on literary as well as purely personal issues.

The possibilities of something really interesting emerging from such satire are more fully realized in Rochester's other two literary satires, especially when he takes after Dryden in *An Allusion to Horace.* The poem is one of the earliest "imitations" of the eighteenth-century kind, applying *The Tenth Satyr of the First Book* of Horace to contemporary English literary figures. Horace had written about satire, defending his having criticized Lucilius and taking comfort in the approbation of the best writers of the early Augustan era. Rochester begins his attack on Dryden with a stylistic assurance such as has been absent from most of the poems we have been considering in this chapter:

> Well, sir, 'tis granted I said Dryden's rhymes
> Were stol'n, unequal, nay dull many times.
> What foolish patron is there found of his
> So blindly partial to deny me this?
> But that his plays, embroidered up and down
> With wit and learning, justly pleased the town
> In the same paper I as freely own. (1–7)

Rochester's specific topic is, then, drama, and we must recall that this precursor of *Mac Flecknoe* considers Dryden largely in that context. The *Allusion to Horace* gains much of its force from not being wholly committed to satire.

The lines just quoted seem to set fair-mindedness as a goal, and many of the judgments on other dramatists seem without animus and remarkably perceptive to have come from a contemporary (ca. 1675–76). He finds Etherege "a sheer original" (33). None, he says, has "touched upon true comedy / But hasty Shadwell and slow Wycherley" (42–43). The epithets at least seem right. The familiar line on Buckhurst (later Earl of Dorset) is worthy of Pope: "The best good man with the worst-natured muse" (60). The return to Dryden begins with vilification (71–80) tempered again by praise. Rochester makes his best point in dealing with Dryden as critic:

> But does not Dryden find ev'n Jonson dull;
> Fletcher and Beaumont uncorrect, and full
> Of lewd lines, as he calls 'em; Shakespeare's style
> Stiff and affected; to his own the while
> Allowing all the justness that his pride
> So arrogantly had to these denied? (81–86)

The distortion of Dryden's attitude toward the earlier playwrights enables Rochester to get at Dryden himself. Part of Dryden's heroic idea was a revival of drama, and Rochester points to Dryden's assumption that he will be captain in the enterprise. More than that, Dryden had supplied Rochester with means for this passage. In his "Defence of the Epilogue" appended to *The Conquest of Granada*, Dryden had reviewed the virtues and, at greater length, the faults of Jonson, Fletcher, and Shakespeare. In doing so, he refers several times to Horace, *Satires* I, x.[27] So quick were men at the time to take hints when Horace, Virgil, and Ovid were involved that Rochester seized the opportunity to take the hint for a satire on the hinter. Dryden got the point all right, and waited till his Preface to *All of Love* (1678) to characterize men like Rochester as wits rather than poets:

> Men of pleasant conversation (at least esteemed so), and endued with a trifling kind of fancy, perhaps helped out with some smattering of Latin, are ambitious to distinguish themselves from the herd of gentlemen by their poetry:
>
> rarus enim ferme sensus communis in illa
> fortuna.[28]

Among Dryden's advantages over Rochester in the realm of satire was his superiority as a writer and thinker. His other chief advantage consisted in just those moral issues that a satirist must count on to support his attack. All that Dryden needed to do was to direct a quotation from Juvenal at

[27] Noted by David Vieth, *The Complete Poems of . . . Rochester* (New Haven and London, 1968), p. 124.

[28] George Watson, ed. *Of Dramatic Poesy and Other Critical Essays*, 2 vols. (London, 1962), I, 226. Dryden's quotation (from Juvenal, *Satires*, VIII, 73–74) charges Rochester with a more serious moral shortcoming: "for in those high places regard for others is rarely to be found" (Loeb trans.).

Rochester's conduct of life. It seems very clear that the two men regarded each other as rivals for literary supremacy in a society of writers and others of the important people of the day. Rochester had great advantages by birth, wealth, and access to high places. Dryden's advantages were solely literary, and the fact that he could triumph tells us everything necessary to be known about the importance literature assumed in the Restoration. Most of the major English poets before Dryden had been middling gentlemen like himself, men who had to yield to the values of aristocracy when those conflicted with literary values. Dryden showed sufficient willingness to cast incense on the altars of the great, when they were content to remain great in their position. But when Rochester pretended to poetic and critical eminence, and when a man of the Earl's life stood in judgment over him, Dryden was seriously challenged and took appropriate measures in return.

Rochester's other fine literary satire, *An Epistolary Essay From M. G. to O. B. upon Their Mutual Poems,* replies to Mulgrave's poem, *An Essay upon Satyr,* in which Dryden had considerable share as a reviser. M. G. is therefore Mul-grave. Why Dryden is designated O. B. nobody knows. Rochester's poem is written as if by Mulgrave to Dryden, very humourously depicting an entirely self-sufficient fool:

> But I, who am of sprightly vigor full,
> Look on mankind as envious and dull.
> Born to myself, myself I like alone
> And must conclude my judgment good, or none.
> For should my sense be nought, how could I know
> Whether another man's be good or no?
> Thus I resolve of my own poetry
> That 'tis the best, and that's a fame for me.
>
> (71–78)

Mulgrave alone seems the victim of this piece. If Rochester did in fact play a role in hiring toughs to beat up Dryden in Rose Alley, he then took the old-fashioned aristocratic way with an inferior.

Except for passages in these poems, Rochester would not likely be well remembered as a satirist. The range of approach and subject, however, is quite impressive, and their "mirth," as Burnet termed one part of Rochester's life, is sprightly and self-sustaining. But Rochester's place among English satirists is earned by *A Satyr against Reason and Mankind.* This poem returns us to the world of his libertine poems and a world akin to Butler's in pessimism. It is also the single major Restoration satire that adheres to the supposed conventions of the formal verse satire.[29] The satire moves by both attack and defense. It attacks the usual view of man as a rational creature and people holding usual views. It defends the satirist's own very different concepts of reason and life.

Rochester begins with an application of theriophily such as was common among French *libertin* writers.[30] Following one of two major theriophilic conventions, he praises beasts for lacking the curse of reason:

> Were I (who to my cost already am
> One of those strange, prodigious creatures, man)
> A spirit free to choose, for my own share,

[29] See Mary Claire Randolph, "The Structural Design of the Formal Verse Satire," *Philological Quarterly,* XXI (1942), 368–84. In addition to this classic article and Sutherland's book (see n. 25, above), see: Ian Jack, *Augustan Satire . . . 1660–1750* (Oxford, 1952); James Sutherland, *English Satire* (Cambridge, 1958); Alvin Kernan, *The Cankered Muse* (New Haven, 1959); and Ronald Paulson, *The Fictions of Satire* (Baltimore, 1967).

[30] See George Boas, *The Happy Beast in French Thought of the Seventeenth Century* (Baltimore, 1933). For a brief application to England, see my *Dryden's Poetry* (Bloomington and London, 1967), pp. 154–55.

What case of flesh and blood I pleased to wear,
I'd be a dog, a monkey, or a bear,
Or anything but that vain animal
Who is so proud of being rational. (1–7)

That proves little more than an introductory sally, although it does prepare the way for a similarly theriophilic passage of greater power later in the poem (114–38). But this time the most moving passage of the whole poem appears near the beginning. It is moving both for its imaginative sweep and for what it tells us of the author's own trials:

Reason, an *ignis fatuus* in the mind,
Which, leaving light of nature, sense, behind,
Pathless and dangerous wandering ways it takes
Through error's fenny bogs and thorny brakes;
Whilst the misguided follower climbs with pain
Mountains of whimseys, heaped in his own brain;
Stumbling from thought to thought, falls headlong down
Into doubt's boundless sea, where, like to drown,
Books bear him up awhile, and make him try
To swim with bladders of philosophy;
In hopes still to o'ertake th' escaping light,
The vapor dances in his dazzling sight
Till, spent, it leaves him to eternal night.
Then old age and experience, hand in hand,
Lead him to death, and make him understand,
After a search so painful and so long,
That all his life he has been in the wrong.
Huddled in dirt the reasoning engine lies,
Who was so proud, so witty, and so wise.[31]

In opposition to that "*ignis fatuus* in the mind," Rochester asserts his notion of true reason, a mental process of

[31] Lines 12–30. Anyone who thinks Restoration poetry one single thing should compare this passage with Milton on the appetites of men and angels, as cited in ch. v; or with Dryden's confession in *The Hind and the Panther*, I, 64–79, which uses very similar imagery.

sensation and will satisfying the body's appetites and human desires to "enjoy." Again the passage is worth quoting at length:

> Thus, whilst against false reasoning I inveigh,
> I own right reason, which I would obey:
> That reason which distinguishes by sense
> And gives us rules of good and ill from thence,
> That bounds desires with a reforming will
> To keep 'em more in vigor, not to kill.
> Your reason hinders, mine helps to enjoy,
> Renewing appetites yours would destroy.
> My reason is my friend, yours is a cheat;
> Hunger calls out, my reason bids me eat;
> Perversely, yours your appetite does mock:
> This asks for food, that answers, "What's o'clock?"
> This plain distinction, sir, your doubt secures:
> 'Tis not true reason I despise, but yours.
>
> (98–111)

The poem received additional strength from its being a reply to an adversary who had argued the views that we tend to share with the seventeenth century. Rochester's defense of libertine behavior here fuses ancient naturalism, Montaigne, and Hobbes among others. But what is important is his own. To my view, Rochester has never received proper recognition for his insight into the primacy of fear in human lives. Once again he implies a contrast with animals:

> For hunger or for love they fight and tear,
> Whilst wretched man is still in arms for fear.
> For fear he arms, and is of arms afraid,
> By fear to fear successively betrayed;
> Base fear, the source whence his best passions came:
> His boasted honor, and his dear-bought fame;
> That lust of power, to which he's such a slave,

And for the which alone he dares be brave;
To which his various projects are designed;
Which makes him generous, affable, and kind;
For which he takes such pains to be thought wise,
And screws his actions in a forced disguise,
Leading a tedious life in misery
Under laborious, mean hypocrisy. (139–52)

A Satyr gains much of its force from two complementary features. On the one hand, it generalizes. It concerns man, his faculties, human life. In that respect Rochester entered into a satiric territory that only the bravest can, a literary territory ruled by Butler in the seventeenth century and Swift in the eighteenth. On the other hand, the source and the verification for the general truth come from felt personal experience. If this satire is in some sense Rochester's *apologia pro vita sua,* he had already written his epitaph in those six powerful lines:

Then old age and experience, hand in hand,
Lead him to death, and make him understand,
After a search so painful and so long,
That all his life he has been in the wrong.
Huddled in dirt the reasoning engine lies,
Who was so proud, so witty, and so wise.

We used to be told not to confuse literature and life, but equal danger lies in not considering literature part of life and part of our understanding of it. If those lines do not also apply to Rochester, then we understand his life less than he did. And anyone who wishes to measure human tragedy may compare that passage with another passage by a poet Rochester's contemporary, that at the end of *Paradise Lost* with its own hands image.

iii. The Harsh Cadence of Rugged Lines

Like its author, the satire of John Oldham proves more difficult to place. If we knew the man better, we might find greater coherence in his poetry.[32] Most people think of Oldham in terms of Dryden's handsome memorial poem printed in Oldham's *Remains* (1684). The young poet had died the year before, "too little and too lately known," as Dryden put it for himself and us. Rochester had died in 1680, probably in September. In 1682 Oldham's elegy for Rochester, "The Lamentation for Adonis," appeared in print, a very different production from "Upon the Author of the play called Sodom." [33] The connection so late with Rochester helps explain why Oldham was unlikely to have come into Dryden's orbit until soon before he died, but we can only guess how Oldham might have appealed to such different men and poets as Rochester and Dryden. In addition, many of Oldham's poems seem to contradict Dryden's own views. Oldham was best known as the author of the *Satyrs upon the Jesuits* and *The Satyr against Vertue*. Oldham's hostilities in the former are, when not simply customary, decidedly Whiggish.[34] The poems hardly represent Dryden's own public principles. Much less does *The Satyr against Vertue* represent his moral views. The attack on virtue follows the Rochester line of arguing against cant about virtue and in

[32] Almost all that is known of Oldham is set forth in about two pages by Harold F. Brooks, "A Bibliography of John Oldham, The Restoration Satirist," *Oxford Bibliographical Society*, V (1936), 1–38. Brooks is now completing his much awaited edition of Oldham's poems and has recently written "The Poetry of John Oldham" in *Restoration Literature*, ed. Love, pp. 177–203.

[33] Oldham's "Upon the Author" was printed in *Poems on Several Occasions* (London, 1680), pp. 129–31, implicitly attributed to Rochester and printed some weeks after his death.

[34] His first published poem had celebrated the marriage of William and Mary.

extolling a version of vice. The pastoral elegy on Rochester's death does not much clarify the situation. It compares Rochester to Spenser, not the first comparison likely to rise in most minds, and it mentions among dead poets an altogether curious assortment: Chaucer, Milton, Cowley, Denham, and Katherine Philips. The only living poet mentioned by name is Waller. It would be difficult to infer very much from this and the other poets mentioned, but it does seem likely that in 1680 or 1681 Oldham knew Rochester pretty well and Dryden not at all.

Oldham was a popular poet. Between 1684 and 1710 there were twelve printings of his *Works*. Two later editions followed in the eighteenth century, and Robert Bell's selection in the nineteenth. The eighteenth-century taste for satirists from the preceding century ran to a surprising extent for such louder writings as *Hudibras*, Charles Cotton's *Genuine Remains* with its hudibrastics and burlesques, and Oldham. It seems that the age of correctness sometimes liked the least correct things from the age of incorrectness. One thing alone remains certain: Oldham tended to keep good company.

Among that company in another sense were Horace and Juvenal. It seems inevitable that Oldham, too, should take a try at Horace's satire on being accosted by a bore. Similarly, he produced versions of Juvenal's third and thirteenth satires, of an epigram by Martial (I, cxviii), and of *Monsieur Boileau's Satyr upon Man* ("Written in October, 1682").[35] In none of these renderings does Oldham appear at his best, but he does show originality in his manner of translating. Following the fashion of Rochester's "allusion" to Horace, Oldham more than anybody furthered by several examples those

[35] Oldham's allusions in this poem to Buckingham's spendthrift nature and to Bethel's stinginess so resemble the characters of Zimri and Shimei in *Absalom* and *Achitophel* that it seems likely that he became acquainted with Dryden about this time.

"imitation" translations that became common in the eighteenth century.[36] By translating persons and events as well as words into English equivalency, Oldham must have seemed to his contemporaries to have novelties that we sense less quickly.

A poet like Oldham requires sifting if he is to claim the attention of readers three centuries after him. One thing in his career that takes on importance in his best poems is his literary ambition. His translations and imitations show him going through the young Restoration poet's exercises. In publishing *Horace his Art of Poetry imitated in English,* Oldham put a foot forward in the revival of critical theory that marked Roscommon's efforts in 1684 and 1685. His *Satyr against Vertue* merely calls attention to himself, as did its later palinodes, the *Apology* and *Counterpart.* The *Satyrs upon the Jesuits* chose a subject at once likely to be popular during the Popish Plot and of a safety unimpeachable. From one point of view, all these productions make up "a *Satyre* without Resentments," or at least a poetry too little imbued with Oldham's own life.[37] But since that life was one with keen literary aspiration, we can see that behind these showy pieces lay the concerns that issued in his best poems.

Those best speak with feeling about things that matter to John Oldham. The finest poem in his first little volume, *Satyrs upon the Jesuits,* is its last, *A Satyr Upon a Woman, who by her Falshood and Scorn was the Death of my Friend.* Whether the situation purported actually existed matters less than that Oldham had found a topic that moved him. The poem has an ancient lineage, both in its misogyny and

[36] See the definitive article by Harold F. Brooks, "The 'Imitation' in English Poetry, Especially in Formal Satire, Before the Age of Pope," *Review of English Studies,* xxv (1949), 124–40.

[37] Even if we lack details of Oldham's life, we can tell when he writes about what matters to him and when he does not.

in its conception of satire as a curse.[38] Its first half shows an energy and a concentration lacking in the rest of the volume:

> I rise in Judgment, am to be to her
> Both Witness, Judg, and Executioner:
> Arm'd with dire Satyr, and resentful spite,
> I come to haunt her with the ghosts of Wit.[39]

He invokes "spightful pow'rs": "Assist with Malice, and your mighty aid / My sworn Revenge, and help me Rhime her dead." [40] The notion of rhyming someone to death is very primitive but had not died by the Restoration. Such collections as *Ratts Rhimed to Death* (1663) or *Rome Rhym'd to Death* (1683) show that some degree of belief remained in the effectiveness of satiric "Malice."

The misogyny of Oldham and his century emerges clearly in a passage of some interest.

> Vile'st of that viler Sex, who damn'd us all!
> Ordain'd to cause, and plague, us for our fall!
> WOMAN! nay worse! for she can naught be said,
> But Mummy by some Dev'l inhabited.[41]

That is a clear echo of the end of Donne's poem, "Loves Alchymie":

> Hope not for minde in woman; at their best,
> Sweetnesse, and wit they'are, but, Mummy, possest.

I give the punctuation of these lines in the 1633 version to show how easy it is to derive different interpretations. Old-

[38] See Robert C. Elliott, *The Power of Satire* (Princeton, 1960). Appropriately, the title page for Oldham's *Works* with the *Remains* has as an ornament the *satura lanx* or well-filled bowl of satire.

[39] *Satyrs Upon the Jesuits*, in *The Works of Mr. John Oldham Together with his Remains* (London, 1684). Pagination in this volume begins afresh with each new part: p. 141.

[40] Ibid.

[41] Ibid., p. 142.

ham clearly read "possest" not to mean "when had sexually," but "by some Dev'l inhabited." The gloss on Donne's much disputed lines holds some considerable interest. The rest of the poem proves rather less interesting. Oldham does not curse as well as he had led us to expect. One or two good things, a bit of scatology, and a great deal that is tired convention make up the second half of the poem. Perhaps the most effective curse follows that on her sexual desires:

> May then . . .
> No madness take her use of Sense away;
> But may she in full strength of reason be,
> To feel, and understand her misery;
> Plagu'd so, till she think damning a release,
> And humbly pray to go to Hell for ease.[42]

At the end of his second collection, *Some New Pieces* (1684), a similar satiric curse is leveled *Upon a Printer* who has misprinted something of his. Once again we get excessive rage, what Dryden kindly termed "the harsh cadence of a rugged line." Oldham seems to feel that harshness is decorous to his genre, and although he wrote in other kinds he now declares that "Satyr's my only Province, and delight, / For whose dear sake alone I've vow'd to write." [43] He develops at some length the satiric version of immortality conferred by verse, for the printer will be "Deathless in infamy." [44] The poem goes on, cursing the printer, creating a vision of his degeneration, and ending with a last curse:

> Forlorn, abandon'd, pitiless, and poor,
> As a pawn'd Cully, or a mortgag'd Whore,
> May'st thou an Halter want for thy Redress,

[42] Ibid., p. 147.
[43] *Some New Pieces* (London, 1684), p. 131.
[44] Ibid., p. 132.

Forc'd to steal Hemp to end thy miseries,
And damn thy self to baulk the Hangmans Fees,
  And may no Saucy Fool have better Fate
  That dares pull down the Vengeance of my Hate.[45]

Such shouting seems to me to conceal a want of thought. In its excess, the wit is verbal exercise rather than an embodiment of experience. Of course, we must remember that Restoration poets did not usually bloom early, and that Dryden's method of heroic satire had not yet calmed the fevers raised by Marvell and Rochester, or by the memory of Hall, Marston, and Donne. But when all excuses have been made, Oldham's reputation cannot be much assisted by any but his last poems. In *A Letter from the Country* in his second collection he bemoans his becoming a poet. If it is clear that he wishes for fame, it is also clear that there are reasons for his not having attained it.

Some of Oldham's poems in his third collection, *Poems, and Translations* (1684) do, however, show a marked increase in the energy of his couplet style. In *A Satyr*, the ghost of Spenser attempts to dissuade him from poetry, and Oldham returns to complaint over his art. This time he seems more wholly to feel what he writes, for the trouble with poetry lies not with itself but (as the end of the meandering title says) with *how little it is esteem'd and encouraged in this present Age*. We can translate that into a felt desire for greater recognition and advancement. The opening lines possess a new rigor and an unprecedentedly rapid movement into the situation:

One night, as I was pondering of late
On all the mis'ries of my hapless Fate,
Cursing my rhiming Stars, raving in vain

[45] Ibid., p. 134.

At all the Pow'rs, which over Poets reign:
In came a ghostly Shape, all pale, and thin . . .[46]

At this we sit up and take notice. The poet honors the ghost of Spenser and asks for some of his spirit. Speaking in the satiric vein of "the fam'd Tale of *Mother Hubberd*," the ghost does not mince words:

I come, fond Ideot, e're it be too late,
Kindly to warn thee of thy wretched Fate;
Take heed betimes . . .[47]

The ghost shuffles between arguing that poets have always suffered and declaring that today things are even worse than before. Seeing that it gets nowhere, Spenser's ghost and the poem end with a curse on our poet. Oldham has gained some detachment even while writing more wholly about himself. It is much the best of Oldham's poems so far mentioned in this chapter.

Oldham's discovery of the hardships of the unfunded intellectual gives us a glimpse of what we might have expected to be true of other times from what remains true today. His best satire sums up his unhappiness. This *Satyr Addressed to a Friend* warns that friend against leaving a secure niche in the university to come into the world. The harsh cadences have smoothed into something like a fluency that was Oldham's last achievement and perhaps persuaded people like Dryden that here was a talent tragically lost. At least he has grown practical, and prudence is a virtue that his writing had not possessed:

If you're so out of love with Happiness
To quit a College life, and learned ease;

[46] *Poems, And Translations* (London, 1684), p. 164.
[47] Ibid., p. 166.

Convince me first, and some good Reasons give,
What methods and designs you'l take to live.[48]

Some padding there certainly is, but he has learned from Dryden that couplets can be marshaled into energetic verse paragraphs. The poet describes the reasonable alternatives to a college fellowship. One can be a parson, but the supply is too great: "you'l hardly meet / More Porters now than Parsons in the street." [49] Teaching in a school earns Oldham's contempt, and being chaplain to the great requires intolerable obsequiousness. The poem concludes with a nice fable of a Wolf and a Dog meeting one night (pp. 144–48). The lean wolf inquires how the Dog prospers so well. He has "*a kind Master*," the Dog replies, describing the luxury in which he lives. The Wolf asks his new friend to put in a good word for him. The Dog promises to do so ("*As I'm a Dog of Honour, Sir*"). But he warns the Wolf to lay by his roughness and learn complaisance. It has grown daylight, and the Wolf observes that the Dog's neck is "all worn and bare." The Dog confesses that he had once been rough and fierce but had been whipped and collared into servility. The Wolf will have none of it:

A Gods name, take your golden Chains for me:
Faith, I'd not be King, not to be free:
Sir Dog, your humble Servant, so Godbw'y.[50]

Whether Oldham had a friend who talked of giving up a college fellowship cannot and need not be known. But Oldham, son of a schoolteacher and an Oxford graduate, dramatizes the dilemma of his own life in the guise of advising a friend. Like the Wolf, he valued an independence he could scarcely support.

[48] Ibid., p. 137.
[49] Ibid., p. 139.
[50] Ibid., p. 148.

Truth requires me to say that by the standards I have tried to exercise Oldham is a poet of shreds and patches and occasional flights such as in the last two poems mentioned, in the poem on Ben Jonson quoted early in this book,[51] and in some of his translations, especially of Horace's *Art of Poetry*. He died too early for us to have any clear idea whether his going to London to set up for a wit would have found success. It was clearly believed that he would, and the support of men like Rochester and Dryden suggests that we should treat the young aspirant with more respect than my remarks will have implied. As a palinode to my strictures, therefore, I shall end with a quotation from the *Satyr* just discussed. It shows how, behind the rattle of his satires, John Oldham glimpsed a Horatian ideal of retired life that testifies at once to perfectly human desires and to his being part of his century.

> 'T has ever been the top of my Desires,
> The utmost height to which my wish aspires,
> That Heav'n would bless me with a small Estate,
> Where I might find a close obscure retreat;
> There, free from Noise, and all ambitious ends,
> Enjoy a few choice Books, and fewer Friends,
> Lord of my self, accountable to none,
> But to my Conscience, and my God alone:
> There live unthought of, and unknown of, die,
> And grudge Mankind my very memory.[52]

It is a fine verse paragraph. Although we may reflect that some wishful thinking may be there, and that like Cowley he might have found the retired life something less than perfect, the humanity and wholesomeness claim respect. Those of us who think our own lives have moved from a poverty like Old-

[51] See above, pp. 19–20.

[52] *Poems, And Translations*, p. 143.

ham's to a small estate with books and friends can have a fondness for Oldham. Such a fondness has led me to insist the more austerely upon his limitations. And when all has been said, few of us will ever earn as a recompense to our failed hopes such praise and clear-sighted evaluation as Dryden bestowed on this unhappy young man in "To the Memory of Mr. Oldham":

> O early ripe! to thy abundant store
> What could advancing Age have added more?
> It might (what Nature never gives the young)
> Have taught the numbers of thy native Tongue.
> But Satyr needs not those, and Wit will shine
> Through the harsh cadence of a rugged line.
> A noble Error, and but seldom made,
> When Poets are by too much force betray'd.
> Thy generous fruits, though gather'd ere their prime
> Still shew'd a quickness; and maturing time
> But mellows what we write to the dull sweets of Rime.
> (11–21)

iv. A Talent for Satire

Toward the end of his epistle dedicatory for *Eleonora*, Dryden has an intriguing comment:

> They say my talent is Satyre; if it be so, 'tis a Fruitful Age; and there is an extraordinary Crop to gather. But a single hand is insufficient for such a Harvest: They have sown the Dragons Teeth themselves; and 'tis but just they shou'd reap each other in Lampoons.

The interesting thing about this comment is that it occurs in a context of praise. Dryden's dedication to the Earl of Abingdon seems until that point to have come with incense in both hands, and the subtitle of the poem runs: "A Panegyrical Poem Dedicated to the Memory of the Late Countess of Abingdon." *Eleonora* itself is modeled on the most lavish poems of praise in the language, Donne's *Anniversaries,* and like those poems employs Neoplatonic and typological means to praise the dead woman. And yet the remark in the dedication has a counterpart toward the end of the poem:

> Let this suffice: Nor thou, great Saint, refuse
> This humble Tribute of no vulgar Muse:
> Who, not by Cares, or Wants, or Age deprest,
> Stems a wild Deluge with a dauntless brest:
> And dares to sing thy Praises, in a Clime
> Where Vice triumphs, and Vertue is a Crime:
> Where ev'n to draw the Picture of thy Mind,
> Is Satyr on the most of Humane Kind:
> Take it, while yet 'tis Praise; before my rage
> Unsafely just, break loose on this bad Age;
> So bad, that thou thy self had'st no defence,
> From Vice, but barely by departing hence.
>
> (359–70)

Obviously the satiric passage heightens the praise of the dead woman. Dryden frequently uses the principle of contrast in plays as well as poems in order to set off as it were a bright portrait with shade. The principle of contrast no doubt involves some basic feature of the working of our minds, but to a person of Dryden's training it would be connected with two other matters, rhetoric and moral judgment. Whatever the particular reason for omission of the lines praising Achitophel in the first edition of the poem, or for their inclusion in the second, their presence does function to set off the bulk of what we are told of the "false *Achitophel.*" Achitophel, we discover, is false to his own best self as well as to the king, to Absalom, to truth, and to common sense. Again, in other poems of praise such as the nearly contemporaneous pair of odes, *Threnodia Augustalis* and the Anne Killigrew Ode, Dryden uses shading so that too bright a picture will not be drawn. Charles II is granted many virtues, including that of a "great Encourager of Arts" (st. xiii). "Encourager" is used very strictly, since the poets themselves found that "little was their Hire, and light their Gain." As one entitled to a pension as poet laureate and historiographer royal and as one who knew that the title was more constant than the payment, Dryden could well add, "The Pension of a Prince's Praise is great." Similarly, after all the grand associations and comparisons for Anne Killigrew, Dryden finally comes to compare her with her contemporary, Katherine Philips, "The Matchless Orinda" (162–64). Judgment is passed, and no longer does Mistress Killigrew evoke comparisons with Plato (50–51). Praise and blame in numerous adjustments required the resources of satire and panegyric, and since the *topoi* for both were very much the same, the complementary procedures often levied on each other.

Dryden's prose remark does not mean that he regards himself foremost as a satirist: "They say . . . if it be so . . . " Yet it is true that in 1692 (*Eleonora*) and the next year or so, Dryden gave signs of being highly disaffected and ready to "break loose on this bad Age." The "Dedication" of *Examen Poeticum,* the third of the Dryden-Tonson miscellanies, seems consistently dyspeptic, and the translation of the first book of Ovid's *Metamorphoses* does not fail to connect the Iron Age with Dryden's own. Dryden has recovered, but not entirely, by 1694, as we can see by the general gloominess of *To Sir Godfrey Kneller.*[53] True, all comes right, or will come right in the end, as Time and Age give what the times and the age seem to deny. The balance of tone can well be found in a sally against Kneller and his art:

[53] For fuller discussion of this difficult poem, see "Dryden's *Eikon Basilike: To Sir Godfrey Kneller* in *Seventeenth-Century Imagery,* ed. Miner (Berkeley and Los Angeles, 1971), ch. IX.

Our Arts are Sisters; though not Twins in Birth:
For Hymns were sung in *Edens* happy Earth,
By the first Pair; while *Eve* was yet a Saint,
Before she fell with Pride, and learn'd to paint.
Forgive th' allusion; 'twas not meant to bite;
But Satire will have room, where e're I write.

(89–94)

The last line has sometimes been quoted out of its witty context and without awareness that Dryden was getting at the enormously vain Kneller. But the line remains generally if not specifically true. In most of his career, satire finds some kind of place in his poems, for the reasons I have given. By the same token, however, he might have said the same of panegyric and of the heroic, which he associated with satire in his "Discourse" prefixed to his translations from Juvenal and Persius.[54] In other words, the heroic ideal prevailed, and as occasion arose, now satire and now panegyric would be employed for moral judgment or to set off each other.

If the rhetorical explanation requires such qualification in terms of Dryden's central heroic idea, I must qualify that as well by attention to the specific fact that these remarks came in 1692 and the year or so following. The five years following the Glorious Revolution in December, 1688, were at once years when extremely important changes were occurring, and years of great confusion, as change often implies. Nobody understood William III very well, and he found opposition in every corner as well as general support. Dryden was not among those who understood William so little as to lampoon him as a homosexual (the unwarranted charge of many Tory or Jacobite satirists) or to levy other such stupid charges.

[54] That satire, like panegyric, is (at least as Dryden wishes his to be) a subspecies of the epic is an idea implicit in much of the "Discourse" on satire. Dryden makes it explicit when he says that elevation is as necessary in satire "as in Heroique Poetry it self; of which this satire [the kind he propounds] is undoubtedly a Species" (Kinsley, II, 665).

But Dryden knew that a new order had come, and he did not like it. He remained a Jacobite, Catholic, and Yorkist in his political and military views. He had reasons for being unhappy with the new order, the loss of a pension (however irregularly paid), and above all the certainty that he had lost full engagement with his times.

This explanation also requires qualification. After all, Dryden's satires do not date from after 1688. *Mac Flecknoe* was at least substantially complete a decade earlier, and *The Medall* was published in 1682. Moreover, Dryden was in danger of his life during the first few years after 1688, and any satire against the government or on sensitive topics would have been suicidal. To use his word, he does snarl in an occasional allusion or prologue. By and large, however, he is not writing satires. Of course there is one major exception, and that really is what his talent for satire and satire's entering wherever he writes is mostly about. He has been working on the translations of Juvenal and Persius, and as usual discovers that the poets he is engaged with are worth special attention. Dryden has the engaging failing of deciding that his soul and that of someone he is translating are very like. In those days it was Juvenal, and shortly it would be Virgil. In the Preface to *Fables,* plainly he and Chaucer are kindred souls, and now he also discovers that he is really more like Homer than Virgil. And he offers the first book of the *Iliad* to see whether the public will not subscribe to his translation of Homer. A certain amount of self-advertising and a certain amount of enthusiasm for what he is doing always combine. Because his guiding conception is a heroic idea rather than, as with Milton, an epic in particular, Dryden subsumes now this, now that under its head, and we are well advised not to mistake the part for the whole.

The fact that Dryden is not primarily a satirist—as are Butler, Pope, and Swift—of course does not imply that he wrote no satires or satiric passages. Since I have already mentioned the rationale behind satiric passages, I may now review Dryden's two satires, *Mac Flecknoe* and *The Medall*, as well as *Absalom and Achitophel*, about one fifth of which is clearly satiric. Putting *The Medall* aside for the moment, we are left with two poems that are not only Dryden's two best known today, but also two that are, after *Paradise Lost*, the best known of the Restoration. Clearly, we do need to consider Dryden's talent for satire. My method in doing so will begin with some less familiar passages that suggest satiric range and technique, and will go on to discuss the three major poems in terms of the implications of their satire.

According to Jacob Tonson the publisher, Boileau's *Art of Poetry* was translated by Dryden's friend Sir William Soame in 1680. Tonson added that Dryden kept the translation by him for six months, revising the whole and especially the beginning of the fourth canto. Tonson was obviously right, for the passage he mentions employs one of Dryden's satiric manners, comic grotesquerie. So droll is the passage, and so little known, that it is worth quoting entire:

In *Florence* dwelt a Doctor of Renown,
The Scourge of God, and Terror of the Town,
Who all the Cant of Physick had by heart,
And never Murder'd but by rules of Art.
The Public mischief was his Private gain;
Children their slaughter'd Parents sought in vain:
A Brother here his poyson'd Brother wept;
Some bloodless dy'd, and some by *Opium* slept.
Colds, at his presence, would to Frenzies turn;
And Agues, like Malignant Fevers, burn.
Hated, at last, his Practice gives him o'er:
One Friend, unkill'd by Drugs, of all his Store,
In his new Country-house affords him place,

'Twas a rich Abbot, and a Building Ass:
Here first the Doctor's Talent came in play,
He seems Inspir'd, and talks like *Wren* or *May:*
Of this new Portico condemns the Face,
And turns the Entrance to a better place;
Designs the Stair-case at the other end.
His Friend approves, does for his Mason send,
He comes; the Doctor's Arguments prevail.
In short, to finish this our hum'rous Tale,
He *Galen's* dang'rous Science does reject,
And from ill Doctor turn good Architect.

(858–81)

Dryden must have liked this sort of thing, because it includes two principles to which he gave frequent attention: perversion (the physician is a killer) and metamorphosis (the corruption of the physician is the generation of the architect). As satire in particular, the passage has some connections with Dryden's stage comedy, and like Dryden's full satires it gives, for all the grotesquerie, a sense of reality. We feel that we need what is there but need no more for total understanding.

At other times, Dryden allows his personality, or some version of it, to be put forward. In *To Sir Godfrey Kneller,* he thanks Kneller for the gift of a portrait of Shakespeare. Dryden declares that he has been inspired in writing his thanks by having the portrait of Shakespeare before him, and hence he can meet any challenge:

His Soul Inspires me, while thy Praise I write,
And I like *Teucer,* under *Ajax* Fight;
Bids thee through me, be bold; with dauntless breast
Contemn the bad, and Emulate the best.
Like his, thy Criticks in th' attempt are lost;
When most they rail, know then, they envy most.
In vain they snarl a-loof; a noisy Crow'd,

Like Womens Anger, impotent and loud.
While they their barren Industry deplore,
Pass on secure; and mind the Goal before,
Old as she is, my Muse shall march behind;
Bear off the blast, and intercept the wind.

(77–88)

The image of the dauntless breast defying the age is the same here as at the end of *Eleonora*. It is noteworthy that as Dryden receives protection from Shakespeare (fighting like Teucer under the great Ajax), so Dryden even in old age will protect the younger painter. Critics and women are derisively dismissed, and the satire of the poem is chiefly directed against the times. As art declined in late Rome, so does it necessarily falter "in a stupid Military State" (51) such as was brought in by the Goths and Vandals, and no doubt by William III. The personal element and the element of the times fuse as Dryden uses political metaphor for the arts:

But we who Life bestow, our selves must live;
Kings cannot Reign, unless their Subjects give.
And they who pay the Taxes, bear the Rule,
Thus thou sometimes art forc'd to draw a Fool:
But so his Follies in thy Posture sink,
The senceless Ideot seems at least to think.

(154–59)

"Kings" and "Subjects" have dual meanings. The subjects of kings and the subjects of portrait painters are equally meant, just as the king as ruler and the king as artist are meant. The bad time for the artist signifies a bad time for the throne of England, and vice versa, in the poem's playing out of the kingdom of letters motif.

Some years later, in his *Fables* (1700), Dryden still often uses satire, but usually it is either glancing or very good humored. From *Mac Flecknoe* onward, Dryden wrote at his best satirically when he had the detachment that could issue in fun for its own sake. While pretending to be writing about the "Military State" of Rhodes in *Cymon and Iphigenia,* Dryden actually characterizes the English militia under the rule and generalship of William III:

> The Country rings around with loud Alarms,
> And raw in Fields the rude Militia swarms;
> Mouths without Hands; maintain'd at vast Expence,
> In Peace a Charge, in War a weak Defence:
> Stout once a Month they march a blust'ring Band,
> And ever, but in times of Need, at hand:
> This was the Morn when issuing on the Guard,
> Drawn up in Rank and File they stood prepar'd
> Of seeming Arms to make a short essay,
> Then hasten to be Drunk, the Business of the Day.
>
> (399–408)

Here we feel no danger, and the tone is altogether without rancor. Dryden's satire embodies, then, certain motifs and certain degrees of his own presence. The range in satiric tone that we have seen extends from the comic to the bitter, and that fairly describes the range in those of his works that are better known as satires.

Some time about 1678 Dryden completed *Mac Flecknoe.* That partial satire, *Absalom and Achitophel,* appeared in 1681. 1682 was Dryden's year of satiric wonders, for in it there were published *The Medall, Mac Flecknoe* in authorized form, *Absalom and Achitophel* again, and *The Second Part of Absalom and Achitophel.* Satiric touches will be found to mark other poems to a greater or smaller degree, as readers of *Religio Laici* (also 1682) and *The Hind and the Panther* (1687) recognize. But the satires proper appear in the early 1680's, just as the translations come a decade later, when Dryden translated five of the most interesting of Juvenal's satires (I, III, VI, X, XVI) and all six of Persius's.

The presence of Juvenal and Persius is especially useful in showing how little neoclassical Dryden's satire is. One searches very hard for Horace, Juvenal, and Persius in Dryden's satires, and after diligent search one finds little of any importance at all. Donne, Marvell, Rochester, Oldham, and others levied, as we have seen, on Horace's satire on being accosted by a bore. Not Dryden. Most of the people mentioned thought that the decorum of satire required the harsh cadence of a rugged line, because that was what they supposed distinguished Juvenal and Persius. Dryden followed another path. Rochester and a few others tried to follow what were thought the rules of formal verse satire, including an adversary, explicit clash of views, a crowded scene, etc. Dryden worked otherwise, and it was left to Pope to bring genius of the "neoclassical" kind to bear on satire. Dryden also did not use a number of satiric motifs that were practiced in his age or before. Some of the most common include the advice to a painter, the dream vision, the dialogue, the satiric epistle, the satiric ballad, and the burlesque. Dryden was obviously as familiar with these as anybody. The fact that he did not use them implies at least that he did not need to. In respect to use of classical forms, Dryden is less neoclassical than Donne, Milton, Pope, and Dr. Johnson. He is more modern and more English.

The superiority of Dryden's satire to that by his English predecessors and contemporaries (with the possible equality of Butler) probably relates to his independence of classical and current models. He was sufficiently original not to have instructed a painter further or to have imagined himself detained by a bore. There is another striking fact. Unlike Donne, Butler, Oldham, Marvell, and Rochester, Dryden does not repeat himself in the kinds or fictions of satire he writes. His two complete satires are totally unlike. *Mac Flecknoe* has a coronation fiction and deals with art, specifically dramatic literature. With a casual gesture, the amused Olympian detachment flicks off the sleeve the offensive insect and all are amused. According to its subtitle, *The Medall* is "A Satyre Against Sedition." It has no fiction running throughout the poem, although the first half is concerned with the significance of the medal triumphantly struck by the Whigs after Shaftesbury's acquittal. Dryden has grown white-lipped with anger. Things have reached the point of total exasperation and fear of anarchy. In such a time, any technique of justification seems called for. The rebel "Chief" —Shaftesbury, though unnamed—must be obliterated. Some would say that the detachment in the one poem and the anger in the other represent satiric stances deliberately chosen. I think that we must agree with that to a point. But the stances also create different poetic experiences, and I am inclined to think that Dryden was writing of himself in *Absalom and Achitophel,* even more than of David and Charles, when he warned, "Beware the Fury of a Patient Man" (1005). In a sense not entirely literal, yet also not entirely figurative, *The Medall* sets out to destroy Shaftesbury. Shaftesbury appears to have destroyed Dryden's equilibrium before Dryden got to him.

It will be evident that *The Medall* is a poem which, for all its merits, seems to me humanly wrong in its first half. The version of Shaftesbury in *Absalom and Achitophel* shows no compunction, but the role it allows him is that of one of the time's "Great Wits." He is "Bold," a driving energy in the state. An enemy indeed, but a Hector, a Turnus, a Satan. And he has a venerable name, Achitophel. The version of Shaftesbury in the first half of *The Medall* denies him the elementary humanity of a name and allows him not so much a personality as a series of roles:

A Martial Heroe first, with early care,
Blown, like a Pigmee by the Winds, to war.
A beardless Chief, a Rebel, e'r a Man:
(So young his hatred to his Prince began.)
Next this, (How wildly will Ambition steer!)
A Vermin, wriggling in th' Usurper's Ear.
Bart'ring his venal wit for sums of gold
He cast himself into the Saint-like mould;
Groan'd, sigh'd and pray'd, while Godliness was gain;
The lowdest Bagpipe of the squeaking Train. . . .
Pow'r was his aym—but, thrown from that pretence,
The Wretch turn'd loyal in his own defence;
And Malice reconcil'd him to his Prince.
Him, in the anguish of his Soul he serv'd;
Rewarded faster still than he deserv'd.
Behold him now exalted into trust;
His Counsel's oft convenient, seldom just.
Ev'n in the most sincere advice he gave
He had a grudging still to be a Knave.
The Frauds he learnt in his Fanatique years
Made him uneasy in his lawfull gears.
At best as little honest as he cou'd:
And, like white Witches, mischievously good.
To his first byass, longingly he leans;
And *rather* wou'd be great by wicked means.

(26–35; 50–64)

It should be clear that one version of Shaftesbury belongs to the heroic and the other to the phillipic. In brief, admiration in the old sense of wonder or awe has been replaced by hatred and fear.

It follows that we must take care not to relate Dryden's satire to his time too simply. (Again we recognize his extraordinary capacity to create "reality.") We can say that in

Achitophel Dryden satirizes Shaftesbury during the Popish Plot, and that is true enough. But we must then say the same of the "Chief" of *The Medall* and that too is true enough. And yet the poems are so different that the historical fact puts the emphasis wrong. What we have are two different experiences and two radically different characterizations. As Jonson had said, the moral art of poetry in satire or panegyric works against the bad, but concerns and addresses the good. Satire at its best discriminates morally and attacks what is bad, wrong, or foolish. Such is Dryden's claim. He is after Shaftesbury because of Shaftesbury's perversion of good things in one poem and because of his total evil in the other, an evil that so illustrates the sad condition of humanity that Dryden comes close to despair. We must, I fear, ask ourselves the question how true that is. We must not ask it naïvely (as if it is all a matter of reading *The London Gazette* or a life of Shaftesbury) but in terms of the truth of interpretations of life. And before we seek to answer that question, we must measure up to the stern fact that Dryden's satire is not some species of game. Whether the morals are good or bad, Dryden is talking about the good and the bad. People were being beaten up, arrested on strange counts, and even murdered.

Because none of us has ever been immortalized by Dryden's satire, we are apt to think that either approach to Shaftesbury involves purely artistic considerations. To think so is to fall into an error opposite to the concern with the effect of the poem on the Popish Plot. Its effect on the plot was small, but the effect of Dryden's satire on individuals was great. By his woefully pointless defense of himself, Shadwell testified to his reduction in *Mac Flecknoe:*

> sure [Dryden] goes a little too far in calling me the dullest, and has no more reason for that, than for giving me the *Irish* name of *Mack,* when he knows I never saw Ireland

> till I was three and twenty years old, and was there but four Months.[55]

The character of Zimri in *Absalom and Achitophel* also hit home. In the "Discourse" prefixed to the *Satires*, Dryden rather airily calls the characterization "ridiculous." Buckingham, he says, "was too witty to resent it as an injury." Dryden had forborne attacking "great Crimes" and had represented instead "Blind-sides, and little Extravagancies." So it all "succeeded as I wish'd: the Jest went round, and he was laught at in his turn who began the Frolick." [56] We might have been warned by recalling Restoration comedy, where the last thing a gentleman can bear is to be laughed at. At all events, evidence has come to light recently showing that Buckingham was far from thinking it all a frolic. He set down some verse, "To Dryden," in his commonplace book:

> As witches images of man invent
> To torture those they're bid to represent,
> And as that true live substance does decay
> Whilst that slight idol melts in flames away,
> Such and no lesser witchcraft wounds my name,
> So thy ill-made resemblance wastes my fame.[57]

Once again we have irrefutable testimony to what I have termed Dryden's ability to create reality. Shadwell's protest and Buckingham's lament show that, to the mind of both, Dryden's art has intervened, replacing as it were their auto-

[55] The remark is in the epistle dedicatory for *The Tenth Satire of Juvenal* (1687); *The Works of Thomas Shadwell*, ed. Montague Summers, 5 vols. (London, 1927), v, 292. It has been argued that Shadwell wrote various poems attacking Dryden, but none possess purely literary interest and their authorship is uncertain.

[56] Kinsley, II, 655. Dryden was right. He dealt with Buckingham's follies, not with his great vices.

[57] First printed by George deF. Lord in his "Introduction" to his edition, *Poems on Affairs of State*, vol. I (New Haven, 1963), liii.

biographical sense of themselves with a new biography that thenceforward became the real person known to the world.

The responses by Shadwell and Buckingham show that they felt misrepresented or hurt by being portrayed as Mac Flecknoe and Zimri. That fact seems to me one principal answer to my question about the human truth of Dryden's poetry, and in particular the satires, which are our present concern. Not to beg any philosophical questions, one view of reality and truth entails precisely this human cognition of it from the victim's standpoint. In other words, to them Dryden has falsified reality, and has failed to tell the truth. To do so in matters moral (and morality bears on literature) is to do something very wrong. I think that we must accept that as part of our answer, and it is indeed the longest lasting risk that a satirist (or praiser) of individuals runs, because from age to age satirists can leave the sorry impression that in judging others they have knowingly misjudged. "Knowingly misjudged." But that raises a separate answer to our question.

Another subjective cognition of reality or truth also must be considered: Dryden's. And the conviction of reality possessed by his poems testifies to his idea of the truth as well as it does to his art. The answer to our question has taken us to a contradiction. Buckingham believed he was thus, whereas Dryden believed Buckingham was so. In the realm of human truth that is, I think, the best simple answer to our question of the truth of Dryden's evaluation. Of course one could seek some kind of historical verification of one or the other versions, and by such an exercise it would probably emerge that Dryden had falsified Shadwell (truly, as he so plaintively says, he is not the dullest), but that he *had* got Buckingham right without mentioning adultery, murder, and other crimes of which he was guilty. But those answers seem less important to me than what Shadwell, Buckingham, and Dryden felt, and what they make us feel by expressing their feelings in poetry and prose. If we take such a view of literary truth, we can then go on to ask how the poet's important beliefs manifest themselves in his writing, and how much affirmation or disagreement we confer on his expressed beliefs.

Setting Shadwell and Buckingham aside, we recur to the nature of Dryden's intellectual temper, his unusual combination of conservatism and progressivism. And since our aim is to get at Dryden's kind of truth in the context of satire, one must first emphasize relativities. I have said that the satirist always risks suspicion, because I feel it to be true. But when we compare Dryden's satire to that by Donne, Marston, and Hall; to that of Butler, Marvell, Rochester, and Oldham; or to that of Pope—we must say that Dryden's is a far nobler version of truth. With the exception of the first half of *The Medall*, what he satirizes ends up being greater than it had been. Greater no doubt in folly, knavery, or evil, but greater. I know of no other verse satire of which that can be said. Indeed, judged by non-dramatic satire from ancient to modern times, Dryden's satiric enlargement seems unique. One explanation for the paradox seems to me to derive from Dryden's experience as a playwright. The achievement is easier on the stage, as Ben Jonson shows. But the primary explanation surely must be that Dryden's satire expresses his mingled conservative and progressive beliefs.

Dryden's conservative belief enters his poems in very subtle ways. In the satiric world of *Mac Flecknoe* a new era is about to begin. That brings hope to the two central characters, but not to us, because we cannot accept their values. The world they possess is one of institutions perverted, crumbled, or threatening fall. The Barbican Tower has become "an empty name." And nothing could prove a more surreal architecture than the "Monument of vanisht minds." In *Absalom and Achitophel*, King David warns Absalom:

If my Young *Samson* will pretend a Call
To shake the Column, let him share the Fall.
(955–56)

The medal struck on Shaftesbury's release resembles him: "so golden to the sight, / So base within, so counterfeit and light" (8–9). Of course the architectural and numismatic images involve the central art-and-nature trope of seventeenth-century poetry.[58] But from the use of architectural imagery in Dryden's personal passage on government in *Absalom and Achitophel* (795–810) we can see that a major function of his imagery of art is to represent civilized values. He believed, and had deep emotional investment in, the stability of human institutions. Fallen towers, shaken columns, and false coins represent the instability, the danger, and the loss so fearful to his conservative temper. Such shaking of nature's germans arouses Dryden's fear and hostility. To counter the disintegration of his conservative palace, Dryden drew on a number of other symbols of value that turn up as images and actions in his writing.

One of the most powerful and consistent is his symbol of the Restoration,[59] emergent in his early poems on the Restoration, recalled by the coronation scene in *Mac Flecknoe*, and by the conclusions to *Absalom and Achitophel* and *The Medall*. Dryden's opera, *Albion and Albanius* deals with the "double Restoration" of Charles II, in 1660 and in the Tory Triumph of 1682. As I have observed before, the restoration of kingship commonly follows the acting-out of a threat to an endangered king in his heroic plays, tragicomedies, and some tragedies. If any central action is shared by the greatest

[58] See the discussion, especially of Dryden, in ch. I, ii, above.

[59] See George deF. Lord, "*Absalom and Achitophel* and Dryden's Political Cosmos," in *Writers and Their Backgrounds: John Dryden*, ed. Miner (London, 1972), ch. VI, to which I am indebted but with which I also disagree.

works of the Restoration, it is just this one central to Dryden's: ruin . . . restoration. *Paradise Lost, Paradise Regained, The Pilgrim's Progress.* The possibility of ruin without restoration haunts the finest satire outside Dryden's: Butler, some of Rochester, Marvell, and Oldham. It seems to me an error to regard deeply held images of experience as either conservative or progressive in nature, because so much depends on the way in which the images are treated.

For the moment, however, Dryden's conservative temper is our concern, and we must therefore see how he shrinks from the possibility of tampering, lest ruin result and chaos come again:

> If ancient Fabricks nod, and threat to fall,
> To Patch the Flaws, and Buttress up the Wall,
> Thus far 'tis Duty; but here fix the Mark:
> For all beyond it is to touch our Ark.
> To change Foundations, cast Frames anew,
> Is work for Rebels who base Ends pursue:
> At once Divine and Humane Laws controul;
> And mend the Parts by ruine of the Whole.

I shall declare again that if this from *Absalom and Achitophel* (801–808) is not conservatism, we shall never find it. To look at matters another way, the restoration often seems to imply recovery by return of that *status quo ante. Absalom and Achitophel* concludes, "Once more the Godlike *David* was Restor'd, / And willing Nations knew their Lawfull Lord" (1030–31). If we can expect ruin from time to time, Dryden wishes restoration to follow in terms just like those lost. Such endings will be found in a number of his works, as we all know. Some aspects of Dryden's conservatism appeal more than others. His desire to preserve the civilized inheritance seems to me so human and so right that I give assent. But his desire to freeze political institutions into stones and then to claim them to be some cathedral or palace which we may touch but not change seems to me a useless magic. Social institutions make possible civilized achievement, and no doubt some are better or worse in that respect than others. But in respect to "Divine and Humane Laws," or justice, that Stuart monarchy so ardently supported by Dryden has lost any claim it once possessed.

In all Dryden's poems, including the satires, the counterpart of his conservatism is his faith in the capacity of the individual to create, of the race to advance, and of all to come ripe. His many progress pieces show just that, and one of their two most frequent images is none other than that architectural one that also figures in his conservatism. Clearly what we can quite sensibly distinguish as conservative or progressive in Dryden's thought and poetry also makes a whole. There would be no point in conserving what lacks value, and there would be nothing valuable to conserve if men could not create. At the end of those progress pieces not employing transcendent imagery (as does "A Song for St. Cecilia's Day") we have those with architectural images (e.g., the Roscommon and Congreve poems), which show that something immortal has been achieved. Dryden has the faith that men and women can achieve in history things of such surpassing worth that the achievements and their creators will continue to exist in history. In that sense the immortal falls short of the eternal, but as we see in "A Song for St. Cecilia's Day," God is Himself the greatest artist, creating the world. Or again, Dryden's symbol of restoration also has progressive implications. The poem to the Duchess of Ormonde rings change after change on the theme, reminding us of the restorations in Shakespeare's last plays. One poet and his subject is restored in another (1–39). A new generation of Ormondes is restored to Ireland (40–59). The Duchess' appearance affirms the restoration of peace and the restoration of man after dangers like Noah's Flood (60–79).

The Duchess herself will be restored in a second coming of the golden age (80–89). Now she has been restored to England (90–100). In particular, after dangerous illness, she has recovered health (101–45). For this, Dryden says in a passage worth quoting again, Blessed be God:

> Bless'd be the Pow'r which has at once restor'd
> The Hopes of lost Succession to Your Lord,
> Joy to the first and last of each Degree,
> Vertue to Courts, and what I long'd to see,
> To you the Graces, and the Muse to me.
>
> (146–50)

And finally, in the Duchess are restored York and Lancaster, Penelope, and Dido. From her procreativity, the Ormonde line will be continued, and the inheritance of her ancestors' Order of the Garter will be renewed. To adopt the terms used earlier, if that attitude is not creative and progressive, then we shall find such things nowhere.

Dryden's satires and satiric passages unquestionably show his conservative side especially clearly, and the first half of *The Medall* shows it to a degree that I find distressing. I shall begin with just that, therefore, to show that even that minimal moment presents the progressive obverse to us. A capacity for great deeds and words, such as Homer speaks of and Dryden celebrates in other poems, implies to any realistic mind the possibility that the capacity will be used wrongly and so be perverted to wrong ends. We need not necessarily agree with Dryden that a given individual has done so, but we must concur in the principle. The point of *The Medall* and other satiric moments in his writing comes to this: the creative force of man has been wrongly used and the heroic idea has been put in danger. In other words, the corruption of individual action is as central to Dryden's satire as is the ruin of institutions. Both will be found in the remarkable outburst at the beginning of *The Medall:*

Of all our Antick Sights, and Pageantry
Which *English* Ideots run in crowds to see,
The *Polish Medall* bears the prize alone:
A Monster, more the Favourite of the Town
Than either Fayrs or Theatres have shown.
Never did Art so well with Nature strive;
Nor ever Idol seem'd so much alive:
So like the Man; so golden to the sight,
So base within, so counterfeit and light.

(1–9)

Man the individual creator has turned into unthinking mass-man: "Ideots . . . crowds." Art is debased to a "*Medall* . . . Monster." Bad art works with ill Nature to produce a false "Idol," at once the medal and the man.

The image of man in Dryden's satires includes two species. The named individual perverts individual creativity and institutions but retains the dignity of being human. The unnamed individual or mass-man either constitutes the mob, the *mobile vulgus*, or as a malign unspecified agency seeks to manipulate that herd. The mob is an irrational force, possessing passions and will without judgment. Individuals (named or unnamed) are motivated by self-interest dictating seizure of power (or other dangerous tendencies). Power pretends to that wisdom which is to Dryden God's essence among His other attributes of will, omniscience, unity, infinity, etc., and to the distinguishing character of man made in God's image, free reason. The mob's parody of divine and human essence emerges more forcibly in *The Medall* than anywhere else in Dryden's writings:

The reason's obvious; *Int'rest never lyes;*
The most have still their Int'rest in their eyes;
The pow'r is always theirs, and pow'r is ever wise.

Almighty Crowd, thou shorten'st all dispute;
Pow'r is thy Essence; Wit thy Attribute! [60]

Man in God's image, rational and free, has been perverted into ignorance and anarchy.[61] This leads Dryden in the much finer second half of the poem to lament, "Ah, what is man, when his own wish prevails," etc. (132 ff.).

"Ah, what is Man!" Or as the chorus exclaims in *Samson Agonistes*, "God of our Fathers, what is man!" (667). Both poets were remembering the Psalmist's question, "What is man, that thou art mindful of him?" (8:4), a question heightened by Job (7:17), and echoed by the Apostle (Hebrews, 2:6). No other literary concern has higher priority, and every genre modern or ancient can avoid it only at the peril of becoming frivolous. From *Aureng-Zebe* to *Amphitryon* Dryden had dramatized the concern. And in *The Medall* what had been implicit, and often triumphant, in earlier works is satirically spoiled.

Dryden's satire deals with the nature of man, then, even more than with the state of institutions. That this is true can be proved by our introspection or by the example of critics constantly recurring to the satiric portraits in *Absalom and Achitophel.* The center of Dryden's poetry and plays lies in people. I have come to think that Dryden's strongest, most enduring personal passion was for his sons. His letters show it, and so in a way do the poems on Oldham and Congreve. It seems all the more remarkable therefore that *Mac Flecknoe* should be based on just such love and pride in one's progeny. A foolish father claims a foolish son:

Let Father *Fleckno* fire thy mind with praise,
And Uncle *Ogelby* thy envy raise.

[60] Lines 88–92; see the California edition, III, 337–39, for discussion of Dryden's philosophical conceptions in matters of religion.

[61] See *The Hind and the Panther*, I, 251–62; and the commentary on the passage in the California edition, III.

Thou art my blood, where [Jonson] has no part;
What share have we in Nature or in Art?

(173–76)

The first two lines quoted echo Virgil (*Aeneid*, III, 342–43; cf. "et pater Aeneas et avunculus excitat Hector"). The ensuing question is comprehensively devastating. We assume that Flecknoe and his son are art-less, but not to be in "nature" is not to be at all. Truly, that is non-sense absolute, and what, indeed, is man?

Absalom and Achitophel affords a number of versions of father-son relationships. The narrator at one point asks why Achitophel should punish himself so with restless, ambitious strivings,

And all to leave, what with his Toyl he won,
To that unfeather'd, two Leg'd thing, a Son:
Got, while his Soul did huddled Notions try;
And born a shapeless Lump, like Anarchy.

(169–72)

These cruel lines give a tragic version of the "Pangs without birth, and fruitless Industry" of *Mac Flecknoe* (148). They also remind us of the brilliant opening lines of the poem, in which the promiscuity of Charles II is at once criticized and meant to be proleptic of Achitophel's production of a monster and David's own problems with Absalom. Out of esteem for that good woman, the Duchess of Monmouth, Dryden greatly softens his satire of Monmouth-Absalom. But he and his readers knew the Bible, recalling the fate of proud Absalom, hanged by his hair in a tree. The only ideal son turns out to be old Barzillai's, "snatcht in Manhoods prime" (833):

Yet not before the Goal of Honour won,
All parts fulfill'd of Subject and of Son;
Swift was the race, but short the Time to run.
Oh Narrow Circle, but of Pow'r Divine,
Scanted in Space, but perfect in thy line!

(835–39)

The heroic conception emerges clearly: "Oh Ancient Honour, Oh Unconquer'd Hand" (844). As in that elegy on another "son," Oldham, Dryden is recalling Virgil's praise of Marcellus:

heu pietas, heu prisca fides, invictaque bello
dextera! [62]

The great and good son has been lost. Epic grandeur remains. When the possibility itself rather than its exemplars has been lost, Dryden exclaims, "Ah, what is man!" It would, I think, be a grave error not to think that Dryden's satire is founded on his conservative sense of folly, wrongness, evil, and a loss of what might have been. But it would be a comparable error to think that such a sense of loss could be felt by him without his possessing high ideals and positive, progressive standards of what might be hoped for from men and women. Without ideals we descend into cynicism or the pessimism of Butler and Rochester. What they tell us about ourselves needs telling. But for Dryden, his satire (including especially that angry, frustrated, and dark poem, *The Medall*) concerns itself with the gap he sometimes found between his heroic idea and reality.

[62] *Aeneid*, VI, 878–79: "Oh, for the goodness, for the old perfect honour, and the stout right hand unvanquished in war." Cf. Dryden's better but freer translation for the *Aeneis* (1214–15), which also creates his sense of the heroic values represented by Ossory: "Mirror of ancient Faith in early Youth! / Undaunted Worth, Inviolable Truth!"

Restoration satire reaches its apogee in Dryden's satires from *Mac Flecknoe* to *The Medall*, and it has a kind of afterglow—or after-lowering—in his translations of Juvenal and Persius for *The Satires* published in 1693. But by that date Dryden was an old man, and no other great satire appeared between 1688 and the eighteenth century.[63] Why this should be is a question that is only now coming to be asked, because it has been only recently that the last years of the century have come to seem so important for understanding changes of taste and attitude along with changes in other spheres of life.

I think that we can see why Dryden ceased to write satire, and perhaps that tells us something about the age as well. The two kinds of satire practiced by Dryden and his contemporaries included that pessimistic or nihilistic satire by Butler and Rochester and the satire waged between the Whigs and the Tories in Dryden's poetic kingdoms. In such a metaphoric, as well as in the strict, sense, Dryden's is Tory satire. That is, it is highly unusual in expressing the views of commanding authority. Most satire comes from those who are on the outside and who resent what they depict as tyranny on the one hand and the mob on the other. The usual satirist is not only outraged but slighted and vulnerable. He assumes his moral and intellectual superiority, but the wicked world does not acknowledge it. Dryden takes no such stance at all. To use his three chief metaphoric strands in *Mac Flecknoe*, the values of monarchy, religion, and art give him full assumption of authority. After 1688, however, a man whom he regarded as a usurper sat on the Stuart throne,

[63] I could find only two or three satires of merit in *Poems on Affairs of State*, vol. v, 1688–97 (New Haven and London, 1971), so very well edited by William J. Cameron. Garth's *Dispensary* (1699) provides a single major exception, if it is major.

and the denomination of Dryden's religion placed his life in peril. His old kind of satire had become impossible to write.

On the other hand, Dryden still believed that his monarchy, religion, and art were the true ones, and that the *de jure* authority still lay with him. The crisis of legitimacy rent the Church of England and English society for two or three decades, and only gradually could people find ways to persuade themselves that *de jure* and *de facto* authority coincided again. Dryden never attempted to persuade himself, and for that reason he could not write satire that spoke without the voice of authority any more than he could now write satire with the voice of authority. There was of course that third possibility, the pessimistic or nihilistic satire of Butler and Rochester. Some who have considered Dryden too hastily have considered that his choice after the Revolution lay between holding onto his Jacobitism and Catholicism or going over to the Williamite and Protestant side. I am sorry to say that such an observation reveals more about the observers than about John Dryden. He had overtures from the government, to be sure, but his crisis was of a very different kind. He could abandon faith, in more than one sense. If he did, then the example of Butler in particular could have led him to a new stage of satiric writing. But he did not abandon faith. Like Milton's concept of a benign providence, his heroic idea required change and a redefinition in broader, less immediate terms. The Augustan ideal became Virgil in English, and the heroic conception of human individuality became a concern with the search for the good life in his *Fables*. I believe it highly ironic that the commercial empire that he had forecast as an aspect of English heroism was coming into being, with a Dutchman as its chief agent. Dryden refused to recognize what he had been first to see from afar. He belonged to an older age of individual enterprise, and such new institutions as William's armies, universal taxation, the Bank of England, and National Debt made no sense to a person born as long ago as 1631. He was saved from blindness by his often remarked-on capacity to develop poetically to the end. And at the end he returned to narrative, to some of the world's best stories, in order to tell the human story and to assess it for what it gave him of the values and hopes he had so long celebrated.

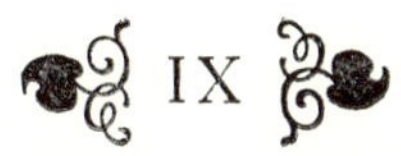

IX

OUR HONOR, VIRTUE, AND CHIEF PRAISE

he who reigns within himself, and rules
Passions, Desires, and Fears, is more a King;
Which every wise and vertuous man attains.
— Milton, *Paradise Regained*, II

As Earth thy Body keeps, thy Soul the sky,
So shall this Verse preserve thy Memory.
— Dryden, *Eleonora*

i. Voices and Actions

Among the voices we have heard from the Restoration poets have been most recently those of the libertines telling of the delights and limits of sensation and the satirists proclaiming what has gone wrong. It is now time to attend to a wider range of voices and to assess the burden of the most important. The great lyric achievement of 1580 to 1640 is not matched by Restoration lyrics. Of course there are songs worth remembering: "Love still has something of the sea," "An age in her embraces passed," "Love in fantastic triumph sat," "Farewell, ungrateful traitor," and so on to Prior's "The merchant, to conceal his treasure." Readers who prefer the lyric above other forms have no lack of collections to choose from.

The strength and the limitation of most of the lyrics during the period depend on a degree of remoteness unusual in lyrics. Many of the lyrics were written as songs to be sung in plays. Others take on such a degree of generalization that although they seem to apply widely, they do so less intensely.

Often the "image-free" styles of Jonson and especially of Suckling were taken new lengths in generalizing, and also from the Cavaliers was taken the "semi-pastoral" that placed the action somewhere between England and Arcady.[1] Such poems do not require that we presume any full congruence between the poet's voice and the speaker's voice, between the person addressed and any historical person. On the other hand, such a congruence is by no means excluded, either. The compromise was particularly well suited to the manners of an aristocracy, and consequently such lyricism was soundly related to its society, but the range of experience in such songs and the intensity with which it is felt are inadequate by high standards. And yet there also existed a quite different strain of lyricism in which the remoteness is of a different kind and the result much superior. The major lyric, as it may be called, begins with Milton's early poems. In them a new degree of narrative appears and, as many people have recognized, so does the heroic. More than that, Milton moves the lyric into the public domain, as his sonnets alone would show. I believe that only a few of his sonnets claim highest respect, but the alteration of lyricism is itself remarkable. The Nativity Ode and *Lycidas* speak, or sing, with voices of authority, and voices indeed such as no one else possessed when Milton's *Poems* was published in 1645. Milton's heir in the major lyric, as in much else, Dryden renovated the public lyric in the last fifteen years of his life by developing the Cowleyan pindaric ode. No one would mistake the voices of Milton or Dryden in their lyrics any more than in their more extended poems. And yet it remains true that the voice of "pure" song is not heard in those lyrics, and that the desuetude of the sonnet after Milton, and by the later Milton, testifies to the public and heroic character of the new styles.

[1] On these two procedures, see *The Cavalier Mode* (Princeton, 1971), pp. 231–37.

Public poetry requires distinct voices to represent personalities in the world, to give a sense of reality. In one short genre, that of the prologue and epilogue, Dryden and a few others like Sir Carr Scrope achieved unrivaled eminence. Dryden wrote nearly a hundred such pieces, and since they extend over much of his career, they have served to provide the critic with a representative sample of Dryden's use of satire and praise.[2] In such pieces, and in plays as well, Dryden developed his talent for creating voices: the girl or woman, the man drunk or sober, the admirer, the insinuator, the pleader, the scatter-brained, the commentator, the critic of Shakespeare. Such negative capability contrasts with the Miltonic egotistical sublime, for although the tone and much else in Milton's poetry alters, the poet's voice is ever the same.

Such voices help define the kinds of values created in Restoration poetry. We can see how this is so by observing that Donne and Jonson also created voices, but of different kinds. We hear Donne's young man address a woman, or his penitent at prayer. We hear Jonson unmistakably praising a woman or advising a friend to the wars. That is, we *over*-hear such things, for they are formally not meant for our hearing at all. Donne and others like him create a private world, as Jonson and others like him create a social. Both such conceptions of men and their limited relations to each other seek far more than does public poetry to create vision, the wholly separate yet universal vision of Metaphysical poetry, or the vision of a precious few of Cavalier poetry. From "The Extasie" to Vaughan, or from the *Epistle to Katherine, Lady Aubigny* to Cotton, Donne and Jonson and their followers excelled in two versions of poetry whose voices told of vision. That sound can become seeing perhaps needs no explaining, but a signal instance occurs at the end of Herbert's "Prayer,"

[2] See the excellent discussion by Arthur W. Hoffman, *John Dryden's Imagery* (Gainesville, Fla., 1962), ch. II.

in which the last image is of church bells heard beyond the stars: for "something understood."

The voices and the lesser visions of the public poets we are considering moved toward the different end of action, and the kind of understanding they sought was either realized or expressed in action. Those who have said that Milton uses little imagery have looked more than they have listened. In Milton's poetry, one listens to conscience. Such hearkening is a form of knowledge, *con-scientia*. In his greatest poem Milton speaks "Of Mans First Disobedience" and in *Paradise Regained* of

> Recover'd Paradise to all mankind,
> By one mans firm obedience fully tri'd.
> (I, 3–4)

Milton was obviously aware of the derivation of "obedience" from *obedire* from *ob-audire*, which could mean "to hear," "to attend to," as well as "to obey."[3] Dryden also plays on the double meaning, as in "A Song for St. Cecilia's Day" (my italics):

> The tuneful Voice was *heard* from high,
> Arise ye more than dead.
> Then cold, and hot, and moist, and dry,
> In order to their stations leap,
> And Musick's pow'r *obey*. (6–10)

Clearly, what is heard is thought of as leading to an action experienced rather than a vision: Belial's thoughts *wander* through that eternity Vaughan *saw*. The heard-act conception derives in part from our familiar experience, in part from literary and philosophical tradition. One of the simplest

[3] Curiously, there are analogies in German *hören* and Japanese *hito ga yū koto o kiku* (to do, literally to hear, what someone says), whereas the French *entendre* more resembles English *see* in the sense of understanding.

literary illustrations will be found in English adaptation of the Virgilian narrative formula "dixerat" (e.g., *Aeneid*, IV, 238, 381, 663). The formula comes after an epic speech and is immediately followed by action on the part of the speaker or those addressed. "He said" is the usual version of the formula in Restoration narrative. In *Annus Mirabilis*, for example, Dryden gives James Duke of York a speech rallying his forces for the second day's battle:

> He said; nor needed more to say: with hast
> To their known stations chearfully they go:
> And all at once, disdayning to be last,
> Sollicite every gale to meet the foe.
>
> (305–308)

Or again, there is *Absalom and Achitophel*, (1026): "He said. Th' Almighty, nodding, gave Consent . . ." Among the examples in Milton's poems, there is this in *Paradise Lost* after a speech by God: "He said, and on his Son with Rayes direct / Shon full" (VI, 719–20). Since his Father has just given the charge to drive the fallen angels to Hell, the Son (receiving divine power with the divine light shed on him) praises the Father: and, "So said . . . ," the dreadful action begins.

To Homer and Aristotle alike, *lexis* and *praxis* or speech and action provide the chief indices of free humanity, and on them they found society, ethics, rhetoric, and happiness. Such presumptions about man underlie the public mode. Words are spoken by people to other people to define what they share or what divides them, and words are fulfilled by action rendering them meaningful or meaningless. One's relation to the world is more ethical in public poetry, whereas in private it is more perceptual. Dryden's prologues and epilogues compare in length with most of the poems by Donne and Jonson, but the fact that Dryden's were written literally to be spoken makes them very different in effect:

Though what our Prologue said was sadly true,
Yet, Gentlemen, our homely House is new,
A Charm that seldom fails with, wicked, You.
A Country Lip may have the Velvet touch,
Tho' She's no Lady, you may think her such,
A strong imagination may do much.
But you, loud Sirs, who thro' your Curls look big,
Criticks in Plume and white vallancy Wig,
Who lolling on our foremost Benches sit,
And still charge first, (the true forlorn of Wit)
Whose favours, like the Sun, warm where you roul,
Yet you like him, have neither heat nor Soul;
So may your Hats your Foretops never press,
Untouch'd your Ribbonds, sacred be your dress;
So may not *France* your Warlike Hands recall,
And have th' excuse of Youth for Ignorance.
So may Fop corner full of noise remain,
And drive far off the dull attentive train;
So may your Midnight Scowrings happy prove,
And Morning Batt'ries force your way to Love;
So may not *France* your Warlike Hands recall,
But leave you by each others Swords to fall:
As you come here to ruffle Vizard Punk,
When sober, rail and roar when you are drunk.[4]

We think with good reason of Donne's poems having a quality we label "dramatic," but what is true of that type or focus is not true of their genre, lyricism.[5] Dryden's prologues

[4] Lines 1–24 of the "Epilogue" with "A Prologue spoken at the Opening of the New House." The "forlorn" (10) was the body of men at the vanguard of an attack and almost certain to be lost; hence the name. But the "Criticks" are also "forlorn of Wit." Notice Dryden's opinion of the Sons of Belial here.

[5] I follow the German distinction between a work's genre (*Gattung*) and its attributive type or focus (*Typus*).

and epilogues were spoken with the plays and must be thought dramatic in a true sense. The poems by Dryden, then, like those by Butler and Milton before him, are public, and in that forum many voices are heard, and the voices are those of personalities who deliver words and act.

As words and deeds create the values of public poetry, in narrative poems speech and action possess complex and fertile relationships. In the *Odyssey* we often find the two nearly impossible to extricate, because the words of Odysseus of the many wiles, *polymētis*, are so calculated that they are implicit with an intended action often quite at variance from the meaning spoken. The *Iliad* first arouses our concern with the words of heated quarrel, and when the action comes after that wind-up, it is furious and bleak. In the *Aeneid*, an oversimplified case can be made for six books of talk and six of action. In any event, diverse models for relating words and action existed from antiquity, and to those mentioned must be added that of Ovid in the *Metamorphoses*, where the discrepancy between human words and divinely imposed change creates a consistent irony, or that of Thucydides alternating set speeches with action to depict and assess both the speaker and the actor. Numerous models existed but, to all minds, rhetoric and philosophy either agreed or disputed over the sphere of action. Even the Calvinists could not allow a mere state of mind and, in seeming contradiction to their *sola fides* position, insisted as much as Aristotle on doing, and indeed they *did*. Our poets held the same concerns, although being poets they often made actions of words, and made words entail action.

ii. The Return of Justice in *Hudibras*

Butler, Dryden, and Milton elicit from Dr. Johnson a series of terms, or conceptions, of the constituents of narrative. We may recall that, although he admired Butler, he found *Hudibras* deficient in action: " . . . there is more said than done. The scenes are too seldom changed, and the attention is tired with long conversation."[6] A narrative requires action, speech, and scenes in the right proportion and with the right handling. Dryden's faults in *Annus Mirabilis* require a different vocabulary: " . . . he affords more sentiment than description, and does not so much impress scenes upon the fancy as deduce consequences and make comparisons."[7] Dryden does not use Butler's seemingly endless harangues, but he too seems to slight action in *Annus Mirabilis* in favor of signifying processes. In his life of Milton, Johnson discusses more traditional aspects of narrative: the moral, the fable, and the characters.[8] From these terms, we can infer not only what is said and done but also how meaning may be derived from what is said and done. Speeches and actions belong to the characters of a poem, whereas descriptions, sentiments, consequences, and comparisons belong to the narrator. Dr. Johnson clearly feels as we do that descriptions and "scenes" belong less obtrusively to the narrator than do comments, which always run the danger of unwelcome intrusion. And yet literary performance never attends to the niceties of critical theory, especially that of a prescriptive kind. What may be termed narrative description may involve action or create character. For example, one of the commonest descriptive motifs, the night-piece (another is the dawn-piece) took from Virgil onward so set a character that introductory formulas were devised in various languages. In rendering Virgil, and in his own poems, Dryden changes "Nox erat . . . " to "Night came . . . ." When night comes, it does so in order either to harmonize with or con-

[6] *Lives of the English Poets,* ed. G. B. Hill, 3 vols. (Oxford, 1904), "Butler," I, 211.

[7] Ibid., "Dryden," I, 431.

[8] Ibid., "Milton," I, 171 ff.

trast with the mood of the characters and the quality of the action about to take place. One can follow this throughout centuries of literature,[9] during which time the world is invariably depicted as sympathetic or hostile but never neutral. By descriptions, then, the poet gently directs our responses. By intrusive reflections he openly suggests the way. The presence and the manner of the entrance of such directives determines the degree to which the author dwells on the significance of his action and also the degree to which the directives retard and diminish the effect of his action.

The greatest of Restoration retarders and diminishers was Samuel Butler. There is no question about that. At the end of the first canto of the first part of *Hudibras,* the introduction of characters is done and we have escaped, with some difficulty, from the first wordy quarrel between Hudibras and Ralpho. At last Hudibras stirs his "sullen Jade" (920, the last line of the canto), so that he and his squire can attack the bearbaiting. The first action, in any ordinary sense, has at last occurred. After so protracted an introduction of characters and after wordy argument, we feel a strong need for action. Let us recall that the argument had been resolved in a very exasperating way, utterly depriving it of any importance it might still have had to us.

> But, *Ralpho* this is no fit place
> Nor time to argue out the Case:
> For now the Field is not far off . . .
> (I, i, 857–59)

Precisely what we had been feeling all along, but why should it then have gone on so long? Hudibras and Ralpho have been arguing out of place and to no end. We are re-

[9] See my "Formulas: Japanese and Western Evidence Compared," *Proceedings of the Vth Congress of the International Comparative Literature Association* (Belgrade, 1969), pp. 405–17.

lieved to think that Hudibras will shut up and get moving. Of course he does neither. He goes on for about fifty lines more. Then the narrator takes over in three similes on his hero's spurring his horse, and at last, more or less, "the sullen Jade has stirr'd." About seventy lines are required merely to spur the horse.

At the opening of the second canto we expect to see some action or wish to know a very good reason why not. And so we begin, after Hudibras spurred his "sullen Jade":

> There was an ancient sage *Philosopher*,
> That had read *Alexander Ross* over,
> And swore the world, as he could prove,
> Was made of *Fighting* and of *Love* . . .
>
> (1–4)

Suffering this indignity, we want to shout at the author, What does this have to do with the story? His reply seems to be, What does anything have to do with anything?—Be quiet, and listen. Then, having mentioned love, he proceeds to throw it away, saying he really has little to offer on that subject. He has more on the subject of fighting, and in particular he attacks "our Authors" and their bloodthirsty heroes. Then a few similes are required, telling us something of "a wild *Tartar*," a giant, and "Beavers," although nothing much about "our Authors," and nothing at all about Hudibras and Ralph. At line thirty-five, Butler momentarily digresses toward action, swearing, "we shall tell / The naked Truth of what befell" (35–36). There follow six lines on how the truth will be told, and at last:

> This b'ing profest, we hope's enough,
> And now go on where we left off.
>
> (43–44)

We left off forty-five lines back, at the end of the preceding canto. To think that Butler hopes that we have had enough of preliminaries!

Then, at long last, the action begins—for two words' length:

> They rode, but Authors having not
> Determin'd whether Pace or Trot,
> (That is to say, whether *Tollutation*,
> And they do term't, or *Sucussation*)
> We leave it, and go on . . . (45–49)

We are so weary with this endlessly evasive Catiline of narrators that we ask why in heaven's name he abuses our patience so. Our hopes are beginning to go with our patience, but let us return for another try:

> We leave it, and go on, as now
> Suppose they did, no matter how.
> Yet—

and we know we are in for it again—

> Yet some from subtle hints have got
> Mysterious light, it was a Trot.
> But let that pass: they now begun
> To spur their living Engines on.
> (49–54)

At this point, a canto and fifty lines on, *Hudibras* has made it to the same point as the first line of *The Faerie Queene*. We have in fact not advanced much beyond the last line of the preceding canto, except to learn that Ralpho is on the move, too. The alert reader will know that the less he hopes for the better.

> To spur their living Engines on.
> For as whipp'd Tops and bandy'd Balls,
> The learned hold, are Animals:
> So Horses they affirm to be
> Mere engines . . .
> So let them be; and, as I was saying, . . .
> (54–58, 61)

So it goes. By now all expectation of action has been beaten out of us. If we persist in reading, we do so on the author's own terms, "as I was saying," awaiting some new simile, or some example of quoted stupidity from sources preposterously authoritative. Robert Burton and Henry James seem relaters of compelling actions by comparison. As it surprisingly turns out, however, the action does begin at the point we last left off. If we remember where that was. The narrator tells us of advance, of gestures, and of the efforts by master and squire to assess the crowd of bearbaiters whom they aim to attack. Having got that far, having to our surprise rattled on in story for about forty lines (in the poem's first thousand), Butler of course finds it necessary to interrupt the rapid pace in order to give "characters" of Crowdero, Orsin, "The Gallant *Bruin*," Talgol, Magnano, Trulla, Cerdon, Colon, and "The numerous Rabble." That work over, the narrator relies on his leather-lunged hero for a speech of 190 lines (493–682). Talgol replies with comparable abuse, provoking Hudibras to defend himself with words. To our surprise, he suddenly interrupts himself for an action: "with hasty rage he snatch'd / His Gun-shot, that in holsters watch'd," leveling "on *Talgol's Skull*" (775–76, 778). To our total lack of surprise, the gun fails to go off. Contrary to that failure, the rest of the canto is filled with "narrative," that is with action. By utter mischance, Hudibras falls on the Bear, who "roar'd, and rag'd, and flung about" (879), so routing all but one of the bearbaiters, the peglegged musician, Crowdero. He is shortly overcome by Hudibras and Ralpho, who put him in the stocks. Butler makes rather a point of the fact that although the sound leg had not entered the battle as a weapon, it is "clapt up," whereas the dangerous peg leg is set free. In such fashion does the second canto of *Hudibras* close with a moral on the fate of Crowdero's two legs:

So Justice, while she winks at Crimes,
Stumbles on Innocence sometimes.
(1177–78)

The moral seems deliberately anticlimactic, utterly stupid, and consciously inconsequential. But it is not. *Hudibras* certainly was designed endlessly to frustrate our normal expectations, but to do so to the end of directing our attention to matters more important than a mere fiction. The interruptions of action tell us what "an ancient sage *Philosopher*" had to say, or what "our Authors" debate on the speed of Hudibras's nag, or what "The learned" have to say about tops being animals and animals engines. In fact, action flickers as a possibility with "we shall tell" and begins only when the narrator insists on himself: "as I was saying." That exasperating narrator, or author, insists that we must trust him rather than all other authorities, just as the first canto had shown we must trust him rather than Hudibras or Ralpho. In case we miss the point, he repeats it, and repeats it again, and yet again. We are given the opportunity to think momentarily with the learned that "Tops and bandy'd Balls" are animals, but not for long. We must, it seems, learn to call Hudibras's "Jade" a jade.

Of course Butler encourages us to think of Hudibras as a knight and his jade a steed, and so on. He does so in order to make us examine what we suppose and what we have been taught by romances to suppose:

> . . . if any man should but imitate what these Heroical Authors write in the Practice of his life and Conversation, he would become the most Ridiculous Person in the world.[10]

We are being told to see things as they are. The lesson is dunned into us by endless iteration, and just as frequently the author gives us opportunities to think that things are *not* as they are, and the narrator sometimes dissimulates with his similes:

> For when a Giant's slain in fight,
> And mow'd orethwart, or cleft downright,
> It is a heavy case, no doubt,
> A man should have his Brains beat out,
> Because he's tall, and has large Bones;
> As men kill Beavers for their stones.
>
> (I, ii, 29–34)

It is a fact that men then did kill beavers for their testicles' imagined medicinal value, and truly it is a "heavy case" that a man should be slaughtered for his size alone. The truth or the fact of the simile (and not all of Butler's are factual or true) exists independently of its application, since the present simile does not apply to the place it is introduced. It may be true, but it is unlike Hudibras. There is something like Milton's negative similes here, but in idea rather than in figurative procedure. Butler expects us to observe something by way of analogous fact and truth. But the essential point is the pointlessness, the lack of application of the fact. Hudibras is neither a giant nor a beaver; moreover, no one gets killed, for all the violence, in *Hudibras*.

Hudibras had begun, it will be recalled, when the narrator shrugged off others and shrugged in his own view, not without considerable dissimulation:

[10] *Characters and Passages from Note-Books*, ed. A. R. Waller (Cambridge, 1908), p. 278.

So let them be; and, as I was saying,
They their live Engines ply'd, not staying
Untill they reach'd the fatal Champaign,
Which th' Enemy did then incamp on,
The dire *Pharsalian* Plain . . . (61–65)

We think we get the point of the allusion to Pharsalia: this story of a bearbaiting does *not* compare with Lucan's plain in *The Civil Wars*. But why "live Engines" for horses, when we have just learnt how stupid and wrong it is to think such an untruth?

So Horses they affirm to be
Mere Engines, made by Geometry.
And were invented first from Engins,
As *Indian Britans* were from *Penguins*.
(57–60)

Butler's note to the passage tells us that American Indians call a bird with a white head a penguin, as in "the Brittish Tongue: From whence (with other words of the same kind) some Authors indeavor'd to prove, That the *Americans* [i.e., Indians] are originally deriv'd from the *Brittains* [i.e., Welsh]." The whole notion is absurd, and yet the author follows from this lunatic comparison (in which two peoples become *Indian Britons* and are somehow derived from birds) back to the equally mad assumption that horses are engines, and having made clear that the minds of others are turned on precisely such matters, he takes a figment of their madness and uses it himself: "They their live Engines ply'd." Certainly the promised naked truth does not make the west of England Pharsalia, as the narrator suggests.

Such dissimulation aids Butler in his craft. By using similes, allusions, and metaphors, he not only interrupts a narrative which shows every sign of being worth little more than interruption (on the evidence, of course, of the interruptions themselves), but succeeds in catching us off balance and pushing us just beyond balance point on the other side. He also manages by this dizzy art to amplify, to enlarge, to reach ever higher by simile, and dissimile, by rumor and report, until the structure topples back into the unedifying truth, which looks the worse for all the pretensions made about it. There do exist, of course, horses, penguins, and a historical Pharsalia. And that reality fills Butler's balloons so that they can burst: "So let them be." It did not matter anyhow. The west of England is *not*, we repeat, Pharsalia. On the other hand, *The Civil Wars* and the *Pharsalia* are interchangeable titles, and the first line of *Hudibras* tells of civil war. Nothing is worse than a true absurdity.

Butler's dissimiles and dissimulation constantly depreciate what might possess value, thereby hazarding our understanding and his. In his economy of means, one does not merely refer to Lucan once with "The dire *Pharsalian* Plain." What connection is there, after all, between a poem beginning "When *civil* Fury first grew high" and Lucan's poem? On reflection, however, it does seem that of all classical epics one knows of, Lucan's is most appropriate for Butler. When Hudibras confronts his enemies, he addresses them with an epic speech:

> What Rage, O Citizens, what fury
> Doth you to these dire actions hurry?
> What *Oestrum*, what phrenetick mood
> Makes you thus lavish of your bloud,
> While the proud *Vies* your Trophies boast,
> And unreveng'd walks _ _ _ _ _ ghost?
> What Towns, what Garrisons might you
> With hazard of this bloud subdue,
> Which now y' are bent to throw away
> In vain, untriumphable fray?
>
> (493–502)

Nothing could be clearer than that this is an echo of Lucan, I, 8–14:

> What fury, Countreymen, what madnesse cou'd
> Moove you to feast your fooes with Roman blood?
> And choose such warres, as could no triumphs yeeld,
> Whilest yet proud Babylon unconquer'd held
> The boasting Trophaes of a Roman hoast,
> And unrevenged wander'd *Crassus* Ghost?
> Alas, what Seas, what Lands might you have tane,
> With what bloods losse, which civill hands had drawne? [11]

Just what is happening in all this may well be questioned.

On the one hand, we observe the process of what I have termed dissimulation. A comparison is suggested between Hudibras and *Hudibras* on the one hand and Caesar and the Senate and the *Pharsalia* on the other. That comparison magnifies the world of Butler's poem, since "What Rage, O Citizens, what fury" brings a higher style to the poem than we had hitherto seen. But the ironic gap proves too wide, and as a result Hudibras and what he represents are further discredited. Each step of the process entails minutely discriminated values, and beyond the whole process itself lies a much larger question: In what sense has Butler revived Lucan, *De Bello Civili*? Like Lucan's poem, *Hudibras* is in some sense incomplete. (But could we stand for any more?) Lucan described the contest between Caesar and the Senate; he apparently meant to end with the assassination of Caesar. Could there be a recollection of Civil War in England and the execution of Charles I?

As long as one puts the matter in terms of a "recollection" and as a question, the answer may be: Possibly. On the other hand, I cannot believe that Butler's aim was that of Lucan,

[11] Following Wilders, p. 350, I quote from the translation by Thomas May (1627). I shall not enter into the complicated question whether "Waller's" belongs in the blank before "ghost."

to lead up to praise of another Nero (see Lucan, I, 33 ff). Also in his usual art of degradation, Butler has taken from Lucan an address by the narrator and has given it to Hudibras. We are given a situation there at the bearbaiting that has led some people to think that the Bear represents Charles I. Again, if we phrase the assertion as a sufficiently vague question, we may respond: Possibly. But most of the evidence contradicts such an allegory. Butler and Hudibras in fact show little interest in Bruin, directing their attention to the bearbaiters. The bear himself might as well be a maypole. Moreover, if we take the Bear as a representative of Charles I, then his attendants must be courtiers, which they are not. Cerdon, for example, is a preacher in a conventicle (435–38). To my mind, no success has been achieved in identifying individual characters in *Hudibras* with historical persons. Whatever their origins in history, Butler's characters achieve their own free life on his terms of depreciation and dissimulation.

The allegory of *Hudibras*, if allegory be the right term, treats only of general matters. The poem pays most of its attention to the squabbles among the anti-royalist, or non-royalist factions in England. Hudibras and Ralpho represent, of course, Presbyterianism and Independency, but even so Butler never fully shows the takeover of the government by Independency. His spoilt romance plot keeps a rigid social order at variance with events. The bearbaiters obviously represent still lower classes, Anabaptists, Brownists, Diggers, and such. Bearbaiting was a stupid but very English amusement, and banned though it had been by the Parliamentary Ordinance of June 3, 1647, it still found favor with those lower classes who represent the non-royalist opposition to Hudibras. In short, Butler puts the middling and lower classes on view, showing the anarchy that exists in a world from which King and God are absent.

It follows that Butler's allegory or allusions do not permit us to identify historical events in his major episodes: the clash over bearbaiting, the Skimmington, the quarrel with Sidrophel, and the debate with the Lady. It can hardly be emphasized enough that, for all its violence, *Hudibras* has no killings (however badly beaten Sidrophel may have been). In that it differs from Lucan's story and from the English Civil Wars. Once again we must account as a species of dissimulation the allusions to Lucan, a likeness that brings a magnification leading to greater depreciation. Hudibras's Lucanian words are selfish and unheroic, spoken by the wrong man to the wrong people on the wrong occasion. The fact of Lucan and the truth of the Civil Wars in the two countries only serve to make Hudibras and his world more grotesque and despicable.

Clearing such uncertainties in the second canto of the first part, we are returned to the earlier question. Perhaps we can now make something of the moral at the end of this lengthy Canto ii:

> *So Justice, while she winks at Crimes,*
> *Stumbles on Innocence sometimes.*

The idea must first be got clear. Just as Hudibras lets free Crowdero's wicked leg (the peg, used as a weapon) and locks up the other, innocent leg, so Justice may close her eyes to crimes, while kicking the innocent. The *locus classicus* for the concept is Juvenal, *Satires*, II, 63: "Our censor absolves the raven and passes judgment on the pigeon!" ("dat veniam corvis, vexat censura columbas"). The line brings to an end the lengthy charge by Laronia against men, who revile women for their errors while committing greater crimes themselves. In Juvenal, Laronia's valid argument routs the would-be Stoics whom she attacks. Is this another instance of dissimulation? That Justice "sometimes" errs hardly requires proof, but both the moral and the allusion require us to ask whether *Hudibras* allows us to conceive of *any* justice in the world.

Butler inescapably insists on the shortcomings of his characters in order to further his larger purposes. By various narrative and antinarrative devices, by similes and dissimulations, he draws himself and his readers far deeper into that despicable world than we care to go. Once this has been shown, as I hope that it has been in some detail, we must consider larger matters. The second canto of Part I shows that an accident enables Hudibras to rout his enemies and put Crowdero in the stocks. Hudibras's crimes are winked at and the pegleg fiddler is stumbled on. Justice has erred. The whole business of the next canto (I, iii) turns out to be a replay of Canto ii with opposite results. When his enemies return, Hudibras fights hard but unfairly only to be defeated by Trulla, who acts with decency and a code of honor. Butler gives us no moral this time, when Hudibras is now clapped into the stocks (I, iii, 1000–1008). No moral is necessary. Justice has opened her eyes; she has returned, taking a humble agent if there ever was one, a whore, to restore the order violated by Hudibras in the preceding canto.[12]

Along with Butler's other characters, Trulla does not lack for words and arguments. But her action reveals what is right, and her action strips the words and acts of Hudibras of their false pretense to virtue. Nothing so decisive happens again in *Hudibras* until the Lady deals with her gross wooer. In *The Ladies Answer* she figuratively and literally has the last word. The capricious and rather sadistic Widow replaces the slut in playing the goddess *Iustitia.* Justice does return to *Hudi-*

[12] Zachary Grey thought that "Trulla" derived from the word for the mistress of a tinker (Magnano who loves her is such: 365). Nash associated "trull" with a camp-follower. The *Oxford English Dictionary* defines a trull as "A low prostitute or concubine; a drab, strumpet, trollop." Since a tinker's drab was the lowest of the low, we have Butler's paradox of Trulla's gallantry and honor.

bras, first as the trull-principle, then as the widow-principle. Butler's poem brings no such new golden age as Virgil's fourth eclogue or Dryden's *Astraea Redux*. Astraea has dwindled into mere woman, and *das ewig weibliche* sets things right in a way other than that imagined by Goethe. Neither great deeds nor great words can be found in *Hudibras*, except when the poem is dissimulating. Justice does rule in *Hudibras*, however. It rules as a signally unfunny joke. Butler's masterpiece is exactly what he wished it to be, a diversion from the insanity and misery of life. If we can keep our senses and find some decency, we owe it to the trulls and widows.

iii. Milton's Empire of the Self

The "Newtonian" principle that each action entails an equal and opposite reaction has no full counterpart in literature, although it has come to be suspected more and more that the conception of a genre also implies the existence of a counter-genre in a tradition and counter-generic elements in a single work. We have seen how counter-narrative pressures require adjustment in narrative and how the pastoral and the libertine, or the satiric and panegyric, may assist each other. One of the reasons why Milton could make his poems so triumphantly whole was that he explicitly put to work the heroic and counter-heroic, adjusting them into a new version of the heroic sanctioned by God rather than by literary tradition, and focused on the empire within man rather than man in the empire.

We may fairly say that Milton is as radical a classicist as Butler is a *romancier*. At the beginning of Book IX of *Paradise Lost*, anticipating the Fall, Milton's narrator (or Milton) finds he "now must change / Those Notes to Tragic" (5–6). As Dryden recognized, Milton broke with tradition, from those rules that Milton himself mentions so approvingly at the end of *The Second Defence*. A new, tragic kind of outcome was necessary for a new kind of epic. With studied disdain Milton declares that he is

> Not sedulous by Nature to indite
> Warrs, hitherto the onely Argument
> Heroic deem'd, chief maistrie to dissect
> With long and tedious havoc fabl'd Knights
> In Battels feign'd; the better fortitude
> Of Patience and Heroic Martyrdom
> Unsung . . . (27–33)

The senses in which this remark is and is not true tell us a good deal about Milton. Let us recall Butler. In writing some manner of utterly spoilt epic, in treating "*civil* Fury," Butler gives only three cantos out of nine (not to mention other supernumerary parts) to battle (twice over the bear, once with Sidrophel), and at no time do we see proper armies arranged for "Warrs." In treating "Patience and Heroic Martyrdom" in *Paradise Lost,* on the other hand, Milton includes two books (V and VI) devoted to the War in Heaven, two on its results and resumption in new form (I and II), and two on its appearance in the very tissue of human history (XI and XII). In fact there is far more of war, arms, guards, and military detail in *Paradise Lost* than in *Hudibras.* For one little sedulous to indite wars, Milton certainly overcame disinclination in a major way.

Milton was of course obsessed by writing not just an epic but, to use his rather terrifying word, the true epic. To stop any blind mouths, he gives the full panoply of war as it had never been depicted before—among the "machines," the celestial characters. And being Milton, he insists that what he has done to such effect is not *truly* epic at all: they do not "justly [give] Heroic name / To Person or to Poem" (IX, 40–41). A "higher Argument" (42) is required, "Patience and Heroic Martyrdom," and "Tragic" tone. We observe in Milton's three principal poems that the central characters—Adam and Eve, Jesus, and Samson—are unarmed. Adam and Eve join hands rather than arms; Jesus rebuffs the military power of Rome and Parthia; and Samson with empty hands and in blindness defeats the giant Harapha. As Milton would no doubt have put it, his central characters are truly armed. Simply put, he spiritualizes, psychologizes heroism.[13] Action is referred to faith. But then heroism had long been understood precisely in terms of the spirit and psyche of a person, the Homeric *arēte*, the *pietas* of Aeneas, the *virtù* of the Italian heroes, the spiritual allegory of Spenser.

No finer critical study of the epic tradition exists than *Paradise Lost*, whose innumerable lessons we are gradually learning. Milton took that inner spirit of classical and Renaissance epics and made war only peripheral. He displaces epic conflict from the plain of battle and puts it into the actions of the individual mind and heart. In doing so he developed at greater length than any other poet the commonplace that to rule oneself is the greatest empire.[14] Milton tells us so in *Paradise Regained* through the mouth of our Savior:

> For therein stands the office of a King,
> His Honour, Vertue, Merit and chief Praise,
> That for the Publick all this weight he bears.
> Yet he who reigns within himself, and rules
> Passions, Desires, and Fears, is more a King;
> Which every wise and vertuous man attains:
> And who attains not, ill aspires to rule
> Cities of men, or head-strong Multitudes,
> Subject himself to Anarchy within,
> Or lawless passions in him which he serves.

[13] See John M. Steadman, *Milton and the Renaissance Hero* (Oxford, 1967); and *Milton's Epic Characters* (Chapel Hill, 1968).

[14] For *loci classici*, see *The Cavalier Mode*, p. 155; the Latin version given there runs "Sibi imperare, imperium maximum."

But to guide Nations in the way of truth
By saving Doctrine, and from errour lead
To know, and knowing worship God aright,
Is yet more Kingly, this attracts the Soul,
Governs the inner man, the nobler part,
That other o're the body only reigns,
And oft by force, which to a generous mind
So reigning can be no sincere delight.

(II, 463–80)

I take this to be Milton's clearest and most general statement on what constitutes human "Honour, Vertue, Merit and chief Praise." Goodness is defined as worship of God and self-rule. It is all so simple, as Milton always is—and yet so extraordinarily complex in the world, whether that world be Milton's, ours, or that we share in *Paradise Lost*. The illustration of this speech through consideration of Milton's unusual handling of voice and action will be my concern.

Criticism of *Paradise Lost* has come more and more to recognize the necessity of our attending carefully to the poem's many voices. We have had emphasized for us the dangers of distraction and erroneous response as well as the assistance provided us by the voice of the narrator.[15] Such dangers, and even more the possible interchange between the roles of voice and action, are greatly heightened by Milton's unusual development of the *Aeneid*-form (see ch. V, above). Because only two books are fully devoted to the natural narrative present, all else recapitulates the past (so chiefly I-VIII), anticipates the future (XI and XII), or here and there brings before us the presence and the words of the narrator. In other words, in ten of the poem's twelve books, we must rely on some voice other than the narrator's as direct relater of

[15] From among many fine studies, see Stanley Eugene Fish, *Surprised by Sin* (London, 1967); and Anne Davidson Ferry, *Milton's Epic Voice* (Cambridge, Mass., 1963).

the story, and in most of the poem Adam and Eve face the same problem of choosing between what is said by various voices. Because what is heard (and in Eden no system of writing exists) provides the basis for choice and action, the listener must be very sure that he has heard aright and that he has fully ascertained the reliability of the speaker. Books IX and X are themselves filled with talk, and they illustrate the crucial nature of right hearing very simply. The central lie in Satan's temptation of Eve amounts to this: he is the serpent and eating the forbidden fruit has given him an intellectual soul. By analogy, the fruit can enable Eve to rise correspondingly in the scale of nature, up to the status of angels or even of God. That lie is repeated at each crucial juncture in her temptation.

The first instance of the lie serves as model for the rest. Satan in the guise of the serpent tells Eve, "I was at first as other Beasts that graze." One day, however, it/he chanced on the wonderful tree, whose fruit hangs so high that conscious effort is required to pluck it. After eating, there came

> Strange alteration in me, to degree
> Of Reason in my inward Powers, and Speech
> Wanted not long, though to this shape retain'd.
> Thenceforth to Speculations high or deep
> I turned my thoughts, and with capacious mind
> Considered all things visible in Heav'n,
> Or Earth, or Middle, all things fair and good.
>
> (IX, 571, 599–605)

This is utterly false. To begin with, the interdiction against the fruit of that tree applies only to Adam and Eve. Moreover, man can be changed not by fruit but by obedience or disobedience, as Raphael had made clear. But above all, Eve hears not the serpent's voice but Satan's, "the Enemie of Mankind, enclos'd / In Serpent, Inmate bad" (IX, 494–95).

Satan supports his central lie with flattery, and the two arts weaken Eve's judgment. Her last reason in her soliloquy justifying her action returns to the lie:

> How dies the Serpent? hee hath eat'n and lives,
> And knows, and speaks, and reasons, and discerns,
> Irrational till then. (IX, 764–66)

Eve acts on what she has just been hearing, forgetting or ignoring what she had earlier heard repeatedly, including the one small exemption from complete freedom, the forbidden act that she then performs.

Satan's friends among the critics do not much discuss his inveterate lying. But the devil speaks truth or cites scripture only in the service of a more radical lie. His first grand speech is uttered "Prone on the Flood" of dark fire (I, 195). Of course it possesses magnificent defiance.

> All is not lost; the unconquerable Will,
> And study of revenge, immortal hate,
> And courage never to submit or yield:
> And what is else not to be overcome?
> (I, 106–109)

The only true phrase is "immortal hate." I am not sure whether Satan deceived himself, whether he seeks to deceive Beelzebub, or whether both deceits are involved. But the narrator makes it perfectly clear that he might have lain forever on the fiery dark flood

> but that the will
> And high permission of all-ruling Heaven
> Left him at large to his own dark designs,

ultimately to bring forth "goodness, grace and mercy" for man (I, 211–13, 218). More than that, the narrator tells us that this speech comes from one "Vaunting aloud, but rackt with deep despare" (I, 126). What Satan does not like is what his sympathizers do not like, the requirement of obedience, that distinctly unmodern, illiberal thing: hearing and doing what is right. Milton does not suggest very earnestly that obedience comes readily to any creature, but he asks us to consider whom we obey and the results of not obeying the words coming from this or that voice. Let us attend a bit longer to Satan's.

The chief action of Book II, "the great consult" (on which unrespectable noun the *Oxford English Dictionary* as usual casts illumination), involves a decision as to what should be done. Moloch, Belial, Mammon, and Beelzebub speak up in turn. We hear in turn recommendations for actions: open war; remaining in Hell, thinking and talking; remaining in Hell, but developing the estate; and seeking revenge on man. Each speaker comes to us either introduced or followed by the narrator's lively condemnation. The whole debate has no point anyway, because the decision had already been made by Satan. A close moment for him comes when Mammon's proposal obviously would earn the votes of any who could exercise them. (Nobody is interested in going through the War in Heaven again.) Beelzebub skillfully enters the debate with "his devilish Counsel," "first devis'd / by *Satan*" (II, 379–80). This skillful pair maneuver the body into approving what was decided on before the meeting: to seduce man to a Fall. (Even Satan is too cowardly to undertake struggle with anyone but creatures weaker than himself.) Having voted for a scheme they did not desire, the fallen angels give their approval to Satan:

Towards him they bend
With awful reverence prone; and as a God
Extol him equal to the highest in Heav'n.
(II, 477–79)

In short, the whole "consult" is false, and the whole question of obedience has been confused as usual. The angels can obey God or obey Satan. They can follow truth or follow lies.[16] Satan lies again to Sin and Death, and yet again to Chaos. And the Father of Lies takes his way to earth, using what freedom he has further to disobey and ruin himself.

Such is the character of Satan before beginning what is commonly described as his process of degeneration in the poem. Milton makes perfectly clear that Satan is a coward, a liar, a dictator, and a cheat. And yet we have a Satan question (see ch. V), and it is enough to say that Milton gives Satan a character of greatness, even in evil, such as exceeds any previous epic hero. In *Paradise Lost* he may be despicable—and the narrator's voice insists on that all along—but to us in our world he is magnificent. The so-called problems in Milton's poems usually testify to his art, and the Satan problem shows in particular how he has created in Satan a real villain offering a real possibility of success: not against God but against man. That is the point. Satan must be a character capable of deceiving Eve and thereby getting Adam to fall. If Satan can genuinely be thought capable of that, then Milton had to assume that Satan also would hold attractions for the descendants of Eve and Adam. Put another way, the reader must be put in the position of regarding Satan as an evil hoax and an evident attraction. He is, therefore, allowed to speak first among the characters of the poem, and second after the narrator. By having Satan's voice enter its claim on us at the beginning, Milton succeeds in mak-

[16] Satan's absence from Hell makes it possible for Belial to hold his philosophical seminar and for Mammon to put his technology to work, neither enterprise being heard of again because they are meaningless. They are mentioned and disdainfully dismissed by Milton so as to observe the to him trivial convention of epic games. Yet the rejection of Moloch's proposal for "open war" shows the lack of courage among *all* the fallen angels but him.

ing Satan real to us and in allowing for all due later correction.

We must follow that idea into somewhat more abstract terms. For literary and philosophical reasons, Milton had a need to make evil seem real and identifiable. For reasons of characterizing Adam and Eve, the fallen angels, and indeed all the characters in the poem, Milton required one character above the rest who could personify evil impressively. Satan becomes a referent, for in him the abstract conception of evil becomes a conspicuous character, a reality in that world every bit as much as are earth or heaven, sunshine, or Eve's hair. It will be evident that the philosophical and religious gains from that were enormous. Satan enables Milton almost wholly to avoid the question of the origin of evil in a world governed by divine providence. Scrupulous as he is, Milton introduces the problem at the first opportunity, in Book III. But as a prudent poet he had already solved, or rather evaded, that insoluble problem by beginning his epic with those unprecedented two books in the underworld and with an impressive villain.

The scene in Heaven in Book III comes as a natural consequence to Books I and II, which have parodied it in advance, as many have observed. In an earlier chapter, I discussed Milton's designs in introducing God into the poem, and I shall now leave this scene as quickly as does Milton himself. The thing needing to be made plain, and to be faced up to, however, is the requirement of obedience. Book III makes clear that obedience is enjoined on angels and men by the one Being wholly entitled to demand it. Further, obedience will bring happiness, is wholly rational, whereas disobedience will bring misery and is irrational. Finally, divine justice is tempered with mercy and love. Mercy and love are present in Milton's God, but until Book XI Milton chooses to depict God more as the Creator and Disposer, the font of justice, and hence reserves the exercise of mercy and love for the Son, who will become our "Redeemer ever blest," as Adam says in his last three words (XII, 573). Such a decision leaves Milton's God just what Milton wishes Him to be: God who must be obeyed. Without doubt, that God has a terrifying aspect that is quite consistent with His absolute distinction from everything else, which must obey Him because all else is contingent on Him. It is ironic to a high degree that those who do not believe in the existence of God believe in Milton's God and disapprove, because they fear such a God. Exactly. "The fear of the Lord is the beginning of knowledge: but fools despise wisdom and instruction" (Proverbs 1:7). The nature of Milton's God has led some recent critics to begin in knowledge, but we owe it to Milton to acknowledge that in *Paradise Lost* the Son provides a precious image of hope, the happiest of escape clauses between our own inclination to disobey and the institutes of divine justice. Because Satan and God have bothered some readers, however, I have made the simple assumption that there are reasons for their being bothered, and that Milton intended them to be. We must also acknowledge, if but in passing, the corresponding hope we derive from the Son, and understand that Milton wished us to have that, too.

There are two presences in *Paradise Lost*, two voices that say relatively little, two actors who act very little, and yet presences who in another sense say and do all. These presences are the two authors of everything in that unique poetic world that contains everything: God and the narrator-poet. As the only omniscient Being, God has no need to hear anything. As omnipotence itself, He can do anything, and has done as it were everything by bringing forth a creation sustained by His omnipotence and ubiquity of providence, in such a way that no intervention is required, unless He decrees special providence through some agent. Calvinist as Milton was to a considerable extent, he recognized that having created man, God could have left matters to run themselves on the system of justice. Man may obey or disobey. Adam and Eve sinned—so they are condemned and to "death devote," and the story is over. But God does intervene with the most special of all His special providences and supplies a Redeemer. Both what He might have done or not done and what in fact He does make Milton's God no less awesome than does the requirement of obedience.

The narrator or poet belongs to a period long after the poem's present and so cannot be considered a character in its action, however intrusive he may seem. And yet the narrator resembles God in knowing that *all* of which the poem consists. The fact that Milton's narrator intrudes his voice so often in the poem testifies to many functions that the voice serves at different stages of the poem. But the most important function of that voice is also the most general. By taking as his role the assertion of "Eternal Providence," Milton through the narrator has a human voice spare the necessity for God's saying such things. Milton offers human testimony on matters divine. Of course the narrator tells us that he is divinely inspired, but apart from being a narrator who, in a sense, says everything about everything, he *does* nothing. Like God, the narrator really does not need to hear anything; and also like God, he need only create and need not act otherwise. In such fashion are all other presences in *Paradise Lost* contingent on the Author of all creation and on the author of the poem treating all creation.

The reader necessarily "hears" those two crucial voices and the others as well, and hearing them he responds. The story of the response in the last fifty years shows that, among other things, Milton's Christianity has troubled readers. Any realistic view of such matters must be that readers are far wiser to be troubled than to be indifferent, for the simple reason that Milton clearly meant his Christianity to matter as crucial support of his epic. Those of us who admire what some respond to unfavorably must regard it as our responsibility to face up to the Christian scheme, to deal with matters like Satan and God the Father, and the central issue of obedience. It will not do for anyone, whatever his attitude, to regard *Paradise Lost* as a treatise on Christian doctrine nor even as an unfictional discourse about philosophical ideas in the fashion of *De Rerum Natura.* Like Dante's great poem, Milton's is a supreme fiction about the whole universe conceived in religious terms. *Paradise Lost* has not yet benefited from the passage of time which enables us to look on Greek tragedy or Buddhist literature with equanimity, and on Dante's much more rigid scheme without agony. To my taste, it is a wonderful thing that Milton's Christian views do live, that they must be faced up to, quarreled over, and, above all, felt. I think it an uncommon tribute to a poet that what he felt mattered most should not fail to matter with great intensity to readers three centuries later.

No small degree of that mattering derives from the lively presences and persuasive voices in the poem. Because of its exaggerated *Aeneid*-form, *Paradise Lost* necessarily depends on relation by individual voices to an extent beyond any other epic. More than that, the voices are so many—not so many as in Dante's poem, but far more loquacious even than Dante's Virgil. And yet, in respect to this most complex art of observing characters hear what was said and what was done, we can say again that the clarity of narration and the ease with which we sort out what we hear are astonishing. In Book V, Abdiel challenges Satan:

Shalt thou give Law to God, shalt thou dispute
With him the points of libertie, who made

Thee what thou art, and formd the Pow'rs of Heav'n
Such as he pleasd, and circumscrib'd thir being?
(822–25)

There is the obedience imperative again. Milton will not let us go. We observe that the question involves a mini-narrative such as we find in many of the speeches and similes of the poem. However brief, it is clear in general import and in the immediate context of Abdiel's argument with Satan. This miniscular narrative about the creation of angels appears in a speech of confrontation before battle; that speech is itself part of a narrative by Raphael; and Raphael's narration is aided by the narrator's own. Plain enough to anyone, it might be said. And that is just my point. What might have gone messy or grown obscure does not. The drama of conflict between Abdiel and Satan retains its force. Raphael remains in character in telling the story to Adam. And the narrator-poet sees to it that the point of the opening of the poem is sustained even in this narrative relation of a narrative relation of a speech.

As the example of Abdiel shows, any voice speaking in *Paradise Lost* takes on a narrative role to some degree, small or large. To such degrees, Milton transfers to his characters part of his own role as poet-narrator. (Of course he often bursts on the scene from which he has just so ostentatiously parted.) Because only two voices in the poem speak with what we can term omniscience (although the Son, Raphael, and Michael participate in divine wisdom also), any giving-over of voice to a character other than God or the narrator implies possibility for error. That possibility occupies four books (I and II, IX and X) as a conspicuous reality, and it is something against which the reader knows he must be on guard. And yet, the reader's experience shows that he believes that it has all been wholly clear to him. Without such clarity, we would suffer confusion to an extreme degree. With such clarity, the participation by so many presences and voices in the conduct of narrative in *Paradise Lost* creates a presumption of first importance to Milton: that knowing in faith and doing by choice may be one.

As examples of surrogate narrators and their functions, it seems wise to take two whose importance to the poem requires no argument. Over half the poem consists of narrations by Raphael and Michael. So familiar is the fact that we fail to observe that Milton has succeeded in solving a problem by putting it on display. A Christian epic had a central problem in what were termed the "machines," the deities or supernatural creatures required by tradition but difficult to put into contact with human creatures and the human world with any credibility. The only objections to Raphael and Michael with which I am acquainted turn entirely on points concerning what they say, rather than on their presence itself, which is amazing, considering all the pains, worry, and failure by poets and critics on the head of machines from the Renaissance through the eighteenth century. Technically, in these angels Milton combines machines, narrators, and the motif of the heavenly messenger.[17]

As surrogates of the poet-narrator, Raphael and Michael provide that greater presence in a poem that a speaking character provides as opposed to a narrator. They furnish a quality of drama—or more accurately, of active presence—to the narration itself. Their voices command past and future, and what they say represents, inwardly, their authoritative knowledge and, outwardly, their obedience, the truth of knowledge in faith. All this contributes to the seemingly

[17] On the theory of "machines," see H. T. Swedenberg, Jr., *The Theory of the Epic in England, 1650–1800* (Berkeley and Los Angeles, 1944); and on the heavenly visitor to earth, see Thomas M. Greene, *The Descent from Heaven* (New Haven, 1963).

effortless sublimity of the poem. Yet such roles as narrator surrogates ignore the central roles of Raphael and Michael. They are angels. An *angelus* or ἄγγελος is a messenger from God (so also in Hebrew). Because the messages taken from God by Raphael and Michael are far from brief, we must also observe that these archangels play roles as surrogate narrators for the divine Poet. Only by narrating to such a radical degree of length and importance can they serve as surrogates of God's voice as well as of a human voice, and so mediate between Heaven and earth, bringing each into verisimilar touch with each other. God's charge to "Raphael, the sociable Spirit" runs in part:

> Go therefore, half this day as friend with friend
> Converse with *Adam*, in what Bowre or shade
> Thou find'st him from the heat of Noon retir'd . . .
> and such discourse bring on
> As may advise him of his happie state.
> (V, 221 . . . 234)

In the very act of charging His messenger, God speaks in earthly terms of Adam's place ("Bowre or shade") and time of day. The divine charge seems so natural, and yet it gets us to accept something that becomes explicit only later in the well known passage by Raphael on accommodation:

> what surmounts the reach
> Of human sense, I shall delineate so,
> By lik'ning spiritual to corporal forms,
> As may express them best, though what if Earth
> Be but the shaddow of Heav'n, and things therein
> Each to other like, more then on earth is thought?

This often commented-upon passage (V, 571–76)[18] follows the other, which seems to have gone unnoticed, by some 350

[18] See in particular, William G. Madsen, *From Shadowy Types to Truth* (New Haven, 1968).

lines. It suggests two seemingly incompatible things: either that spiritual and corporal forms are distinct but comparable, or that the spiritual ("Heav'n") and corporal ("Earth") differ rather in gradation than in nature. The whole of God's speech charging Raphael (V, 224–45) implicitly suggests the second possibility raised by Raphael. More important, Raphael and the narrative technique of the poem support it. God speaks to His angels and they to man. But as we have seen, God speaks of place and time as if they were as familiar in heaven as on earth, warm middays and all. Later, Adam narrates his encounter with God just after his creation (VIII, 295 ff.), one of the most daring stories in this or any poem.

Milton's use of angelic narrators brings far closer than otherwise possible those spiritual and corporal forms of the total universe. At the other extreme, Milton personifies Chaos and Death, even troubling himself with descriptions of them that take the creation, like their corporeality, to the vanishing point. Such wholeness, such integrity, testifies to a conception of the world in which only one dualism is ontologically real: Creator and creature. Other differences exist and must be recognized: angel and man, spirit and matter, heaven and earth, man and woman, humankind and beasts, etc. But these merely fit into a hierarchy of creation in which it is possible to rise at least from earth and humanity to heaven and eternity. And twice in the poem Milton resolves much even of the distinction between God and man. In Book III and in Book XI, he resolves any ontological conflicts by the simplest of Christian expedients: enter the Son of God, the Messiah. In Book III the Son offers to lay aside his great dignities to become man. In Book XI, after Adam and Eve's prayers of contrition, he speaks to God in his role as priest, interceding between sinful man and offended deity.

See Father, what first fruits on Earth are sprung
From thy implanted Grace in Man . . .
let mee
Interpret for him, mee his Advocate
And propitiation, all his works on mee
Good or not good ingraff, my Merit those
Shall perfet, and for these my Death shall pay.
(XI, 22 . . . 36)

Grace and penitence, prayer and the priesthood of the Savior, these help create that active inwardness that so marks *Paradise Lost.* In the central Christian story Milton found means for a narrative transpiring from heaven to earth and from earth to heaven: the whole thing, a public epic of inward man.

We accept the individual narrative surrogates and other voices for their integrity of personality. Satan must never be trusted, Michael is stern, the Son holds to the very center of truth, and so on. Only the human characters undergo real change, for only beneath the lunar sphere comes that mutability associated with the Fall. The change in Adam and Eve is a familiar one and the point of the poem with such a title. There is another human being who also alters frequently in the poem, and his changes have not been much remarked: the narrator himself is full of moods. Of Satan nearing the world, he says:

Thither full fraught with mischievous revenge,
Accurst, and in a cursed hour he hies.
(II, 1054–55)

Excited and angry the narrator may be, but we have already heard him in a yet more emotional state:

O shame to men! Devil with Devil damn'd
Firm concord holds, men onely disagree

Of Creatures rational, though under hope
Of heavenly Grace. (II, 496–99)

In the hymn to light at the beginning of the next book, the narrator appears before us in a different temper still. In all this we discover that man is the variable creature, and such variability unites not only the narrator with Adam and Eve, but them with the reader. The passage just quoted makes no sense unless we assume that Milton the narrator is addressing us in our fallen state, out of concord, lacking even the joined hands of Adam and Eve at the end of the poem. The result of such narrative conduct is to put us at one with the narrator and to lead us to participate with him in the humanity of Adam and Eve. No wonder Satan impresses us. The devils impress the narrator, and Satan seduces Eve. Or to take the end of the poem, by then the narrator need only narrate, because in the purest of narratives in the whole poem no word is spoken except by the narrator telling what we could almost tell ourselves of what is almost happening to him and ourselves. With great tact, Milton denies his narrator any intrusion of his own concerns after the Fall.

Milton's narrative procedure involves his putting himself before us as a distinct and flexible personality. The flexibility permits him to admit various surrogates in the narration, and at the same time to insure that any voice heard sounds in our ears in the right tone, as adjusted by a narrator who is inspired by the Holy Spirit and yet participatory in our variable humanity. As narrator, Milton both participates in our responses and humanity and yet also participates in the divine wisdom so as to guide our responses. Poetry could scarcely be more public. He is also a presenter of other voices and presences in such fashion that he underscores the Satanness or the Raphaelness or the Sonness of those other characters, voices, and presences. As a result of the successful conduct of so many personalities, Milton is able to make narration of speech and, as a corollary, action of speech. Such an achievement can be possible only in a poem in which narrative works toward discovery of inner faith, in which Milton's Protestantism refers action to faith and its ethical counterpart, obedience.

In Books IX and X Adam and Eve strike us as being alone as they never have been before. They are alone in the sense that everything is up to them and in the sense that all the great action of the exaggerated *Aeneid*-form has coiled into a spring releasing at this moment. But by making his epic one of voices that are actions, and by making it into an inward story of faith and obedience, Milton manages to make all the other voices and presences bear on the episode of the Fall. God's commandment, Satan's presence—and yet more the presence of the narrator in whose humanity we share—make it the moment that Milton designed it to be. Satan being what he is, and Adam and Eve being what they are, our participation makes it certain that this *agon* is ours as well. We would have sinned with Adam, too, and in fact we do in reading. Our faith would not have been sufficient; we should have disobeyed. In the story of the Fall, we also fall, as the doctrine of Original Sin implies. And yet the Fall involves the double peripeteia of fall and rise, and we share as well in Eve's beautiful contrition and taking of blame on herself.

If any character in the poem is underrated, it is Eve. We had, as it were, fallen before she does, but she in her sweet repentance leads Adam, the narrator, and us out of the utter ruin to which we have been reduced. Her faith saves us long before Adam responds positively to Michael's stern lecture. Adam's discovery of the fortunate character of the Fall is as nothing next to Eve's making the last major adjustment. With her repentance we—narrator and readers alike—arrive at the immensely assuring assumption that we participate in repentance and divine grace. Her voice is the voice of love, and that makes possible faith and hope such as had not been possible since our Fall. Eve's voice is the voice of the one action—that of love—that unites her and Adam, along with the narrator and reader, in the profoundest sorrow and the profoundest hope. Such attitudes mingle in the incomparable ending of *Paradise Lost,* and quite apart from Milton's Christian insistence, they mingle in any epic conception of human life. Whether we consider Eve as the first to sin and the first to repent, as our general mother or as the type of Mary and hence the fertile source of our deliverance, all that is tragic and all that is hopeful in our lives can be referred to her. In a real sense, all readers of *Paradise Lost* are male, and equally all readers require Eve, whether in sinning or in regeneration.

iv. To Create Afresh the Inward Man

Paradise Regained and *Samson Agonistes* give us simpler versions of the same process of inward heroism. *Samson Agonistes* rather than *Paradise Regained* follows *Paradise Lost* in the biblical-historical sense of Samson's coming between the Fall and the appearance of the Redeemer. Like Adam and Eve, Samson has sinned, and in the early portion of the drama he sinks further in the moral ruin of despair, as his conversations with the chorus and his father attest. In the encounter with Dalila, he begins his rise and so marches on to the ruin of another kind that is also a triumph. Whatever we think of the ending, Samson has borne witness to God at the Temple of Dagon. This contoured action obviously resembles *Paradise Lost* more than *Paradise Regained,* because in the latter poem the hero is not a mere mortal, and the structure is yet more episodic along a level until the very late climax. In all three works, however, the empiry of the self, an obedient faith in Providence, is essential.

It is just this relation between man and God, with seeming disregard for others, that has led a fairly prominent minority to consider the ending of *Samson Agonistes* to be "indeed morally disgusting."[19] I agree heartily that a Cromwell's assumption that his virtue and privy acquaintance with God's designs, and his conclusion that others should obey him, were detestable. I also think Milton arrogant in his prose. But we are considering God and poetry, larger matters indeed. Critics hostile to that ending cannot accept what they regard as Samson's vengefulness and his large slaughter of the Philistines. The biblical account of Samson certainly strikes me as an unedifying account of a folk hero. And it is safe to say that not since "Upon the Circumcision" had Milton begun with so inherently recalcitrant a subject. Yet *Samson Agonistes* is as successful as the earlier poem is boring. Critics of the morality of the play's ending must be granted to be right in their major premise: killing is wrong. But in practice such critics, who might perhaps discover "redeeming social significance" in lesser works, fail to see that the drama does not concern killing or vengeance at all. Nor does it, on the other hand, make Samson into a Christ figure, an innocent sacrifice for others: precisely because Samson is not innocent. Such typology might have been involved but is not. To take another possibility, Samson's role might be (but is not) about love: "Greater love hath no man than this, that a man lay down his life for his friends" (John 15:13).

If I understand the temper of seventeenth-century England, any moral question raised by the play's ending would

[19] John Carey, with Alastair Fowler, ed., *The Poems of John Milton* (London, 1968), p. 335. By the end of his introduction, Carey does discover that the imagery makes "a major contribution to the moral maturity of the work" (p. 343).

have centered on a different issue: suicide. In "The Argument" Milton obviously worries far more over this issue than the "genocide" of one hysterical critic. When (according to Milton's argument) "an Ebrew" messenger enters, he relates "the Catastrophe, what *Samson* had done to the *Philistins*, and by accident to himself." In the drama we learn that Samson pulls down the roof of the temple upon the Philistines, and that

> *Samson* with these inmixt, inevitably
> Pulld down the same destruction on himself.
> (1657–58)

Such "by accident" or "inevitably" betrays a nervousness in Milton not to be found over the deaths of so many Philistines. Of course Milton's tenderness on one matter does not preclude callousness on another. But I venture to think that as we are actually reading *Samson Agonistes* we are affected far less by this action's happening offstage (or rather being merely read about) than we are by seeing Hamlet thrust his sword through Polonius behind the arras and then, finding he had not slain Claudius, treat the matter as Polonius' fault. Not that I think we condemn Hamlet completely, but that what we behold directly (or discover while reading) affects us far more. If we are going to insist on the letter of morality, without attention to an author's emphasis, more idols than Dagon will fall.

In short, the criticism is very wrong but very illuminating. It shows that to some degree, as with the indifferent forbidden fruit, Milton simply does not regard the external circumstances to be that important. As the Lady says in *Comus*, only "such as are good men can give good things" (703). Of course Milton pays attention to the great differences between Samson's father and Samson's wife in terms of their effect on the hero, and the Samson story did happen to have quite a catastrophe as its basis. But the crucial matter is faith, the subject of Hebrews 11, which begins:

> Now faith is the substance of things hoped for, the evidence of things not seen. For by it the elders obtained a good report. Through faith we understand that the worlds were framed by the word of God, so that things which are seen were not made of things which do appear. (1–3)

Nothing could be more central to Protestantism of almost every kind than those three verses (see, for example, Anglican Articles XI and XII); and to a mind that found some aspects of Neoplatonism congenial and whose hero was blind, those verses provide a kind of inevitable gloss on what the drama was about. Verses 4–32 enumerate the "elders" or Old Testament figures who "obtained a good report." Paul includes Samson in a composite group toward the end:

> And what shall I more say? for the time would fail me to tell of Gedeon, and of Barak, and of Samson, and of Jephthae; of David also, and Samuel, and of the prophets: Who through faith subdued kingdoms, wrought righteousness, obtained promises, stopped the mouths of lions. (32–33)

Samson Agonistes concerns a crisis of faith in Samson rather than death records in the annals of the Philistines. And since the hero weathers the crisis triumphantly, there can be no irony or disagreement over what the last choral ode says: "All is best, though we oft doubt," etc. In fact we agree with the Chorus over the inscrutability "Of highest wisdom," and understand that a providential God has been working His mysterious purpose of grace and has worked in a man of faith:

> His servants he with new acquist
> Of true experience from this great event

With peace and consolation hath dismist,
And calm of mind all passion spent.

(1755–58)

If either vengeance or suicide had been the concern of the drama, its ending would be bitterly ironic, as no one will ever convince the world that it is. The poem chiefly concerns the alteration in Samson from an impotent, self-betrayed Nazarite who has violated the pledge of his dedication to God. So lowly a person, sinful, blind, despairing, purges his strong passions by received grace and by steady faith to become God's agent. The strongest temptations Samson faces are those resulting from his present captivity and blindness. The initial encounter with the Chorus and the one ensuing with his father almost overcome Samson with that sin which destroys faith, despair. Later, "His Giantship," Harapha, tempts Samson to yield to the passion of fear. Samson does not fear, however, and the difference between his response to his father and to Harapha is extraordinary. Earlier almost crushed by despair, he now shows no fear at all. Let us follow his responses to Harapha a bit:

I know no Spells, use no forbidden Arts;
My trust is in the living God who gave me
At my Nativity this strength . . .
while I preserv'd those locks unshorn,
The pledge of my unviolated vow. (1139 . . . 1144)

All these indignities, for such they are
From thine, these evils I deserve and more,
Acknowledge them from God inflicted on me
Justly, yet despair not of his final pardon
Whose ear is ever open; and his eye
Gracious to re-admit the suppliant. (1168–73)

My Nation was subjected to your Lords.
It was the force of Conquest; force with force
Is well ejected when the Conquer'd can.
But I a private person, when my Countrey
As a league-breaker gave up bond, presum'd
Single Rebellion and did Hostile Acts.
I was no private but a person rais'd
With strength sufficient and command from Heav'n
To free my Countrey.

(1205–1211)

Two questions call for answer. How has the remarkable alteration come about? And what kind of change has taken place?

Theologically speaking, Samson effects the change only after it has been made possible by God. Dramatically speaking (and there is no contradiction, as these passages show), the question involves the operation of Samson's inner self in the succession of temptations. Now alteration between the despair of Samson's response to Manoa and the triumph he achieves over Harapha can be explained only by what happens between those episodes, the appearance and rejection of Dalila. She brings the temptation of the body, the kind before which Samson has always been weak. Samson clearly feels great apprehension over his weakness for her and keeps her far off. To gain control over her means nothing *essential* in Milton's scheme; to gain control of oneself means everything. To rule himself, Samson must rouse himself to an inward strength more important than his physical strength and indeed the premise of that outer strength. In the Dalila episode we find the "middle" that Dr. Johnson declared the poem to lack. We can say for Johnson that, looking at the play in terms of external actions, no episode has any more importance than another, and the poem is all middle or no middle, whatever we wish to say. But as always Milton concerns himself with the interior state of mind that constitutes action in *Samson Agonistes* as much as in *Paradise Lost* and *Paradise Regained.* Of course he always gives us external action as well. But the large circumference of Milton's world centers on grace and faith.

Samson's change can best be explained by reference to what Milton called, in *The Christian Doctrine,* "Renovation" (I, xvii) and "Regeneration" (xviii). Samson lived of course under the Law rather than under the Christian dispensation, but Milton's concept of "special calling" involves a renovative concept applicable to Samson: "God's special calling is that whereby he, at the time which he thinks proper, invites particular individuals." [20] Regeneration (which according to Milton comes only from God the Father) obviously bears on Samson's case, as Milton's description of its "intent" shows:

> The intent of SUPERNATURAL RENOVATION is not only to restore man more completely than before to the use of his natural faculties, as regards his power to form right judgment, and to exercise free will; but to create afresh, as it were, the inward man, and infuse from above new and supernatural faculties in the minds of the renovated.[21]

Remove the Christian emphasis, and this describes perfectly what happens to Samson. Milton later describes a special version of regeneration, with all but one of his proof texts taken from the Old Testament. "Sanctification" bears particularly on Samson: "Sanctification is sometimes used in a more extended sense, for any kind of election or separation [as a Nazarite, Samson is technically "separated"], either of a

[20] *Christian Doctrine,* in the Columbia *Works of John Milton,* vol. xv (New York, 1933), 349. See through p. 355.

[21] Ibid., p. 367.

whole nation to some particular form of worship, or of an individual to some office."[22] Samson's remarks to Harapha quoted at length above clearly show that Samson is "called" and "sanctified." Milton's use of largely Christian concepts in the characterization of one of the Judges of Israel may seem anachronistic. But his concepts themselves were flexible enough, and Old Testament figures were in fact invoked constantly by Milton and other Christians, not necessarily typologically but for the examples they gave for right conduct of life, and because the Scriptures of the Hebrews were taken to be Christian as well.

The challenge to the morality of *Samson Agonistes* proves useful, because it raises the question of just what the work is about. When moral and aesthetic issues directly conflict, we usually prefer the moral. But in *Samson Agonistes* the conflict is devised by the critics rather than the poet, just as is the dispute whether Hamlet dies damned. If the question is asked, we must say that a man guilty of several murders who dies unshriven must be damned. But the question is conspicuously not asked at the end of *Hamlet,* and to ask it is critically mischievous. So with *Samson Agonistes* and "genocide." We see from *Comus* forward that the action central to Milton's work, the action he considered more heroic than the actions of earlier epics, is inward. Theologically speaking, Milton was orthodox in regarding that "action" as first and essentially one by God, for man only participates in grace by virtue of God's offering it to him (whatever the Calvinist or Arminian disputes about its general availability). But man participates by faith, which makes right reason and free will possible and infuses "new and supernatural faculties" in the mind or soul. So renovated, Samson is called by God to smite the Philistines, and His providence for Israel in that is as much "th' unsearchable dispose / Of highest wisdom" as

[22] Ibid., p. 375.

was His delivering of Israel to the Philistines in the first place. If there is a problem of morality in *Samson Agonistes*, that is because the problem of morality exists in the world. Milton did not lack for a philosophical basis of morality, God, but by definition man cannot explain God's aims, and Milton succeeded as well as has any writer in accounting for evil in a providential world. Milton knew the book of Job well, and the last affirmation by the Chorus begins in a way reminding us of the affirmation that we are brought to by the story of the man of Uz: "All is best, though oft we doubt . . . . " We feel with the Chorus that we can do no more than attend on "th' unsearchable dispose." In observing that inward action of the renovated hero, however, we also arrive at "peace and consolation . . . calm of mind all passion spent."

The hero of *Paradise Regained* has already acquired "supernatural faculties" to a degree impossible for any other creature, and there cannot occur any such change as takes place in Samson. At the end Milton of course achieves a splendid climax, but by theophany rather than catastrophe and tragic reconciliation (with the exception of *our* falling for Satan over the temptation of pagan wisdom). The triumph by Jesus over Satan also means that its story differs fundamentally from that of Adam and Eve. Instead of telling of one failure, Milton has repeated victories to relate. Once again, we must recognize that the inward state is all, and although we find the separate temptations carefully distinguished to the point of our rejecting most but falling for one, they are all one relative to the steadfast faith of Jesus. As a result, *Paradise Regained* takes on a ritualistic, repetitive movement unlike those of Milton's other two greatest works. Not only that, the narrator's role also becomes ritualistic, for what other than praise can one give to such a hero?

The novel hero and his actions make *Paradise Regained* differ from *Paradise Lost* in other ways of act and voice in narration. But what concerns us most toward the end of this discussion of Milton can only be the kinds of values and experiences his brief epic gives us. Everyone can sense that in it Milton appeals to fresh matters: awe, reservation, and wonder celebrated by ritual. No one has ever preferred the poem to *Paradise Lost*, partly because that poem includes (if not so strongly) the elements distinguishing the shorter epic and much else besides. And yet I think it very true that in *Paradise Regained* Milton made fewer mistakes than in *Paradise Lost*. Perhaps he made none of any matter. And increased experience with its sparer style and austere economy of means brings ever growing esteem. With everything that it contains and does to recommend it, *Paradise Regained* nonetheless leads us to judge the poem by its terms, or scope, in comparison to the longer epic. *Paradise Lost* admits much more, it risks much more, and it involves much more. By such things as admission and risk I do not refer merely to characters, plot, time, and place. More of Milton, and more of us, is admitted and hazarded in the experience. We are more deeply involved. Yet, what Jesus says in *Paradise Regained* unquestionably holds for *Paradise Lost* and, for that matter, *Samson Agonistes* as well:

> he who reigns within himself, and rules
> Passions, Desires, and Fears is more a King;
> Which every wise and vertuous man attains.
>
> (II, 466–68)

We see again how wonderfully simple the mature Milton always seems, for all his grandeur and his very different literary emphases in his three principal poems. Providence and faith occupy all corners of his work, and the center as well. The public mode has been made completely inward, and man's soul becomes the issue in the most public of forms, the heroic poem. Providence of course is an attribute of God, and faith the necessary requirement of man. And in faith kindled in man, Milton celebrated our "Honour, Vertue, Merit and chief Praise."

v. Dryden's Esteem of Merit, Man, and Love

In considering Butler's values, we have only one major poem for concern, and in considering Milton's we have three of length and complexity. In assessing Dryden from the same viewpoint, we have so many poems to be included, at least in any generalization, that the task proves far more difficult. Dryden creates countless voices urging, describing, justifying, reprobating, and praising actions. Given so many voices and actions, some kind of orderly approach must be taken, even at the cost of missing the great variety and of falsifying chronology. Like every major poet, Dryden is concerned with man, and like most poets he creates numerous voices for himself and his characters. We can begin with consideration of those poems in which something like his own voice is heard, that is, in panegyric, satire, complimentary address, and narrative. Given what I have termed his great idea, his poems normally treat human merit and the meaning of love.[23]

Although never really private and intimate in his poetry, Dryden is constantly personal, whether the personality be his own or that of some other character more or less fully historical (or fictional). It will assist us to begin with him at his most personal and with him explicitly concerned with merit and love. At the conclusion of his poem *To My Dear Friend Mr. Congreve*, he speaks of himself:

> Already I am worn with Cares and Age;
> And just abandoning th' Ungrateful Stage:

[23] "Merits" may of course also have a theological meaning, as in *Religio Laici*, 195; and "love" may be a delusive passion as well as a cardinal virtue.

Unprofitably kept at Heav'ns expence,
I live a Rent-charge on his Providence:
But You, whom ev'ry Muse and Grace adorn,
Whom I foresee to better Fortune born,
Be kind to my Remains; and oh defend,
Against Your Judgment, Your departed Friend!
Let not the Insulting Foe my Fame pursue;
But shade those Lawrels which descend to You:
And take for Tribute what these Lines express:
You merit more; nor cou'd my Love do less.
(66–77)

So personal is the revelation that even without having the date on the title page of Congreve's *Double-Dealer*, we could date the poem with some accuracy. The situation in a way reverses that in "To the Memory of Mr. Oldham." There the senior poet recalls the merits of the dead junior poet whom, out of the love that had grown between them, "I began to think and call my own" (2).

Before Dryden, Cowley had celebrated Crashaw in a poem Dryden echoes at the close of *Mac Flecknoe*, and from this stanza xvii of Cowley's fine poem, *On the Death of Mr. William Harvey*, Dryden recalled tributes that he modified and conferred on Oldham and Anne Killigrew:

Wondrous young Man, why wert thou made so good,
To be snatcht hence ere better *understood*?
Snatcht before half of Thee enough was seen!
  Thou Ripe, and yet thy *Life* but *Green!*
Nor could thy Friends take their last sad Farwel,
  But Danger and *Infectious Death*
  Malitiously seiz'd on that Breath
Where *Life, Spirit, Pleasure* always us'd to dwell.

Cowley simply has not caught the air of deep affection that Dryden conveys. *Mac Flecknoe* almost eerily resembles the poem to Congreve in the expression of affection by a senior to a junior writer, as it does in subject and metaphor. Paternal love for a meritorious son by adoption after the Roman fashion seems to lie behind these poems. Of course the son of Flecknoe does not reciprocate affection, and the merits of both are made to count as demerits. But the fact that Dryden could base *Mac Flecknoe* on the love he felt for his own sons and for such literary sons as Oldham and Congreve shows that his satire does possess that positive, humane quality that most readers have felt, and that I find absent altogether from the first half of *The Medall*. Of course the late climax of *Mac Flecknoe* (a kind of parody in advance of the theophany of *Paradise Regained*) shows the son so far from loving the father that he summarily gets rid of him.

When in 1717 Congreve at last fulfilled Dryden's charge to be kind to his remains by issuing *The Dramatick Works*, he prefixed something of a brief preface by way of a dedication, echoing Dryden's association of merit and love. Congreve has been concerned in "the Remains and elegant Labours of one of the greatest Men that our Nation has produced."[24] When he praises Newcastle for erecting a monument to Dryden, whom he had never met, Congreve distinguishes himself as a person with greater obligations:

> . . . as I had the Happiness to be very Conversant, and as intimately acquainted, with Mr. *Dryden*, as the great Disproportion in our Years could allow me to be; I hope it will not be thought too assuming in me, if in Love to his Memory, and in Gratitude for many friendly Offices, and favourable Instructions, which in my early Youth I received from him,

he were to take the role of praising Newcastle's act.[25] In all this Congreve is no doubt as eager to play the polite gentle-

[24] Congreve, dedication, sig. a1^{v}.
[25] Ibid., sigs. a3^{v}–a4^{r}.

man as he is to speak sober truth. But he cuts across all suspicion when he anticipates that the censorious may tax him "of Affectation and Officiousness": "I have but one thing to say either to obviate, or to answer such an Objection, if it shall be made to me, which is, that I loved Mr. *Dryden*." [26]

A few poems by Dryden and the reaction from Congreve establish a useful point. When Dryden writes about human merit or about love, he writes about values wholly real, alive to him and to his contemporaries, and therefore to us. As *Mac Flecknoe* shows, he could parody the very things most dear to him in order to test them as well as the pretenders to them. Another version of his enduring concern will be found in one of the poems included in *Fables: Sigismunda and Guiscardo* deals principally with the tyrant Tancred and his only daughter Sigismunda. He loved her so much that he long delayed her marriage, not wishing to lose her to a husband. "At length," however, she was married. By a sudden turn, her husband soon dies, and she returns to her idolizing father. All is love, but the merits of the case put both father and daughter into some doubt. Dryden presents Sigismunda as a flawed paragon. "The Princess"

> Did all her Sex in ev'ry Grace exceed,
> And had more Wit beside than Women need.
>   Youth, Health, and Ease, and most an amorous Mind,
> To second Nuptials had her Thoughts inclin'd.
>
> (32–35)

Consequently she approaches Guiscardo, so far beneath her in rank. They hastily summon and hastily dismiss the priest. After a time the secret love is personally discovered by Tancred, who thinks her guilty of whoredom. But what really bothers Tancred (when he learns that she is married) is that she should have chosen "A Man so smelling of the Peoples

[26] Ibid., sigs. a5^v–a6^r.

Lee" (317). If that is what troubles him, what motivates him is something akin to incestuous attachment, and he feels himself besmirched by her behavior, "an Offence of this degenerate Kind" (353).

The mixture of unbending pride and concealed attachment makes Tancred a fine psychological study anticipating Browning and the contemporary novel. Sigismunda proves a worthy daughter, wholly opposed to her father and willing to die with her husband:

> My Words to sacred Truth shall be confin'd,
> My Deeds shall shew the Greatness of my Mind.
> That I have lov'd, I own; that still I love,
> I call to Witness all the Pow'rs above:
> Yet more I own: To *Guiscard's* Love I give
> The small remaining Time I have to live;
> And if beyond this Life Desire can be,
> Not Fate it self shall set my Passion free.
> This first avow'd; nor Folly warp'd my Mind,
> Nor the frail Texture of the Female Kind
> Betray'd my Vertue: For, too well I knew
> What Honour was, and Honour had his Due:
> Before the Holy Priest my Vows were ty'd,
> So came I not a Strumpet, but a Bride;
> This for my Fame: and for the Publick Voice:
> Yet more, his Merits justifi'd my Choice.
>
> (394–409)

She returns Tancred's scorn over Guiscardo's low birth by accusing her father's judgment (he had said as much of her) of "herding with the common Crowd":

> Thou tak'st unjust Offence; and, led by them
> Dost less the Merit, than the Man esteem.
> Too sharply, *Tancred*, by thy Pride betray'd,

Hast thou against the Laws of Kind inveigh'd;
For all th' Offence is in Opinion plac'd,
Which deems high Birth by lowly Choice debas'd.
(480–85)

Her entire speech, almost two hundred lines long, argues in a way reminiscent of the Wife of Bath's Tale for true merit rather than false. In doing so, she also justifies her own action, which is as much her aim as the talk of letting down the family blood is Tancred's way of expressing his attachment. The lurid ending of the story continues the strong coloring of the feverish passions of the father and daughter. Both make much of merit and love, and in making much they deceive themselves more wholly than others. The reader keeps his judgment intact, distinguishing what is said from what is meant, as also what is meant from what is truly meritorious. Whatever his poetic form, Dryden recurs to those things that we prize in people and to the emotional attachments that we develop to strengthen, to transcend, or even to deny the standard of human merit. The *Fables* differs only by articulating its many voices into action and a freer narrative than Dryden had practiced before.

In distinguishing between poems in which Dryden's own voice can be heard, as narrator or speaker, and those in which another character's voice is heard, I return to an old-fashioned distinction. Of course one must recognize that the Dryden who speaks in a satire and the Dryden who speaks in a religious confession are in some sense two different Drydens. But I venture to suggest that any of *us* now castigating a contemporary and then praising another contemporary would appear two different people to the same degree, at least if we had the artistic power to re-create ourselves for others. Dryden's power to create reality has been discussed earlier (ch. VI, and we must recognize that the major reality is not only

Sigismunda but also John Dryden himself in such poems as those to Oldham or Congreve.

In his songs for plays and even in the few not for plays, the voice is convincingly not Dryden's, but someone else's. The songs form a distinct group, related to the plays themselves in having as it were separate, free, unhistorical characters speak. They speak largely of physical passion in anticipation, achievement, and regretful memory. The dramatic character of such songs provides their strength, which is minor, and their weaknesses, which are major. Each claims respect for its realization of its kind and end, but after the songs for plays by Shakespeare, Jonson, and a few other earlier dramatists, and after the love poems of Donne and Marvell, we are entitled to find the kind and end relatively deficient. A typical example of a song for a woman expresses her state of mind at having been betrayed. She has yielded to male entreaty, and she gets the rejection that comes in Restoration comedies for women who do not wait out marriage. The best things to be said about the well known "Song" from *The Spanish Fryar* ("Farwell ungratefull Traytor") include its clarity of situation and expression, along with the mixture of the woman's sense of having been wronged qualified by her lingering passion. Whatever the merits of such a song when set to music, the human music of Herrick's "Corinna's going a Maying" has been lost. (On the other hand, in the plays themselves, Dryden finds great scope for really human development.) What is usually, properly, and yet limitedly meant by love—boy and girl or woman and man in lyricism—invoked Dryden's personality more often than Butler's or Milton's, but not in lyrics. Milton and Dryden simply required much larger structures, and in dramatic as well as narrative poetry the love they much more convincingly develop is of a kind they fully understood, the love between adults who live within the world rather than young people who inhabit private realms. By the high standards that we are entitled by his poetry to exercise, Dryden's love songs have as their chief value the evidence they provide of his depth of feeling in other genres more suitable for the public mode. They are otherwise relatively negligible.

The "dramatic" element in Dryden's nondramatic poetry holds as much importance as the narrative in revealing Dryden at his best. A poem like *The Hind and the Panther* consists mainly of speeches between rivals, recalling for us such diverse works as *Hudibras, An Essay of Dramatick Poesy*, and *Paradise Regained*. In some of his late songs, especially those for operas and similar productions, Dryden achieves a new richness, that is a reality, that proves more satisfying. In *King Arthur*, the opera written with Purcell, for example, the songs constitute a narrative of "British" triumph over the "Saxons." Yet the individual songs enact dramatic scenes. The hit of the opera, the "Pudding and Dumplin" song, involves Comus and three peasants (designated "1 Man," etc. in speech tags), and it creates a real sense of rural England. The peasants feel resentment over the ecclesiastical tithe, but they manage to have a roar over an English harvest festival. Opera and reality of a familiar Drydenian kind prove to be congenial:

Enter Comus *with three Peasants, who sing the following*
Song in Parts.

Com. Your Hay it is Mow'd, and your Corn is
Reap'd;
Your Barns will be full, and your Hovels
heap'd:
Come, my Boys, come;
Come, my Boys, come;
And merrily Roar out Harvest Home;
Harvest Home,
Harvest Home;

And merrily Roar out Harvest Home.
Chorus. Come, my Boys, come, *&c.*
1 *Man.* We ha' cheated the Parson, we'll cheat him agen;
For why shou'd a Blockhead ha' One in Ten?
One in Ten,
One in Ten,
For why shou'd a Blockhead ha' One in Ten?
Chorus. One in Ten,
One in Ten;
For why shou'd a Blockhead ha' One in Ten?
2 [*Man*]. For Prating so long like a Book-learn'd Sot,
Till Pudding and Dumplin burn to Pot;
Burn to Pot,
Burn to Pot;
Till Pudding and Dumplin burn to Pot.
Chorus. Burn to Pot, *&c.*
3 [*Man*]. We'll toss off our Ale till we canno' stand,
And Hoigh for the Honour of Old *England:*
Old *England,*
Old *England;*
And Hoigh for the Honour of Old *England.*
Chorus. Old *England, &c.*
The Dance vary'd into a round Country-Dance. (ix, 32–60)

No one would identify Dryden with such speakers. Equally, no one who knows Dryden would fail to recognize his hearty sense of the English lower classes, his mark of real life and poetry. Many of his songs were printed separately with their music. Pepys wrote songs and even set them, and he often played his flute. Evelyn also wrote songs, as did others. It was a highly musical age, blessed by a number of good composers and by England's greatest composer. But it was an age of songs that were sung, as with the Elizabethan courtly makers, rather than spoken, as were the intense, private "Songs and Sonnets" of Donne as a means of creating their intense vision. If the songs that became madrigals were mannered in the "Petrarchan" way, it might have been expected that songs performed by professional musicians and singers in the Restoration might also be mannered, in another way. Dryden's love songs for plays fulfill the expectation, but his lyrics that make something positive of the social and public canons of performance quite transcend expectations, because in such a world Dryden (like Milton) was more at home.

Not surprisingly, therefore, Dryden's finest lyric poems embody his heroic idea and are therefore apt to be narrative in character. He first discovered the major lyric in what became his favorite form, the Cowleyan pindaric, in his splendid translation of Horace's "Tyrrhena regum progenies" ode (III, xxix).[27] The odes that follow (on Anne Killigrew, *Threnodia Augustalis*, the two for celebrations of St. Cecilia's Day, and such others as that on the death of Purcell or of Anastasia Stafford) prove that Dryden is a major lyric poet, and that like Milton he shared the lyric gifts of his century, even if those had to be exercised under the new conditions of the public mode.

All these odes take as their chief subject human merit, the merit belonging to those who have achieved something the world will wish to remember rather than private, intense, and universal feelings. The great actions require the poet's own

[27] The Delphin Horace, *Opera*, my copy "Editio Decima" (London, 1740), describes the verse-form as "tricolos tetrastropos," rather like Marvell's *Horatian Ode*. Dryden translated only four poems by Horace, but those were central to seventeenth-century views of Horace: see *The Cavalier Mode*, pp. 119–20. The classicist Michael Grant has written that in these translations "John Dryden, in his way, rings a uniquely authentic and permanent echo of Horace" ("To Meet Modern Needs," *Times Literary Supplement*, March 31, 1972, p. 362).

voice or adequate surrogates, as the love songs had not. Milton's alteration of the sonnet into a public trumpeting of his contemporaries often succeeded in playing the new Restoration music of greatness, but often the sonnet form simply proved inadequate to a poet whose designs were so grand. Dryden's development of the more capacious ode realized the aims of Milton and Cowley, while also seducing a number of lesser poets into a kind of free verse that had not yet arrived at a meaningful hour. For Dryden the pindaric ode and the poem of complimentary address became the lyric expression of his heroic idea, and a medium as well of his higher mimesis and the creation of positive values. Those who have acted, who have done great things, achieve immortality, when at least the poet's voice in such poems would confer immortality on them. Again and again Dryden's art doubles on itself, with his lyric and address affirming artistic achievement. The art celebrated may be Anne Killigrew's sister arts of poetry and painting. More often it is music, symbol of that harmony that Dryden sought in all his "poetic kingdoms." The *musica mundana*, or world harmony, and the *musica humana*, the grand harmony "closing full in man," are celebrated in "A Song for St. Cecilia's Day." Timotheus controls the world of Alexander the great, and in the Purcell ode, the power of that great musician's harmony would be sufficient to tune Hell into order and goodness. In *Threnodia Augustalis*, the kingly merits of Charles II include "clemency and Love" (260), peace (280–91), freedom (292–307), unblemished succession (308–26), learning (327–45), and cultivation of the arts (346–63).

Anyone well acquainted with Charles II recognizes his intelligence, curiosity, and keen sense of the possible in human affairs. In the practical realm he was the best of the Stuart kings and, Elizabeth I apart, he was the best English prince after Henry VIII. We know this, and we also know that his indolence and addiction to pleasure were dismayingly excessive. His sexual promiscuity and his taking money from Louis XIV have won so much attention that few people have been aware that his opposition was doing much the same thing: the notorious bawd, "Mother Cresswell," was of chief service to Whigs. Adjusting all this to reasonable proportions, one must get Charles into Dryden's own perspective. Given Dryden's heroic idea of England, Charles appears to us a rather shoddy figure, especially in view of his abilities. Interested in everything, lavish with promise and praise, he exploited, slighted, or ignored many of the best people in his reign. This carelessness rather than promiscuity must be the major charge against him: he wasted people. What then are we to make of Dryden's praise of him, or of the celebration on the other hand of such a morally impeccable but unquestionably minor poet as Anne Killigrew? It very much appears that in Dryden's poems of praise we discover equivalents of Milton's problems, or Milton's readers' problems, with Satan and God the Father.

In his *Epistle to Dr. Arbuthnot* Pope bravely and honestly faces up to the question that his satire has corrected nobody to any appreciable degree. The English Horace of the seventeenth century, Ben Jonson, suffered contrary self-questioning over the fact that he had praised people beyond their deserts. The poets' ideas of good and evil do not always fit with their poetic representations of them, and men as intelligent as Jonson, Dryden, and Pope should not be thought behind us in awareness of the fact. In his *Epistle to Master John Selden*, Jonson acknowledged that he had praised people "past their termes." "But," he declared, "twas with purpose to have made them such" (21–22). That provides one answer to our problem, but only a partial one for a poet as clear-sighted as Dryden. As we have seen, Jonson provides a second answer, also of limited applicability (although much more important to him, Dryden, and Pope) in writing "To William Earle of Pembroke" that his moral art has been directed "Against the bad, but of, and to the good" (3). If we consider the people Dryden praised or satirized, we can see that he could make a larger claim than Jonson or Pope to have exercised an art of moral discrimination. That is truly important, but still not enough. Dryden might have wished to make Charles what he hoped him to be, and he might have seen true virtue in Anne Killigrew, but he knew as we do that Charles had faults that no poet could mend and that Anne Killigrew's moral virtue did not make her a great poet. No matter how carefully we consider the matter, we have not yet come on a wholly satisfactory explanation.

Of course Dryden's poems themselves provide us with the answer. His attention to historical detail creates the "reality" of the person, and even in the context of praise that reality finally turns to truth, showing us that Charles did not support the men he knew deserved it, and that Anne Killigrew in the end is at best a second Katherine Philips. Both such reality and truth enter into the praise of John Oldham and even of William Congreve. But the chief basis of Dryden's praise as a moral art consists in his emphasis upon that ideal which the individual who is praised at once stands for and imperfectly represents. A supernal or immortal order of standards provides the class to which the individual can be assigned (king, poet, etc.) by virtue of his best qualities. The "reality" makes us believe the person exists. The truth enables any reader to account for the disparity, while the higher order shows what ought to have been. Limited but real merits provide the basis for Dryden to celebrate in imperfect individuals the ideal merits of their species. Such merits, limited in the individuals, unlimited in Dryden's vision of what might be, were the continuing basis of his heroic idea.

Dryden's unparalleled optimism was subject often enough

to question and even crisis, but a major part of it derives from a firmly providential view of history especially concerned with creation and the day of judgment. Like many poets, he also derives hope from typologies, especially of a retrospective, recapitulative kind, and from a sense of Christian glorification. What sets him apart from other poets before him is his hope for what man might do between creation and glorification. No English poet, before or after him, ever wrote so many progress pieces in verse and prose. For whatever reason, we assume that poets will be unhappy, disaffected with the world. Dryden obviously did not think everything perfect in his age, and his satire certainly affected those at whom it was directed. But on balance Dryden affirms human possibility, not long ago or at some distant future, but right now. Only such a sense of historical possibility and individual merit can explain why and how he recognized in Purcell the greatest composer England had known. It would be difficult to exaggerate the significance of Dryden's alluding to *Paradise Lost* and *Paradise Regained* in poems written shortly after their appearance: he recognized that they were classics upon their publication. He also gave quick recognition to even lesser contemporary poets like Cowley and Davenant, recalling their lines in such a way as to show that the reader was expected to know them as well as Virgil or Horace. Pope of course had most of Dryden by memory, but his poetic levies on Dryden normally involved use of a word-hoard kind rather than allusion.

Such faith in historical men and women of his own time cannot be sufficiently emphasized for any understanding of Dryden's values. Of course he demanded, as a conservative, that institutions be preserved. But he also called for and celebrated greatness among his contemporaries. And he was right. In science, in the art of war, in commerce, in music, in architecture, and in poetry it was a great age that Dryden lived through. Perhaps nothing illustrates his sense of human capacity and achievement better than his refusal to write ordinary death elegies. Because the persons he celebrates were important to him for their merits, he of course felt and expressed loss. But the loss is swallowed up by the sense of triumph and lasting achievement. The whole point of life to Dryden was personal achievement, immortality, and eternal salvation. The poem on Oldham is commonly read as a Romantic lament, but in fact it concerns the meeting of the heroic (in Virgilian allusions) and of nature (early ripeness), with the implication out of Martial (an implication clearer in the lament on Ossory and the ode on Anne Killigrew) that those of unusual merit die young. Such faith in individuals is supported by Christian providence and eschatology, as is evident in the endings of the Anne Killigrew Ode, "A Song for St. Cecilia's Day," or numerous passages in *The Hind and the Panther*. Those "birds of Paradise" the "sacred Poets," will one day hear "the Golden Trump" and, with Anne Killigrew, "streight, with in-born Vigour, on the Wing / Like mounting Larkes, to the New Morning sing." The singing poet merges with the Christian soul.

> We shall not all sleep, but we shall all be changed, In a moment, in the twinkling of an eye, at the last trump: For the trumpet shall sound, and the dead shall be raised, and we shall be changed. . . . O death where is thy sting? O grave, where is thy victory? (1 Corinthians, 15:51 . . . 55)

The religious element varies in its degree of explicit presence, and in general one can say that it comes more to the fore after Dryden's conversion, as *Eleonora* and the Anastasia Stafford ode show particularly well. Both employ typology and allusion to bring in suggestions of human participation in divine attributes. Eleonora, Countess of Abingdon at once recapitulates all three persons of the Trinity and functions

Neoplatonically to unite heaven and earth by her dual role as pattern of God and for man. "The Pattern" was Dryden's original title for the poem, and as we have seen he uses her in the dual senses of the Greek "idea," as pattern (εἶδος) and as ideal form or archetype (ἰδέα).

Celebrating Anastasia Stafford's marriage at Christmas-time, Dryden asks:

When nature, in our northern hemisphere,
Had shortened day-light, and deform'd the year;
When the departing sun
Was to our adverse tropique run;
And fair St Lucy, with the borrow'd light,
Of moon and stars, had lengthen'd night:
What more then summer's day slipt in by chance,
To beautify the calendar?
What made a spring, in midst of winter to advance,
And the cold seasons leap into a youthfull dance,
To rouse the drooping year?
Was this by miracle, or did they rise
By the bright beams of Anastasia's eyes,
To light our frozen clime,
And, happily for us, mistook their time?
'Twas so, and 'twas imported in her name;
From her, their glorious resurrection came,
And she renewed their perisht flame.
The God of nature did the same:
His birth the depth of winter did adorn,
And she, to marriage then, her second birth was born.
(1–21)

The associations between Anastasia Stafford and Christ go far beyond the Christmas timing. "Her name," "Anastasia," derives from the Greek word for resurrection, ἀνάσταοις. Also, in the Roman Catholic Church (and this is Dryden's most

Catholic poem), the second Nativity Mass, or Dawn Mass, commemorates the martyrdom of St. Anastasia on Christmas Day. Her martyr's deathdate is also, hagiologically speaking, her birthdate, her *dies natalis,* and the marriage date of her soul with Christ. Dryden's light imagery derives in part from the Introit of the Second Nativity Mass: "A light shall shine upon us this day. . . ." And the regeneration he speaks of relates to the epistle for the mass (Titus 3:4–7):

> But after [our sinful behavior] the kindness and love of God our Saviour toward man appeared, . . . that being justified by his grace, we should be made heirs according to the hope of eternal life.

Divine love and providence occupy most of the Stafford ode, and what they do not is occupied by Anastasia Stafford and her family revealing by their piety the same love and providence. Those unfamiliar with typology, and especially that of the late Renaissance and of England, might feel blasphemy in such seeming equations. Donne certainly stretched things a bit for Elizabeth Drury, and it is remarkable that for *Eleonora* Dryden should call so unerringly upon the eulogistic sections of the *Anniversaries.* The Stafford ode also shows how Dryden (unlike Donne) presumes a benign order around the dead or married person, a benignity enabling others as well as the person celebrated to participate in the benefits of merit: "that being justified by his grace, we should be made heirs according to the hope of eternal life." The concept of human merit in Donne's poems of compliment has been termed "metaphysical," and his practice "a metaphysical inquiry into the bases of human worth." [28] Dryden celebrates rather than inquires, and he is so far from finding an unbridgable discrepancy between historical and metaphysical

[28] Barbara K. Lewalski, "Donne's Poetry of Compliment," in *Seventeenth-Century Imagery,* ed. Miner (Berkeley and Los Angeles, 1971), p. 47.

realities that he combines them to the point of their being lost sight of by many readers. His sense of human merit makes us heirs of the conserved, historical past, of our liberal historical moment, and "of eternal life."

Having emphasized the religious basis of Dryden's sense of human merit in reference to poems written later in his career, I shall now seek to emphasize briefly the historical basis by attention to his early poems. It is simply a matter of convenience, because both points can be made throughout his career. I have already made clear what I understand to be the literary deficiencies of the early poems. There is not much to recommend Dryden's earliest extant poem, "On the death of the Lord Hastings," except that it is better than the others printed with it and that it shows as if by accident the role that praise was to have throughout his career. The poem on Cromwell shows that we can participate in greatness by actively appreciating it:

> Yet 'tis our duty and our interest too
> Such monuments as we can build to raise;
> Lest all the World prevent [anticipate] what we should do
> And claim a *Title* in him by their praise. (13–16)

Dryden regarded merit according to ethical standards, as should be obvious enough, but we can understand his art somewhat better if we presume that above ethics lay the supernal realm of value giving validity to the ethics, and beside the ethical principles lay the historical realm of action in which the ethics were to be put into function and praiseworthiness to be determined. The details of ethical principles had long since been codified by the rhetoricians and philosophers. Certain topics recur: ancestry, education, noble deeds, testimony from enemies, etc.[29] From Aristotle on, epideictic

[29] On these and other matters related to the art of praise, see O. B. Hardison's excellent study, *The Enduring Monument* (Chapel Hill, 1962), pp. 30 ff.

or demonstrative oratory was conceived of in terms of praise or blame in relation to merit or evil, and this tradition made it altogether easy for Dryden to use the father-son topos to satirize Shadwell or to praise Oldham and Congreve. According to Aristotle's *Rhetoric*, epideictic discourse deals with "virtue and vice . . . the noble and the disgraceful" (I, ix, 1). Further, "praise is language that sets forth the greatness of virtue" (I, ix, 33). And, as I have been emphasizing, "praise if founded on actions, and acting according to moral purpose is characteristic of the worthy man" (I, ix, 32; all Loeb trans.). In the praise of Cromwell, Dryden obviously wished to present the worthiness of the man. Noble birth was out of the question as a topic of praise, but character could then be made to seem all the more important: "His *Grandeur* he deriv'd from Heav'n alone, / For he was great e're Fortune made him so" (21–22). Perhaps because of the doubtful legitimacy of Cromwell, Dryden develops as he does not do later the Machiavellian concept of strength of character (*virtù*) and fortune or destiny, which he modifies, however, in more orthodox religious and classical details. Lacking ancestry of importance, Cromwell gains lustre from his noble deeds. Such "praise" indeed "sets forth the greatness of virtue," and neither to the poet nor to us does it much matter that Cromwell is dead, for Dryden has so extended the happier sides of funeral elegies as to transcend despair.[30] Cromwell's merits therefore come to mean everything, overshadowing loss, death, and even "thee / O Time."

The relation between the art of praise in its historical setting and the supernal or metaphysical sanction that gave history its validity was a relation made possible by many means. Not a few of those means seem somewhat exotic

[30] Hardison also shows (pp. 113–15) that J. C. Scaliger distinguished five parts to funeral elegies: praise, delineation of loss, lamentation, consolation, and exhortation.

today: alchemy, astrology, musical symbolism, and other mystical lore.[31] Throughout the Renaissance, and with the impetus of the Interregnum experience when Dryden was growing up, these and similar intellectual solvents helped dissolve constraining dualisms such as body and spirit or time and eternity. Like Milton, Dryden kept such things more or less under control, using "speculative music" when writing about musicians, for example, and so honoring larger decorums. But none of these hazy or clear but irrational schemes of thought was any substitute for experience and an energizing conception. Dryden's poetic world became "a just and lively image of human nature" when he conceived that great idea. Divine providence and eschatology, the reality of the historical present, the possibility of progress and immortal achievement, typological and other associations of the human and the divine—these guided by the Graeco-Roman classics, the Bible, and traditions of celebration—make up one large area of Dryden's celebration of human merit. But none of them would have mattered to us had he not grown as a poet beyond the limits of his early Restoration poems and if he did not communicate his belief in such ideas. For although it remains indisputable that great poetry requires maturity, depth of feeling, and height of thought, these three together do not guarantee great poetry. To adopt phrases in

[31] On Dryden and alchemy, see Rosenberg, "*Annus Mirabilis* Distilled," as cited in ch. VI, n. 18, above. On astrology, see Dryden's letter to his sons in Rome in *The Letters of John Dryden*, ed. Charles E. Ward (Durham, N.C., 1942), pp. 93–94; the Anne Killigrew Ode, lines 6–11, 39–43, 174–77; and numerous other poems. On musical symbolism, see John Hollander, *The Untuning of the Sky* (Princeton, 1961); D. T. Mace, "Musical Humanism, the Doctrine of Rhythmus, and the St. Cecilia Day Odes of Dryden," *Journal of the Warburg and Courtauld Institutes*, XXVII (1964), 251–92. On numerological symbolism, see Alastair Fowler and Douglas Brooks, "The Structure of Dryden's 'Song for St. Cecilia's Day, 1687,'" *Essays in Criticism*, XVII (1967), 434–47.

Dryden's neglected poem to Sir Robert Howard (1660), "the providence of wit," or "Art," must still "cultivate the richest ground" (34, 55, 56).

Dryden's attention to human merit expressed his particular concern with good and evil. The concern pervades so many poems in so many kinds that any simple approach can only be representative. In what follows I shall seek somewhat arbitrarily to isolate one group of poems that shows such concern. His concern with human merit naturally led to satire when demerits were in play and to religious confession at moments of self-assessment. Again and again, however, he avoids the abstract consideration of virtue as such, for he was quite simply a poet rather than a divine or a philosopher. Another means of identifying merit was ready to hand in his congenial habit of discovering merit in historical individuals. If his belief in his heroic idea was at all real, it required men who exemplified it. As early as "To my Honored Friend, Sir Robert Howard," he had found that he could achieve his aims by addressing someone he admired with praise (and with an undercurrent of qualification to measure both the real and ideal). Such poems are commonly termed verse epistles, but Dryden's versions vary as much from the Horatian norm as do his poems on the dead from the usual lamentation-plus-consolation routine of the elegy. The verse epistle has proved, in any event, to be highly elastic, even in the handling by such far more classically inclined writers as Jonson and Pope, and the best criticism of the form has usually succeeded most in dealing with individual poems.[32]

[32] Two studies seek to examine the criteria for the verse epistle or the poem of address: Jay Arnold Levine, "The Status of the Verse Epistle before Pope," *Studies in Philology*, LIX (1962), 658–84; and Miner, "Dryden's *Eikon Basilike: To Sir Godfrey Kneller*," *Seventeenth-Century Imagery*, ch. IX. See also Mark Van Doren, *John Dryden* (New York, 1946), ch. IV; Earl R. Wasserman, "Dryden's Epistle to Charleton," *The Subtler Language* (Baltimore, 1959), ch. II; Alan Roper, *Dryden's*

Dryden's "verse epistles" can be more accurately termed poems of complimentary address. Even "complimentary address" overlaps with panegyrics, and Dryden's panegyrics take such forms as the ode and the epicede, sometimes in the same poem. Yet there is a difference between addressing a living person and writing a poem to the memory of someone recently dead. For the latter, the poet's contemporaries expect him to exercise familiar rituals. In writing poems to living people, the poet must expect that even readers not his contemporaries will enter more rigorous judgments. With some effort, then, and without absolute rigor, we can distinguish five elements in those works of Dryden's that I have termed poems of complimentary address. They are addressed to some person historically real and alive, so distinguishing them from Ovid's *Heroides* and commemorative poems. They take rise from an occasion of some importance to Dryden and the person addressed. They concern a topic or topics derived from the addressee, the occasion, and the interests of the poet. They pay compliment by testimony from the poet, so establishing his bond with the person addressed and with readers. And they are written in verse paragraphs usually made up of Dryden's version of the heroic couplet modified by triplets, alexandrines, and other variations.

Apart from concern with human merit the poems satisfying the five criteria do not limit themselves to any easily specifiable group of values. Dryden's sense of important values gradually altered during his career and naturally varied with the individual addressed. Given such variables, the simplest way to begin is to set down the dates of the poems, with

---

Poetic Kingdoms (London, 1965), pp. 104–84 (the fullest discussion of individual poems); and again Levine, "John Dryden's Epistle to John Driden," *Journal of English and Germanic Philology*, LXIII (1964), 450–74.

the names of the people addressed in lieu of the often cumbersome titles. As it happens, the poems fall into chronological groups of some significance, and I shall also designate those:

1650–53
- 1650 To John Hoddesden
- 1653 To Honor Dryden

1660–67
- 1660 To Sir Robert Howard
- 1662 To Lord Chancellor Clarendon
- 1663 To Dr. Walter Charleton
- 1667 To the Duchess of York

1674–77
- 1674 To Lady Castlemaine
- 1677 To Nathaniel Lee

1684–87
- 1684 To the Earl of Roscommon
- 1685 To John Northleigh
- 1687 To Henry Higden

1691–1700
- 1691 To Sir George Etherege (in "ramble" couplets)
- 1692 To Thomas Southerne
- 1694 To William Congreve
- 1694 To Sir Godfrey Kneller
- 1698 To George Granville (Lansdowne)
- 1698 To Peter Motteux
- 1700 To the Duchess of Ormonde
- 1700 To John Driden of Chesterton

It may come as a surprise that Dryden wrote nineteen such poems and that they span his career from its earliest attempts to its last triumphs. But such is adequate reason for isolating these poems. No decade of Dryden's known career lacks examples, but in very general terms the poems improve as time passes. However, the poems of the 1660's do show a rise in genuine seriousness, and the poems of that decade address men and women on topics involving social, intellectual, and political values. On the other hand, with the exception of the poem to Roscommon, the addresses of the 1670's and 1680's are slight affairs, which is surprising in view of the fact that their topics cluster on just those literary matters that often evoked the finest responses from Dryden. But he was then at the center of momentous events, and the poems seem to be casual productions. We observe that in the 1660's Dryden wrote four addresses, and if they do not rank among his major poems, that fact provides yet additional evidence not of their lack of seriousness, but of his slow development of powers in such poetry. In the next two decades, he wrote relatively fewer addresses, only five in all, and for the reason given they do not claim sustained attention. Other poetic approaches were claiming his attention and better satisfied his needs.

The contrary holds for the addresses of the last decade of his life. Complimentary address becomes more frequent—he wrote eight such poems between 1691 and 1700—and we have come to see that some of them are among the finest poems of the century.[33] In that decade, Dryden no longer has the impetus, important though it was, of the new man, that Neander of the 1660's for whom verse address was a way of knowing and getting known. On the other hand, in the last decade of his life poetic address has become a convenience, perhaps a necessity, for an old man seeking to join hands with people he esteems in a world increasingly separated from him. In the preceding two decades, he participated in that harmonious world of politics, religion, history, science, and

[33] My failure to treat these poems seems to me the major defect of my *Dryden's Poetry* (Bloomington, 1967).

art. In the last decade of his life Dryden felt exiled, not like Ovid to Pontus, but in his own land.[34]

The nucleus of that achievement in the nineties is formed by the *Congreve, Kneller, Ormond,* and *Driden* poems. These four clearly respond to Dryden's needs and express his values. The first two address fellow artists at a time when Dryden feels that the poetic scope that is his due has been denied to him. The second pair address friends of the last years of his life, although the two Drydens were of course related by blood, and Dryden had poetically served three generations of the Ormonde family. In each of the poems the relation between the poet and the person addressed is developed with great care: father and son, king and prince, in the Congreve; fellow artists, and fellow kings, in the Kneller; kinsmen and active patriots in true kingdoms of virtue and poetry, in the Driden; immemorial male poet praising beautiful, good womanhood in the kingdom of humanity, in the Ormonde. In each instance, the praise of the person addressed is of great importance, and its brightness is often set off by the darker shading of satire. But the person praised is made to stand for the virtues for which he or she is praised. If, for example, Congreve and Kneller were not respectively the greatest younger playwright and greatest painter of the day, the poems would lack that deep integrity in history and in metaphysical or enduring value that they so evidently possess. The poems do one other principal thing: the virtues and values do not only exist historically and metaphysically alone, nor as attributes of the person praised; they also allow Dryden full participation in them as an equal sharer in an ideal and public world.

Having lost the easy participation in the public world that

[34] Dryden's reference to Ovid and the imagery in the epistle dedicatory to *Eleonora* show that he adopts the Ovidian exile to himself. His comments on the age at the end of the dedication show why.

he enjoyed during the almost three decades between 1660 and the Revolution, Dryden at last found it possible to create public worlds of his own by means of poems of address. Each of those worlds is distinct from the others, and of course from the larger world, and yet since Dryden is the same person in each, and since he had fully known the larger world, politics can enter each, and his *foci* of values in kingship, religion, and art therefore remain operative values as well as metaphors. Each of the special worlds seems entire, as it were, in its terms, laws, and history. Each is the possession of two people, the person addressed and the poet. The two do not exclude others, nor does their world exclude other worlds, as is so frequent in Donne's poems. But the two and their world set the terms on which all else is to join them.

Dryden's technique seems simple enough. He singles out four prominent people whom he knows, choosing a special occasion, for example of Kneller's giving him a picture of Shakespeare he had copied. The poet then celebrates the painter for his creation of portraits that come to life. Such an achievement is founded on, and developed into, principles of merit that determine the character of the newly wrought world. The "constitution" of the kingdom of painting is expressed in its history from the rudest beginnings to the present time, and at each possible juncture the art of poetry is expressed by the art of painting, and vice versa. The Kneller poem, like the other late addresses written to men, employs a darker shading than the verse addresses in the previous three decades. Art has reached a crisis point like that it had reached once before. We observe how very differently the Roman allusion functions now, as compared to its use in *Annus Mirabilis* or *Absalom and Achitophel*:

> *Rome* rais'd not Art, but barely kept alive;
> And with Old *Greece*, unequally did strive:

Till *Goths* and *Vandals*, a rude *Northern* Race,
Did all the matchless Monuments deface.
Then all the Muses in one ruine lye;
And Rhyme began t' enervate Poetry.
Thus in a stupid Military State,
The Pen and Pencil find an equal Fate.

(45–52)

Plainly, England remains the second Rome, "a stupid Military State" under William III.

The Kneller is the darkest of the four poems, and yet it also moves in Dryden's wonted way into the future:

More cannot be by Mortal Art exprest;
But venerable Age shall add the rest.
For Time shall with his ready Pencil stand;
Retouch your Figures, with his ripening hand.
Mellow your Colours, and imbrown the Teint;
Add every Grace, which Time alone can grant:
To future Ages shall your Fame convey;
And give more Beauties, than he takes away.

(174–81)

We are not so much surprised from all that precedes in the poem that the optimism here is chastened as that the poem should close optimistically at all. Time the devourer of things, to recall Ovid's famous phrase, is astonishingly the one who ripens painting. How this can be seems not clear at all until we ask what is missing from the close of the poem. Obviously there is no mention of poetry, of the poet, or of the particular poet writing. The omission is all the more striking, since Dryden was never hesitant to mention himself, much less his art, in poems even less personal than these of address. The modesty, if that is what it is, implies quite simply that it is unnecessary to speak of himself and his art. Time and Age will help that, too, although it seems from the absence of reference that in all likelihood they will need to do less for Dryden's poetry than for Kneller's painting. Dryden quite simply dismisses his age as "a stupid Military State" and looks forward to an era of peace and cultivation of the arts, when his poetry will be valued for its achievement, and the artist-king will be restored to his kingdom.

The occasion of the poem to Congreve was the publication of *The Double-Dealer* (1694), which at first was thought too bitter a play and had no great popularity until Dryden's high estimate, with that of some others, brought popular opinion into a juster appreciation. The well known opening of the poem again focuses on a moment of time and incorporates that sense of an age of art that Dryden had introduced into English critical thought:

> Well then; the promis'd hour is come at last;
> The present Age of Wit obscures the past.
>
> (1–2)

The whole long first (of three) verse paragraph develops and qualifies the senses in which Congreve completes the great idea that Dryden held of the Restoration. Among the ambiguities requiring adjustment are included the meanings of "present" and "past." We wonder whether the "present" is as it were Congreve's age alone or the age of Congreve *and* Dryden; and again whether the past consists of the Elizabethan-Jacobean dramatists or (alternatively) of Dryden and the earlier Restoration dramatists preceding Congreve. A series of very subtle adjustments becomes the business of the poem, and some have in fact proved too difficult for any of us to put into words successfully, even though we sense what Dryden is up to.

Dryden quickly moves into his accustomed cultivation metaphor for the progress of art, here the drama, and arrives at his frequent architectural metaphor for its realization. The "second temple"—the drama that Dryden and his fellows had created—improved on the first in refinement and in other respects, but on balance it was different from and not equal to the first—the earlier drama. A series of critical pairs (skill vs. strength, judgment vs. wit, etc.) carefully adjusts the process of evaluation, sometimes in ways extending the architectural metaphor (skill vs. strength), and at other times asking us to refer to the powers of mind requisite to any achievement (judgment vs. wit). Congreve in one sense completes the second temple, and in another sense he builds a third. At least that is the only way I can interpret the very difficult syntax:

> The second Temple was not like the first:
> Till You, the best *Vetruvius*, come at length;
> Our Beauties equal; but excell our strength.
> Firm *Dorique* Pillars found Your solid Base:
> The Fair *Corinthian* Crowns the higher Space;
> Thus all below is strength, and all above is Grace.
>
> (14–19)

The first two lines quoted appear to say that Congreve at last makes the second temple excel the first, and the shift from the past tense to the present seems to underscore just such a contrast. At the same time, however, the our/your opposition suggests a distinction between the second and a third temple. To make matters yet more difficult, Dryden's architectural description fits features of St. Paul's Cathedral and St. Peter's Basilica alike, both of which had been rebuilt, the former still being worked on (and hence a second temple), the latter and older now the symbolic center of Dryden's new faith. If we find such difficulties in making the assessment, then we must assume that Dryden did also, and was most concerned in setting forth all important matters that entered into the complex comparisons. The conclusion of the first paragraph (31–40) deals with a somewhat simpler matter, Congreve. Congreve's achievement (whichever temple it may involve) is being made while he is still young. His sudden rise does not aggrieve contemporary dramatists: "We cannot envy you because we Love" (34). The theme of great merits not provoking envy in someone loved is then played in variations from Roman history and (with an uncharacteristic mistake in chronology) from Italian painting. Such comparisons have as their effect a generalizing from drama to wider life, from England to European civilization, and from Congreve to great artists of many kinds.

The second and third paragraphs develop new versions of the former metaphoric strains, but the tenor or purpose shifts as Dryden examines his relationship with Congreve. Again we have a complex of metaphor or analogy, turning on deposition and succession. Dryden manages to suggest that he (James II, Edward II, Tom I) having been deposed, Congreve (William III, Edward III, Tom II) reigns. At least, Congreve would reign *de facto* as he does *de jure*, if a usurper had not entered in. The distinction between *de facto* usurpers and *de jure* monarchs permits us to distinguish evaluatively between the various pairs named. The Tom I-Tom II sequence, obscure as it is, helps solve the problem of tone.[35] Whether or not the Toms are Tom Shadwell and Tom Rymer (which Dryden would have surely thought an improvement rather than a decline) or, as I am tempted to think, Tom Sternhold and Tom Shadwell (which, however, involves no immediate succession),[36] it is clear at least that in this instance a bad is meant to be replaced by an equally bad or worse. In other words, from a *de jure* replacement on the whole good

[35] For detailed interpretation of the poem, see Roper, pp. 165–84, the best discussion, although not altogether clear on the two Toms.

[36] See *Religio Laici*, 456.

(Dryden by Congreve), we are taken through a number of *de facto* parallels revealing a worsening in quality and a failing of justice for the poet-kings.

For all this, Dryden takes consolation in being succeeded by his "Son" (43). Whether Congreve participates in the second temple or the third, Dryden suffers from great sadness that after the Revolution circumstances make it impossible for him to continue his epic of England. The "Throne of Wit" has gone wrong as much as the throne of England after 1688. We see very clearly that Dryden's association of monarchy and art in the 1660's and 1670's was serious and literal as well as metaphorical. On the other hand, if Dryden must yield to others, Congreve should be the one yielded to. The young man clearly has what Shakespeare had: genius. (Not an ill-considered remark, in view of the evident superiority of Congreve's first two plays to Shakespeare's.) Congreve does seem "to better Fortune born" (71) and, as Dryden looks ahead to the future, he asks his friend to defend his memory:

> Let not the Insulting Foe my Fame pursue;
> But shade those Lawrels which descend to You:
> And take for Tribute what these Lines express:
> You merit more; nor cou'd my Love do less.
>
> (74–77)

The three-part (past, present, future) movement of the poem relates it to the *Kneller* and to the movement of most of Dryden's poems. But in the *Congreve* Dryden must take heart from a future consolation basically sadder but more human than that in the *Kneller*. Instead of the unstated confidence of the ending of the poem to the painter, Dryden adopts Congreve as a son by virtue of merit and expresses his love for his heir. All the poem's uncertainties of detail come to rest on merit and love. I doubt that any precedent can be found for the poem (except *Mac Flecknoe*!). When else had the first writer of the age handed over the laurels he would still have wished to wear to the one contemporary who deserved them by merit and had won them by love? It is one of Dryden's finest moments, an illustration also of the personality of the public mode.

Behind such poise and warmth there lie events that most people are unaware of today. Simply put, Dryden was in danger of his life after the Revolution. His friend Pepys was in custody for three months in 1690 on suspicion of being a Jacobite. Dryden was certainly a Jacobite, as the *Congreve* and *Kneller* show. And he was guilty of treason (as Pepys was not): for having become a Catholic. Dryden dedicated *Don Sebastian* to Philip Sidney, Earl of Leicester, a Protestant and Whig friend, dating it January 1, 1690, almost exactly one year after William III had come to England with a Protestant wind. As in the poem to Congreve (1694), so in the dedication Dryden develops a series of metaphors to describe the relations between Leicester and himself, whose very different London houses neighbored each other. In one analogy, Leicester's patronage, or protection, resembles the patronage of Spenser by the earlier Philip Sidney. But the chief comparison is that of Leicester to Atticus, the great friend and helper of Cicero. Dryden's fiction is that his epistle dedicatory is a proper letter like one of the many written by Cicero to Titus Pomponius Atticus, a fiction accounting for the dating in Latin at the end of the piece. And just before that date, Dryden inserts a pastiche of two of Cicero's letters to Atticus.

Cicero's letters date from 58 B.C. Having deeply committed himself against Catiline and his cause, Cicero had lost support from the Roman nobility at the crucial time when Julius Caesar was fast rising to power. The nobles were reluctant to support one of the "new men" and were jealous of Cicero's own recent rise in eminence and of its symbol, his splendid house just built in Rome. Cicero could have changed directions (as he had done before) and found an ally in Caesar, but he refused the overtures made him from that quarter. Whereupon Caesar's followers, especially Publius Claudius, began to attack Cicero in public. On Cato's advice he fled Rome at the end of March, arriving at Thessalonica on May 23. The two letters to Atticus appropriated in part by Dryden are brief ones, written on the road. Here is Dryden's conclusion:

> Be pleas'd therefore, since the Family of the *Attici* is and ought to be above the common Forms of concluding Letters, that I may take my leave in the Words of *Cicero* to the first of them: *Me, O Pomponi valdè poenitet vivere: tantùm te oro, ut quoniam me ipse semper amâsti, ut eodem amore sis; ego nimirium, idem sum. Inimici mei mea mihi non meipsum ademerent. Cura, Attice, ut valeas. Dabam Cal.*
> Jan. 1690.[37]
>
> (O Pomponius, I grow heartily sick of life. . . . One thing alone I ask of you, that since you have always loved me for myself, you now preserve your affection for me. I am still the same. My enemies have robbed me of what belongs to me, but not of myself. Take care of your health.
> Sent January 1, 1690.)

Dryden and Leicester knew that Cicero returned to Rome and after a time was purged by Caesar on the urging of Cicero's enemies.

Given the pressures being placed on Roman Catholics even then being rounded up in London and the provinces, and given also the audacity with which Dryden confirms his Roman Catholicism in the prologue to *Don Sebastian*, the

[37] *Don Sebastian* (London, 1690), sig. A4^{r}. Dryden echoes *To Atticus*, III, iv and v, making a few changes. The translation given accordingly alters the Loeb translation and indicates the break between the two letters.

parallel between himself and Cicero does not seem far-fetched. Cicero the *novus vir* and Dryden the Neander ironically found themselves imperiled in a revolutionary state. Dryden's preface to Leicester resembles the poems we have been considering in that it adapts a form of the letter as a means of defining a public role and world for himself at a time of peril. In prose or verse, Dryden writes as friend to friend, drawing upon the tradition that friendship provides the basis of harmony in the state.[38] The imagery of kingship or succession in the *Congreve* and *Kneller* touched on tradition as well as real and evident dangers to impart reality to such analogies. It took Dryden the same length of time, five years, that it took William III to get his affairs in order after the Revolution, and by the time we reach the two addresses to the Duchess of Ormonde and John Driden, our poet has weathered his storm in triumph, translated Virgil, and created a fresh world in his *Fables, Ancient and Modern.*

The *Ormond* and *Driden* appear in *Fables,* a collection that will be the last concern of this book and of my account of seventeenth-century poetry. The *Fables* greatly enlarges the worlds capable of development in poems of address by admitting the heroic. In that collection the whole subject of love also assumes greater preponderance in relation to merit. In addition, the *Fables* possesses an unusual ordering making them into an integral whole.

vi. Last Perspectives on the Human Comedy

Throughout Dryden's career a number of motifs recur, seen now in this way and now in that. The relation of father and son, the sister arts, kingship and poetry, world and hu-

[38] The idea is owed to Aristotle through his Peripatetic school; see *The Cavalier Mode,* pp. 256–60; and from those pages let me repeat acknowledgement of my debt to David Latt, who drew my attention to the importance of the letter to Leicester.

man harmony, the two Romes, passion and merit, death and immortality—such concerns have marked the pages of this concern with Dryden's values. As I have said, in *Mac Flecknoe,* in the "Oldham," and in the *Congreve,* we have the motifs of father and son and of succession in the kingdom of letters. I believe that I am the first to remark on such resemblances among the three poems, but they are so obvious that they have probably been observed before. Certainly once the resemblance is pointed out it cannot be forgotten. The three poems differ markedly on other grounds, one being a satire, the second memorial verse, and the third complimentary address. *Mac Flecknoe* dates from about 1678, "To the Memory of Mr. Oldham" from 1684, and *To my Dear Friend Mr. Congreve* from 1694. From all this it emerges forcibly that Dryden was much given to looking again and again on like topics but from different perspectives.

The principle of multiple perspectives possesses far greater importance than Dryden's mimetic theory, which held that a better or worse likeness might be taken of the same nature. Instead of that, Dryden's actual practice shows that certain important *foci* of thought and ideals were capable of being seen in quite different ways, depending on the situation, the individuals involved, and the state of Dryden's mind. But in the process of being seen differently, they undergo some change while also thereby altering the perspective itself by virtue of their own strength as values. If father-and-son relations of merit and love are important, if true succession in the kingdom of letters is necessary, then a perspective like the Flecknoe-Shadwell one differs from the perspectives in the other two. But those other two also differ from each other in that the Dryden-Oldham succession is aborted by the death of Augustus' heir Marcellus, whereas in the Dryden-Congreve instance usurpation had ended Dryden's *de facto* rule and he can only give his son *de jure* right. So the perspective changes our sense of the presence and play of the two values in the three poems. On the other hand, the values are active rather than neutral, and they serve to reverse the chess board, as it were, by asserting what must be understood of this perspective or that. Such values as Dryden held to were not always affirmed by experience. Sometimes a Shadwell seemed to parody them (in which case the values effectively placed and displaced him). Sometimes a Shaftesbury or a William III genuinely seemed to threaten the values, and in such cases Dryden was, as we have seen, on the attack or the defense. His values aided him, but it is also true that the terms on which they lived underwent some alteration.

Like Milton's conception of providence, Dryden's heroic idea simply had to continue if his life was to have point. Both men met the challenge and overcame it, but they did so by extending the terms and by admitting more of tragedy than they had originally planned to attribute to the divine and human comedies. As Dryden's early career shows him adding one kind of resource to another (the Augustan conception, typology, etc.) until his heroic idea is fully formed, so his late poems, and above all his *Fables*, show him reconciled to a more distant view of the heroic effort, and ready to love mankind the more for showing fewer merits and for taking seemingly forever to arrive at a just life.

Dryden's steady concern with human merit and the affection it breeds, as well as the immortal achievement that it claims, works through a series of perspectives and crises, then, affecting all of them and being affected in return. If colors of good never become those of evil, similar looking hues may vie for what is in reality something at the other end of the spectrum. Having brought Dryden once again to that point of his life when he devoted himself to making Virgil English, we may profitably consider, however briefly, the Dido story once again. The heroic ideal and merit are pitted against a tragic passion and a lesser merit. In a sense Dryden is re-writing *All for Love* in the Dido story, and he must concern himself with two versions of the world, one gained after much struggle, the other lost after the woman had risked everything. Within the fourth book of the *Aeneid* Dryden found rival perspectives of life, and the great popularity of the Dido story shows that her faults may, on balance, be seen from a perspective in which she is more humanly attractive than Aeneas. The *Fables* carries that principle of multiple perspective to more complex dimensions, and we must therefore inquire into the principles Dryden gives us for understanding the whole multiperspective human comedy. It will be recalled that Book IV of the *Aeneid* has its own highly symmetrical structure, giving it an integrity within the entire epic. The *Fables* has no such exact symmetry, but it does have principles of coherence and it does follow the Dido story in the sense of giving unity to a world enlarged beyond the public version of the heroic idea. The heroic conception of Dryden's own time has altered into the human comedy as a whole, including intimations of eternity. And the new story requires a new kind of telling.

The telling of *Fables Ancient and Modern* brought Dryden back to narrative practice freer even than that in *Annus Mirabilis*. Indeed, many of the fables show Dryden telling stories in the purest version of narrative he had ever employed. One reason for the high esteem its readers give *Fables* is the evident joy Dryden took in telling fine old stories well. Ovid, Boccaccio, and Chaucer comprise a triumvirate not readily excelled as story-tellers. On the other hand, Dryden also included poems of his own (those to the Duchess of Ormonde and to John Driden, "Alexander's Feast," and "The Monument of A Fair Maiden Lady"). In addition, he rendered in poetry what Boccaccio had written in the other harmony of prose, and his "Character of A Good Parson" adopts Chaucer's poor parson of a town into a nonjuring divine like Bishop Ken.

There appears to have been no quarrel with the basic interpretation of *Fables* I advanced a few years ago. After examining various classical concepts of *narratio*, and showing how all the poems in *Fables* could be entered under the head of one form of "narrative" or another, I remarked that only Dryden's versions of Ovid's stories fall in the original order of telling and that the *Metamorphoses* provides more tales than either Chaucer or Boccaccio, as well as a model for Dryden's collection. The individual poems are themselves linked one to the next by various connecting devices, and the whole is founded on concern with perspectives of the good life.[39] Just as Milton had come to use the *Aeneid*-form for his greatest narrative work, so Dryden chose the *Metamorphoses*-form for his. We have recently learned that Ovid is an epic poet as well as Virgil,[40] and Dryden regarded Chaucer's Knight's Tale as well as Ovid's tales of change as heroic poems.[41] What the *Metamorphoses* furnished Dryden was a model precisely of differing perspectives in which the principle of transforma-

[39] See Miner, *Dryden's Poetry*, ch. VIII. Judith Sloman, who was completing her excellent University of Minnesota dissertation just as my book came from the press, has given a very articulate "Interpretation of Dryden's *Fables*," *Eighteenth-Century Studies*, IV (1971), 199–211. It will be plain that I share her conviction that Dryden maintains an astonishing degree of historical and heroic emphasis in the collection.

[40] Brooks Otis, *Ovid as an Epic Poet* (Cambridge, 1966), an excellent study, which clearly illuminates Dryden's interpretation of the *Metamorphoses*, although the *Fables* is not mentioned.

[41] Dryden states flatly that the Knight's Tale is "of the epic kind": see Preface to *Fables*, in *Of Dramatic Poesy and Other Critical Essays*, ed. George Watson, 2 vols. (London, 1962), II, 290. And Dryden repeatedly discusses individual stories from the *Metamorphoses* in the heroic context; see, e.g., Watson, I, 99; II, 238–39.

tion was a constant. Dryden does not relate any literal metamorphosis outside the Ovidian stories in *Fables*, but we have seen how the use of differing perspectives on various motifs of value had the effect of somewhat altering our understanding of the values and of assessing if not wholly altering the new perspective.

As one who has shared the Romantics' high regard of *Fables* since he first read it, and who has suggested that it makes a single whole, I am eager that its variety also be emphasized. The point can be made, and a number of others will also be made more easily, by setting forth (in abbreviation) the titles Dryden uses, along with parenthetical comment on their sources.

Dutchess of Ormond (Dryden)
Palamon and Arcite (Chaucer's Knight's Tale reorganized)
John Driden (Dryden)
Meleager and Atalanta (Ovid, *Metamorphoses*, VIII)
Sigismunda and Guiscardo (Boccaccio)
Baucis and Philemon (Ovid, VIII)
Pygmalion and the Statue (Ovid, X)
Cinyras and Myrrha (Ovid, X)
Iliad, Book I (Homer)
The Cock and the Fox (Chaucer, The Nun's Priest's Tale)
Theodore and Honoria (Boccaccio)
The Flower and the Leaf (then attributed to Chaucer)
"Alexander's Feast" (Dryden)
The Twelfth Book of Ovid His Metamorphoses
The Speeches of Ajax and Ulysses (Ovid, XIII)
The Wife of Bath Her Tale (Chaucer)
Of the Pythagorean Philosophy (Ovid, XV)
The Character of a Good Parson (Chaucer, much enlarged)
"The Monument of a Fair Maiden Lady" (Dryden)
Cymon and Iphigenia (Boccaccio, introduced by Dryden's address to the Duchess of Ormonde)

So to set down the titles emphasizes the variety better than any other means. We have a sense of evident possibility, of constant renewal in a fresh realm, and of enormous range of time and characters. Such variety produces a capacious world governed by a heroic wisdom and mellow style that make up the miracle of Dryden's last years.

The variety can only be felt a precious and unusual creation to come after the enormous discipline of mind that had made possible the heroic idea and that had defined a Restoration poetic at once related to Milton's and distinct from it: we have only to think of the control of *Absalom and Achitophel.* By the same token, however, it must be shown that the variety of *Fables* possesses integrity. There is no need to rehearse the specific connections among all twenty-one poems.[42] But it must be admitted that the succession, say, of the *Iliad,* I, by *The Cock and the Fox* seems more various than ordered. The *Iliad,* it will be recalled, begins with debate over the possession of women. Readers are not likely to recall that the first book ends with a debate between Zeus and Hera (Dryden calls her Juno), who go to bed. Dryden extends the celestial scene, as usual making the heathen gods look ridiculous. Then, in *The Cock and the Fox* Dryden takes us forward, to the next morning as it were. We first encounter the hero and heroine awaking on their perch, then the debate between husband and wife, and later the scene of momentous action.

Let us now recall the dismal scene when the Fox runs off with Chanticleer:

> Not louder Cries when *Ilium* was in Flames,
> Were sent to Heav'n by woful *Trojan* Dames,
> When *Pyrrhus* toss'd on high his burnish'd Blade,
> And offer'd *Priam* to his Father's Shade,
> Than for the Cock the widow'd Poultry made.
> Fair Partlet first, when he was [borne] from sight,

[42] As in *Dryden's Poetry,* pp. 296–300.

With soveraign Shrieks bewail'd her Captive Knight.
Far lowder than the *Carthaginian* Wife,
When *Asdrubal* her Husband lost his Life,
When she beheld the smouldring Flames ascend,
And all the *Punick* Glories at an end. (699–709)

Most of the passage is occupied with catching Chaucer's splendid comic-heroic tone of this epyllion as Troy and Carthage fall again in the barnyard. The connection between an *Iliad* or a Carthaginiad and the barnyard turns out to be far closer than we had thought, and just as Dryden had, as it were, brought the world of pagan gods and heroism closer to the barnyard, so he takes Chanticleer closer to the heroic world. One tragic, yet epic, line is solely his: "And all the *Punick* Glories at an end." From afar we hear the strains of an older version of the heroic:

Thus mighty in her Ships, stood *Carthage* long,
  And swept the riches of the world from far;
Yet stoop'd to *Rome*, less wealthy, but more strong:
  And this may prove our second Punick War.
(*Annus Mirabilis*, 17–20)

Or let us consider one of Dryden's other additions to Chaucer's tale.

  Ye Princes rais'd by Poets to the Gods,
And *Alexander'd* up in lying Odes,
Believe not ev'ry flatt'ring Knave's report,
There's many a *Reynard* lurking in the Court;
And he shall be receiv'd with more regard
And list'ned to, than modest Truth is heard.
(659–64)

The pindarics on William and Mary are mostly unendurable today for other reasons than their being "lying Odes." But we also know Dryden's great mirth with Alexander in his own ode, "Alexander's Feast," and we might remember that Alexander was a favorite model for William's panegyrists. We are meant to entertain the possibility that William is subject to "lying Odes" and crafty foxes in this instance, and of his playing the role of Pyrrhus sacking Troy in the other. Of course Aeneas escapes to form the New Troy, and Chanticleer escapes to a riper wisdom in the hencoop. And we discover new forms of the heroic idea in a public world at once diminished into a cock and enlarged to encompass numerous historical periods.

Dryden at once captures the spirit of his authors and makes them his own. His *Palamon and Arcite* makes thousands of changes in the Knight's Tale, and measurably alters the story by making three parts of Chaucer's four. And yet I have had a Chaucerian critic tell me that Dryden's conception of the Knight's Tale as an epic seemed to him the single most important insight into the poem. Such appropriation at once increases the variety by introducing changes in what was already sufficiently unlike, and also brings all the stories into orbit around Dryden's own concerns. The best illustration I can think of to prove beyond cavil that Dryden's changes introduced variety is that he has been caught out coloring his work with—of all poems—*Pharonnida*.[43] Chamberlayne's poem had been published the year before Charles II returned and was not republished until the last century. I can only assume that as he sat down with Boccaccio, Dryden must have felt his mind go back to something similar. Perhaps he went

[43] In his edition of *The Poems of John Dryden*, 4 vols. (Oxford, 1958), IV, 2072–74, James Kinsley seems to have been the first to relate *Pharonnida* to Dryden's translation of *Sigismonda and Guiscardo*. In his excellent but unpublished *thèse complémentaire*, "Dryden Traducteur et Adaptateur de Chaucer et de Boccace" (Sorbonne, 1960), Antoine Culioli confirms Kinsley and also finds resemblances between passages in *Pharonnida* and *Cymon and Iphigenia*: see pp. 17–24.

to a copy of *Pharonnida* wondering if it was still the extraordinary tale he had read, or perhaps he simply remembered details. As far as I know, no other poet has ever drawn on that remarkable story, and it is wonder upon wonder to think that Dryden should have done so late in life.

Dryden's total method of appropriation involves, then, such very different methods as adding to or rearranging Chaucer, turning Boccaccio into poetry, and echoing *Pharonnida.* Such ways of proceeding mean more to a poet than other ways that we like to talk about because they mean more to the reader. But having emphasized them with my trump, *Pharonnida,* I wish to proceed to other features of what may be termed Dryden's integration of *Fables.* It will have been observed that, apart from "Alexander's Feast," Dryden's own poems in *Fables* appear at the beginning and at the end of the collection, along with major "fables" by other authors. Along with *Palamon and Arcite* go the two addresses to the Duchess of Ormonde and Driden. The collection concludes with four poems: *Of the Pythagorean Philosophy, The Character of a Good Parson,* "The Monument of a Fair Maiden Lady," and *Cymon and Iphigenia.* In the simplest terms, the opening cluster emphasizes the heroic and historical sides of the collection, whereas the closing cluster represents the philosophical and religious sides. Neither side holds a monopoly on the emphases, because the great speech by Theseus in *Palamon and Arcite* (III, 1024–1134) superbly adapts Chaucer's adaptation of Boethius' adaptation of Stoicism and Platonism. And *Cymon and Iphigenia* not only replays the motif of love rivalry begun in *Palamon and Arcite* but also begins with that *poeta loquitur* to the Duchess of Ormonde, so bringing the whole collection back to its beginning.

Another factor of high importance in Dryden's integration involves the reappearance of certain characters. Repeatedly we interest ourselves in three kinds: the pair of lovers, rivals in war or love, and the exemplary character or teacher. The Duchess of Ormonde and John Driden are exemplary; so are the Good Parson and the Fair Maiden Lady. So also are the figures of Theseus and Numa in the poems included with those opening and closing groups, *Palamon and Arcite* and *Of the Pythagorean Philosophy*. To put it one way, the shadow of Dido and her heroic passion falls right across the *Fables*, but so also does that of Aeneas, of man seeking heroic achievement. And the light that plays such shadows is Dryden's own concern with what the good life may be, how it can be found, and what are the philosophical and religious principles on which it rests. The treatment of love moves in one little sequence from the idyll of *Baucis and Philemon* to the story of *Pygmalion and the Statue*, in which unnatural love for a statue made with one's own hands turns natural by divine intervention, and on to the lurid incest of *Cinyras and Myrrha*. The love exemplified by the Good Parson, on the other hand, is Christian charity:

> Yet, of his little, he had some to spare,
> To feed the Famish'd, and to cloath the Bare:
> For Mortify'd he was, to that degree,
> A poorer than himself, he would not see.
> True Priests, he said, and Preachers of the Word,
> Were only Stewards of their Soveraign Lord;
> Nothing was theirs; but all the publick Store:
> Intrusted Riches, to relieve the Poor. (50–56)

That, like most of what we find in the *Good Parson*, belongs to Dryden rather than Chaucer, although I believe that it does not falsify Chaucer's account, which is moving in another way for its simplicity among so many accounts of worldly ecclesiastics in the General Prologue. Whether or not Dryden modeled the character on Bishop Thomas Ken may be a question; but that we have come to believe so once again emphasizes that higher mimesis, that power to create reality that Dryden could exercise even in creating so ideal a character. Similarly, the love exemplified by that historical person, the "Fair Maiden Lady," combines chastity, charity, and devotion to God.

The peculiar magic, the rich humanity of the *Fables*, in all its strivings and failures, fears and ideals, can be illustrated by the fact that after we have heard of Pythagorean doctrines of change and of the saintly Parson and Maiden offering us Christian standards above change, Dryden will not let us rest in simple idealism. *Cymon and Iphigenia*, the last of the fables, follows immediately, opening with these lines:

> Old as I am, for Ladies Love unfit,
> The Pow'r of Beauty I remember yet,
> Which once inflam'd my Soul, and still inspires my wit.
> If Love be Folly, the severe Divine
> Has felt that Folly, tho' he censures mine. (1–5)

In addressing himself more or less to the Duchess of Ormonde, Dryden presents the tale as an exemplification of the old motif of love as education:

> Love first invented Verse, and form'd the Rhime,
> The Motion measur'd, harmoniz'd the Chime;
> To lib'ral Acts inlarg'd the narrow-Soul'd:
> Soften'd the Fierce, and made the Coward Bold:
> The World when wast, he Peopled with increase,
> And warring Nations reconcil'd in Peace.
>
> (33–38)

Charity and chastity cannot be the final values for most men and women, yet love can ennoble to the point of bringing back Dryden's heroic ideal. In this triumph, man finds sufficient sorrow. For although Cymon is made a rational and noble creature by love, to win Iphigenia he must undertake something akin to the Rape of the Sabine women—war and killing—leaving behind "Gore," "loud Groans, and lamentable Cries" (607, 611). In the initial *poeta loquitur*, Dryden had said that "Love's the Subject of the Comick Muse" (24). The poem shows that the human comedy includes violence and tragedy. If most of us, and indeed the race itself, cannot subsist on charity and celibacy or chastity, we must expect to enact a comedy with such dark shadows and fervently hope to share in the Parson's text, "Eternal Mercy" (29; see also the following to line 41).

In the middle of *Fables* there appears a story that treats love in a way more comic to most views than the concluding story. Dryden has an arresting expansion of Chaucer's brief allusion to the incest of Chanticleer with his sisters, which of course comes as no news to any farmer:

This gentle Cock for solace of his Life,
Six Misses had beside his lawful Wife;
Scandal that spares no King, tho' ne'er so good,
Says, they were all of his own Flesh and Blood:
His Sisters both by Sire, and Mother's side,
And sure their likeness show'd them near ally'd.
But make the worst, the Monarch did no more,
Than all the *Ptolomeys* had done before:
When Incest is for Int'rest of a Nation,
'Tis made no Sin by Holy Dispensation.
Some Lines have been maintain'd by this alone,
Which by their common Ugliness are known.
(55–65)

A remarkable passage indeed (and no less for the ironic jingling in 63–64). Chanticleer as "Monarch" with "Six Misses" (or mistresses) reminds one inescapably of Charles II and the opening lines of *Absalom and Achitophel.* Gilbert Burnet had argued in a secret court debate that the problem of succession posed by Queen Catherine's sterility should be solved by polygamy.[44] And later, the irrepressible Burnet hinted darkly that Charles had been guilty of incest with his sister, the Duchess of Orleans, on her visit to England.[45] Dryden had heard the story, and like modern historians believed it a scandalous untruth—except for the Bourbons with their unattractive mouths (his accusation was no doubt also untrue, with whatever minor exceptions, although they did marry among themselves closely). Such scandalous goings-on evaporate into the barnyard air of that morning after Chanticleer's bad dream. A more ethereal comic Muse has triumphed.

A much more serious version of love is given by Theseus in his speech at the end of *Palamon and Arcite,* one of the most beautiful passages in seventeenth-century poetry, basing the entire universe on divine love: "The Cause and Spring of Motion, from above / Hung down on Earth the Golden Chain of Love . . ." (III, 1024-25). In a world of constant change and succession (III, 1054–77) humankind wastes itself, and death itself may be welcome release before our fame has been sullied (III, 1089–97). "What then remains . . . ?" (III, 1111). And so at last Theseus finds the means to bring happiness out of woe and harmony from the strife between the two friends over Emily.

> Ordain we then two Sorrows to combine,
> And in one Point th' Extremes of Grief to join;
> That thence resulting Joy may be renew'd,
> As jarring Notes in Harmony conclude.
>
> (1115–18)

[44] See *Dryden's Poetry,* pp. 119–20; and with the passage quoted, cf. *Don Sebastian,* v, 523–24.

[45] See *Burnet's History of My Own Time,* ed. Osmund Airy, 2 vols. (Oxford, 1897–1900), I, 538–39.

The last line fairly sums up, if any half dozen words can, the conception of the *Fables*. Admitting so much variation in characters and tone, the *Fables* yet provides Dryden's fullest ideal of a harmony formed of human discords.

The harmony of the *Fables* admits the most in way of discord of any of Dryden's creations, and it realizes the largest dynamic order. No small part of the harmony is created by the mellow, ripe style of the collection. We may recall for the total career of Dryden, who recalled so much himself, the opening lines of the last choral ode of *Samson Agonistes*:

All is best, though we oft doubt,
What th' unsearchable dispose
Of highest wisdom brings about,
And ever best found in the close.

(1745–48)

In the last year of his life, Dryden's position was not unlike Milton's as he wrote *Paradise Lost*. Dryden was old, suffering from disease, and exiled in his own much hoped for *patria*. It would not be too much to say, I think, that in summoning his powers for one last major creation, he eased the intensity with which he had regarded his age by combining with his lifelong concerns of his nondramatic poetry that tragicomedy that marked most of his finest dramatic work.[46] But such concerns were admitted only by becoming narrative and by fitting, without undue pressures, into his heroic and historic idea, creating a new and yet higher mimesis of the human condition and of man's search for the good life. Although they are Dryden's freest fictions, the poems in *Fables* and especially the collection as a whole, comprise his fullest realities. The public, heroic idea exercised less immediate pressure in *Fables Ancient and Modern* as the century and the poet's

[46] See John Loftis in *John Dryden* (Writers and Their Background series), ed. Miner (London, 1972), ch. II.

own life neared their periods, at last becoming the more universal, and more affecting, human story.

I must admit to suffering from one of Dryden's failings, the belief that the author one is at present reading is especially to be recommended to the world because he has special importance to oneself. In looking back over this account of seventeenth-century poetry, I recall my attempt to espouse Cowley (which was, I think, not wholly successful, and by my fault, not his), Charles Cotton, and William Chamberlayne. Any reasonable person must concede that Donne and Jonson, with Milton and Dryden, are the greatest poets of the century, not just for their poems but for the way in which their poems ever after have adjusted the way in which they, their contemporaries, and we look upon ourselves in our world—what I have designated "mode." Such a stance is at once emotional, intellectual, and religious, and when one combines these three elements one can only say that Milton exemplifies them best of all, for if there is any problem with his emotional quality, the problem is not with deficiency but kind. Blind though he was, he saw the most, and in terms of creativity, order, and magnificence we may never see the likes again in English poetry. All the same, I confess to a spontaneous pleasure in reading Donne, a sense almost that the poet has wished me right there, which is a secret he shares with Chaucer. And perusing Dryden yet again, I recall my first encounter after returning from military and civilian service in Japan. Here was a poet who showed that such things as I had felt to be important—Depression, war, politics—could be made important in poetry. As time passed, I discovered the *Fables*. Whether because I am once again just fresh from them or because I am just right, I think that collection the finest poetic achievement in the century apart from *Paradise Lost*. In its variety, its comprehensiveness, and especially its humanity it is, as the Romantics recognized, something almost free of connection with any century. Of course it belongs to Dryden and to that age which he, if any man, could declare had drawn to its close:

> 'Tis well an Old Age is out,
> And time to begin a New.[47]

[47] *The Secular Masque*, 96–97, altered from italics. These are presumably the last verses written by Dryden.

APPENDIX

Two Summaries of William Chamberlayne's *Pharonnida*

1. George Saintsbury, *Minor Poets of the Caroline Period*, 3 vols. (Oxford, 1968), I, 7–10.

[Saintsbury wrote that he read *Pharonnida* three times to enable himself to write the précis that follows, and even he who was so dedicated and so admiring of the poem flagged at the end. This account should be compared with that by A. E. Parsons, given next. (The notes are those of Saintsbury and Parsons.)]

Book I, Canto i.[1] Aminander [Ariamnes], a Spartan lord, hunting on the shore of the Gulf of Lepanto, sees a naval combat between Turks and Christians; and when the combatants, wrecked by a squall, are still fighting on the beach, rescues the Christian heroes Argalia and Aphron.

Canto ii. Another lord, Almanzor, the villain of the piece, finds two damsels, Carina and Florenza, in a wood. He offers violence to Florenza, and her lover, Andremon, though coming in time to save her, falls before his sword. But Argalia, who has been sleeping near, is waked by the scuffle, takes her part, and severely wounds Almanzor, despite the succour of his friends. Forces come up, and, appearances being against Argalia, take him into custody.

Canto iii. He is conveyed to the capital, where, according to the custom of the country, it is the duty of the king's daughter, Pharonnida, whose mother is dead, to preside over the tribunal. She falls in love with Argalia at first sight, but he is condemned, receiving three days' respite as an Epirot, a

[1] Observe the *five* books, and the *five* cantos in each. This was one of the curious "heroic" punctilios, to bring the construction nearer to the *five* acts of Drama.

citizen of an allied state, which is confirmed by ambassadors from Epirus then present.

Canto iv. This is however not sufficient to obtain his pardon: and he is about to suffer when Aminander reappears with Florenza herself, who tells the whole story. Argalia is set at liberty and is about to depart with the ambassadors (who have become "Calabrians" and who have told what they know of his origin) when a fresh adventure happens. Molarchus the Morean (now Sicilian) admiral, who has been charged to convoy the envoys, invites the king, princess and court on board his flag-ship and makes sail, having formed a design to carry off Pharonnida. This he does, although there is a fierce fight on board, by throwing her into a prepared boat and making off, while the crew do the same, having previously scuttled the ship. Argalia, however, with the help of his friend Aphron, though at the cost of the latter's life, secures one of the boats, rescues the king, and lands on a desolate island, where they find that Molarchus has conveyed Pharonnida to a fortress. Argalia, always fertile in resource, makes a ladder of the tackling of some stranded boats, scales the walls, slays Molarchus, and rescues the princess.

Canto v tells of a halcyon time at Corinth, where Pharonnida and Argalia, who is captain of her bodyguard, fall more and more deeply in love with one another, till the usual romance-mischance of a proposed betrothal to a foreign prince interrupts it: and the book finishes with this agony further agonized by Argalia's appointment on the very embassy destined to reply favourably to the Epirot suitor.

In Book II, Canto i we return to Almanzor, who forms a plot to abduct the princess, succeeds at first by turning a masque into a massacre, but is defeated by the rising of the country people, who half ignorantly rescue her. But her ravisher, in

Canto ii, thinking he has gone too far to retreat, sets up a rebellion and garrisons the castle of a city named Alcithius, which the king at first retakes, but which only serves him as a place of refuge when Almanzor has beaten him in the field. He has just time to send to Epirus for help before the place is invested.

Canto iii. It is almost reduced by famine, and the besieged are meditating the forlorn hope of a sally when Zoranza the Epirot prince arrives with a large army, the vanguard of which, commanded by Argalia and supported from the castle, disperses the rebel forces, though not at first completely. After a glowing interview between the lovers the hero has to expel the remnant of the foe from a strange cavern-fastness where he finds a secret treasury with mysterious inscription.

Canto iv. Another interval of war. The unwelcome suitor is called off by troubles at home: and the lovers (Argalia still commanding the princess' guard) enjoy discreet but delightful hours in an island paradise.

Canto v. Episode of two Platonic-Fantastic lovers, Acretius and Philanta, on whom a practical joke is played. Intrigues of Amphibia, who excites the king's jealousy, and induces him to send Argalia at the head of a contingent to Epirus. After pathetic parting scenes, Argalia leaves Pharonnida, and the poet "leaves the Muses to converse with men," that is to say to fight the Roundheads at Newbury.

Book III, Canto i opens with a semi-episode of the rival loves of Euriolus and Mazara for Florenza, and Mazara's consolation with Clarina, Florenza's companion at her original appearance. In

Canto ii the princess, unwarily reading aloud a letter from Argalia with her door open, is overheard by her father, who is furiously angry and sends letters of Bellerophon to the Prince of Syracuse [Epirus] as to Argalia. Zoranza, nothing loth, makes Argalia captain of the fortress Ardenna, with a secret commission to the actual governor to make away with him. He is saved from death for the moment by a convenient local superstition, and carried off (still prisoner) by an invading fleet, which fails to capture Ardenna. But Pharonnida is strictly imprisoned in the castle of Gerenza. In

Canto iii Argalia, after a rapid series of adventures at sea and in Rhodes, is captured by the Turkish chief Ammurat and sent to his wife Janusa in Sardinia to be tortured and executed. But Janusa falls in love with him, and this and the next Canto [iv] contain the best known and perhaps the most sustained chapter of the poem, Argalia being not merely

"Like Paris handsome and like Hector brave,"

but also like Joseph chaste. [Canto v] The passage having ended happily for him, tragically for Janusa and her husband, he seizes ships, mans them with Christian slaves, rescues the Prince of Cyprus from a new Turkish fleet, returns to the Morea, and after a time resolves, aided by his Cyprian friend, to release Pharonnida. In this, at first, they succeed.

Book IV, Canto i. Episode of Orlinda and the Prince of Cyprus. Pharonnida and Argalia enjoy a new respite in a retired spot, but are attacked by outlaws, who wound Argalia and carry off the princess. Their chief is Almanzor, who in

Canto ii tries to force Pharonnida to accept him by threats, and immures her in a living tomb from which she is rescued by Euriolus (mentioned before) and Ismander, on whom and Aminda there is fresh episode continued into

Canto iii by entrances of certain persons named Vanlore,[2] Amarus, and Silvandra, but not concluded. The rest of Canto iii, Canto iv, and

Canto v contains an account of Argalia's recovery, and long

[2] It will be observed that Chamberlayne's nomenclature, mainly of the odd rococo-romantic type popular in the seventeenth-century literature, is still more oddly mixed. This particular name must have been a favorite, for it recurs in [Chamberlayne's play] *Love's Victory.*

conversations, in which he reveals what he knows of his youth to a friendly hermit.

Book V, Canto i. Meanwhile Pharonnida has retired to a monastery and is about to take the veil (has actually done so after a fashion) when Almanzor attacks the convent and once more carries her off, but surrenders her to her father that he may obtain his own pardon and plot further.

Canto ii. Argalia goes to Aetolia, of which he is the rightful heir, and fights his way to his own.

Canto iii. He is however rejected as suitor and attacked by his rival Zoranza. But Almanzor procures both this prince's murder and that of King Cleander (who is never named till very late in the story). Then Pharonnida in Canto iv undergoes her last danger, and in Canto v is finally freed by Argalia as her champion from Almanzor, whom he at last slays, and from all her other ills by marriage with her deliverer.

2. A. E. Parsons, "A Forgotten Poet: William Chamberlayne and 'Pharonnida,'" *Modern Language Review*, XLV (1950), 296–311.

[Parsons supports his view that the poem has a "disguised political meaning" with two not necessarily mutually dependent interpretations. He holds "that we have unmistakably topical passages embroidering the main theme" (p. 298) and that after revision "the real mainspring of the plot is the political situation" (p. 310). The portions italicized in his précis identify what he believes are "interpolated passages and scenes," with "conjectural substitution" included within brackets. His précis will be found on pp. 306–308, and, as a test for possible tendentiousness, should be compared with Saintsbury's.]

Book I

Canto i. Argalia and his friend Aphron arrive in Morea.

Canto ii. Argalia rescues Florenza, lady-in-waiting to the

local Princess, wounds her assailant, Almanzor, and is taken before the Princess' court.

Canto iii. Argalia and Pharonnida love at sight. He is condemned to death. Ambassadors from Epirus arrive to treat for marriage with the Princess. They recognize Argalia as a countryman and adopted son.

Canto iv. Florenza's evidence clears Argalia, he is set at liberty and *is just about to leave in the train of the Epirot lords when the Spartan Prince entertains them with a naval display, during which the Sicilian admiral tries to abduct Pharonnida; she is rescued by Argalia and* (canto v) *has a dream vision in which she sees her future and that of Argalia and the ultimate union of the three crowns of Sicily. Argalia is sent on an embassy to Epirus to arrange about Pharonnida's marriage and* leaves in the train of the Epirot lords. Almanzor is banished.

Note on Book I. It will be observed that in each version Argalia is now in Epirus in company with Pharonnida's authorized suitor. The "Sicilian" passage with the attempted abduction of the Princess in a richly decorated ship on the occasion of a naval display is taken from Barclay's *Argenis.*

Book II

Cantos i-iii. In Argalia's absence Almanzor abducts the Princess who *is rescued by the peasants on her father's estate, joins her father and is immediately afterwards beset with him in the Castle of Alcithius by Almanzor who has raised all the disaffected subjects of the Prince and is now in open arms against him. Almanzor poses as the champion of an overtaxed and oppressed people,* [is carried off to a robber's cave whence she] is rescued by Argalia, returning in company with the Epirot Prince. When the robbers are dislodged from the cave, the princes with Argalia, exploring the subterranean passages connected with it, find an underground chamber containing the figure of a mighty king who points to a prophecy declaring that "Old Morea's triple crown" is soon to be "united on one royal head."

Canto iv. Argalia, in high favour with the Prince, is made commander of Pharonnida's guard.[3]

Canto v. *Episode of the Platonic lovers who have become foolish by reading too many romances.* (This has no connexion with the story.)

The Prince's jealousy is aroused and Argalia is sent to help the Epirot Prince with a Spartan contingent against the Aetolians. The lovers part with tears.

Book III

Canto i. *Episode of Florenza and two suitors Mazara and Euriolus.*

Canto ii. The Prince surprises Pharonnida's love for Argalia and sends to the Epirot Prince (here called the Prince of Syracuse), on whose behalf Argalia is fighting, to have him killed. Attempted assassination of Argalia in the Castle of Ardenna, a city lately taken from the Aetolians. Argalia is captured by Turkish pirates. Pharonnida, who betrays her grief at the news of Argalia's disappearance, is closely imprisoned by her father in the Castle of Geranza, and Florenza is banished.

Canto iii. Argalia escapes from the Turks and takes part in the defence of Rhodes. *He is recaptured and imprisoned. The Sultan's concubine Janusa falls in love with the captive and threatens him with torture since he will not yield to her desire.*

Canto iv. *Ammurat, overhearing the Christian's steadfast answers, first secures his release and then kills himself and his*

[3] Book II, iv, 98–100 promise that the Princess's fate is to be sad but no longer tragic. In the final version of the poem very much the worst part of her troubles is still to come.

now repentant wife. Argalia, now in Turkish dress and in a Turkish ship, sails towards Palermo.

Canto v. He rescues the Prince of Cyprus who was captured by Turks on his way to pay court to Pharonnida. Pharonnida and Argalia escape with the help of the Cyprian Prince. They meet with Florenza.

Note on Book III. This book, in which the story is continued after Chamberlayne's return from the wars (probably in 1645–6), is headed "A tragi-comical poem." The scene, as regards the Prince (now first named—Cleander) and Pharonnida, is now in Sicily. There is little interpolated matter, other than the Turkish episode, and the story goes straight on. The atmosphere is that of romance. The lovers are now together and free, but in danger from pursuit.

Book IV

(With Book IV begin new type, different arrangement, and fresh pagination.)

Canto i. *Episode of Orlinda, sister of Zoranza, and the Prince of Cyprus.* The escaping party is attacked by bandits, and Pharonnida and Florenza are carried off. Argalia is left for dead.

Canto ii. Pharonnida, in the power of Almanzor (now a chief of bandits), suffers attempts on her constancy and chastity. She is buried alive with the supposed corpse of her lover. She escapes with Florenza, Euriolus and Ismander.

Canto iii. *The story of Ismander and Silvandra.*

Canto iv. Argalia is rescued by a monk who recognizes his jewel and relates to him the story of his birth as Prince of Aetolia and his father's misfortunes and retirement to a monastery.

Canto v. *The monk then tells Argalia of his father's recent efforts to regain his throne (after an exile of twenty years or more), of how a powerful subject (Zarrobrin) had established military control and was oppressing the Aetolians under the name of "protecting" them, and secretly aimed at the throne.* A supposed heir to the throne had been proclaimed.

The monk describes the defeat of the royal army and the capture of the Prince (Argalia's father) by Zarrobrin.

Having ended his tale the monk opens Argalia's jewel and shows him the miniature of his father.

Note on Book IV. The pseudo-prince put forward by Zarrobrin is not required in the final version and Chamberlayne has rather a scramble to get rid of him. He probably loomed much larger in the original version. There are indications in the second part of the monk's tale that Chamberlayne is drawing on first-hand knowledge of Penruddock's Rising.

Book V

The poet tells us that he has taken up the poem again after a delay and interruptions which almost prevented its completion.

Canto i. Pharonnida, in company with Florenza, goes to profess as a nun. They are seized by Almanzor and brought back to Cleander. Almanzor is forgiven and reinstated.

Canto ii. (Chamberlayne refers to the historical truth of Argalia's story and the wickedness of the days in which he is writing.) Argalia *takes service with Zarrobrin, who is now ruler or "Protector" of the Aetolians, and helps him defeat* [defeats] the Epirots under Zoranza and then restores order among the Aetolians. *Zarrobrin, seeing that the Aetolians have not forgotten their Prince, determines to overawe them with a show of military power. He convenes a court of soldiers and the King*[4] *is forced to undergo the indignity of a*

[4] When Chamberlayne is too acutely conscious of the reality of his theme he sometimes, as here, slips into the error of calling his Prince the King.

mock trial. He is condemned to death by beheading, is brought to the scaffold and is rescued by Argalia just as the axe is about to fall.

Argalia is recognized as the heir to Aetolia, and Zarrobrin and the pretended Prince are killed. Argalia sends ambassadors to ask for Pharonnida in marriage.

Canto iii. *She is, however, against her will, promised to Zoranza. The Prince of Cyprus plans to help her escape. Almanzor contrives the murder of Cleander and Zoranza and makes Pharonnida and Amindor (Prince of Cyprus) appear guilty of the crime.*

Canto iv. *Pharonnida and Amindor are tried for murder and high treason, and condemned to die unless a champion appears within twenty days.*

Canto v. *Argalia, first convincing himself of Pharonnida's innocence by disguising himself as a priest and hearing her last confession, appears as a champion at the last moment,* he overthrows Almanzor, is found to be the rightful heir to the throne of Epirus, and by his marriage with Pharonnida the three crowns are united.

Notes on Book V. In Canto iv Chamberlayne pronounces on the iniquity of subjects who would pass sentence on their sovereign. The passage (ll. 389–408) contains a direct reference to the trial of Charles I.

In canto v we have an instance of Chamberlayne's rationalization of the more exotic elements of Greek romance. Thus the Trial of Chastity, undergone by the Greek heroine after she has been condemned to death or sacrifice, is here reduced to the episode in which Argalia in guise of a priest hears her last confession.

MAJOR EDITIONS USED AND CONSULTED

THE texts used are for the most part modern "old-spelling" editions or, in their absence, old or modernized editions readily available to me. For convenience sake, in my quotations I have sometimes substituted or interpolated material in square brackets, and I have taken liberty with titles, especially with regard to italic usage, and also preferring, for example, *Paradise Regained* to *Paradise Regain'd*.

Asterisks distinguish the editions used for quotations, determination of canon, etc.

Authors follow in alphabetical order of their surnames, except that for the nobility I have used the most familiar style, preferring "Rochester," for example, to "John Wilmot . . .".

SAMUEL BUTLER (1612–1680)

Hudibras. Ed. Zachary Grey. 2nd ed. London, 1764.

Hudibras. Ed. Treadway Russell Nash. 2 vols. London, 1847.

**Hudibras*. Ed. John Wilders. Oxford, 1967.

**The Genuine Remains in Verse and Prose*. Ed. R. Thyer. 2 vols. London, 1759.

**Characters and Passages from Note-Books*. Ed. A. R. Waller. Cambridge, 1908.

**Satires and Miscellaneous Poetry and Prose*. Ed. René Lamar. Cambridge, 1928.

**Characters*. Ed. Charles W. Daves. Cleveland and London, 1970.

WILLIAM CHAMBERLAYNE (1619–1680)

**Pharonnida*. London, 1659.

**Pharonnida*. Ed. George Saintsbury. In *Minor Poets of the*

Caroline Period. 3 vols. Oxford, 1968 (vol. I). (The text is given as in the 1659 ed., with some assistance from Saintsbury, especially in line numbering.)

JOHN CLEVELAND (1613–1658)

**The Poems of John Cleveland.* Ed. Brian Morris and Eleanor Withington. Oxford, 1967.

ABRAHAM COWLEY (1618–1667)

**Poemata Latina.* London, 1668.

**The Works.* London, 1700.

**Poems.* Ed. A. R. Waller. Cambridge, 1905.

**Essays, Plays and Sundry Verses.* Ed. A. R. Waller. Cambridge, 1906.

SIR WILLIAM DAVENANT (1606–1668)

**Sir William Davenant's Gondibert.* Ed. David F. Gladish. Oxford, 1971.

**The Works.* London, 1673.

SIR JOHN DENHAM (?1615–1669)

**Expans'd Hieroglyphicks . . . Cooper's Hill.* Ed. Brendan O Hehir. Berkeley and Los Angeles, 1969.

DORSET, THOMAS SACKVILLE, EARL OF (1638–1706)

See under Rochester.

JOHN DRYDEN (1631–1700)

The Works of John Dryden. Ed. Sir Walter Scott. 18 vols. Edinburgh, 1808.

The Poetical Works of John Dryden. Ed. George R. Noyes. 2nd ed. Boston, 1950.

**The Works of John Dryden.* "The California Edition," 20

vols., in progress. Ed. Edward Niles Hooker, H. T. Swedenberg, Jr., *et al.* Berkeley, Los Angeles, and London, 1956ff.

**The Poems of John Dryden.* Ed. James Kinsley. 4 vols. Oxford, 1958.

**Of Dramatic Poesy and Other Critical Essays.* Ed. George Watson. 2 vols. London, 1962.

Sir George Etherege (?1634–?1691)

**The Poems of Sir George Etherege.* Ed. James Thorpe. Princeton, 1963.

**The Dramatic Works of Sir George Etherege.* Ed. H.F.B. Brett-Smith. 2 vols. Oxford, 1927.

Sir Francis Kynaston (1587–1642)

Leoline and Sydanis (1642). In *Minor Poets of the Caroline Period.* Ed. George Saintsbury. 3 vols. Oxford, 1968 (vol. II).

Andrew Marvell (1621–1678)

The Poems and Letters. Ed. H. M. Margoliouth. 2 vols. 2nd ed. Oxford, 1952.

**Complete Poetry.* Ed. George deF. Lord. New York, 1968.

**The Rehearsal Transpros'd* (both parts). Ed. D.I.B. Smith. Oxford, 1971.

John Milton (1608–1674)

Paradise Lost. Ed. Thomas Newton. 2 vols. 3rd ed. London, 1754.

Paradise Regain'd, etc. Ed. Thomas Newton. London, 1752.

Milton's Paradise Lost Illustrated with Texts of Scripture. Ed. Thomas Gillies. 2nd ed. London, 1793.

**The Works of John Milton.* "The Columbia Edition." Ed. Frank Allen Patterson, *et al.* 18 vols. New York, 1931–38.

*_The Complete Poems and Major Prose._ Ed. Merritt Y. Hughes. New York, 1957.

*_The Complete Prose Works._ "The Yale Prose Milton." Ed. Don M. Wolfe, _et al._ 5 vols. in 6. New Haven, 1953–71.

The Poems of John Milton. Ed. John Carey and Alastair Fowler. London, 1968.

HENRY MORE (1614–1687)

*_Philosophical Poems._ Cambridge, 1647. (Scolar Press Reprint, 1969).

JOHN OLDHAM (1655–1683)

*_The Works . . . Together with His Remains._ London, 1684.

MULGRAVE, JOHN SHEFFIELD, EARL OF, later MARQUESS OF NORMANBY, DUKE OF BUCKINGHAMSHIRE (1684–1721)

*_The Works._ Ed. Alexander Pope. 2 vols. London, 1723. (See also under Rochester.)

FRANCIS QUARLES (1592–1644)

*_Divine Poems._ London, 1642 (with the "histories" of Jonah, Esther, Job, and Samson).

ROCHESTER, JOHN WILMOT, EARL OF (1647–1680)

Rochester's Poems on Several Occasions. Ed. James Thorpe. Princeton, 1950 (contains numerous poems not by Rochester but represents the conception of the poet held by his contemporaries).

Poems. Ed. Vivian de Sola Pinto. London, 1953.

*_Restoration Carnival._ Ed. Vivian de Sola Pinto. London, 1954 (contains poems by Rochester, _Dorset, Sedley,_ Etherege, and _Mulgrave_ and valuable particularly for those italicized).

The Complete Poems. Ed. David M. Vieth. New Haven and London, 1968.

SEDLEY, SIR CHARLES (1639–1701)

The Poetical and Dramatic Works. Ed. Vivian de Sola Pinto. 2 vols. London, 1928 (see also under Rochester).

INDEX

The entries include names, topics, and titles (under their authors' names) of works by Restoration poets. The word "discussed" designates more extended discussion of a poem. Royalty are specified by their regnal names, nobility by their most familiar title, and classical persons by a single name except in cases where fuller specification may be necessary to avoid confusion.

This book has been composed and printed by
The Maple Press Company
Designed by Jan Lilly
Edited by George Robinson
Typography: Electra and Bodoni
Paper: Warren's Olde Style
Binding by The Maple Press Company

Library of Congress Cataloging in Publication Data

Miner, Earl Roy.
The restoration mode from Milton to Dryden.

Includes bibliographical references.
1. English poetry—Early modern (to 1700)—History and criticism. I. Title.
PR541.M5 821'.4'09 73-14865
ISBN 0-691-10019-5